The Highest Perfection

The Highest Perfection

A History of De La Rue

Peter Pugh

Published in the UK in 2011 by
Icon Books Ltd,
Omnibus Business Centre,
39–41 North Road, London N7 9DP

ISBN: 978-184831-335-4

Typeset in Classical Garamond by Marie Doherty

Printed and bound by 1010 Printing International, China

Contents

Introduction

When I was asked to research and write the history of De La Rue and its subsidiary, Portals, I was very excited. Most of the companies for whom I have written histories were founded in the 20th or mid-to-late 19th centuries. Here were two that were founded in 1813 (De La Rue) and 1712 (Portals). Furthermore, both companies had been dealing with other important and interesting companies and operating on a world scale. This was going to be both testing and very interesting.

Fortunately, the companies had been assiduous in collecting and keeping valuable archives, and the many present and former executives whom I interviewed were knowledgeable and helpful. Finally, there were many fascinating photographs and fine samples of the meticulous work they have produced.

As the companies were both dealing with governments and national banks, they have been involved in world history and I have tried to put them in their context. No company exists in a vacuum. There have been a number of interesting, not to say eccentric, characters who have worked for both companies, and I have tried to portray them in their adventures. Money itself is an interesting subject and the printing of it inevitably attracts both those of the highest integrity and those who can best be described as 'adventurers'. You will find plenty of both types in the book.

Both companies developed as family businesses. The Portals lasted many generations with sons following fathers. After two very talented generations, Thomas the founder and his sons Warren and William Frederick, known to all as Colonel Billy, the de la Rues ran into difficulties and the company had to be rescued by a financier, Sidney Lamert, and a very able businessman who came from a competitor, Waterlow. You will see what a masterly job these two did, first in the difficult years of the 1930s and then through the Second World War and beyond.

They were succeeded by another hugely talented leader, Arthur, later Sir Arthur, Norman, known to everyone as Gerry. He steered the company through the 1950s and 1960s as Managing Director and then through the 1970s and on until 1987 as Chairman. He was helped and succeeded by another very strong and forthright character, Peter Orchard.

This is no humdrum corporate history but the story of twists and turns, ups and downs, good guys and bad guys, and it is still going forward on its successful way.

I hope you enjoy reading it as much as I enjoyed writing it.

Peter Pugh
February 2011

MONETARY VALUES

Money and its value is always a problem when writing about a period that stretches over a number of years, in this case nearly 300 years, particularly when parts of that period have included some years of very high inflation. Furthermore, establishing a yardstick for measuring the change in the value of money is not easy either. Do we take the external value of the £ or what it will buy in the average (whatever that may be) weekly shopping basket? Do we relate it to the average manual wage? As we know, while prices in general might rise, and have done so in this country every year since the Second World War, the prices of certain products might fall. However, we are writing about a business, and money and its value crop up on almost every page. We therefore have to make some judgements. We can only generalise, and I think the best yardstick is probably the average working wage.

Taking this as the yardstick, here is a measure of the £ sterling relative to the £ in 2011.

Apart from wartime, prices were stable for 250 years, but prices began to rise in the run-up to the First World War.

1665–1900 multiply by 120
1900–1914 multiply by 110

1918–1939 multiply by 60
1945–1950 multiply by 35
1950–1960 multiply by 30
1960–1970 multiply by 25
1970–1974 multiply by 20
1975–1977 multiply by 15
1978–1980 multiply by 8
1980–1987 multiply by 5
1987–1991 multiply by 2.5
1991–1997 multiply by 1.5

Since 1997, the rate of inflation, by the standards of most of the 20th century, has been very low, averaging, until very recently, less than the Labour government's originally stated aim of 2.5 per cent which was later reduced to 2 per cent. You don't need me to tell you that some things such as telephone charges and many items made in the Far East, notably China, are going down in price while others, such as houses, moved up very sharply from 1997 to 2008, before falling back in the financial crisis. In the UK in 2011, general inflation is rising again.

Chapter One

Where Are We Now?

The largest in the world
Absorbing others
Manufactured all over the world

THE LARGEST IN THE WORLD

This is the story of De La Rue, a company celebrating its 200th anniversary in 2013, and of Portals, which will be 300 years old in 2012. Both companies have magnificent histories of which they can be proud. Furthermore, there are very few large companies that have lived and thrived for so long. After this introductory chapter we are going to tell the story of the early life of Portals, because they existed, and were clearly involved with the Bank of England, in the 18th century, whereas De La Rue was not founded until the early 19th century.

Where are they today?

De La Rue is the largest commercial currency printer and papermaker in the world, involved in production of more than 150 currencies as well as a wide range of security documents such as passports, authentification labels and fiscal stamps. De La Rue is also a leading provider of cash-sorting equipment and software solutions to central banks, helping them to reduce the cost of handling cash. It is even more significant in this financial industry than it was when it celebrated its 150th anniversary in 1963. This is what it said about itself then:

> In a century and a half, the world has seen revolutionary changes. Granted a Royal Letters Patent for the manufacture of playing cards by the typographical process by William IV in 1832, the House of De La Rue has produced packs of playing cards for members of the Royal Family, for European Kings and Queens and for Indian princes. In 1843, in the time of Nicholas I, a member of the de la Rue family travelled to

St Petersburg to initiate the Russians in the art of printing playing cards, shipping a press and printing inks. In the last decade, banknote counting machines have been sent to the USSR.

In a century and a half, to mention but a few activities, stamps have been printed for India for seventy-one years; passports have been supplied to Aden; notes and banknote counting machines to Spain; notes, stamps and banknote counting machines to Portugal; passports to Gambia; Nigeria; Zanzibar, also banknotes; stamps to the Cape of Good Hope; notes and banknote counting machines to Iran; passports and banknotes to China; printing presses and banknote counting machines to Japan; stamps and banknote counting machines to Australia; currency, stamps and banknote counting machines to New Zealand; stamps to Antarctica; currency and stamps to Haiti; currency to Brazil; currency and counting machines to Ecuador; banknote counting machines to the United States, and printing presses to the US Treasury Bureau of Engraving and Printing; similar presses are also used by the Bank of England.

The production of stamps on the part of De La Rue originated in 1853, when their first contract was received from the Inland Revenue for the supply of fiscal stamps. Contracts for the postal requirements of Great Britain and India followed in 1885 and lasted for fifty-five and seventy-one years respectively; and 1951 saw the production of the first United Nations stamps. The printing of paper currency on the part of De La Rue originated in 1860, with the production of its first notes – £5, £1 and 10s – for the Government of Mauritius. 1914 saw the printing of the first notes below £5 issued since 1822, the 10s and the first £1 note on watermarked paper for eighty-nine years. In the Second World War, tens of thousands of cases of currency and stamps were printed for the exiled Governments of France, Czechoslovakia, Greece, Poland and Yugoslavia, for use on the liberation of their countries. Stamps were also printed for Norway, issued by the exiled Government in London for use on correspondence posted at sea on Norwegian merchant ships, and, in certain circumstances, from Norwegian camps in Great Britain.

The post-war era marked a new age. Given time, man continued with the business of living and earning his living. New conditions came into being, new interests and new requirements; a development in taste and an appreciation of progressive trends. It may be said that, in keeping with traditional foresight, the House of De La Rue envisaged and met the needs of the changing society and of a changing world, experimenting with new methods and perfecting new materials undreamt of a century and a half ago. This branching out has, for example, affected many a home, bringing comfort, warmth, cleanliness and elegance, and efficiency in the service of industry. It also contributes to the security of the realm by guarding and transporting the nation's money and valuables. In constant touch with the dazzling achievements and possibilities of the harnessed and latent resources of science and technology, it is perhaps timely to mention here that Formica International laminate-based potentiometers were used to track Commander Alan Shepard's space rocket; and in keeping with the times, *THE WORLD OF DE LA RUE* [a book produced by the company at the time] shows delicately coloured, gleaming earth surfaces and dark oceans. This is how our planet looks to the adventurer on high: the astronaut.

ABSORBING OTHERS

In 1963 De La Rue had just absorbed a long-time competitor, J. Waterlow and Sons, and in 1986 it bought another perennial rival for banknote business around the world, Bradbury Wilkinson, a subsidiary of American Bank Note. So keen was the then Managing Director, Peter Orchard, to absorb Bradbury Wilkinson, known to everyone as 'Brads', that he agreed to pay the price demanded by Ed Weitzen, the President of American Bank Note, without question, and without insisting on due diligence. Needless to say, De La Rue's Finance Director, John White, was horrified, a concern somewhat justified when it was discovered that Bradbury Wilkinson was not quite the force it appeared to be.

In the 1990s De La Rue further strengthened its position by buying, first, Portals, the papermaker, and then Harrisons, another competitive security printer. Certainly in the case of Brads and Portals it could be argued (and was argued by many, especially in the City) that De La Rue paid too much. Others appreciated the long-term strategic benefits of the two acquisitions and felt that the short-term financial pain was worth it.

MANUFACTURED ALL OVER THE WORLD

Over the years De La Rue has operated from and manufactured in many places, though it currently produces banknotes and components in six locations: in the UK at Overton in Hampshire (paper), Gateshead in the north-east of England, and Debden in Essex; and in Malta, Kenya and Sri Lanka. As we shall see, all the factories combined to produce a new currency for Iraq in record time in the middle of 2003 following the downfall of the Saddam regime. From its original base in Bunhill Row in the East End of London, which again, as we shall see, was almost obliterated in the Blitz in 1940, the company has, at one time or another, manufactured in over 25 other locations around the world including: Leeds, Dublin, Gateshead, Dunstable, Crawley, Gatwick, Overton, Debden, Westhoughton (threads), Basingstoke, Bathford Mill, Windsor and Tewkesbury in the UK, Brazil, Colombia, Malta, Kenya, New Zealand, Singapore, Hong Kong, Sri Lanka, Mexico, Argentina, the USA and South Africa.

Manufacturing in Leeds was the result of the bombing of De La Rue's factories in Bunhill Row at the end of 1940, when their friendly rival, John Waddington, who were based in Leeds, forgot the rivalry and stepped in to help. Victor Watson wrote in *The Waddingtons Story*:

> In December 1940 the De La Rue main factory was completely gutted during the first big London fire raid and within days Waddingtons were printing and finishing foreign banknotes which had been the main output of this particular factory. Although playing

cards, also produced in these buildings, had never been mentioned, or even thought about, when the two managing directors met together at the burnt-out site with the remains still smouldering, a characteristic gesture was made by Victor Watson who said, 'For every pack of cards produced for John Waddington we shall manufacture one for De La Rue.'

Manufacturing in Dublin was also the result of the bombing of Bunhill Row, as Alan Nolan offered the services of his company, Browne and Nolan. De La Rue printed from this plant until the 1980s.

The Leeds plant was supplanted by the brand-new 200,000-square-foot factory De La Rue built in the 1960s. At its peak, the Gateshead plant employed 1,700 people, but this gradually diminished as the company took advantage of lower costs in the plants it set up overseas in the 1970s, 1980s and 1990s, including Malta, Singapore, Hong Kong, Sri Lanka and Kenya. The Singapore and Hong Kong factories were sold at the end of the 1990s.

The factory in Malta has been a huge success. This is what long-time executive of De La Rue, Nicol McGregor, had to say about it:

When the opportunity was given to me to go to Malta to set up a new factory I saw that as a tremendous opportunity to do things the way they ought to be done, and not the way they were done in Gateshead – not even the way they were done in Dublin – but the way that I and the other people working with me felt should be done.

Malta was a building site when I went. David Rowe-Beddoe phoned me up and said, 'We're building a new factory in Malta, I want you to go and set it up.' And that was a tremendous thrill to feel that you were being sent to do something completely new, green field site, or rather a dusty brown site.

I went there with Len and Winnie Weston, who had been chosen to train the print and finishing team respectively, and one or two other expatriates followed as we gradually built up a team and started the factory going. I went out in April '75, we took over the first part of the factory in September and were finishing notes there by the end of the year. And I recall that we finished 44 million notes in the financial year '75/76 which we were very proud of.

McGregor then stayed in Malta for five years and said of his time there:

I was obviously ready to come back at the end. But it was a very challenging period throughout. We have to remember that De La Rue was pretty nervous about this, right from the initial investment – it was a major step to take and the company was not rich at that time. The original plan, in fact, was to transfer secondhand autos [older-generation banknote presses] from Gateshead and to put them down in a cheap location and use sweated labour. However, in one of those moments of foresight that the company has had from time to time, people sat back and said, 'No, this is not the right way to do it – if we're setting up a new factory we want to have the best equipment.' So a late decision was taken to install brand new De La Rue Giori multicolour presses which didn't exist anywhere else in the Group, and we were given this new kit to work with. So we had to work out new working practices to operate the kit for the first time, which was one of the great challenges.

At the time, the redoubtable Dom Mintoff, who professed publicly to have no liking for the British, was Prime Minister, but McGregor found that in reality, the anti-British threats were mostly for local consumption:

> We were working there under the Mintoff regime, which most British companies took a very dim view of. Many of them came to see me when they were looking at Malta as a prospective country to invest in, and went away incredulous that De La Rue had decided to invest in Malta, which seemed to them to be a most unstable country with the risk of expropriation from this nutty socialist prime minister. But in fact De La Rue's faith was very well founded. We had received all the assurances that we needed that our investment was going to be safe, we had been given very attractive incentives to invest there, cheap building and so on, and we actually had nothing but help from the government because they needed the investment and wanted it to be successful.

The company now has the largest banknote design facility in the world at its plant in Basingstoke. It has always led the banknote world in its design expertise, and still does today.

For 60 years after the Second World War, the main strategy of the De La Rue Board was diversification (the company's diversification actually began in the First World War, but it was rather haphazard at that stage). The feeling was that the days of the banknote were numbered and that cash would be replaced by plastic cards and electronic transfer of money. In the event, though the use of both plastic cards and electronic transfer have expanded enormously, so has the use of cash. De La Rue conducts research into people's use of cash, and a recent survey in 2009 showed that cash remains the preferred means of payment for 58 per cent of people in the UK. This seems just as true in the rest of the world. For example, according to the World Payments Report of 2006, the aggregate number and value of ATM cash withdrawals grew at an annual rate of 5.9 and 7.1 per cent respectively from 2000 to 2004.

There were many attempts at diversification during these 60 years, with some, such as Crosfield Electronics and many of the companies in what became known as the Cash Systems division, at least related to De La Rue's main business. Others, such as Potterton Boilers and Formica, were completely unrelated. Finally, in 2008, De La Rue sold its Cash Systems division and it was 'back to basics'.

De La Rue did not begin life as a banknote printer. Indeed, its early fame was as a printer of general stationery. Thomas de la Rue, the founder, began his business by publishing *Le Miroir Politique* in Guernsey in 1813. He moved to London and in 1821 was printing general items including stationery. He was also a fancy goods manufacturer. Most significantly, in 1813 he was granted a Royal Letter Patent by King William IV to manufacture playing cards by using the typographical method of production. A born entrepreneur, Thomas de la Rue printed a special golden edition of the *Sun* newspaper to celebrate the coronation of Queen Victoria in 1838. The Great Exhibition of 1851 was an important event for De La Rue. Thomas's son, Warren, was involved in the organisation and was able to exhibit on the large De La Rue stand the envelope-folding machine that he had invented. 1853 was another important year for the company, as it won the contract to print adhesive fiscal stamps for the UK's Board of Inland Revenue. These stamps were the first to be surface printed and the first to be perforated. Following up this success, by the mid-1850s De La Rue was printing postage stamps for countries throughout the world, including the Cape of Good Hope, Mauritius, Trinidad, Western Australia, Ceylon, Saint Helena, the Bahamas, Natal and St Lucia.

1860 was the momentous year when De La Rue printed its first banknotes. They were for Mauritius. By this time, De La Rue was printing general stationery, playing cards, postage stamps and banknotes; and to cope, it opened a new factory in Bunhill Row in London. The company continued to grow and prosper but, as is so often the case, the third and certainly the fourth generation of de la Rues were not of the same calibre as the first two, Thomas himself, his brilliant son Warren, and his other effervescent son William, known affectionately as 'Colonel Billy'.

The first two decades of the 20th century proved to be difficult, and by the early 1920s De La Rue was in financial trouble and in danger of collapse. Fortunately, an investor who had made money during the bull market based on rubber in 1910–14, Sidney Lamert, stepped in to rescue it. With the help of a former Waterlow employee, Bernard Westall, Lamert steered the company through the depressed years of the 1920s and 1930s and the Second World War.

Thereafter, led by the energetic Arthur Norman, known as 'Gerry', De La Rue expanded throughout the world towards the magnificent company it is today. The diversification policy was pursued, and some of the acquisitions, notably Formica and Crosfield Electronics, at times contributed worthwhile profits. More often, the acquisitions had a tendency to drink the profits made by the backbone of the company, banknote printing. From the mid-1990s the diversification strategy was abandoned completely. The plastic card business was sold to the French banknote printer, Oberthur, while the banknote and stamp printer, Harrisons, a subsidiary of Lonrho, was purchased.

Before this acquisition there had been five major banknote printers in the world – De La Rue, Giesecke und Devrient in Germany, Oberthur in France, British American Banknote in Canada, and Harrisons in the UK. At the same time as De La Rue bought Harrisons, Giesecke und Devrient bought British American Banknote, reducing the number to three. Also at the end of the 1990s, Giori was bought by Koenig and Bauer, and De La Rue's association with banknote press manufacture came to an end.

A constant companion to banknote printing is counterfeiting, and De La Rue has always had to stay one step ahead of the counterfeiters. These criminals were given a new opportunity with the development of the photocopier, especially the colour photocopier, and it was partly to fight this that De La Rue saw the benefit of buying Portals, the long-established banknote paper manufacturer. Portals had also built into their paper some qualities that counterfeiters would find very difficult to reproduce.

On to Portals and back 300 years to 1713. Isaac Newton, Master of the Royal Mint, was still alive.

Chapter Two

The Portals Arrive in England

Portals, 1712–1914

'His bones were broken one by one'
The making of bank paper
The South Sea Bubble
The Bank of England
Supplier to many banks
Forgeries
'Servants at the Mill must starve'
A contract in India

'HIS BONES WERE BROKEN ONE BY ONE'

The Portals came from France and were effectively, as Huguenots (Protestants), refugees from the persecution put in place by King Louis XIV. Louis – the Sun King – reigned from 1643 until 1715 and his reign is seen by many as a golden period in French history. Nevertheless, Louis was not noted for his tolerance. As far as he was concerned, 'L'État, c'est moi' ('The State, it is I'), and as far as the religious beliefs of his subjects went, it was to be 'Un seul roi, une seule foi' ('One king, one faith'). In 1685 he revoked the Edict of Nantes, a decree promulgated in 1598 by Henri IV to restore internal peace in a France riven by wars between Roman Catholics and Protestants (Huguenots). The Edict defined the rights of the Huguenots, granting them full liberty of conscience and private worship, liberty of public worship where previously granted, full civil rights including the right to hold public office, royal subsidies for Huguenot schools, special courts with both Catholic and Huguenot judges, retention of the Protestant Church in France, and Huguenot control of some 200 towns and cities.

Having revoked the Edict, Louis sent out his dragoons to enforce conformity to Catholic ways. Sir Francis Portal described it well in his book, *Portals, the Church, the State, and the People*:

> At the same time as revoking the Edict of Nantes he let loose such a carnage of persecution as can only be compared with the massacre of St Bartholomew just over a hundred years before. This new terror was commonly known as Les Dragonnades, from the dragoons who sought out Huguenot families in their homes and hiding places all over the country and put them to death in the cruellest ways. Prominent among the victims was Antoine Chamier, a grandson of Antoinette de Portal. He was arrested at a prayer meeting, and condemned to be put to death on the 'wheel'. There, his bones were broken one by one, in an ordeal which lasted three whole days. Only then was he given the coup de grâce which put an end to his suffering. [...]
>
> Other victims whose names have come down in history were Louis de Portal, and his wife Jeanne de la Porte. He was the Seigneur de la Portalière in the province of Dauphiné, and at the time he and his wife were living on the route which the dragoons followed on their way to the massacre referred to above. Their house was burnt over their heads and both Louis and his wife had their throats cut.

The branch of the Portal family with which we are directly concerned, that of Jean François de Portal, also suffered mightily. Many of them were murdered, but Guillaume and his younger brother, Henri, hid in a disused bread oven when the dragoons arrived. They then fled to Bordeaux where they were concealed in empty casks on an outward-bound ship. It's not certain, but it seems that they went to Holland first, before moving to London. Guillaume took orders in the Church of England, and his son Abraham became a tutor to George III when he was Prince of Wales, and was a famous silversmith, poet and friend of Hogarth and Sheridan. As Sir Francis put it:

> This line is the senior branch of the Portal family in England, and its descendants in the present generation include Marshal of the Royal Air Force Viscount Portal of Hungerford, KG, GCB, OM, DSO, MC (a Director of Portals Ltd) and his brother Admiral Sir Reginald Portal, KCB, DSC.

Henri moved to Southampton and became apprenticed at a paper mill at South Stoneham nearby, owned by the White Paper Makers' Company. In 1711 Henri Portal became a naturalised Englishman. The certificate read:

> These are to Certifie that Henry [note change of spelling; by this time England was at war with the French] Portall of South Stoneham in this County gent Did at this Generall Quarter Sessions of the peace, in open Court, take the oaths of Allegiance and Supremacy And the Abjuration Oath And likewise repeat and Subscribe the Declaration required by an Act for Naturalizing foreign Protestants.

THE MAKING OF BANK PAPER

In the meantime, Henry Portal had impressed a local squire, Mr William Heathcote of Hursley Park, with his intelligence and hard work, and Heathcote leased him Bere Mill, originally a corn mill, on the upper reaches of the River Test, close to the London–Exeter road and about a mile from the village of Whitchurch. Portal moved to Bere Mill in 1712 and took a number of Huguenot papermakers with him from South Stoneham.

1712, therefore, is the year when Portals was founded. As it happens, it was also the year that Frederick the Great of Prussia was born. In spite of the fact that Prussia was small, with a population of only 2.5 million, thanks largely to Frederick it exercised a greater influence in Europe in the 18th century than that size merited.

Frederick was an important figure on the European scene, transforming Prussia from a small state in a European backwater into a modern economy. By the middle of the century, Prussia was important for the British and therefore for Portals.

Henry Portal prospered and six years later was able to take a 99-year lease on Laverstoke Mill, a mile to the east of Bere Mill. He signed an agreement to build a new mill on the site, pay an annual rent of £5 (about £600 in today's money) and provide 'one Reame of fine foolscap paper neatly cut'.

William Heathcote really did prove to be a wonderful patron to Henry Portal, introducing him to his uncle, Sir Gilbert Heathcote, who just happened to be the Governor of the Bank of England. The Bank had recently begun to issue banknotes, and with Heathcote's recommendation behind him, Portal signed a draft contract in November 1724:

Draft Contract with Mr Henry Portal
For the Making of Bank Paper

27 November 1724

> I HENRY PORTAL of Bere Mill near Whitchurch in the County of Southampton Papermaker do hereby contract and Agree to and with the Governor and Company of the Bank of England.
>
> That I will make for the Use and Service of the said Governor and Company such number of Rheams of Paper for Bank Notes of the like goodness or fitter for their Service than the paper now used for that Purpose as they the said Governor, and Company shall think it fit to require and shall and will deliver the said Paper when made and finished at the Public Office of the said Governor and Company in London at and for the Price of Eight Shillings per Rheam and no more. They the said Governor and Company paying and allowing the Kings Duty for Excise the Charges for Felting Cloth and the Water Carriage for the same from Newbury to London.

THE SOUTH SEA BUBBLE

Henry Portal's success in securing the Bank of England contract took place in the immediate aftermath of what became known as the South Sea Bubble.

The South Sea Company had been set up in 1711 by the government as an effective alternative to what was perceived as the monopolistic Whig Bank of England. For eight years the company did little except supply slaves to Latin America, but in 1719 it was decided to offer shares to the general public. The PR man who masterminded the promotion was Sir John Blunt, and, just as with the 1980s privatisations, investors had to pay a little up front and the remainder by instalments. The issue was heavily over-subscribed, and there was an outcry when it was discovered that men of influence had received an extra allocation. The government itself made loans to the public secured on the shares themselves, provided the money was used to buy more stock. If this was not the fuel for a short-lived boom and an almighty crash, it is difficult to think of a better one. Pouring oil on the flames was the oleaginous Blunt, who talked of high dividends and the ending of the war with Spain.

At the beginning of 1720 the shares stood at £128. By March they were £330, by May £550 and by 24 June £1,050. At that point, the government, after all its members had sold at or near the peak, brought in an Act to prevent similar enterprises. Crash! Within weeks the price was back to £175 and by the end of the year, at £124, lower than it had been at the beginning of the year.

There was, as always, an inquiry and the Chancellor of the Exchequer, the Duke of Argyll, was found guilty of infamous corruption and sent to the Tower. And, as always, there were some heart-rending anecdotes. Sir Isaac Newton who, among his many other achievements, served as Master of the Mint, said at the beginning of 1720: 'I can calculate the motions of the heavenly bodies, but not the madness of people.'

He sold his shares in the company having made a profit of £7,000 (£840,000 in today's money) – a solid profit of 100 per cent. However, as the shares took off he bought back in, a decision that cost him £20,000 or £2.4 million in today's money.

In contrast to Newton, Thomas Guy, a bookseller dealing in bibles and books of common prayer, as well as buying sailors' tickets (credit notes issued by the Navy in lieu of pay) at deep discounts, made a fortune out of South Sea Company shares. In April 1720, his holding was worth £54,000, but over the next two months he sold it for £234,000 – about £28 million in today's money. To the benefit of generations of Londoners since, he founded and endowed Guy's Hospital.

Amid all this excitement, Henry Portal kept his cool and secured the contract with the Bank, and his company was on its way.

THE BANK OF ENGLAND

The Bank of England had been founded in 1694 largely as a response to the money needs of the War of the Grand Alliance against France. However, for decades before this, promissory notes, known as Goldsmith's notes, were used for making payments between merchants and traders. In 1677 there were no fewer than 44 goldsmiths in London engaged in this activity. The Goldsmith's notes were in manuscript form and, as their circulation was very limited, they did not serve the purpose of a general note issue.

When the Bank of England was founded there were already a number of bankers operating throughout Europe, but none of them except one was a bank of issue, so that the Bank's notes were the first of their kind in the UK.

Marco Polo spent seventeen years in China in the 13th century and was greatly impressed with the idea of 'paper cut into pieces of money'. He wrote of the notes in circulation under the Great Khan Kublai. Apparently they were printed in black ink on the peculiarly dark-grey paper produced by pulping the bark of the mulberry tree, and bore the authorising seal in bright vermilion.

This is what was written in *The Banknote*, published by De La Rue in 1971:

> The history of banking is as old as civilised man and is closely connected with his efforts to overcome a difficulty or crisis of some sort. Much has been published about the political, social and economic history of banking but little has been said about the practical and technical history of banknotes. The purpose of this brief story is to attempt to fill some of this gap.
>
> Records exist of banking deposits and loans four thousand years ago in Babylon, and there is evidence that the Chinese and the Greeks and the Romans had banking facilities several centuries before the birth of Christ. Paper came comparatively late in the history of man and we can therefore assume that the ancestors of paper currency were the clay tablets of Babylon, various objects (rare or practical) which were used as value tokens and, later, the leather currency used by the Chinese and the Romans. Leather currency probably bore some sort of printing in order to give it value but history does not relate how this was done.
>
> The first true paper money is said to have appeared in China about AD 700, and it is likely that these were merely statements of debt or credit, which were negotiable. [...]
>
> In Europe the introduction of paper money came very slowly. The marriage of paper to print started in the 15th century, but this was confined to the production of wood-cuts, etchings, books and pamphlets; there was no real necessity for printing paper money. It was then the common custom for merchants and wealthy men to deposit their money and valuables with goldsmiths who would give them a written receipt, which in England became known as Goldsmith's Notes. They could be exchanged for payments between merchants, but there was no question of a design, although some of them had a hand seal of authenticity stamped on them. A seal to show authenticity goes back thousands of years, and it is of interest to note that present day designers of banknotes are sometimes required to introduce an official seal in the designs. [...]
>
> It was the development of banking which set the scene for designing and issuing paper money. By the 17th century there were many banks in Europe, but it was not until 1661 that a Swedish bank actually issued the first banknote. It was an abortive

> attempt which lasted only three years, because of financial difficulties. [...] The Bank of England was founded in 1694 and within a few months they were issuing their own banknotes. The design was extremely simple, just a few lines of engraved text with spaces for handwritten date, number signature and the name of the payee. The printed text merely said that the Bank promised to pay a specified sum at the Bank's premises. The top centre of the note showed the engraved figure of Britannia, which embodied the characteristics originally created by the Romans for use on the coinage of Britain in the first century of AD. The vignette of Britannia throughout the centuries has had many varying forms, but it is still the seal of the Bank of England.
>
> The first notes were printed on plain paper and in the following year (1695) the bank ran into counterfeiting difficulties. The forgers were probably dealt with by the time-honoured custom of hanging but the technical response to the problem is interesting. The Bank promptly arranged for a specially designed watermark paper to be made and this seems likely to be the first time a watermark was used as a measure of security.
>
> In those days, banknotes were engraved on copper plates and printed, one or two at a time, on a hand-operated press. Basically the press consists of a flat-bed which is made to pass between two cylinders, the upper cylinder being adjustable to obtain the necessary pressure. To operate the press the plate is first warmed and inked and then surface-wiped, leaving the engraving full of ink; damp paper is placed on the plate, which is then made to pass between the two cylinders under considerable pressure, thus producing the print. By this method a good workman could turn out about 1,500 sheets a day, which was adequate for the needs of the times. It is interesting to note that this kind of machine was used in the 16th century by artists to produce copies of their engravings and etchings; similar machines were used in the 18th and 19th centuries to produce banknotes.

At the Bank of England at the end of the 17th century, the first notes were written by hand, with a few lines of engraving. On 30 July 1694 the Court of Directors ordered 'that the Running Cash Notes be printed'. The method used was plate-printing, and copper plates were engraved for notes of £5, £10, £20, £50 and £100. When we take into account inflation and multiply by 120, at £600, £1,200, £2,400, £6,000 and £12,000 in today's terms, these were high-denomination notes.

The figure of Britannia, which formed the subject of the vignette, had been adopted by the Bank as their seal, and the Court of Directors ordered 'that the Seale which was now shewn to this Court ... being Britannia sitting and looking on a Bank of mony ... be the Common Seale of the Company in all their transactions'. The figure resembled very closely the design by John Roettier, which embodied the characteristics of the original Britannia, created, as we have seen, by the Emperor Hadrian for use on the coinage of Britain in the 1st century AD. The figure is bare-headed – originally to distinguish it from the helmeted figure of Roma – and is armed with a spear, while the left hand holds an olive branch. In the Bank's version, the shield is fittingly emblazoned with the Cross of St George instead of the 'old' Union flag, which appears on the coin of 1672, and the 'Bank of mony' is represented by a pile of coins at the side of the figure. This vignette of Britannia, which, in the course of years, has taken varying forms, has been a feature of every printed Bank of England note from the very beginning.

The first order from the Bank of England for 12,000 printed notes in seven denominations (£5, £10, £20, £30, £40, £50 and £100) was placed on 5 June 1695. The issue was short-lived, because in August 1695 a forged note for £100 was presented for payment, and on the 14th of that month it was ordered 'that all the Running Cash Notes for the future be written by some of the Cashiers, and that noe more of the printed ones bee delivered out'.

The directors of the Bank reacted quickly and within a week decided that 'a mould be made for making Ten reames of paper', and a special committee was appointed to 'consider of the forme of the Mould'. This was how the idea of a special watermark, which became an outstanding feature of all Bank of England notes, came about.

The paper was made, as was all paper of good quality at that time, from linen rag with a proportion of cotton. The process of manufacture was by dipping a wire mould into a vat of pulp, the solid part of which, as soon as the surplus water had drained between the wires, was 'couched' onto a bed of felt to undergo its preliminary drying. It was then pressed, dried and 'tub-sized' by being passed through a weak solution of animal size.

The wire mould was contained in a wooden frame, upon which another wooden frame, known as a deckle, was fitted, in order to prevent the pulp, while still in a liquid state, from running over the edges. It would, however, penetrate slightly between the two frames, and thin out gradually into what is known as the 'deckle edge', a well-known feature of all hand-made paper. The design of the watermark was reproduced in stout wire, worked into the required pattern and sewn onto the mould with extremely thin wire, with the result that the wet pulp, and consequently the finished paper, was thinner where it had lain upon the wire pattern, producing the phenomenon of a design lighter than its surroundings when held to the light, and darker when placed on an opaque background. Watermarks at this period were usually employed as manufacturers' marks, or to distinguish the dimensions of the paper – for example, foolscap paper was originally watermarked with a representation of such a cap – and it seems likely that the Bank was the first private corporation to use a watermark on its own as measure of security.

Forgery, as might be expected, was a constant source of trouble. By an Act of 1697, the forgery or alteration of a banknote was declared to be 'a felony without benefit of the clergy'. However, the prospect of capital punishment did not seem to deter potential forgers. Counterfeiting continued, while erasure and alteration – the words and figures of the amount were in manuscript – were a constant source of anxiety. In 1722 the Bank, with a view to finding a means of combating this form of crime, adopted the unusual course of sending a cashier to Newgate prison in order to interview a forger who had been found guilty of erasing and altering a banknote, and had been sentenced to death. The condemned man, who was young and well educated, was found to be cooperative, and provided some useful information.

He suggested, for example, that erasure would be made practically impossible if the amount of a banknote were to 'appear on the reverse of the note in figures against the figures on the front', and it is interesting to note that although no action was taken at the time, this device was tried, nearly 100 years later, as a security measure.

The forger also criticised the paper, which he said was spongy and ill-coloured and made erasure by chemicals easy. The Bank decided to look into this problem. The original banknote paper had been supplied by Sutton Courtney Mill, but the owner, Rice Walkins, had died in 1705 and perhaps the quality of the paper had deteriorated. By a happy coincidence, as we have seen, the Governor of the Bank, Sir Gilbert Heathcote, was introduced to Henry Portal by his nephew. Portal's paper proved to be of much better quality than that coming out of Sutton Courtney Mill. It was harder and of better texture, and the watermark had a definition and clarity not found on the other paper. The design of the watermark remained the same, except that the words 'Bank of England' in the panel at the foot of the note were in roman capitals rather than in italics.

At this time there were probably about 200 small paper mills dotted around the country, none of them employing more than a handful of people. Papermaking had established itself at the end of the 15th century in mills operated by water power. Most mills would be used to grind corn also.

Bere and Laverstoke mills would have employed fewer than ten people each. One or two people would have worked on sorting rag, with perhaps another two or three on stamping and grinding operations – what was later called breaking and beating – and the remainder would have been in the vat house, where the skilled journeyman – the vat man – was the boss. He would have been supported by his coucher and the 'dry-worker' or dryerman who operated in a separate drying loft.

SUPPLIER TO MANY BANKS

From 1724 until 1813 the paper went by 'water carriage' from Laverstoke Mill to London. Enclosed in 'elm chests with locks and bound with iron' and transported on twelve miles of unadopted road to Newbury, it went by barge on the River Kennet to Reading, and then by the Thames to London.

The difficulties of travelling by road during the 18th century are illustrated by this entry in his diary of 1755 by Henry Portal's son, Joseph:

> 10 November 1755. Carr. it to Lond° in my own waggon and went the first day from hence to Egham which was too farr and I believe occasion'd the death of one of my horses which dy'd of the frett comeing home. Next time to go no further than Bagshot the first day and to get done by ye week after Michaelmas at latest if possible for the roads was very badd and made it much worse for my horses.

From 1725 to 1819 the Bank of England sent a representative to the mill to oversee the production of the banknote paper. He was known as 'Ye Bank Officer'. The first was Mr Carruthers, and Portal noted in 1725: 'For Boarding Mr Carruthers 17 weeks at 10/– [50p or £60 today], £8.10.0.'

Laverstoke Mill concentrated on producing paper for Bank of England banknotes, while Bere Mill's customers were the provincial banks as well as leading stationers both in London and the provinces. Joseph Portal, who inherited the business when his father died in 1747, supplied a large number of private banks, which at that time printed their own banknotes. He also supplied the Bank of Ireland, the General Bank of India by order of Messrs Drummonds, Charing Cross, and the Bank of Hindustan.

Joseph had appreciated the importance of Sir William Heathcote to the family business, writing to him on 1 November 1747, just after his father's death:

> I presume ere this you have heard of my father's death, and as you Hon^{r}. was principally instrumental in procuring him the making of Bank Paper, and afterwards when he was opposed, in preserving it to him the making the Bank Paper [a reference to Jubb – see below], I most humbly begg the continuance of your favour to me, and my Mother, if there be occasion; for, as it comes in course to be made next Summer, tis not unlikely that someone or other will take this advantage of his death to get it from us.

Jubb was clearly a competitor, as can be seen from this note at the bottom of the 'Coppy of the Bank Bill' of 1737:

> NB – There was an opposition made at this time by One Jubb at Yewell paper mill by which means ye Price was lowered 1s.p. Ream, and the duty, Felting and carr^{g} to London all struck off and to be p^{d} and done by ye Maker.

And in August 1749 Joseph wrote again to Sir William, saying:

> As I am making the paper for the Bank this Summer and shall soon go to Town with it in order to take my money it may not be amiss to make the Governor a present of a Haunch of Venison. I begg of you to give an order to send to Hurseley for it when I have an opportunity to convey it with speed to London.

Portals was still having to cope with the Ye Bank Officer. The only problem was that the Officer did not have enough to do and would find excuses to have 'parties' with the employees. A journal entry by Joseph Portal in 1755 gives some idea of the problems that this entertaining could cause:

> Wee began making Monday, May 26th, and the following Fryday Mr Poole gave a treat at Ye White Hart to all the men and women and children that workt at Both Mills. This day was found Inconvenient, for some of them gott drunk and no work was done at any mill on Satterday.

> N.B. Next time we have ye feast the Satterday before we begin making to avoid the like mischief again.

There may have been negligible inflation by late 20th century standards, but nevertheless Joseph Portal felt the need in 1772 to request higher payments from the Bank of England because of increased cost in production. He recorded that 'the Governor and Directors ordered me Thirty Guineas [£31.50 or £3,780 in today's money] over and above my Bill as a Douceur but it should have been Fifty'.

As well as extra costs, Portals were experiencing some difficulties in delivering the paper to the Bank. Here is an entry from Joseph Portal in one of the accounts books:

> Next time to unload at the Bank front door to let them be carried in on their little Trucks, a Chest at a time and not draw round to Bartholomew where it is very troublesome and could not get into the Bank Court with the Waggon but was forced at last to put them into a Cart and twas with great difficulty Mr Fisher turned ye Waggon about again.

Joseph coped well with all the inflationary pressures and continued to build the business. He bought the Laverstoke estate in 1759 and was appointed High Sheriff of Hampshire for the year 1763. He developed the idiosyncratic habit of inserting into his bank and other accounts books certain 'Receipts' and 'Standing Memorandums' such as:

> A Receipt for the frett in a Horse – Take one pint of Sack and one ounce of Venus Trakle well stir'd till ye Trakle is desolv'd and Drench him with it.
>
> Doct. Meades Receipt for the Bite of a madd Dog – Take of the grey ground Liverwort and Long Pepper each two ounces and make it into a Powder and keep it in a Bottle Close stopt. Give a Dram of the Powder every morning in milk or Broth for 9 days running as soon as possible after the Bite. This above for a Man, but for Hoggs and Sheep half as much and for a Horse etc half as much again.

Joseph died in 1793 at the age of 72, and left his estate to his eldest son, Harry. He died after only a few years and the estate passed to the second son, William. The third son, John, took over the business and immediately invited his cousin, William Bridges, to join him as a partner. Bridges seems to have been very much the junior partner, managing the mill while John secured the business.

Sir Francis Portal gives us an insight into the Portal family status in Hampshire at this time, noting that the redoubtable Jane Austen approved of them (even if they were in trade!):

> What sort of picture, then, can we form of John when he inherited the business at the age of twenty-nine? We can assume, I think, that he was both able and reliable: otherwise he would not have been successful in carrying out the responsibility for fifty-

five years, including periods of difficulty almost amounting to crises for the mills. For more personal references to the setting in which he lived, let us turn to Jane Austen, who grew up at Steventon, about 2½ miles from Overton. She and her family used to attend the dances in the Assembly Rooms at Basingstoke, and writing about one of these to her sister Cassandra, on 9 January 1796, she says, '... After this necessary preamble I shall proceed to inform you that we had an exceeding good ball last night ... In addition to our set at the Harwoods' ball, we had the Grants, St Johns, Lady Rivers and her three daughters and a son, Mr and Miss Heathcote, Mrs Lefevre, two Mr Watkins, Mr J Portal, Miss Deanes, two Miss Ledgers, and a tall clergyman who came with them, whose name Mary would never have guessed.' During Christmas 1798 she writes to her sister about another of these dances: '... There were nearly sixty people and sometimes we had seventeen couples. The Portsmouths, Dorchesters, Bolton, Portals, and Clerk were there, and all the meaner and more usual etceteras'. In 1817, towards the close of her life, she writes from Chawton, to her niece Caroline in north Hampshire, in a letter dated 26 March: 'How very well Edward is looking! You can have nobody in your neighbourhood to vie with him at all, except Mr Portal.'

Portals continued to supply the Bank of England with paper with the same watermark, but at the end of the 18th century a few alterations were made; and in 1800 William Brewer, who became the Bank's mould-maker, suggested to the Bank that the laid lines in the Bank of England's note should be waved instead of straight. Another security device was added by the inclusion in the watermark of the denomination of the note in bold roman capitals.

The early years of the new partnership, Portal & Bridges, were busy ones. The French Revolution caused economic ripples not only in France but elsewhere, and in 1793, faced with a currency shortage, the Bank of England issued notes for £5. This was followed in 1797 with the issue of £1 and £2 notes, causing a leap in demand for paper from Portal & Bridges. At the same time the firm experienced increased demand for loan paper and notepaper from the Banks of Ireland, India and Hindustan, and country banks.

They obviously coped, as is made clear by this entry in A.D. Mackenzie's book, *The Bank of England Note*:

> [I]ncreased requirements of paper seemed to present no difficulties for Portal & Bridges, who responded at all times to the repeated demands for paper that were constantly made upon them.

Nevertheless, in 1807 the Bank of England considered a plan for printing the notes four on a sheet instead of the customary two. Both the paper and moulds were manufactured accordingly and the Bank's presses adapted.

In the 18th century, as we have seen, Portals benefited from the growth of British commerce, and consequently the increasing importance of banking and the Bank of England.

There were three factors in the expansion of British business: a growing domestic demand for American and Asian consumer goods, especially sugar, tea, tobacco and coffee, and north European raw materials such as timber; a growing European market for re-exports of the products imported from America and Asia; and a growing protected market for British products in the colonies in America and Africa. And London finance was closely involved. As *The Picture of London* wrote at the beginning of the 19th century:

> London is the centre of the trade of the whole world, and more ships sail from it in a year than from all other places in the world united. It has fifty times more trade than ancient Carthage, than Venice in its glory, than all the Hans towns or Amsterdam could ever boast.

Furthermore, many of those at the top of the finance and merchant houses were, like Portals and the De La Rues, of European origin: either Huguenots, Dutch Jews or Germans.

At the centre of it all was the Bank of England. As David Kynaston wrote in the first part of his four-volume history of the City of London:

> Another central pillar of the City now taking shape was the Bank of England, established in 1694 by opportunistic merchants in order to fund the war against France. Over the next century there were few pauses for peace, the national debt grew inexorably, and the Bank of England not only managed that debt but became a government bank, looking after the accounts of most of the departments of state. Moreover [which was of great benefit to Portals], backed by its considerable bullion reserves, it issued a large volume of notes, becoming the dominant influence in the London money market. In the course of the eighteenth century it came to seem indispensable: in 1745, as the looming presence of the Young Pretender threatened a potentially fatal run on the Bank, a powerful group of merchants met at Garraway's and agreed to accept its notes as payment; in the financial crisis of 1763 the Bank for the first time acted as lender of last resort; and in 1781 the prime minister Lord North famously referred to it as 'from long habit and usage of many years ... a part of the constitution.'

At the end of the 18th century and for the first fifteen years of the 19th, Europe was continually at war, and this further strengthened the position of London and Britain as the dominant force in world trade. The French occupation of Amsterdam in 1795 was fatal to the claims of financial supremacy of that city.

According to Kynaston, there were three key events in the 1790s:

> In 1793 a monumental commercial crisis was only avoided through Pitt and the Directors of the Bank of England coming up with a timely issue of Exchequer Bills; three years later Pitt's ennoblement of Smith [Robert Smith, a prominent banker] was a tacit recognition of the importance of financial advice; thirdly in 1797, the beginning

of Restriction (by which the drain on the Bank's gold reserves made it necessary to stop paying out gold in exchange for the Bank's notes).

FORGERIES

As we have seen, forgery was a constant source of concern, and it became acute in the early years of the 19th century. The Napoleonic wars and their aftermath brought an increase in economic uncertainty and therefore crime, as wars always do.

At the turn of the century the number of forged notes per year was rising to about 4,000, although the Brewer modifications described above drove it down to 3,000 by 1803, where it stayed for a number of years; then, in 1811, it rose sharply to 9,000, and in 1812 to 18,000. By 1817 it was 31,000. By this time, the general public, incensed by the number of hangings of mostly very poor people who had been duped into passing notes made by the real forgers (who, needless to say, mostly escaped unscathed), were bombarding the Bank with suggestions. The populace was already outraged by the inflation caused by the Napoleonic wars (wars are always inflationary), and it was further outraged by what it saw as excessive brutality towards so-called forgers.

William Cobbett wrote in his *Political Register*:

> This villainous Bank has slaughtered more people than would people a State. With the rope, the prison, the hulk and the transport ship, this Bank has destroyed, perhaps, fifty thousand persons, including the widows and orphans of the victims.

One correspondent wrote to the *Examiner* and suggested that all hangings for forgery should be carried out by a Director of the Bank. Leigh Hunt, the editor, wrote:

> Our correspondent professes to have been some time debating with himself, whether it would be still more effective if the Forger were to hang the Director.

In December 1817 the Bank appointed a 'Committee to examine plans for the Improvement of Bank Note, and for the prevention of forgery'. By 1819 no fewer than 108 projects had been examined, as well as 70 varieties of paper. Sir William Congreve, a member of the Royal Commission on Security Printing, submitted a plan that would wed collaboration between mould-maker and papermaker.

Needless to say, Portal & Bridges were closely involved in all this activity. The firm of Applegarth & Cowper were granted £5,000 (£600,000 in today's money) to continue their work of colour printing, and they made demands with regard to the banknote paper, insisting on a special quality and certain texture. Portal & Bridges were forced to install new plant to accommodate their wishes.

Brewer, the mould-maker, came to Laverstoke Mill to work with John Portal (Bridges died in 1819) and put into practice Sir William Congreve's suggestions. These mainly consisted of 'triple paper', of which the distinctive feature was a coloured watermark. Three separate sheets of extremely thin paper, one of them coloured by the use of stencils, were dipped and couched one on another, with the coloured sheet in the middle, so that, after pressure, they dried as one sheet. As a result, the paper, which showed the watermark only faintly, would, on being held to the light, fully reveal the colour that was embedded between the outside layers.

Many experiments were carried out, and finally the chosen method was three dippings and one couching. The results were shown to the Bank, but they were unhappy about the colour. John Portal was against it also, on the grounds of cost. The complicated production process would necessitate extra plant and staff, in itself a forgery risk. The price of the paper would double and, as it was heavier, the duty payable would increase as well. In the end, although it was embarrassing because Sir William Congreve's suggestion had been approved by the Royal Commission, the Bank had to inform him that they were not going to adopt his paper. Furthermore, in 1821, after forgeries of Applegarth & Cowper's colour notes had been discovered, the Bank put a stop to their experiments also. Brewer's implementation of Sir William Congreve's suggestion remained the only alterations made.

However, John Portal, who had succeeded in extracting £2,000 (£240,000 in today's money) from the Bank of England as a grant for all his experimental work, now put forward a new idea. This involved radical change in the design of the banknote watermark.

In 1801, when the waved lines and the denomination in words had been embodied in the watermark of the £1 and £2 notes, the remainder of the design, i.e. the looped border and scroll in the margin, had remained unchanged. John Portal's idea was to dispense with both these features and to substitute a broad and simple design of waved lines, enclosed in a panel with waved edges, covering the whole expanse of the paper except for a very narrow margin. The denomination of the note would be shown in roman capitals similar to those used for the £1 and £2 notes, and in the same place across the middle of the note. The words 'BANK OF ENGLAND' would appear, also in large roman capitals, at the head and foot of the panel. Also, by increasing, almost imperceptibly, the thickness of the paper, it would be possible to make more prominent both the waved lines and the lettering.

The Bank loved it, strongly approving the clarity of the watermark and the simplicity of the design. They immediately decided to adopt it, although it was 1824 before sufficient paper was produced and the printing completed so that an issue could be made. This new design was a great success: it remained untouched for 30 years and then became the basis of the design that endured until the second half of the 20th century.

In 1825 a number of provincial banks failed, causing a run on the Bank of England and a reduction in the Bank's stock of gold. There was a huge demand for currency, leading to such a shortage of notes that the £1 note was produced again to help relieve the crisis.

'SERVANTS AT THE MILL MUST STARVE'

By this time Portals were tied very closely to the Bank of England. Indeed, in 1815 the Bank requested that the company sever all connections with the provincial banks. John Portal was obviously pleased to be close to the Bank, but it meant that the company would suffer if the Bank's orders dried up. For example, in 1821 both the £1 and £2 notes, first issued in 1797, were discontinued, and John Portal wrote to the Governor of the Bank:

> Dear Sir,
>
> In the present state of things I am of course retarded in my Northern Tour [a projected holiday previously mentioned] until I hear again from you – the difficulties to contend with must be got over before with any satisfaction I leave home.
>
> The men now at work for me at the Mill, are I believe truly not to be matched in any one respect – and it is no more than right to give them encouragement adequate to their merit. I certainly can prevent them starving by continuing their pay though the Mill is laid still – and I would do this willingly and without troubling you, did I not know that the consequences of this would inevitably be to drive them to the Ale-house for employment, and after contracting habits of Vice and Idleness, it would be quite in vain to hope to recover them to the industry, and steadiness for which they are at present so peculiar. They are at present, I may say, doing their work beautifully, and it is so delicate and nice a kind, that when thrown out of the practice, it would be a length of time before they would again arrive at the same perfection …
>
> [He goes on to ask whether an order might be made to entail a] halfday's work, which would keep those hands in, and would be no great detriment to you, and I would willingly pay them their whole day and abide the loss, rather than incur the inconveniences I have mentioned – and I think you will be happy to acquiesce in my suggestion on this head. – Your forgiveness for my importunity will oblige.
>
> Dear Sir
>
> Yours very truly
>
> JOHN PORTAL

The Governor rescued Portals with an order, but the same potential crisis arose again in 1838. John Portal wrote to the Governor when the Bank were delaying orders because of a possible change to the notes:

> If you are in doubt as to the precise note to be made use of at the Bank in future [a new issue was still under consideration], I am far from wishing you to give an Order to make Notes which may be useless. At the same time – allow me to say – it is my duty to inform you that the Servants at the Mill (if thrown out of work) must starve, if they have no order from the Bank; as they are exclusively – I may say – 'Servants of the Bank'.

To parry this difficulty, at least for some weeks – I trust you will forgive me if I suggest putting the men at work upon Dividend Warrant paper at this time – instead of next year, if you approve of this proposal, to which I consider there can be no objection. I flatter myself you will be happy to make this charitable accommodation, by sending the Dividend Warrant moulds to the Mill, they may be put to work immediately.

I am, Dear Sir,
Your very Obedient
Faithful Servant
JOHN PORTAL

A 'charitable accommodation' was made and an order for dividend warrant paper received, but it was not enough to keep the mill fully occupied. John Portal, by this time 74 years old, was faced with a real crisis. Luckily, his brother William came to the rescue. He wrote these two letters to John:

Dear John,

I beg leave to return your Cheque for the balance of our account to the 31st December last, and wish you a pleasant Holiday with it; and I beg that in future you will not credit me with the Charge on the Mill, which I relinquish henceforth altogether.

Yours very Affect^ly
W. PORTAL

The second letter goes further.

My dear John,

Your connection with the Bank seems precarious, and as it may in some degree enable you to pursue the course you think best in that matter with less anxiety, I freely give you up my life-interest in Charlcot Farm, and also in Southington Farm, with the half-years-rent due on each at Michaelmas last, subject of course to the usual outgoings.

Yrs, My dear John
very Affect^ly
W. PORTAL

This help from his brother saved the firm, but they were still under a great deal of pressure – and probably regretting bitterly that they had abandoned their connections with the other banks. Just how bad things were is revealed by this letter from John Portal to the Governor of the Bank on 7 January 1840:

> My dear Sir,
>
> Now upwards of a year and a quarter since any Bank Notes have been made. I should therefore foresee that the stock at the Bank must be running short.

He went on to remind the Governor how the company had worked day and night when the Bank needed notes urgently, and concluded:

> The Mill Servants of the Bank I also plead for, they have been out of work these last four weeks.

Fortunately, the Bank responded and by the end of the year Laverstoke Mill was busy again.

There was another financial crisis in the mid-1830s, leading to an increase in banknote forgeries, and in 1838 the Governor of the Bank of England expressed concern about the watermark. He recommended that while the design of the watermark should remain otherwise unchanged, the denomination across the middle of the note should be in opaque letters instead of being only outlined. William Brewer and John Dusautoy, John Portal's partner since the death of William Bridges, were consulted by the Bank and agreed that such a paper could be made. Experiments were carried out and samples produced, but the Bank seemed to lose enthusiasm and the project died.

However, William Brewer's son, also called William and also a first-class mouldmaker, continued work on the shaded watermark in collaboration with John Smith, a die-sinker used by the Bank, and in 1849 they patented their device. Two years later, as Messrs Brewer & Smith & Company, they signed an agreement with the Bank whereby the latter acquired the sole right to use the invention. By this time Wyndham Portal had succeeded his father in running the business.

John Portal died, at the age of 83, in 1848. Again, the estate was left to the eldest son, Melville, and the business to the third son, Wyndham, who had been working at the mill since 1841. The second son, Robert, went into the army and became one of the few survivors of the Charge of the Light Brigade at Balaklava in 1854. He joined Wyndham as a partner in 1863.

We have all heard about the horrors and the folly of the Charge of the Light Brigade, but it is interesting to have a quote or two taken from a letter to his mother the day after the charge, from Robert Portal, as a participant:

> By a perfect miracle, I, among a few more, was not touched by anything, except a piece of shell caught me in the back, but it was quite spent and did not hurt me in the least. Our Major was killed, as also a Lieutenant Sparke; Captain Hutton shot through both thighs. To give you an idea of the loss sustained by the Light Cavalry Brigade, – in round numbers we mustered on parade 800 soldiers, last night we numbered 180. I numbered in my troop this morning on parade ten mounted men. I have twenty left in the troop, but the horses are nearly all sick and wounded. Captain Nolan was shot

> dead the first shot, and we think it was a judgement on him for having been the cause of our getting into such a mess. Lord Lucan is dreadfully cut up about it, but says that he 'can show the order in writing, which is his only comfort'. The number of wounds and deaths among the officers is too horrid to think of. Poor Morris, who joined here a fortnight ago, having just recovered from his cholera attack at Varna, and who had just succeeded to the command of the 17th Lancers in consequence of the sudden death by cholera of Major Willett, was shot in the head. I passed him lying on the ground when we were in full gallop, but of course could do nothing. He was found and brought in, and was not quite dead, but quite out of his mind. I must write to Arthur Taylor by this mail about him. The horse I was riding (Paddy) was shot with a Minié ball through the fleshy part of the leg, but he brought me back all right nevertheless. It was altogether the maddest and most extraordinary order ever given to Cavalry, and there is to be an inquiry instituted at once. Lord Raglan, who came down here last night, was furious, and said loudly that 'the Cavalry had been wantonly sacrificed'. They might now send us home I think. The French were looking on at this wonderful charge and held up their hands in astonishment. They said 'it was most splendid, but it was not war'. I slew one Russian by running him through the vitals with my sword; several more were scratched a little. If they had any pluck at all, not one of us, if we had been ten times as strong, could ever have come back again.

Wyndham had been working on experiments on the new paper, and the Bank's acquisition of the Brewer & Smith patent led to the first issue of a note incorporating a 'shaded' watermark in 1855, the shaded portion being the denomination of the note in roman capitals within a centre panel. The broad and simple design of waved lines, first introduced in 1824, covered the rest of the note (see illustration).

While the work preparing for this new banknote paper was going on, an agreement was made between the Bank and Wyndham Portal for the Bank's mould-making department to be transferred to Laverstoke Mill. The move took place in 1852 and William Brewer Jr was put in charge of the new Mould Office. This obviously brought Portals even closer to the Bank of England.

A CONTRACT IN INDIA

Between 1854 and 1861, Laverstoke Mill was completely rebuilt and new sizing and drying machines were installed. Nevertheless, the paper continued to be made by hand. Business for Portals was booming, not least because it won a new contract in India. Following the insurrections in India in the late 1850s, during which the infamous Black Hole of Calcutta incident occurred, a new government of India was formed in 1860. This government decided to issue a new currency note that would circulate alongside the existing notes of the banks of the three Presidencies: Bengal, Madras and Bombay. The Bank of England undertook the printing, and the paper was supplied by Portals with the light-and-shade watermark following the pattern used for the Bank of England. It included the facsimile signatures of Lord Canning, the Governor General, and James Wilson, the Financial Member of the Council.

Conditions in India were different from England and the notes struggled to cope with repeated re-issue, constant handling by the local population, and the humid atmosphere during the monsoon season. There were also instances of forgery. In 1864 the Bank held discussions with the India Office and Wyndham Portal, and although it was agreed that the existing paper was tough and of excellent quality, a new design was agreed and new notes issued in 1867. The paper was slightly tougher, the signatures in the watermark were discontinued, and it no longer bore a vignette.

The next big event after the rebuilding of Laverstoke Mill and the award of the Indian contract was the first serious internal security breakdown. Two Portals employees stole some paper, passing it to a forger who was able to produce notes on genuine Bank of England paper. An intensive police investigation led to the capture of the criminals and Wyndham Portal revised the whole system of security at Laverstoke Mill, eventually setting up a Security Control Diary. The system proved to be so successful that it stayed in place for over 100 years.

Then came an Act of Parliament in 1880 authorising the issue of Postal Orders. The Post Office asked the Bank of England to print them and Portals to supply the paper. Combined with the Indian rupee contracts and an increase in Bank of England business, this extra demand led to the installation in 1885 of a Fourdrinier Paper-Making Machine to manufacture the Postal Order paper. (The Fourdrinier family were also Huguenots from France.)

The Fourdrinier Paper-Making Machine was the first papermaking machine to make continuous paper. Prior to this machine, paper was made in single separate sheets.

Instead of placing the stock, or watery pulp, onto individual screens, the Fourdrinier machine used a continuous screen, or wire, made of woven wires, that moved like an endless belt. The stock was sprayed or dropped onto the moving wire. The water was drained and sucked out through the porous screen. The stock was usually about 3 per cent solids when it was placed on the wire and about 7 per cent solids by the time it got to the end of the wire.

At the end of the wire, the stock was picked off the felt from above (at the couch roll) by a felt which was moving at the same speed. Often, the stock went through a series of rollers that squeezed and/or sucked more water out of the stock. This section was called the press section. By the end of the press section, the stock was usually 40–50 per cent solids.

The stock then moved into the dryer section. The dryer section was made up of a series of dryer rolls or one large dryer. Dryers were heated from the inside by dry steam and from the outside by hot air. The stock was usually about 95 per cent solids by the time it came off the last dryers.

The original Fourdrinier machines had to hang the paper in long sheets to dry. Eventually, the paper was scraped off the dryer and wound onto the dry end winder as part of the continuous process. Often, the paper had to be rewound on rewinders to make the paper's thickness and grain consistent.

The process of the wet end wire, placing stock on a continuously moving wire, was the initial innovation of the Fourdrinier machine. This innovation made today's high-speed paper machines possible.

The *Paper Trade Review* wrote of this development:

> The fact that the famous Laverstoke Mills should put in a machine, is an indication of the times. Its reputation as a vat mill is unassailable. We believe, however, that the recent issue of Postal Notes has led to this new departure. Doubtless other Government Security Papers are also required. Whatever may have first led to this addition to the production of the Laverstoke Mills, the celebration of the two hundredth anniversary of the Edict of Nantes [This was incorrect: it was the 200th anniversary of Louis XIV's *revoking* of the Edict of Nantes] is an appropriate time for so remarkable a change in what must be one of the oldest as well as the foremost vat mill in Great Britain.

In 1885 the Bank of England allowed Portals to manufacture banknotes for the Bank of Scotland and, the following year, the company also began supplying the Bank of Ireland. With the business flourishing, the 19th century ended on a happy personal note when Queen Victoria created Wyndham Portal a baronet. Sir Wyndham died at the age of 83 in 1905 and was succeeded by his two elder sons, Sir William Portal, Bt., and Spencer (later Sir Spencer) Portal, Bt.

One of William's first actions was to revive Bere Mill, where the company had started. Production of paper at Bere Mill had stopped in 1815 following the agreement with the Bank of England that Portals would stop producing trade papers and banknotes for provincial banks. Now William decided to introduce electricity into Laverstoke Mill and, in 1906, installed a turbine in Bere Mill to transmit the power. In the same year the company leased Bramshott Mill, Liphook, and William Portal wrote to the Governor of the Bank:

> You will be interested to hear that we purchased last week, the lease of Bramshott Paper Mill ... It contains an excellent Paper machine, which is practically new, (it is 2 years old) and which is of the <u>same</u> type as that which we already have here for the manufacture of Postal Orders.
>
> We are taking immediate steps for putting the Mill itself in a condition suitable for our requirements and, when all is ready, we shall devote it to the making of Postal Order paper.

Chapter Three

The Founding of Thomas De La Rue

1813–1850

A humble start
Thomas founds his first business
London and straw hats
Now playing cards
The move to Bunhill Row
Thomas arrested for debt
Some stability
Postage and envelopes
'The highest perfection'

A HUMBLE START

Thomas de la Rue made a very humble start in life. Born in Guernsey, an island in the English Channel, in 1793, the year the King of France, Louis XVI, died on the guillotine, he was the seventh of nine children of Eleazar and Rachel de la Rue. He was born and spent his early years in Le Bourg in the parish of La Forêt, the second-smallest parish on Guernsey, whose whole population was only 16,155. La Forêt's population was a mere 552. The de la Rues were poor, with Eleazar scratching out a living on a smallholding. Eleven of them slept in just two rooms.

In 1802, the de la Rues sold their farmhouse and bought a house in the centre of St Peter Port, the capital of Guernsey. At least this provided more possibilities of employment to the many children, and on 1 March 1803 Thomas became apprenticed to a master printer, Joseph Antoine Chevalier. The agreement for the length of the apprenticeship stipulated seven years. For the first two years he would have to work for nothing, in the third year he would receive two shillings a week, then three shillings in his fourth, and six shillings in his final year. (It is difficult to offer a judgement on what this would be in today's money, but I would estimate a shilling at about £6.) For these sums he would have to work six days a week.

Monsieur Chevalier's main production was the *Gazette de l'Ile de Guernsey*, the first printed newspaper on the island, and it was printed in both French and English. Thomas was effectively a jack-of-all-trades in the business, and as such received a good general grounding in the art of printing. By 1811, Thomas's apprenticeship was over, and while he was looking for a new position he met Tom Greenslade, who had emigrated from Bishop's Nympton, a village in Devon in south-west England. By this time Guernsey was booming, and Thomas and Greenslade decided that the island could support another newspaper, which they described as a 'journal politique et littéraire'. Greenslade took on Thomas, by this time eighteen years old, not only for his knowledge of printing, but more importantly because Thomas promised to attract the subscribers. By September 1812, Thomas had secured enough subscribers and the paper, called *Le Publiciste*, was launched. It was a weekly, on sale 'tous les samedis chez T. Greenslade au bas du Pollet et chez T. De La Rue au haut de la Rue de la Fontaine'.

THOMAS FOUNDS HIS FIRST BUSINESS

Unfortunately, Thomas and Greenslade fell out and they produced only thirteen editions, the last appearing on 19 December 1812. Thomas stormed off, but Greenslade continued to publish with the help of a new assistant. In February 1813, Thomas published a competing journal, *Le Miroir Politique*, price 3d (1.25p or £1.50 in today's money). He must have secured some financial backing but, if so, his backers were happy to remain anonymous. At nineteen, Thomas was already his own master and he lost no time in attacking not only his former employer, Greenslade, with the words: 'Désirant de plus sincère de mon coeur d'avoir plus tien de commun avec T. Greenslade' ('Desiring more truth from my heart than the dialogue with T Greenslade'); but also the other newspapers on the island with: 'Quatre journaux françois! C'est assez, c'est beaucoup; c'est trop peut-être pour cette île.' ('Four French newspapers! It's enough, it's plenty; it's perhaps too many for this island.)

His competitors did not like this, and both the *Policiste* and the *Mercure* attacked him in turn. In spite of this, indeed perhaps because of the publicity, Thomas's paper thrived and within two months he was advertising for additional help. Furthermore, he was able to announce that the *Miroir Politique* would soon appear in fine print on paper 'd'un qualité supérieur'. This was so well received that he published a special edition of the Liturgy and the Psalms – the only volumes, alongside the Prayer Book and the Bible, to be found in the average Guernsey home.

We will never know whether Thomas thanked Greenslade, before they quarrelled, for introducing him to Jane Warren. She came from the same village in Devon as Greenslade. Indeed, they were distantly related. Because of its remoteness in an age when the vast majority of people did not travel far from their own village, almost everyone in Bishop's Nympton was related to someone else in the village. Lorna Houseman, in her book *The House that Thomas Built*, explained the whole scenario surrounding the de la Rue family's involvement with the Warrens:

> Ironically it was Greenslade who was involved in Thomas's meeting with his future wife, Jane Warren ... [her] family was still more numerous than Thomas's and, in so far as he owned no property of his own, her father was less well-endowed than Eleazar ... Because of the size of their family the Warrens had cause to rejoice that the young Guernseyman had taken a daughter off their hands. Twenty-four year-old Jane, born in a generation which believed, like Elizabeth Elliot in Jane Austen's *Persuasion*, that after her mid-twenties a woman 'felt her approach to the years of danger', also had reason to feel relieved. But what of Thomas, who had not even celebrated his twenty-first birthday and was four years her junior? Why should he want to marry an older woman from an impecunious family in this remote Devonshire village?
>
> The Warren girls had some attraction. For Jane's sister Sarah married twenty-four year-old Paul de la Rue, Thomas's younger brother, when she was thirty-one, well over Jane Austen's danger limit. Obviously the two sisters were neither ill-favoured nor unaccomplished in the eyes of the de la Rues.
>
> There was also another reason for the de la Rue brothers to marry out of Guernsey. They lived at the time when the island's social conventions were still rigidly adhered to. Wedding outside the appropriate families was frowned upon, and early marriage strongly discouraged; children constituted a source of free labour for their parents. In such matters it was the materfamilias who had the final word. As Eleazar was his wife's inferior not only in wealth but health, Rachel's word carried more than usual weight. Whereas Eleazar survived for only another two years, Rachel lived for another twenty. Had Thomas and Paul not chosen outside the island she would have selected their brides for them 'The young people who broke away from this system', says a Guernsey historian, 'were those who learnt a trade and were adventurous enough to emigrate'. The de la Rue boys did both these things.

LONDON AND STRAW HATS

Thomas could not see a future for himself and his family (Jane gave birth to a boy, whom they called Warren, in honour of her family, early in 1815) in Guernsey. Guernsey's prosperity was dented by the defeat of Napoleon at Waterloo in that year. There were no more French ships to be captured, and the returned soldiers and sailors as well as the idle privateers brought heavy unemployment to the island. Thomas decided to move to England and sold his *Miroir Politique* to his brother-in-law, John Champion, who had married his older sister, Rachel. In early 1816, Thomas's wife gave birth again, this time to a daughter whom they named Jane after her mother. When Thomas left Guernsey with his wife and two infant children he left behind his mother, who was taken in by the long-suffering Champions.

Thomas and his family probably moved to Bishop's Nympton for a time, but this was never going to satisfy a man of his ambition and, after raising money in nearby Barnstaple, he moved to London. His next problem was deciding in what trade he should start a business. Printing was the obvious one, but starting a newspaper in London was a totally different proposition from starting one in Guernsey. One deterrent was the recent raising of tax on newspapers from twopence to fourpence. (This made the tax alone in today's money about £2!) The government's reason for raising this tax was not to create revenue but to try to reduce the number of newspapers, most of which were highly critical of the government. Furthermore, economic conditions after the end of the long Napoleonic wars were not good. The whole of Europe was suffering and was too poor to buy enough British exports, the national debt was an astronomical £860 million (no less than £100 billion in today's money!) and, as in Guernsey, the demobbed soldiers and sailors pushed up unemployment. It was not a perfect time for starting a business.

The country reeled under the blow of a stunted harvest to add to the trade depression and a glutted labour market. In his book *The Real Oliver Twist*, John Waller describes the conditions in the Nottingham area:

> The summer of 1815 had brought a fearful drought, which destroyed potatoes and other root crops. The harvesting of grain began early, but rainstorms then set in with such strength and persistency that work had to be abandoned and the crops left to rot in the fields. Severe shortages and high bread prices were the result. All over the country, horses were slaughtered for meat or left to starve, cottagers killed their pigs, and many were reduced to eating turnips and nettles. In the capital, crowds of 'poor women, without cloaks or bonnets, some with scarcely cloaths to cover them', gathered to demand cheaper bread. In Nottingham, a desperate scramble for flour ensued. Mobs railed against the millers, grain barges were plundered, and knots of hungry women hurled stones at the premises of bakers. They then joined their menfolk in ambushing a detachment of yeomanry carrying a cartload of grain. Several cotton mills were also attacked on the grounds that they had caused the hardship which left most of the population too poor to buy the essentials of life.

Asa Briggs, renowned historian of 19th-century Britain, agreed:

> In 1816 and early 1817, there was a gloom in the countryside and distress in almost all industrial areas. At Birmingham 'nearly a fifth part of the population' were receiving weekly relief; in the iron-producing area of the Black Country there was the 'silence of unmingled desolation' inside many of the great ironworks and the cries of angry men outside.

And London itself would have been a great contrast to the more gentle ways of Guernsey and Devon. George III was very old, and suffering from what was then thought of as a mental disease. (Recently doctors have suggested it was porphyria, a blood disease.) The Prince Regent, as with many princes who have to wait too long to attain full power, was wasting his life in heavy spending and debauchery; while throughout London there was drunkenness, lax morality, and a plethora of chancers and tricksters ready to prey on unwary strangers. The capital was physically squalid, a labyrinth of narrow streets bounded by Hyde Park Corner and the New Road in the west, stretching to Shadwell in the east, and from a little beyond Old Street in the north to St George's Church, Southwark in the south. Robberies and brawls were commonplace. Beyond the city, a great part of Finsbury, Lambeth and St George's fields had only recently been reclaimed from marshland. Walworth, Peckham and Camberwell in the south, Hackney and Stepney in the east, Islington in the north and Kensington and Chelsea in the west were outlying villages, reached only with difficulty by roads not always passable and rarely safe.

What trade did Thomas choose? The *London Street Directory* tells us:

> De la Rue, T.
> 40 Crown St.
> Finsbury Square
> Straw hat manufacturer

This was not as mad as it sounds. Thomas was nothing if not alert to opportunities, and he would have noticed that straw hats, once seen as rather 'common', had become fashionable thanks to the scarcity of other materials during the Napoleonic wars. Upmarket hats had been made of beaver fur, but the source had dried up when the United States indulged in its own war against the British in 1812. The straw hat became fashionable both in France and Britain.

Thomas de la Rue became a straw hat manufacturer and tried all sorts of ideas, including making them waterproof by studying Macintosh's patent 'for rendering substances impervious to water'. He also looked at a substitute for leather invented by a Mr Hancock and a special dye created by a Monsieur Le Roi de St Germain. While experimenting with straw hats he did not forget paper, and he wondered whether straw could be used in its manufacture. He wrote down in the notebook he had bought in Barnstaple a French patent for such a process. He also carried out experiments in paper bonnets and in different colour dyes. Finally, in 1828 he wrote in his notebook: 'Adding a little talc in the liquor will add more brilliancy – it stands well – it is what I propose to myself for playing Cards!'

NOW PLAYING CARDS

This is the first mention of playing cards, which were to become so important for him. Certainly by 1830 Thomas was convinced that he was not going to make his fortune in hats, and he moved into the stationery business. Nevertheless, he did not abandon hats altogether. He went into stationery with two partners, friends he had made in Barnstaple: Samuel Cornish and William Frederick Rock. They set up in Queen Street, Finsbury and were described as 'Cardmakers, Hot Pressers and Enamellers'. Hot pressing was the production of a glossy surface between two plates, while enamelling meant the hard, smooth finish on the paper of playing cards.

1831 was an important year in the history of De La Rue. Thomas registered an ace of spades at Somerset House. This was the first public appearance of a De La Rue playing card, and in the following year 'His present most Excellent Majesty King William the Fourth' granted him a Royal Letters Patent for 'certain improvements in making or manufacturing and ornamenting playing cards'.

Before this development, playing cards had either been stencilled by hand in watercolours or printed in one colour and then hand-tinted. Whichever method was used, the process was laborious, expensive and inaccurate.

Thomas now registered patents concerning inks and printing. They were verbose, but as Lorna Houseman correctly wrote:

> The real contributions of Thomas's 'Improvements' were the 'Ring', the superior quick-drying oil-inks employed, the new method of glazing the cards by passing them between copper sheets through powerful rollers instead of the antique method of glazing by friction with a flint, and the use of enamelled paper.
>
> One of the problems of colour printing was that of 'register', i.e. ensuring that the pink of a royal face on a court card neither overlapped its outline nor failed to meet it, thereby engendering an ugly white gap. Thomas solved this by making a steel block or 'ring' into which was cut an oblong the exact size of a playing card. When a measured piece of lead was inserted in this aperture and pressed down on the original plate the lead, now bearing the image, could be extracted and fifty-two reproductions in reverse fitted together in four plates of precise size.

The Thomas de la Rue patent is very important because it led to his becoming known not only as 'the father of the English playing card' but also by some as the founder of modern English colour printing.

Thomas de le Rue was undoubtedly an innovator, and in 1829 he produced a large, royal octavo edition of the New Testament, 25 copies of which were embossed in pure gold powder. It was an amazing piece of work, but at £15 a copy (£1,800 in today's money) there were no buyers among the public. One was given to King William IV and Queen Adelaide at Brighton to celebrate their accession, and Timperley's *Dictionary of Printers and Printing* judged it to be a 'typographical wonder', with the gold alone worth five guineas (£630).

Only one copy was actually sold. Lord Spencer – great, great, great grandfather of Diana Spencer, later Princess of Wales – bought one for the library at his grand house in Althorp, Northamptonshire. Thomas was left with some gold powder, as only 104 copies were ever printed, even though he tried to relaunch it in 1834 and again in 1836. Nevertheless, all was not lost, as it enhanced his reputation as a printer of quality and luxury.

What it did achieve was a legal action brought against him by a Mr Horner, who claimed in the Court of Exchequer that in the course of manufacturing the gold New Testament his stereotype plates were ruined by printing on the hard enamelled vellum found for him by Mr de la Rue. Unfortunately for Horner, a copy of the book 'excited the administration of the Court so much' that proceedings were suspended while it was passed to the bench, on to the Bar and finally to the jury. The jury found in favour of the defendant and 'the learned Judge expressed a hope that the defendant would be able to furnish him with a copy of the work, the elegance of which he greatly admired'. Not for the first time, Thomas de la Rue had turned on the charm when it really mattered.

Having established himself as a playing card printer, Thomas spent the three years from 1832 to 1835 altering the designs of the playing card faces, which had remained unchanged for generations. His idea was to put some life into the faces of the kings, queens and knaves. At the same time he modernised their court dress and put feet on the queens.

The important card game of the day was whist, and the bible was *Mrs Battle's Opinions on Whist* by Charles Lamb. Mrs Battle did not want new designs, and asked: 'Why two colours when the mark of the suit would distinguish without it?'

Charles Lamb tried to support Thomas, saying:

> But the eye, my dear madam, is agreeably refreshed with variety. Man is not a creature of pure reason – he must have his senses delightfully appealed to. All these might be dispensed with [meaning Thomas's designs] and with their naked names upon the drab paste board the game might go on very well, pictureless, but the beauty of cards would be extinguished for ever.

However, Mrs Battle was a very determined woman and Thomas felt obliged to try to concur with her wishes. He is said to have 'incurred heavy losses in the endeavour to create a more elegant taste in playing cards'. Nevertheless, in a way, he was victorious. If he could not have his more lively kings and queens, and knaves and queens with feet, he would have more interesting backs on the cards. He invested in designers, 'choosing some of the best artists in London and giving them as much as twenty or thirty pounds [£3,600 or £4,800 in today's money] for a design no larger than a hand's breadth'.

The writer who put this down also noted that:

> Mr de la Rue's idea had been to excite and cultivate the public taste. In these more elegant forms of printing, formerly in England few or no manufacturers thought of going to the expense of employing designers. Others had merely copied French originals.

(It might be interesting to note here what the rates of pay were in the printing and binding industry in Britain in the mid-19th century. In relation to other industries and occupations, printers and binders were well paid. They were not quite at the top. This position was reserved for scientific, surgical and optical instrument-makers, alongside scale-makers and leather case-makers, watch-makers, jewellery-makers and engine-drivers, who earned 35 shillings a week (£1.75, or £210 in today's money). The printers and binders were second on 28–30 shillings (£1.40–£1.50, or £160–£180 today), alongside hat-makers, ivory-, bone- and wood-workers, earthenware-, arms- and tool-makers, iron-workers, cabinet-makers and upholsterers, musical instrument-makers, and bakers' and butchers' men.)

THE MOVE TO BUNHILL ROW

If 1831 had been a significant year for the future of De La Rue, 1833 was another one, for in that year the partnership of De La Rue, Cornish and Rock moved from Crown Street to 110 Bunhill Row, Finsbury, which they rented from a Mr James Esdaile for £230 per annum (£27,600 in today's money). De La Rue would be associated with Bunhill Row for more than the next 100 years. In the event, Thomas did not take up the rental in Bunhill Row until the following year, probably because he was busy, not only moving house but also changing partners. For twelve months he operated everything, including his family life (and by this time Jane had given birth to another four children) from 20 Finsbury Place. There was the family, the partnership of De La Rue and Rock, now calling itself 'Leghorn Manufacturers' (the *Oxford Dictionary* defines 'leghorn' as a hat of fine plaited straw), and a new partnership, De La Rue, James and Rudd, listed as 'Cardmakers, Embossers and Wholesale Fancy Stationers'. The embossing meant paper-hanging, for which Thomas was working on a new process. By 1835 Cornish and Rock had ended their partnership with Thomas, and we know that Rock made £5,000 (£600,000) from his three-year association.

When Thomas and his partners moved into 110 Bunhill Row, Jane moved her family into 108 Bunhill Row; so, at last, she had a house to herself with no warehouses and offices underneath. For his part, Thomas seems to have found secure ground. As Lorna Houseman put it:

> Bunhill Row was an agreeable street with a distinguished history of its own. The shaded expanse of Bunhill Fields opposite, with its avenue of plane trees, dated its burial ground from the time of a prehistoric tumulus, hence the name Bone Hill. In the seventeenth century it was opened to provide a cemetery for London dissenters, and contains the graves of Bunyan and Defoe. Down the road the Honourable Artillery Company set up its headquarters, its drill ground providing another open space. In the same street the blind Milton composed *Paradise Regained*, and it was here that he died soon afterwards.
>
> This was the site that Thomas chose for the founding of his house and dynasty. There he and his sons, grandsons and great-grandsons mapped the fortunes of De La Rue, until nearly all Bunhill Row and considerable portions of neighbouring property became assimilated into their empire.

However, all was not wine and roses yet.

THOMAS ARRESTED FOR DEBT

We have lived through some difficult economic periods since the Second World War, but they pale beside the crises that Thomas de la Rue faced in the 1830s and 40s as he tried to move his company forward. Here is Asa Briggs again, putting them in their context:

> The English social and economic crisis of 1837 and 1838 was serious enough in its practical implications without the need of apocalyptic Owenism to give it extra colour. Although it was the economic implications of the crisis which had the most significant political consequences – the formation of two great extra-parliamentary pressure groups, the Chartists and the Anti-Corn Law League – it was the social implications which fascinated a generation of prophets of catastrophe and captured the attention of the more critical members of society.
>
> The economic crisis of 1837, like the further crisis of 1842, involved more than the statistics of industry and trade; it touched the mainsprings of human emotion and imagination.

The early 1830s had been good times with plentiful harvests and strong trade, particularly with the United States. However, 1836 proved to be a turning point. The run of good harvests came to an end, and a financial crisis, beginning in the USA, broke the trade boom. This brought a serious recession in 1837, with businessmen forced to sell goods at prices below what they had paid for them.

By April of that year, Liverpool merchants were complaining in a petition to Parliament that 'the distress of the mercantile interest is intense beyond example and it is rapidly extending to all ranks and conditions of the community ... the prudent with the imprudent ... spinners and labourers with the manufacturers themselves', while from Birmingham the cry came that 'unless remedial measures will be immediately applied a large portion of our population will shortly be thrown out of employment ... with alarming consequences to all classes of the community'.

There was a slight recovery in the next four years but the recession returned with a vengeance in 1842, described by some as the worst year of the whole of the 19th century. Fortunately the next few years, with the exception of 1847, brought some recovery. By this time the boom in railway construction was dominating economic activity. However, even here, there was bust as well as boom. Here is Asa Briggs again:

> By 1845 there was much talk of a 'railway mania', far bigger than the canal mania of the 1790s but inevitably involving wild speculation as well as substantial genuine investment, and in October 1845 the railway bubble was pricked. A crisis in the railway share market was followed by the reappearance of unemployment in Lancashire and the Midlands and a rise in the expenditure on poor relief. More serious financial and economic difficulties ensued in 1847 and 1848, when the need for large grain imports to meet bad harvests led to a loss of gold, credit stringency, and some business

> failures. While the price of corn rose to 100s a quarter, a shortage of raw cotton led to short-time working in the Lancashire mills. Old tensions reappeared and social conflicts became once more acute.

Amid all this turmoil, the new partnership of De La Rue, James and Rudd faced serious difficulties too. On 29 April 1837 the account books noted: 'De La Rue and Company assigned all machinery and stock in trade and book debts to T.B. Crompton and William Sedgewick.'

Crompton and Sedgewick became Thomas's two main creditors for the next two years. They were substantial businessmen. The larger creditor of the two, Thomas Bonsor Crompton, was a millionaire cotton manufacturer and paper-miller. He was a big operator not only in Lancashire but also in London, where at one time or another he owned most of the established newspapers, including the *Morning Post* (eventually bought by the *Daily Telegraph* in 1937). They applied pressure on Thomas and, under this pressure, Thomas dissolved his partnership. On 2 May 1837 a notice appeared in the *Gazette* announcing the end of the partnership of De La Rue, James and Rudd.

Thomas now turned to two of his employees. One was Alfred Augustus Fry, the company's accountant, though also a man of scholarship who had, in conjunction with his son Danby, created 'a new arrangement and classification' of all the words in Johnson's *English Dictionary*. The other was Jonah Nathan, the key salesman. Crompton and Sedgewick seemed happy to go along with this, and wrote to Nathan on 6 May authorising him to collect all book debts while at the same time telling the customers that they should maintain their relations with De La Rue. They concluded: 'The business now placed upon a firm footing, you can have no difficulty in showing to your friends the advantage of confirming their connection with the house.'

However, all was not yet sweetness and light. On 25 May, Thomas was arrested for debt and incarcerated in the Bailiff's House. Such a house was called a 'Lock-up' or 'Sponging House'. Kept by the Bailiff, supported by his 'Bum', such a house was a half-way point between freedom and imprisonment. Thomas de la Rue would not have liked it; fortunately for him, he was there for only one night before Mr Sedgewick came riding to the rescue in his hansom cab, accompanied by his solicitor who said later: 'After much trouble, we obtained the liberation of Mr de la Rue giving undertaking to officer etc.'

Mr Sedgewick paid the fine of one guinea and was reimbursed by Augustus Fry. For the moment the debt, whatever it was, remained unpaid. Sedgewick's motivation, which would have been supported by Crompton, was to make sure that Thomas did not go bankrupt, in which case he would not have been able to repay them. Crompton was owed the very considerable sum of £9,500 (about £1.14 million in today's money).

Undaunted, Thomas continued to bargain with Crompton and Sedgewick throughout the summer of 1837. They wanted assignment of Thomas's white lead patent. He refused to give it to them. A vital ingredient used in the enamelling of new playing cards, he had been working on it since 1833. At the time it was fiercely expensive, a guinea an ounce, and Thomas was working on ways of making it cheaper. He perfected a process which he patented in 1837, just when both his and his country's fortunes were at their nadir. His argument to Crompton and Sedgewick was that they could ask only for such goods as he possessed at the time the debts were incurred, and not for money received as a result of this patent.

The patented method was certainly startling in its result, reducing the price from one guinea to just sixpence. Bizarrely, the good news travelled to Guernsey, where, on 11 June 1838, the *Guernsey Star* wrote:

> We are happy to state that Mr de la Rue, formerly a printer in this island, and well known as an inventor of the new playing cards, has recently discovered a method of preparing white lead, the new patent of which he has sold for thirty thousand pounds, reserving for himself one sixteenth of the profits. Many of our readers who know the ingenuity of Mr de la Rue will rejoice that this brilliance has crowned his labours.

In the meantime, Thomas reached a compromise with Crompton and Sedgewick whereby the property of his firm, including the complete stock of warehouse and factory, was vested in them as trustees for him and his interests. In return he asked them to guarantee his bills of exchange to tide him over his immediate difficulties, pay him a salary of £6 a week (£720), and allow him to stay in his house in Bunhill Row.

In spite of this arrangement the wrangling continued until June 1838, when Thomas decided to let Crompton have a share of the white lead patent if he would write off the debt of £9,500. This was only after strong words had been spoken on both sides. In spite of his status as a successful and wealthy businessman, Crompton did not want to discuss matters face-to-face with Thomas de la Rue. The latter's fiery temper was obviously bad enough at one remove and Crompton did not want to endure it at close range.

Elsewhere, Thomas's financial position seemed to be improving. One of his debtors, a Mr Cave, paid £2,500 (£300,000 in today's money) and a Mr Charles Button said he was willing to advance £7,000 (£840,000) plus a further £1,500 so that Thomas could relaunch his company. Apparently 'he thought it of so much consequence to Mr de la Rue to be free from the Trust' (i.e. the agreement to repay Crompton and Sedgewick). Finally, Crompton and Sedgewick agreed to wind up the trust, and although Thomas still owed Crompton £2,500, the latter agreed to accept Thomas's unsecured covenant that he would repay this sum. How was Thomas faring on the £6 a week that his two major creditors allowed him? It sounds very little, though it was equivalent to about £720 in today's money (or £37,000 a year).

It was not a king's ransom, and by this time Thomas and Jane had six children, but plenty of people survive quite well on less.

SOME STABILITY

One of the first acts of the revived De La Rue operation was to produce an edition of the *Sun* newspaper, printed in gold, to celebrate the coronation of Queen Victoria in 1838. Fortunately, in contrast to the ill-fated New Testaments of a few years earlier, it was a sell-out. Indeed, they went for a premium, with commemorative copies selling at five shillings (25p or £30 in today's money) and more. Thomas had persuaded Messrs Clowes and Sons of Stamford Street (still in business in spite of some difficult times recently) to make some of their printing machines available, and no fewer than 100,000 *Sun*s were printed and rushed over to Bunhill Row to be gilded. A marquee was erected in the open yard there to cope with the influx, and copies were spread out to dry over every available inch. This rush job lasted six days and over 100 men and women were brought in to help. All in all it was a brilliant success, and the mercurial Thomas, in one of his bursts of generosity, gave his ex-creditor William Sedgewick six copies of the golden *Sun*.

So Thomas was launched again, largely thanks to the investment by Charles Button. Who was he?

He was a wealthy chemist and importer of 'operative and manufacturing chemical apparatus'. He had many interests, among which he listed 'underwater cables' and sharing a patent for 'Certain Improvements in the Means of Appliances used in the Conveying of Telegraphic Intelligence between Different Places'. One of his scientific papers was called 'A Series of Tables of the Elementary and Compound Bodies Systematically arranged'. His co-author on this paper, and here is the key to his involvement with Thomas, was none other than Warren de la Rue, Thomas's eldest son.

Button and Warren were friends, though Button was much older. During their friendship, Button became convinced that the firm of De La Rue would benefit from Warren's input. Button was right.

What were Warren de la Rue's qualities, and how had they been developed?

Thomas had decided that Warren should be educated at a private school in France. His own education had been extremely limited and he wanted to do much better for his son. When he was sent to Sainte-Barbe school in Paris, Warren did not speak French. He may have been born in French-speaking Guernsey, but his parents had left for England when he was only two and had not taught him French. His first school reports in 1829 said that he was trying hard at French and that he was doing well at arithmetic. Generally he was proving to be an able and willing student, as this report shows:

> Cet enfant montre déjà plus de maturité que son age n'en comporte, la conduite très régulière, caractère bon, sensible, honnête avec ses maîtres et prévenant envers ses petits camarades. [This child already shows a maturity above his age, conduct very stable, good character, sensitive, honest with his masters and kind to his younger comrades.]

Although in his second year, perhaps affected by the onset of puberty, he brought forth from his masters the comment, 'quelques petits reproches', nevertheless they wrote that he is 'rempli d'intelligence' and forecast: 'Cet élève est capable de faire un sujet distingué, qu'il ne manque pas sa destinée.' His drawing was slow, his history 'faible', but his arithmetic outstanding.

Warren did not stay long at his school in France. 1830 brought a mini-revolution in the country as the middle-class moderates finally rebelled against the reactionary King Charles X and installed Louis-Philippe in his place. There was street fighting around the school, in which some of the senior boys became involved. It was enough for Thomas to bring his son home and to employ him in his struggling business. The first recorded evidence of his working at 110 Bunhill Row was his signature in 1835 on the contract of a Thomas Rockett, who was working as a card-maker at 45 shillings a week (this was the equivalent of £270 a week).

In spite of working for his father, Warren continued his scientific experiments, no doubt encouraged by Thomas, especially if they would benefit the business. His first scientific paper, on the Daniell electric battery, was published when he was 21.

The traumas of 1837 and 1838 affected Warren adversely, along with everyone else, and his salary went unpaid for a time. However, when Warren effectively brought Charles Button to the rescue of his father, Thomas put up £2,965 as Warren's share of the capital. His own was £6,877 and Button's the largest at £7,351.

Warren took the opportunity to get married. His bride, Georgiana Bowles, had also been in Guernsey, but her father was considerably wealthier than the de la Rues had been. When the Bowles family moved to London they bought a large house in Islington, from which Warren and Georgiana were married in 1840. Lorna Houseman gave an excellent précis of Georgiana's life and her benefit both to her husband and the De La Rue company:

> Young Mrs Warren de la Rue's good looks were delicate, Dresden China variety, and upon first meeting her some of her husband's friends were apprehensive about his choice of so fragile though so charming a partner. They did not think that she would be keeping him company for long in this world.
>
> As it turned out, however, it was his beloved Georgie who nursed Warren devotedly through illness of old age, attacking his international correspondence with gusto, and punctiliously answering on his behalf the kind inquiries of scientists from half Europe. A childhood attack of smallpox appeared neither to have weakened her constitution, nor marred her beauty. Travelling tirelessly with Warren, she rattled across Russia in a coach and comforted him in his wearisomely drawn out Italian business negotiations, the ultimate success of which, as her brother-in-law justly pointed out, owed more than a little to her patience and tact. Georgiana was a forerunner of a long line of company wives supporting their husbands around the globe. In her nineties she would cut short her enthralling tales to her grandchildren to ask anxiously after Bleriot's progress across the Channel. She died when she was ninety-eight.

With his business relaunched, the reinvigorated Thomas, still only in his late fifties (this was perhaps older in 1840 than it is today), took out another patent, this time for 'Improvements in printing calicoes and surfaces'. Within it are the words:

> In printing bankers checks, bills etc, bank notes, post office envelopes or any work requiring great difficulty of invention the wire fabric or tissue may be made with plain or ornamental ground.

Security printing. Here was his future. In a sense he was already in it, because the printing of playing cards requires the security of sameness that prevents cheating. His calico invention, using a Jacquard loom to create 'a cloth of wires', enabled him to produce these criss-cross lines 'like the checks in tartan' for the repetitive, all-over patterns of playing card backs, and ultimately for all kinds of security printing. *Chambers' Edinburgh Journal* wrote: 'Mr de la Rue is prouder of his wire cloth invention than of any other improvements he may have introduced.'

POSTAGE AND ENVELOPES

It was still fourteen years before De La Rue produced its first adhesive postage stamp, and twenty years before its first banknote, but envelopes were a different matter.

1840 was also the year in which Rowland Hill's idea for pre-paid Penny Postage was introduced. Before then, the payment for postage was something of a lottery. As often as not, the postage charge was paid by the recipient rather than the sender. Hill's idea was said to have been prompted by the story of an illiterate woman whose son had emigrated to Australia. He wrote to her regularly, but she never paid for the letter because she would have had to pay not only for the postage but also a reader; and anyway, she already knew the one thing she wanted to know – her son was alive and capable of writing to her.

Rowland Hill made his proposal to the government, which set up a Commission to examine it. They voted favourably, and the Prime Minister, Lord John Russell, told the House of Commons in 1839 that the government accepted the Commission's proposal and the Post Office envelopes would be issued. A competition held to decide the best designs was won by William Mulready RA. The envelopes, with elaborate drawings by Mulready, were made of thread paper and produced by John Dickinson. They were not a success.

Fortunately for De La Rue, Warren was friendly with Edwin, Rowland Hill's brother, and through this connection he learned that concentration on envelopes without design or stamps was the way forward for the moment. During the 1840s Warren and Edwin worked on creating an envelope-making machine.

Originally envelopes were used flat and unfolded. The customer would have to fold them. Later they were produced folded, this process done by hand. The invention of Warren and Edwin meant that more envelopes could be folded in an hour than had previously been folded in a day.

The *Engineer and Machinist* wrote this of Warren de la Rue's patent application for 'improvement in the manufacture of Envelopes' in August 1850: 'These improvements in the manufacture of envelopes refer more particularly to the gumming, or application of adhesive matter to the flaps requiring such application during the process.'

'THE HIGHEST PERFECTION'

We have already seen that Thomas de la Rue was no slouch when it came to securing publicity both for himself and his company, and in the 1840s he went into overdrive. There was no doubt that card-playing in Victorian families was becoming increasingly popular, and Thomas decided that articles in leading journals were the way to make sure that the De La Rue brand secured a healthy share of this market. On 16 April 1842, *Bradshaw's Journal* published an article under the title, 'Visit to Messrs De La Rue's Card Factory'. It was a very detailed article, and it began by eulogising over the skills of British manufacturing generally:

> Nor should we forget that it is from her superior productive skill, that England, with a comparatively small territory, and a soil less fertile than many of her neighbours, has become the master of the world, and to this in part she owes as well her political supremacy amongst the empires of Europe, as her influence over the demi-barbarous populace of the remotest parts of the habitable world.

It went on to talk of the 'skill and ingenuity of the Messrs De La Rue', which had brought to playing card manufacture 'the highest perfection'. The article described at length the manufacturing process, beginning with the preparation of the paper, which was subjected to pressure and then brushed over with white enamel to give it a highly polished finish. This was followed by the printing of the playing card fronts, which were divided into two groups, the 'pips' (i.e. the numbered cards) and the 'têtes' (the court cards). The pips were relatively easy to print, and as they had only one colour (either black or red), were worked together at the hand press. The court cards, containing five colours, were not so simple, but this was where Thomas's patent was important.

As *Bradshaw's* put it:

> The colours are printed separately and are made to fit into each other with great nicety, for this purpose a series of blocks is provided, which if united would form the figure intended to be produced. By printing successively from these blocks, the different colours fall into their proper places, and the whole process is completed. The printed fronts then go off to the drying rooms for three or four days.

The backs were printed in the same way, using Thomas's Jacquard calico method to produce:

> Repetitive tartan and criss-cross patterns from a single block engraved with straight lines and printed in one colour, which is afterwards crossed with the same or any other colour by again laying the sheet on the block, so that the first lines cross the second printing at any required angle.

Finally, in quantities of four or five reams at a time, the newly pasted sheets of cards were subjected to the gradual but powerful pressure of a hydraulic press of 100 tons, worked by a steam engine. This dispelled any air bubbles lurking between the layers of pasteboard. If any special quality was required, the backs of the cards were waterproofed with varnish.

> Then the cards were given solidarity. Between the fronts and the backs were pasted two ordinary layers of paper. To be of an especially smooth quality, the paste employed is cooled by steam, even the pasting performed with a large brush in a series of systematic movements is something of a work of 'art'.

Bradshaw's noted that the finest-quality cards were called 'Moguls', the next best 'Harrys', and those with imperfections, 'Highlanders'. The Moguls were supposed to be named after the Mogul emperors, Harrys were kings, after Henry VIII, and Highlanders were princes, after Bonnie Prince Charlie.

Bradshaw's concluded the article with:

> The whole of Messrs De La Rue's establishment is carried out in a manner perfectly unique. Steam power is used wherever practicable in the various departments of the business.

In 1853, De La Rue had the great good fortune to have six pages entitled 'A Pack of Cards' written by no less a figure than Charles Dickens, by this time famous not only in England but throughout the English-speaking world, published in his own journal, *Household Words*. Dickens noted that De La Rue used Owen Jones to design some of its playing card backs. Jones was a Welsh architect who would become well known for his illuminated gift books, and whose *Grammar of Ornamentation* achieved great fame. He began working for Thomas in 1844 and, over the following 23 years, created no fewer than 173 different playing card designs for the firm. For example, Charles Dickens expressed delight with the 'dainty little pictures' that he produced on cards for the royal family.

Others to give publicity to De La Rue included *Chambers' Journal*, produced by the Scottish publishers William and Robert Chambers, which noted that the company printed other things besides playing cards. One was railway tickets. Railways were being built throughout the country, even if the Duke of Wellington decried them as 'enabling the lower classes to travel about needlessly'. Thomas de la Rue was alive to the possibilities of such a growing market and in 1841 secured his first order from the London and Blackwall Railway. According to *Chambers' Journal*, by

1846 De La Rue were printing tickets for 'nearly all the railways in the United Kingdom'. By 1856 the firm was printing 1.5 million tickets a week.

The other sideline noted by *Chambers' Journal* was visitors' cards. People were already using playing cards to leave messages. Thomas reduced the size of the cards, making them more portable, but used his enamelled playing card paper, which bent less easily than the flimsier, pre-De La Rue cards.

In July 1846 *Chambers'* published an article entitled 'A Day at De La Rue's', following the visit of a journalist to Bunhill Row. Here are some of the journalist's comments:

> It was a visit of curiosity. I wished to see one of the remarkable establishments in London – an establishment which could only flourish in the midst of a great and wealthy people, De La Rue and Company's manufactory of fancy stationery. The art of writing letters is pretty nearly as old as the hills; but, till within the last twenty years, there was no such thing as a tastefully-got-up epistle. There was a deficiency in the mecanique of letter-writing. In Norway, to the present day, when a person wishes to write a note, he cuts a piece from a large sheet of paper; and something of this sort was prevalent in England forty or fifty years ago. It was considered a great advance in taste when a papermaker at Bath got up what he called his 'Bath post' – a smooth yellow paper, quarto size, with a small stamp in the corner of the sheet.
>
> Matters remained at this point till a comparatively recent period, when the whole business of the stationer underwent a rapid and most extraordinary change – the establishment of the penny post alone causing the introduction of many new auxiliaries to epistolary correspondence. It cannot but be interesting to know who has led this great movement – who has filled the ladies' writing cases with finely tinted note papers – who has given to the world the envelope, the enamelled calling-card, and the numerous other elegancies which now fill the shop-window of the stationer. Different active spirits have contributed their respective inventions in this useful department of art, but the mastermind has been that of Thomas De la Rue.
>
> Entering by the large gateway of this interesting establishment, I was, by the kindness of one of the partners, conducted over the several departments of the works – the whole nestling in a cluster of old edifices, and forming an amusing hive of industry; steam-engines, machinery, and animated beings, commingling in restless and varied movement. The purpose of nearly all that strikes the eye, is to cause paper to assume new forms and appearances. Of this article, forty-five thousand reams, valued at £30,000 [£3.6 million in today's money], are consumed annually – a quantity so great, that it would require three mills for its production.
>
> It will perhaps afford still more impressive considerations of the completeness of the arrangements, when I observe that the first place into which I was conducted was a large apartment devoted exclusively to the making and mending of machines. Mr Warren De la Rue, by whom some of the most ingenious machines have been constructed, superintends this and other mechanical departments.
>
> Adjoining this department is a mill-like apparatus for grinding colours, and materials for enamelling; and further on, in two upper apartments, is a laboratory, with

retorts, mixtures, and a store of bottles sufficient to set up a chemist's shop; here is also a chemical library of French and English books, which are in constant requisition. It is deemed somewhat of a favour to be admitted to this department; for many projects for executing new and peculiar tints and surfaces, likewise processes for electrotyping, not generally known, are here daily in operation.

Above the electrotyping room is one occupied with die-sinkers, and engravers-men busy with hammers, punches and chisels, executing objects to be employed in some of the more elegant kinds of printing. Besides these artists, many individuals, I was told, were employed out of doors in designing patterns. Novelty and taste are never for a moment neglected. Mr De la Rue mentioned to me that he sometimes gives as much as £20 or £30 for the drawing of a design not larger than your hand. The best classic models of antiquity are sought out.

Perfect novelty, however, is a governing principle. The object of the concern is to maintain a high character for the originality – to copy from no one, English or Continental. Formerly, in England, few or no manufacturers thought of going to the expense of employing designers, and consequently designers did not exist amongst us. In the chief manufacturing towns there might have been here and there a dissipated man of genius, who, when he could be laid hold of quite sober, would, for a guinea or so, furnish a design, such as it was; but there was no principle in the thing, and almost every manufacturer copied from French originals; the more enterprising of them bribing French workmen to send early copies of what they had begun to execute.

The necessity for competing with Continental manufacturers in the home market consequent on the late free-trade measures, has, among respectable men, put an end to this meagre and shabby state of affairs. Every respectable tradesman, who desires to avoid following among the mere herd of imitators, not only employs skilled designers, but is constantly racking his brains how he is to maintain his place in the market. It sounded new to me, in general principles of trade, to be told that no man can now expect great success in any fancy manufacture unless he competes with himself. Competition with others won't do any longer. The true art consists in not waiting to be stimulated by rivalry, but in bringing out fresh novelties at proper times, one after the other, and so gaining a command, as it were, over the public taste. I was taken with this idea of Mr De la Rue; it showed in his craft.

Having been conducted through the preparatory departments of the establishment, I was now introduced to what forms a principal branch of manufacture. This is the making of playing cards, which engages a considerable number of hands, and several machines and presses.

Mr De la Rue, some years ago, introduced the improved plan of printing the cards with inks, or colours in oil, by which means no degree of rubbing or moisture of the hand can move the figures. At one time, playing cards were plain on the back; now, they have generally backs printed with fanciful figures; and therefore each side of the card requires its own appropriate printing.

The printing of playing cards, numerous as are the impressions they must undergo, is but a small part of the manufacture. Having seen the printed sheets carried away to the drying room, we proceeded to the pasting process. Here there are two long tables, with a number of men at work. Each of these had on his left a pile of the mingled sheets, and on his right a tub of paste. Lifting a sheet with his left hand, and laying it on the bench before him, he speedily smeared it over with the great paste-brush he held in his right; next were laid down two sheets, only the upper-most of which was pasted; and thus there arose a great pile of pasted sheets, with unpasted intervals. The whole operation was performed in a rapid and business-like way, with all the regularity of a machine. The brush, which seemed to be made of soft bristles, was as large as the besom of a housemaid, but without any handle; and I was assured that so methodic do the men become in their movements, that the brush in each case performs precisely the same curvilinear evolutions. Coarse as this branch of labour appears, it is reckoned one of skill, and is accordingly well paid. The weekly wage of a good paster is about two pounds; some can realise about fifty shillings [£300 in today's money].

The second floor exhibits a busy scene of rolling and other apparatus, with great quantities of pasteboards and sheets in different stages of advancement. When a cardboard reaches this department, it is for the purpose of being rendered perfectly smooth on the surface. Two surfaces smoothed in the same manner will not glide over each other so well as if they be smoothed differently. In smoothing the cardboard, therefore, it is passed between two rollers, the lower of which is of metal, and the upper of paper; both are equally smooth but they impart a certain variety in the dressing, to cause a sufficiently easy gliding of the cards face and back. The paper roller is prepared in a way which no one could expect. A great pile of sheets being pasted together, squeezed to the hardest possible consistency, and dried, the mass is fixed on a spindle, and turned on a turning lathe; the result is a smooth, round beam, the surface of which consists entirely of edges of paper, but the whole of as close a texture as a piece of finely polished wood.

Removed from the pressing-room, the boards next migrate to the cutting apparatus. With this machine a man cuts them, individually, first into long slips, and next across into single cards. With such accuracy is this operation performed, that although the cutter turns out 20,000 cards in a day, all are of precisely the same dimensions. The sorting into qualities next takes place, and requires much sharpness of hand and eye.

The consumption of playing cards in the United Kingdom is, to all appearance, stationary notwithstanding the continual increase of population; it would, however, be rash to ascribe this altogether to a gradual diminution of card-playing propensities. It is believed that there is a prodigious sale of cards with surreptitious stamps; and it is Mr De la Rue's opinion, founded on knowledge of the trade, that, were the duty reduced from a shilling to threepence per pack, the Government would derive ten times the amount of revenues from this branch of manufacture.

This publicity was building up the company nicely for the great event of the middle of the 19th century for Britain, the Great Exhibition of 1851.

Chapter Four

A Golden Age

1851–1900

The Great Exhibition
Colonel Billy
Warren de la Rue
And now, banknotes
North or South or neutral?
Working at full capacity
Thomas de la Rue dies
Monopoly?
Applied his scientific knowledge

THE GREAT EXHIBITION

The Great Exhibition of 1851 was important for Britain and it was important for De La Rue as well. It was opened on 1 May 1851 by HRH Prince Albert, husband of Queen Victoria. By this time he had established himself as a popular and, perhaps more important, a significant member of British society.

Charles Mackay wrote these words to celebrate the opening (to which Henry Russell supplied music):

> Gather, ye Nations, gather! From forge, and mine, and mill!
> Come, Science and Invention; Come, Industry and Skill!
> Come with your woven wonders, the blossoms of the loom,
> That rival Nature's fairest flowers in all but their perfume;
> Come with your brass and iron, Your silver and your gold,

> And arts that change the face of earth, unknown to men of old.
> Gather, ye Nations, gather! From ev'ry clime and soil,
> The New Confederation, the Jubilee of toil.

The exhibition building, the Crystal Palace, was itself a triumph of technology and therefore an ideal setting in which to exhibit the best of British expertise.

This is what the excellent historian, Asa Briggs, had to say about the Great Exhibition and Britain's place in the world at the time:

> The triumphant facts of industrial progress were proclaimed for all the world to see in the Palace of Industry of 1851, the Great Exhibition, which set out 'to present a true test and a living picture of the point of development at which the whole of mankind has arrived ... and a new starting point, from which all nations will be able to direct their further exertions.'
>
> The Exhibition, with its 13,000 exhibitors and its six million visitors, not only brought the facts to life, but invested them with a new romance ... [It] was designed to display the works of other nations besides the English – pottery from Sèvres as well as from Etruria, fine black lace from Barcelona as well as printed calicoes from Manchester. There was no more vigorous assertion of national confidence than the internationalism of 1851.

The key organiser of the Great Exhibition was Henry, later Sir Henry, Cole. What was his background?

First, he was a writer of children's books, but more significantly, he was an assistant keeper at the Record Office and the reorganiser of the Post Office who had also worked with Rowland Hill on the Penny Post and may have designed the Penny Black. He was the editor of numerous periodicals (among them the *Journal of Design and Manufactures*), designer of prize tea services, an etcher and a watercolour painter. He was profoundly interested in the improvement of British industrial design and a great believer in exhibitions to promote those designs. Under his leadership the Society of Arts organised an exhibition of art manufactures in London in 1847, another in 1848 and a third in 1849. Manchester and Birmingham held similar exhibitions. Everything was ready for the big one in 1851, which Cole conceived and Prince Albert fully supported. A Royal Commission was appointed.

And how did they choose the 'Crystal Palace'? 245 different plans were submitted, but the committee did not approve any of them, drawing up its own plans and inviting tenders from builders for what would have been a hideous brick building. When they published the plans, the reaction was one of scorn and derision. The committee dithered but the indefatigable Cole contacted Joseph Paxton, an architect in glass. Paxton and his men worked day and night and submitted plans for a huge glass palace. While the committee deliberated, Paxton sent a copy of the plans to the *Illustrated London News*. Such was the enthusiasm that the committee was left with no choice but to abandon its own plans and accept those of Paxton.

John W. Dodds in *The Age of Paradox* described the Crystal Palace as follows:

> That conception had everything. Using iron and glass, in standardized and interchangeable sizes, it could be built within the time limit. It could be taken down afterwards (a stipulation of the Commission) with relatively small effort and with a high salvage value. The interior space, with its galleries, was perfect for exhibition purposes. And above all it was a daring, imaginative creation – soaring, ethereal, brilliant. The die-hards who resisted the idea of any building in Hyde Park had complained about the necessity of cutting down trees. So Paxton incorporated in his plan a great transept which would enclose the large elms, alive. This was the only major change since he had jotted down his original design on blotting paper while attending a committee meeting of the Midland Railway!
>
> The assembling of the building was ingenious and its erection rapid. New machinery was designed to groove the 'Paxton gutters', which served both as frames for the glass and led the rainwater to the hollow iron supporting columns. These in turn carried it to the iron pipes which were both the structural base of the building and the main drainage system. No mortar and no bricks were used. Adjustable louvres provided ventilation.
>
> There were still carpers who complained that the building would not be safe: a hailstorm or even a stiff wind would break the glass; gunfire across the Park would collapse it; the structure would buckle under the weight of the people in the galleries; the vibration either of moving machinery or of the large pipe organs would shake the glass out like cards. Even those who liked the building had moments of doubt; nothing like this had ever been tried in architectural history. But Paxton knew what he was doing. Even before the building was completed a hail-and-wind storm did not move a single pane of glass. Huge carts were filled with cannon balls, weight eight tons, and were rolled in test up and down the galleries with impunity. The whole corps of Royal Sappers and Miners marched over and around the bays in close order, and even marked time 'in the most trying manner.' Still the construction suffered no injury.

Why did De La Rue become so deeply involved? In 1850 Warren de la Rue, by this time already an important member of the Royal Chemical Society, was elected to the even more prestigious Royal Society. Prince Albert himself was a leading light, and the Society was used as a platform by amateur and professional scientists. For example, Michael Faraday was a member and Warren knew him well, allowing Faraday to use his private laboratories for his experiments. It also gave Warren an entrée into the European science scene and enabled him to employ the distinguished Dr Hugo Müller of Leipzig (of whom more in a later chapter). The Royal Society became involved in the Great Exhibition, with the planning dominated by Fellows of the Society.

The key organiser, as we have seen, was Henry Cole, also a Fellow, as was Owen Jones, already carrying out design work for De La Rue. Jones was appointed superintendent of works. Thomas and Warren sat on several committees under Cole, one of them deciding which items submitted from around the world could be shown. For its part, De La Rue showed no fewer than 289 items, all listed in the official catalogue. Through their influence, Thomas and Warren secured a key position for the company in the central aisle of the English exhibition, and in the middle of their stand stood their new envelope-making machine in full operation. The *London Illustrated News* wrote:

> None other can boast of bigger congregations ... There are few things in fact which Paxton's glass shade contains more attractive to the curious than this.

And it was not only the British press that publicised De La Rue. Germany's *Illustrierte Zeitung* of Leipzig wrote, after describing its folding and gumming processes, that the machine could be run by 'one boy and a maid', and 'can always attract inquisitive persons to whom the finished envelopes are generously distributed'.

Again, Thomas and Warren used their contacts to make sure that one of the largest write-ups in the official catalogue was for their envelope-making machine. But it was not just for this machine that De La Rue were noticed. An *Illustrated Cyclopaedia of the Great Exhibition* noted:

> Of highly-glazed and tastefully packeted writing papers, Messrs De La Rue and Co were the principal exhibitors.

Thomas and Warren were both appointed Jurors of the Exhibition and were on the prize-awarding panels. Thomas was even deputy chairman of the panel judging what was called Class 17, which was for the category of Stationery, Printing and Bookbinding. Naturally this panel could not give a prize to De La Rue, but it noted:

> The position of Mr de la Rue as a juror has not allowed the jury to recommend that the Council Medal be awarded to him, which in their opinion he so justly deserves.

Instead, Thomas received a special medal, presented by a commission presided over by the Prince Consort, for his services to the exhibition as a whole. He also received a bronze medal for his invention of iridescent film. The jurors said it was a beautiful illustration of the production of colour on a thin transparent surface such as is transiently seen in an ordinary soap bubble.

De La Rue also received a bronze medal for the excellence of the whole exhibit, and another for the envelope-making machine; while Warren received a medal for his work as a Juror.

The Jurors' reports said, inter alia:

> Messrs De La Rue & Co as paper finishers displayed every description of the best writing papers produced in England. The mode of perforating thick paper and cardboard was first applied by Monsieur Marc la Rivière, a Swiss watch-maker ... but Mr de la Rue suggested its application to paper and cardboard.

Altogether, the Great Exhibition, a huge triumph in totality, was an enormous success for De La Rue as well. The de la Rues themselves were so delighted that they bought the picture by Henry Selous of the exhibition's opening by Queen Victoria. It showed Thomas on the right-hand side and Warren in the background. When Warren died, his younger brother William gave the picture to the Victoria and Albert Museum in Kensington, London.

De La Rue followed up its success in the Crystal Palace by showing at the New York Exhibition in 1853 and the Paris Exhibition in 1855. In New York, the firm received medals for diaries, calendars and vegetable parchment, and in Paris it won two gold, two silver and two bronze medals. To round off this success, Thomas de la Rue was made a Chevalier d'Honneur.

COLONEL BILLY

We have read of Warren's achievements both inside and outside the family firm. How was William Frederick, Warren's younger brother by ten years, faring? He had joined the Volunteer regiment of the 4th Tower Hamlets Rifles and became known as 'Colonel Billy'. Lorna Houseman described Colonel Billy as follows:

> He has been described as 'an Elizabethan born out of his age, with the charm that overcomes obstacles both human and material – the Cavalier as well as the Colonel'. In a family already noted for its charm, his was the most irresistible of all; spiked with a caustic wit, it was quite spontaneous. Its effect in business was powerful. If Warren, who was considered 'a diplomatist of the highest order', lent 'tact … and suavity of manner' to the De La Rue partnership, his younger brother contributed breezy authority combined with bonhomie.

He began work in the firm at an early age. Indeed, there is evidence of his helping out at Bunhill Row during the financial crisis of the late 1830s when he was only twelve. At fifteen he became a travelling salesman for the company, and he was also closely involved in the management, writing to his older brother when Warren was in Italy:

> Your telegram of the 17th was utterly unintelligible, you did not say where you were staying … we first thought you had been captured by brigands and that £50 was your ransom money.

And he followed this up with:

> I hope you will not hurry back while you are enjoying yourselves. All is going well and I want you to have a good stock of health when you do come back. I think you were not looking well in Paris.

The two brothers worked well as a team, the one standing in for the other whenever one was travelling. In 1850, Colonel Billy married Emma Tanner, the daughter of a prosperous family living in Charterhouse Square. They moved in to the family house in Bunhill Row when Thomas and Jane moved to the West End in the early 1850s, and he was on call at any time, as is made clear by this report from Edwin Hill in 1856: 'Mr William de la Rue, whose house adjoins the office, would undertake the safe custody of the die in the night.'

However, by 1864, Colonel Billy and his wife Emma had had enough of 'living over the shop', and moved to fashionable Harley Street.

WARREN DE LA RUE

We have already seen that Warren de la Rue was a bright pupil at his French school and that he continued with his scientific experiments when Thomas brought him back to England and employed him in the firm. His focus was the Royal College of Chemistry, the college that was the first unit in the order of formation of the Royal College of Science and the Royal School of Mines, which eventually in 1907, with the City and Guilds College, became the Imperial College of Science and Technology.

In July 1845 at a public meeting, undoubtedly attended by Warren, it was agreed that a College of Chemistry should be founded. Prince Albert, no less, consented to being made President of the Council, and August Hofmann became Professor of the new college. Hofmann grew to be a close friend of Warren and influenced him greatly. Many documents at Imperial College in Kensington attest to this.

At the same time Warren became a student, and he would later be described in glowing terms by Sir Frederick Abel:

> Among the most prominent of the first students at the college, there was one who at once exercised a very marked beneficial influence in establishing a spirit of emulation, combined with good fellowship, among the younger students, and who speedily became one of Hofmann's most intimate and most useful friends; it is almost needless to say that I refer to Warren de la Rue. A bright example to all in industry and unflinching in perseverance, manipulative skill and methodical work.
>
> No man has made himself more universally beloved than de la Rue. There can be no doubt that he laboured as importantly, as he did unobtrusively, for the good of the college in the days of its greatest troubles. He was a powerful support to the professor in his battles against formidable difficulties.

Warren remained at the college for three years as a student and for a few years thereafter as assistant to Hofmann. During his student years he experimented with cochineal, and he read the results of his researches to the Chemical Society. Hofmann referred to the results as 'beautiful and elaborate research', and went on to say:

> Mr de la Rue succeeded for the first time in obtaining the colouring matter of cochineal in a state of chemical purity; and proved by decisive experiments that the substance is free from nitrogen, the element which is present in pollution.

At this time, Warren also tackled other subjects – photography, astronomy, physics and mechanics. However, his most famous invention was his photoheliograph. With this he applied photography to the recording of celestial phenomena. The photographs, when measured by a micrometer (which he invented), provided some exact astronomical data. He built his own private observatory, first at Canonbury House and then at Cranford in Middlesex, where he installed a bigger observatory with a reflecting telescope made to his design. Apparently, a daguerreotype of the moon (an image produced by an early photographic process employing an iodine-sensitised silvered plate and mercury vapour), taken by an American and exhibited at the Crystal Palace, fired his imagination. He began to experiment with his own methods of lunar photography.

It was not just in scientific advances that Warren de la Rue was making a name for himself. He was also a respected businessman. Lyon Playfair, the organiser of the juries at the Great Exhibition, had subsequently been appointed Secretary of the Science and Art department at the Science Museum in South Kensington in 1853. Having met Warren at the exhibition, he would have been impressed by his business acumen, and he wrote to him from Marlborough House asking his opinion on the state of the paper trade in Britain. In his professional way, Warren spent a month carrying out intensive research and sent a reply. Among other things, he said:

> It would appear that railways and steamboats consume a very large quantity of waste for wiping machinery which formerly found its way to the paper mill. But the most important of all competitors are undoubtedly the Americans who of late years have purchased largely in our own market.

He also noted that 'the growing thirst for literature' was increasing the demand for paper, and advised that 'new fibrous materials' would have to be found to augment the traditional materials of rags for paper production. (We have seen that in the 1840s De La Rue themselves were consuming 45,000 reams of paper a year.)

Warren and Professor Hofmann experimented with vegetable parchment, which Hofmann found greatly superior in strength to real parchment, being 'capable of resisting the tooth of time for many centuries'.

We have already seen how Warren worked with Edwin Hill in developing an envelope-making machine that transformed the speed at which the envelopes could be produced. He later improved the machine on his own by adding a gumming device.

De La Rue's success at the Great Exhibition would have been helpful in bringing about the next big step forward for the company. We have seen how the inventor of the Penny Postage, Rowland Hill, had shown little faith in adhesive postage stamps. However, in the months after the Great Exhibition, perhaps prompted by some of the developments he had seen, he changed his mind. In April 1853, the Board of Inland Revenue decided to use adhesive stamps on drafts and receipts and, as there was no room to produce them at Somerset House, they awarded a four-year contract to De La Rue to produce them at Bunhill Row. Why they did not ask Perkins

Bacon & Co., the producers of the first stamps (the Penny Black and Twopenny Blue), is not clear. The Board was obviously confident enough in De La Rue to allow them to use their new typographical process, the same one used by Thomas for his playing cards. The Hills, who were close to the De La Rues, would have been party to this decision.

De La Rue claimed that their process was more practical and economical than that of Perkins Bacon. First, their process used special fugitive ink that disappeared if a fraudster tried to clean the stamps for use a second time. They also claimed that their treatment of stamp paper was better suited to perforation. (They knew that Perkins Bacon had been experiencing problems in this area.) The final telling point was one of price. Sir Henry Cole said that the De La Rue method would save the Exchequer £10,000 a year (£1.2 million today). Pressed by the costs of the Crimean War (governments are always pressed by something), the Chancellor of the Exchequer was asking Sir Rowland Hill to increase Post Office revenue.

AND NOW, BANKNOTES

In the 1850s, the company that enjoyed almost a monopoly in supplying stamps to Britain's still expanding legion of overseas colonies was Perkins Bacon. De La Rue *had* gained a foothold in India in printing stamps for the powerful East India Company, but the Crown Agents dealt exclusively with Perkins Bacon.

As happens in a monopoly situation, Perkins Bacon became either careless or over-confident; and in 1858, in their rush to meet the growing demand for penny and two-penny English stamps, they did not consult the newly appointed Agent General, Penrose Julyan, when showing a new colonial stamp to the Treasury. Julyan was not a man to take lightly what he perceived to be an insult, and he insisted that Perkins Bacon surrender to him their stamp dies and plates for the Cape of Good Hope, Mauritius, Trinidad, Western Australia, Ceylon, Saint Helena, the Bahamas, Natal and St Lucia. He then wondered to whom he should award the contracts.

De La Rue had just completed a small stamp order for Ceylon efficiently and on time, and Julyan was also impressed when he looked at the company's security record for the Inland Revenue. He also found Colonel Billy, a man of action like himself, to be just the sort of person with whom he would like to work. Trust built up between them so that they conducted business without formal agreements, and whenever one of the colonies wanted stamps, Julyan handed the order over to Colonel Billy. He gave him the courtesy title of 'Engraver to the Agents General for the Crown Colonies'.

Then Mauritius asked the Crown Agents if they could supply paper currency as well. Perkins Bacon were already a banknote printer and De La Rue had never printed one in its history. Nevertheless, Julyan was not a person to forgive easily, and at the end of 1859 he gave De La Rue the contract to print Mauritian five-pound, one-pound and ten-shilling notes. De La Rue took this order very seriously and produced the notes by copperplate on paper from Turner's mill at Maidstone. They were bound in books of 500, each with a counterfoil, and resembled cheques rather than banknotes. Every one was signed individually by the Treasurer.

The design was a milestone in banknote design. The notes were printed on heavily watermarked paper with the value printed in green or blue and the main working in black engraving. The usual 'promise to pay' was on a panel of micro lettering and a black-and-white line panel showed the value. The coat of arms was included in the title, and the side of the design was embellished with a complicated stylised floral ornament. Spaces were made in the design to include three numbering boxes, the hand-written signatures of the Treasurer and Auditor General, and the date of issue. The introduction of colour and the excellence of the engraving, particularly aimed at deterring the forger, set a style in design that was followed for many years. There are no records of these notes ever being forged.

It was not just a case of Julyan finding any company as long as it was not Perkins Bacon. De La Rue's success in winning the business was due to their development of technology associated with typography or surface printing. The company had invested heavily in skill, tooling and machinery, which placed it ahead of the competition. When De La Rue was asked to print stamps by the copperplate or recess-printing process, the company saw it as a way to increase its business, trusting that in due course, as plates wore out and new designs were needed, the customer would recognise the great advantage offered by typography and would therefore place further orders to be produced by this method with designs that suited De La Rue's tooling and machinery. De La Rue's preference for typography was not just because of the investment the company had made in that process, but because it felt it was a simple way of printing stamps.

An article in *The Art Journal* in 1859 would not have done De La Rue's reputation as a first-class manufacturer and employer any harm either:

> The manufactory which we lately visited, is one of the largest, and certainly the most complete in the world ... Extending behind the houses in Bunhill Row, it now stands upon nearly an acre and a half of ground; and the several floors, which are crowded with machinery, represent a space of about five acres. This space comprehends the various departments which are devoted to a trade finding customers in every part of the civilised globe; and we must, in brief, endeavour to convey to our readers some idea of one of the most complete and best conducted establishments to be met with in this country, employing hundreds of men and women, boys and girls.
>
> One feature worthy of the highest commendation, and one which we could desire to see copied in all the large establishments of the United Kingdom is the marked attention which the employers have given to the social conditions of the employed. The men were indeed, by the promised remission of half an hour from the general day's work, persuaded to abandon the use of beer during the hours of labour ... A sickness fund and a library for the use of all, are well organized; and altogether this hive of industry is working with the utmost harmony and profit to all concerned.

To keep this factory busy, the De La Rue sales team, led by Colonel Billy, were working hard to win orders. We have already seen that Colonel Billy was a natural salesman, and he kept his eye on international affairs because new countries or new monarchs would almost certainly mean new opportunities for business. For example, when King Leopold I of Belgium died in 1865, Warren and Billy were in touch with his successor, King Leopold II, about a new issue of stamps. At this time there was also the prospect of a united and independent Italy, and Colonel Billy travelled to its first capital, Turin, in 1862. He sent a proposal 'for the production of postage and other stamps for the Kingdom of Italy for a contract of seven years' to the Minister of Finance, Commander Sella. He suggested that the stamps should initially be manufactured at the De La Rue factory in Bunhill Row and be the same size and quality as the company supplied to the British government. He also suggested that an Italian agent could supervise the production. The possibility of securing the Italian business was considered so important that Warren went out to Italy to help his brother, and Thomas came out of his retirement to hold the fort at Bunhill Row while his sons were away. They were successful, and Warren wrote to his father giving Billy the credit: 'William's point of the wedge has been driven home ... it is to him that we owe the order.' In truth, it was a combination of Warren's scientific knowledge and Billy's natural salesmanship that made them a formidable team.

Colonel Billy returned to Italy in December 1863, this time taking his wife Emma and daughter Ellen, and supervised the establishment of a printing plant in the buildings and grounds of the Palazzo dei Martiri in Naples. A senior Italian official, Cavalieri Perazzi, went to Bunhill Row to learn the art of printing. The Italians were so delighted with the help Warren and Billy gave them that they awarded them both the Order of St Maurice and St Lazare, and Camillo Cavour, generally considered the father of modern Italy, referred to Billy as *mon ami*. In 1866 the company received an order for five-lire notes.

NORTH OR SOUTH OR NEUTRAL?

The British have always had mixed views about the American Civil War in the 1860s. The simplistic, if incorrect, view that it was all about ridding the South of slavery is surely given the lie by the announcement by Abraham Lincoln in his inaugural address as President on 4 March 1861 that he would not interfere with the institution of slavery in the southern states. Admittedly, Lincoln appeared to change his mind when in September 1862 he proclaimed that the slaves in the rebellious states would be legally free at the beginning of the year 1863. As nearly always in war, the real causes were economic. The southern states wanted to protect their businesses from those pesky, tax-gathering northerners. Whatever the causes, the United, or Disunited, States of America were already important enough for the progress, or otherwise, of their own economy to have serious consequences elsewhere. For example, in 1860 no fewer than 530,000 of the working population (equivalent to perhaps 1.5 million in today's bigger workforce) in Britain depended directly, and many others indirectly, on the cotton industry, and about 80 per cent of the supplies of raw cotton came from America. Disruption in the supply was not in British interests, whatever one's views on slavery.

The British government, led by Lord John Russell, maintained a neutral position but was faced on several occasions with the difficulty of deciding how to deal with British companies or individuals who did not maintain such a stance and supplied one side or the other. We have already seen that De La Rue were fully alive to the opportunities around the world as new states appeared. Here was a new one, as by February 1861 the seven southern states, with Jefferson Davis as President, had formed themselves into the Confederate States of America. By April the war against the Federalist North had started (and a very bloody war it turned out to be), and by the end of the year a Major Ficklin had arrived in England with a view to buying necessary supplies, including stamps.

Ficklin seems to have been given a forceful introduction to De La Rue, as Lorna Houseman points out in *The House that Thomas Built*:

> Although Ben Ficklin has been called the 'Mystery Man of the Confederacy', he wasted no time being mysterious with the De La Rues. Within a matter of days he moved in on them, and made Bunhill Row his headquarters. From there on February 11th he dispatched no less than eight telegrams, and sent out for twelve copies of Spense's *On the American Union*. On March 12th he requested De La Rue, through their Paris agents to obtain for him: 'Twelve dozen First Class Quality Kid Skin Gloves' in sizes varying from 6¼ and 6¾ in different colours and '3 dozen similar pairs all in white'. What B.F. Ficklin wanted with 180 assorted pairs of ladies' gloves we shall never know. De La Rue made no comment, but took care to charge them to the Major's account, both in francs and pounds.
>
> On March 18th he asked for a loan. The firm lent him £1,000 [over £100,000 in today's money] in cash, and three days later another £1,238 7s 1d. At this time the capital of De La Rue was £73,000, so that the amount of ready cash could not have been more than £10,000. The loans were therefore comparatively large. De La Rue also paid the men recruited by the Confederacy in Scotland, who were to travel to America to manufacture its stamps with De La Rue equipment.
>
> At the outset of the American Civil War British sympathy was fairly equally divided between both sides. Later in the war Queen Victoria declared the Federalists to be 'such ruffians', and the bulk of upper class and industrial England, especially the cotton magnates, agreed with her. But Colonel Billy was ready to assist the Confederates from the outset. One wonders why.
>
> The answer must have lain in personal relationships. Colonel Billy was especially close to the Winans's; he and his family had just returned from travelling with these American cousins in Europe. He had undoubtedly enjoyed their hospitality in America on his 1850 visit. They were not only leading Confederates, they were also excessively wealthy as a result of their rail-roads. Had Ben Ficklin failed to honour his bills the Winans's could have covered them many times over. This is every reason to suppose that it was at their instigation that Colonel Billy agreed to so immediate an involvement.

> At the time Warren was abroad again. Colonel Billy wrote from Bunhill Row to give him a picture of the home front. Major Ficklin, he said, was dominating the scene and taking up most of his time. But still, the Major was paying his debts. He 'gave us a cheque for £5,000 ... I have paid away for him about £2,500 but he will give me another £2,000 in a day or so'. The company would make a profit on the Confederate order, in itself worth nearly £5,000. With a light heart Colonel Billy went up to Glasgow to see Ficklin off.

The stamps that De La Rue supplied to the Confederates were designed by the company's brilliant French designer, Joubert de la Ferté. Jean Ferdinand Joubert de la Ferté engraved for De La Rue, among other things, the Queen Victoria heads used on the early Victorian postage stamps. Born in Paris in 1810, he worked in both France and England, mainly engraving pictures by well-known French and British artists. His grandson, Air Chief Marshal Sir Philip Joubert (Jean Ferdinand had become a British national in the 1850s), wrote this of him:

> A few years later he began to work for De La Rue and with them he engraved the famous head of Queen Victoria which graced so many British and colonial stamps of the period. It is of great beauty and simplicity and it is probable that no other engraver of stamps has achieved a purer or more attractive form.

The American stamps he designed were the Five Cents Blue with its head of Jefferson Davis, and the Orange One Cent, with the head of John C. Calhoun (former Senator and Vice-President). The Five Cents Blue was the only American stamp printed abroad that remained in use for any length of time.

Records show that Colonel Billy mentioned the despatching of 'a very large quantity of goods [including] all the American order of Ficklin'. These were the first instalment of 5 million Five Cents Blues, and they were safely delivered into the port of Wilmington, North Carolina thanks to the skills of the Confederate Navy Captain John Wilkinson, sailing his blockade-runner, *Robert E. Lee*, past the ships operating the blockade.

The next shipment was not so lucky, as Lorna Houseman shows:

> The following March another blockade runner, the ill-fated *Bermuda*, left Liverpool. The passenger list included the Scottish printers hired by De La Rue, and the cargo represented the fruits of Ficklin's De La Rue-aided shopping expeditions. It contained tea, coffee, drugs, surgical instruments, saddlery and cutlery bearing such legends as:
>
> JEFF. DAVIS
> OUR FIRST PRESIDENT
> The Right Man in the Right Place
>
> Stowed away in the hold were some boxes from Bunhill Row. Inside them were the rest of the five million Five Cents Blues and the first Orange One Cents.

> The ship arrived in St George's, Bermuda, and lay up there for five weeks. While venturing in the direction of Charleston on April 27th 1863, she was captured by the Federalist ship *Mercedita*. She was taken to Philadelphia, adjudged a legal prize by the Federal Court, and sold with all her contraband cargo – all, that is, except for the stamps from De La Rue. According to an order from the Attorney General, these were ordered to be reduced to pulp.
>
> Among the Reports of Cases Argued and Adjudged in the Supreme Courts of the US in December 1865, is one on the *Bermuda* case. It throws another light on the story: 'At the time of the capture and after the boat was boarded, the captain's brother by his order threw overboard two small boxes and a package which he swore contained postage stamps ...'
>
> 'On the vessel', continues the Report, 'were several persons called in various letters "government passengers" being in fact "artists" from Scotland. One of them carried a letter written from a Mr C. Straker of the Stationery department, 80 Bishopsgate Within, 26 Leadenhall St, London ...' This letter, addressed to the Confederate Government by the aggrieved Mr Straker, complained of a Confederate Commissioner (Major Ficklin) who 'served me shabbily and ungentlemanlike. I had many interviews with him and gave him all necessary information; furnished him with a list of requirements, compromising myself with several workmen and put myself to many inconveniences. He admitted my price being proper and correct and led me to believe that he would give me his order, but having got out of me all that he could he then entrusted the order with another house' (De La Rue). There is something curiously affecting about Mr Straker's impotent cry addressed to the leader of a lost cause, concerning the stamp issue which came to be known philatelically as 'The Lost Shipment', in a letter which lost its way and was never delivered.
>
> Mr Straker might have felt better had he known there was one bill for which the crafty Ficklin did not pay Colonel Billy. In addition to the stamps seized on the *Bermuda* there was also a small matter of a 'Super Royal Printing Press in satin-lined Tympan Box with Six Inking Rollers'. For these the Confederate States owed De La Rue £294 8s 4d ever after.

At a dinner at the Savoy Hotel in February 1934 held to celebrate De La Rue's 102nd anniversary, Chairman Sidney Lamert told his guest – in reply to a Mr John Drinkwater recalling that De La Rue had supplied the rebel southern states – that one fact that Mr Drinkwater had not recorded was that De La Rue had not been paid for the stamps. Lamert surmised that it would be a simple matter to work out how far that sum, at compound interest, would go to offset the debt that Great Britain owed to America.

WORKING AT FULL CAPACITY

As well as contracts in the newly independent Italy, the 'hoped-to-be' independent southern states of America, and the colonies under the buying control of Agent Penrose Julyan, demand for other De La Rue products in the early 1860s kept the company very busy. They rented all the neighbouring houses in Bunhill Row and bought two freeholds in Blue Anchor Alley. At the same time they set up offices in Liverpool and Paris. (Because of the difficult American situation they closed their New York branch in September 1861, losing £100 (£10,000) on the 'Sale of Mr P. Supple's furniture on his leaving New York in consequence of the Civil War'.)

The stationery business was booming alongside the new security printing projects. The Indelible Diary, originally developed for use by Warren and Colonel Billy, proved popular with other well-to-do middle-class Victorian men. And in November 1862 Colonel Billy was able to report that notepaper work was expanding steadily. The Commissioner of the Rajah of Mysore had just ordered '5,000 reams of f.cap paper with watermark ... Moreover he says he requires annually from £1,500 to £2,000 [over £150,000 to £200,000] of ordinary Stationery for the public offices'. As we have seen, the *Art Journal* was able to refer to De La Rue at Bunhill Row as 'this immense establishment'. Furthermore, between 1857 and 1866 De La Rue's output of railway tickets doubled, while the packs of playing cards produced increased from 93,060 in 1856 to 265,048 in1868.

The British empire was to prove a very important source of business to De La Rue, as indeed it was to many other British manufacturers. Much has been written about the rise and decline of the empire. The simple facts were that by 1921 the British held sway over 458 million people in 60 countries, which was then about 25 per cent of the world's population, and the empire stretched over 14.2 million square miles, which, by coincidence, was about 25 per cent of the world's land surface. It was seven times the size of the Roman empire. However, in Lord Palmerston's famous words, this empire had been acquired almost 'in a fit of absent-mindedness'.

Queen Victoria was not entirely happy about some of the acquisitions. She remarked to Disraeli: 'We don't want Fijians, they're all cannibals.' Apparently Disraeli replied: 'No madam, they're actually all Methodists.' Whatever her views on certain of her new subjects, she was certainly happy to accept all the gifts that came her way, and probably approved of the advice given to the colonists – 'Keep the Sabbath and anything else you can lay your hands on.'

Trevor Lloyd, in his book *Empire*, summarises the creation of the British empire extremely well:

> For almost four hundred years Britain ruled substantial areas of the world outside Europe. In the first 150 years, from 1600 to 1750, expansion was a matter of setting up small but prosperous trading posts and settlements very close to the sea, supported by naval strength and close contact with friends in England. After 1750 imperial rule began to move inland and for the next 170 years, up to the end of the First World War, a steadily increasing part of the earth's surface was ruled from London. The naval and industrial power which made this possible also meant that Britain could exert a great deal of influence in the world outside the empire, but this was a matter of diplomacy rather than direct rule.
>
> Up to the beginning of the nineteenth century British expansion can be seen as an important but secondary part of the overseas expansion of Europe which began with

> Columbus's discovery of the route to the Americas in 1492. Spain took the lead, closely followed by Portugal; France, England and the Netherlands became involved about a hundred years later. Until 1800 these five European countries all ruled overseas empires. Between 1790 and 1830 all of the other European empires were seriously weakened so that by the middle of the nineteenth century the British Empire was not only the largest empire the world had ever seen, it was the only flourishing and functioning empire in existence.
>
> In the late nineteenth century and the first decades of the twentieth century there was a new outburst of general European expansion, but it brought with it ideas that destroyed empire. Democracy and nationalism, mixed in varying proportions, built up the determination of people ruled from Europe to run their own affairs, and undermined the willingness of the imperial powers to hang on to their possession. Within fifty years of the peak of imperial expansion in 1920 the overseas empires had almost completely disappeared.

However it was acquired, the fact remains that by the second half of the 19th century, the British empire was substantial, and De La Rue seized the opportunities for business.

THOMAS DE LA RUE DIES

Suddenly, in the summer of 1866, Thomas de la Rue's health deteriorated sharply, and in three weeks he died of what his death certificate called 'break-up of constitution'. His first wife, Jane, had died of apoplexy in 1858. Within a few months, Thomas, by this time aged 66, had married a much younger Alice Marie, one of three daughters of a Swedish gentleman called Carl André. Alice Marie was young enough to be Thomas's daughter. The wedding took place in Stockholm and, with no other de la Rues present, was witnessed by the British Consul.

Three months after his wedding (needless to say, the de la Rues were shocked by it, especially by the 'new wife being a Roman Catholic'), Thomas retired and he and his wife divided their time between Westbourne Terrace, Hyde Park and their country house near Sandy in Bedfordshire. On retiring he nearly fell out with his sons, as he made some tough financial demands that included an annuity of £3,500 (over £350,000 today) plus 5 per cent interest on the £30,000 (over £3 million) he left in the business. Warren was moved to write: 'You have retired on terms which any disinterested person would pronounce liberal', and 'in the arrangements which followed a lengthy discussion of terms, you fully and ably protected your own personal interests'.

Furthermore, from the shooting lodge near Inverness rented by his cousins, the Winans's, Warren wrote to Thomas:

> You allude to your separation from the business in Bunhill Row in terms not warranted by the facts. For a number of years you enjoyed a large monopoly of shares in the business, namely four-ninths of the Whole, the other three partners having five-

> ninths to divide amongst them and at a period when I feel I was actively promoting the prosperity of the business and when that was by no means equivalent to my services; during the last term it was two-ninths and William's one-ninth, which at that period we would not have been contented with, with any other partner than a father … It appears to me that if my children were in my place and I in yours that it would be a subject of pride on my part to feel that after many years of labour I could retire with such a magnificent income and leave my children in such a prosperous business to which I was linked by name and feeling.

Regrettably, father and sons never really made it up before Thomas died. Moreover, we have to suspect that Thomas's marriage to Alice Marie did not help. (Incidentally, she remarried within a year of Thomas's death. Her new husband was Sir Richard Temple Rennie, a successful barrister whose father had been Governor of the Falkland Islands. She then disappeared from the De La Rue orbit.)

Thomas's two sons, Warren and Colonel Billy, felt that they had put the business on a sound footing, and in the second half of the 1860s they pursued their other interests. Warren became an important figure in the scientific body called the London Institution, located in the City. At the same time he and Dr Hugo Müller continued with a series of electrical experiments. Warren let Müller run the De La Rue laboratories and left the running of the company to Colonel Billy, while he became President of the Royal Chemical Society. At the same time he used his money, energy and influence to push forward research at the Royal Astronomical Society.

In spite of his commitments at Bunhill Row, Colonel Billy became involved in other businesses. He was a director of the National Mercantile Assurance Society, which was just merging with the Eagle Star Insurance Company, and he became a director there as well. Within three years he had been appointed Deputy Chairman and then Chairman. By 1870 he was Chairman of Eagle Star, Senior Partner of De La Rue and, as Engraver to the Crown Agents, was responsible for advising on all colonial security matters. Tragically, he then developed cancer of the liver and died within a few months at the young age of 46. A disaster for his wife and family, Colonel Billy's death also brought upheaval to the De La Rue business. Warren had virtually retired from it to concentrate on his scientific interests, and the other partner, Jonah Nathan, was due to retire soon as well.

Fortunately, Warren was able to call on his two sons, Warren William and Thomas Andros, both of whom followed the de la Rue traditions of moving into the business after their studies were completed (Warren William was educated by tutors at home, while the more conventional Thomas Andros went to Rugby and Cambridge).

Warren William was particularly able, and Warren was able to say of him at 23, when he had been in the business just four years, that 'he had developed so rapidly that he was able to take over his Uncle's work entirely'. He was also appointed Engraver to the Crown Agents. As Lorna Houseman noted:

Warren William was a slogger.

His attention to detail amounted almost to a fetish. He had been in Colonel Billy's shoes one month when he was already worrying about the firm's methods of recording Colonial transactions. In October 1870 he requested permission from Crown Agent Sir William Sargeant to make and keep a perfect record of all the Crown Colonies Stamp printing plates 'with an impression of each form printed on its own paper and in the proper colour'. It disturbed his tidy mind not to be able to make an instant reference to these without 'inconvenience and loss of time'. Sir William demurred, Warren William persisted, and by the end of November the required Colonial specimens lay neatly pigeon-holed in Bunhill Row.

That the coming era was a golden age for the firm was partly due to the meticulousness with which Warren William kept the customers satisfied.

In spite of De La Rue's continued success, Perkins Bacon were still printing all the stamp denominations in Britain, including the One Penny. However, as the next date for a new tender approached, De La Rue received a large PR boost from the journal *The Globe*. On 7 March 1877 it published an article severely criticising the quality of the Perkins Bacon stamps, saying that its paper was 'inferior to that of any other kind' and that its colouring material was soft and dusty, 'which renders the use of any considerable number anything but pleasant'. Furthermore, it did not stick well because it was too thick and stiff. Finally, much to the delight of De La Rue, which manufactured the receipt stamps, the *Globe* article concluded: 'Everyone who has had the satisfaction of using a receipt stamp must be well aware of the superior character of this stamp over the other.'

Shortly afterwards, the government invited seven firms, including Perkins Bacon, Bradbury Wilkinson, Waterlow and De La Rue, to tender for a One Penny Order. As well as postage stamps printed for the Post Office, De La Rue and other printers also tendered to the Inland Revenue for financial documents.

De La Rue told the government that almost all 'the great States of Europe' had sought advice from De La Rue, and the number of stamps it had supplied to India and the Colonies ran into 'billions' without a single complaint of forgery. It also made much of the superiority of its letterpress method of printing (in which it had invested heavily) over the copperplate method of Perkins Bacon. De La Rue won the tender and then worked hard to produce a stamp of the highest quality. The red colour they proposed to use had a copper base, and to ensure that it was harmless they called in three leading toxicologists, Doctors Dupré and Murrell of the Westminster Hospital's School of Medicine, and Dr Ringer, Professor of Medicine at University College. The Board of the Inland Revenue were impressed with these efforts and noted that De La Rue had not become complacent or conceited. Mind you, the numbers were worth it. From November 1879 to 30 June 1881, no fewer than 1,462,584,000 One Penny stamps alone were delivered.

This meant that De La Rue needed more room and more printing capacity. It added the Crown and George Works to its Bunhill Row factories, as well as the new Star Works, which, as it wrote to the Board of the Inland Revenue, 'stands unrivalled in the nature of the accommodation it affords'. In total the company now had five factories working flat-out for the British Inland Revenue. Needless to say, De La Rue tried to secure a long-term contract, but the Revenue would only increase the contract from seven to ten years. Nevertheless, the future for the company looked very rosy in the early 1880s.

Mainly for reasons of security, printing stamps at Bunhill Row was divided into four sections. There were those for the Inland Revenue, those for India, those for the Crown Agents, and finally a 'Trade Printing Shop'. The Crown Agents employed a Chief Inspector of Stamps who worked and lived at Bunhill Row (rather like the inspector from the Bank of England who lived near the plant at Portals), and under him were an assistant, six male examiners and twelve female examiners. The male examiners supervised the contracts by going to the Engraving and Plate-Making departments, releasing plates, locking and unlocking the machines, and issuing the watermarked paper from the Crown Agent store. Whereas the Inland Revenue and India departments dealt with long runs of a limited range of stamps, the Crown Agent department was dealing with short runs of many different stamps.

As the Crown Agent work accounted for only about 1.5 per cent of their business, we may wonder why they took so much trouble over procuring and processing it, especially as many of the stamps had to be printed by the recess method. Perhaps they saw it as a challenge – and, after all, when you are in business, every order is an order. And De La Rue took pride in their ability to print by the recess method. They used it for stamps for British East Africa and Zanzibar in 1896 and for Malta and Tasmania in 1899. The last was the first complete issue of purely pictorial stamps. De La Rue improved on it in the Jamaican One Penny stamp of 1900, which reproduced by recess a photograph of scenery, thus pioneering a type of stamp that would become increasingly popular.

Warren de la Rue retired in 1880 and the following winter became seriously ill with pneumonia. He recovered, but from that time on the fortunes of the firm were definitely in the hands of Warren William and Thomas Andros. Both were married by this time. Warren William's marriage to Helen Norton was not a success and they divorced after seven years. Perhaps fortunately, there were no children. On the other hand, Thomas Andros's marriage to Emily Speed was a great success.

Perhaps of concern for the future of the firm, both Warren William and Thomas Andros had outside interests that were not necessarily conducive to business success. Warren William, like his Uncle Billy, was keen on horse-racing. He maintained a large house including stables at that centre of horse-racing, Newmarket in Suffolk. When his horse Trayles won the Ascot Gold Cup, the Alexandra Plate and the Goodwood Cup all in the same year, he named a house after the horse and built twin models of its head over the gateposts. This single-mindedness on horse-racing cost him his marriage and a small fortune. Not that he seemed perturbed, seemingly happy to return to a bachelor existence and dividing his time between his houses in Newmarket and York Terrace, Regent's Park, where, apparently, a special lift was built for the sole purpose of sending his false teeth down to his valet to be cleaned.

He was also probably attracted to the Newmarket scene by the presence of the Prince of Wales, the leader of 'society' in the last quarter of the 19th century. Both as Prince of Wales and when he became King Edward VII, he was extremely keen on horse-racing. Sir Edward Grey would say of him:

> The humblest devotees of horse racing in a Derby Day crowd knew that King Edward was there to enjoy the national festival in precisely the same spirit as themselves … There was, in fact, a real sympathy and community of feeling between himself and his people.

His enthusiasm was welcomed by those who frequented Newmarket and Epsom, Warren William de la Rue among them. To them it was a welcome relief compared with the moral rectitude of the Prince's mother and father.

For his part, Thomas Andros found that the social life of upper-class Londoners suited him and his wife perfectly, and they became great party-givers, especially at their new house in Cadogan Square. He could be somewhat eccentric like his brother, and insisted that all the other residents of the square change their number so that his house could be number 52, like the number of playing cards in a pack.

The two brothers' lack of close attention to the business was epitomised by their absence from Bunhill Row when the top brass came to the head office on the occasion of the jubilee ceremony in 1890 for the 50th anniversary of Rowland Hill's 1840 Penny Postage. 10,000 jubilee postcards were printed, all of which sold within three hours. The dignitaries were taken on a tour of the works by De La Rue partner W.T. Shaw. Neither Warren William nor Thomas Andros was present. Thomas de la Rue must have been spinning in his grave!

With regard to jubilees, three years earlier Queen Victoria had celebrated her Golden Jubilee and De La Rue had made a huge effort to perfect the first two-coloured stamps to mark the occasion. A set of the stamps was carefully mounted and sent to Windsor Castle for the Queen's approval. Lorna Houseman recounted what happened next:

> J.S. Purcell, Controller of Stamps, wrote to acknowledge them:
>
> > 'I am commanded by the Queen to thank you for the book of Postage Stamps which you have sent to Her Majesty and for giving her notice of the proposed change of design.
> >
> > The Queen looked at the new stamps but did not give me any opinion upon them.
> >
> > Perhaps she may do so later.'
>
> Explained the Controller apologetically: 'I am afraid the Queen's mind is more set upon the Churchill incident than upon our stamps.' The Churchill was Lord Randolph, who was then Chancellor of the Exchequer, and one with an attitude of

> rigid economy. Queen Victoria was waiting breathlessly to see whether he would apply this to the grants for the royal children and grandchildren.
>
> Since Lord Randolph was staying at the Castle when the De La Rue stamp package arrived, it is understandable that the Queen did not give it her attention, for, she said, the Chancellor proceeded to behave 'in a very improper manner'. At dinner he outlined to her the Government's plans for the next session, went up to bed, and 'that very night in my House, on Windsor paper he deliberately wrote his resignation and sent it to Lord Salisbury', an act which might have toppled the Government and brought back her detested Gladstone. Not until she recovered from the shock could she manage to turn her attention to lesser things, and approve the Jubilee stamp issue.

Fortunately for De La Rue, even if Queen Victoria was not giving their stamps her full attention and apparently not appreciating their efforts, India asked the company to depict the Queen, by now Empress of India, on bi-coloured stamps. (This was as much a case of security as patriotism. The One Rupee stamp had been subject to increasing attempts at forgery.) De La Rue submitted no fewer than 298 bi-coloured stamp essays, of which only one would be chosen. The India Office showed its appreciation by continuing to award De La Rue its stamp contracts for another 30 years.

MONOPOLY?

Nevertheless, there were those who felt that the stamp monopoly that De La Rue seemed to be enjoying should be investigated. In the House of Commons, the member for Prestwich asked why the Board of Inland Revenue had awarded De La Rue the consolidated contract for all British stamps in 1880 when others had offered lower prices.

The Chancellor of the Exchequer, George Goschen (famous for his conversion of the National Debt in 1888), told the House that 'owing to the fall in prices and improved processes of production it is tolerably certain that when the contract expires in 1890, considerable savings will be effected'. Warren William attacked the Member for Prestwich, a Mr Mowbray, saying:

> The statement which you addressed to the House of Commons last Monday, with reference to certain of our Government Printing Contracts, having received new prominence from its republication in a distorted and still more injurious form in yesterday's *Daily News*, we deem it necessary to address you on the subject.

He then went on to say that Mr Mowbray had not the slightest idea what he was talking about, because he would need specialised knowledge about stamp-printing and clearly he did not have that knowledge. For example, the Member was presumably not aware that in the London School Board printing contracts there was a difference between the highest and lowest tenders of 57 per cent. A subsequent government inquiry accepted De La Rue's evidence unequivocally.

Indeed, *The Times* was full of praise for De La Rue's work in ensuring the quality of the stamps produced:

> The stamp scheme recommended by the joint committee was approved by Mr Shaw-Lefevre in May 1885, just before his resignation of the office of Postmaster-General ... The elaboration etc. of all the designs that were considered by the committee and the execution of the work of manufacture has throughout rested with Messrs De La Rue and Co., the Government contractors, to whom all praise is due for the very excellent manner in which a most difficult task has been brought to completion.

Nevertheless, the company could not but be aware of the criticism of its potential monopoly position and consequent pricing power, and in November 1888 De La Rue wrote to the Inland Revenue:

> London, 110, Bunhill row, E.C., Nov. 9.
>
> Sir – We beg to confirm that we are willing, under a re-arrangement of the existing English and Indian contracts (except the stamped papers contract just concluded, and taking effect from Jan. 1 next), so to reduce our prices as would enable thoroughly good stout postcards to be sold to the public at 7d per dozen and the existing thin postcards at 6½d per dozen, at the same time leaving a substantial profit to the Post Office.
>
> Under a re-arrangement of prices we should have to ask to be allowed to increase the prices of the adhesive stamps, and one or two minor lines in which the market has gone against us.
>
> We could only re-arrange the existing English and Indian contracts, which have two years in the one case and two-and a half years in the other to run, from the 31st of December next, upon a new contract for ten years from the 1st of January next being granted to us, which would virtually extend the present contracts by eight and seven-and-a-half years respectively,
>
> We are, Sirs, your obedient servants,
> THOS. DE LA RUE and Co.

This was followed by a further letter to Sir Algernon West KCB, Chairman, Board of Inland Revenue at Somerset House:

> Sir – With reference to our letter of the 9th inst., and your answer thereto of the 16th inst. (not printed), the reply made by the Chancellor of the Exchequer to Mr Jennings in the House of Commons on Friday last leads us to believe that the decision conveyed to us may not be final. We therefore feel it due to ourselves, although we are not prepared at the present juncture to furnish details of prices, to state that we would guarantee under a re-arrangement and extension of contracts that the total net reductions, after allowing for the increase on adhesive stamps, &c., should amount to not

less than £30,000 per annum, which means a corresponding savings to the revenue, and would enable thoroughly good stout postcards to be sold, to the public at 7d per dozen, and the existing thin postcards at 6½d per dozen.

The fact of our being able to offer this large reduction is due to the fall in material costs and to the introduction of machinery (mostly of our own invention and construction) which has superseded costly hand processes.

We would remind you that, as reported in the papers, a slight error crept into the Chancellor of the Exchequer's reply in the House of Commons on Friday. He appears to have stated that we had asked for a ten years' extension of our contracts, the fact being that we asked for new English and Indian contracts for ten years from the 1st of January next, which, as pointed out in our letter of the 9th inst., would be an extension of eight and seven-and-a-half years respectively upon the existing contracts.

We have carefully read the report of the committee upon the Revenue Estimates, and we find that the recommendation finally agreed to, as to throwing contracts open to public competition, &c., was considerably modified from the original draft, and now reads, 'for as short periods as the interests of the public service and the nature of the article contracted for permit.' We assume that this was done advisedly, the committee no doubt recognizing the fact that in work of this nature it would be impossible to invite competition for contracts for short periods, having regard to the large amount of capital to be sunk in the plant, &c., necessary to the proper carrying out of such work.

We may also add that the prices of materials are now considered to be at the lowest point, and that there are not wanting indications of a probable advance in the future.

We are, Sir, your obedient servants,
THOS. DE LA RUE and Co.

A letter to *The Times* in 1900 also suggested that De La Rue should not be too complacent about its monopoly position with the Inland Revenue:

TO THE EDITOR OF THE TIMES

Sir, – March 31, 1890, I asked the Postmaster-General whether the new contract with Messrs. De La Rue and Co., for the supply of stationery and stamps had been signed: and whether he had any objection to lay the contract upon the table of the House of Commons.

The Postmaster-General replied that the contract had been signed and was in full effect. He added, 'No public advantage would be derived from laying it on the table.'

Let us now quote 'Hansard', March 19, 1888:-

'Mr Hanbury gave notice that he would call attention to Messrs De La Rue's contracts on going into Committee of Supply and move for correspondence.'

This afternoon in the House of Commons I asked 'the Secretary to the treasury (Mr Hanbury) if he would state to the House what is the cost per 1,000 of the

1.1 Henry Portal had impressed a local squire, Mr William Heathcote of Hursley Park, with his intelligence and hard work, and Heathcote leased him Bere Mill, originally a corn mill, on the upper reaches of the River Test, close to the London–Exeter road and about a mile from the village of Whitchurch. Portal moved to Bere Mill in 1712 and took a number of Huguenot paper-makers with him from South Stoneham.

1.2 In 1785 Joseph Portal built the 'Little White Tenement' next to the Mill as a residence for the Bank Officer.

1.3 John Portal, who had succeeded in extracting £2,000 (£240,000 in today's money) from the Bank of England as a grant for all his experimental work, now put forward a new idea. This involved radical change in the design of the banknote watermark.

1.4 John Portal's second son, Robert, went into the army and became one of the few survivors of the Charge of the Light Brigade at Balaklava in 1854. He joined Wyndham as a partner in 1863.

1.5 In 1901 Wyndham Portal was honoured with a baronetcy for his public service in many fields.

1.6 Overton Mill in the first half of the 20th century. As it became clear to the more far-sighted that another war was inevitable, Portals erected two buildings on the north side of Overton Mill early in 1939 on behalf of the Bank of England.

1.7 The founder, Thomas de la Rue (1793–1866).

LE MIROIR POLITIQUE;

Journal Hebdomadaire.

No. 19. GUERNESEY, SAMEDI 12 JUIN, 1813. Vol. I.

CONFERENCE,

ENTRE NAPOLEON ET L'AMBASSADEUR AUTRICHIEN, COMTE VON BUBNA.

Dans le *Correspondanten* du 7 de Mai dernier, on annonça le départ de Paris du Ministre Autrichien, Comte Von Bubna, ainsi que celui de l'Ambassadeur extraordinaire, le Prince de Schwartzenberg.

Ce dernier remit à Bonaparte une lettre écrite de la propre main de l'Empereur François, *(Francis)* contenant les propositions finales de l'Autriche pour la paix, propositions néanmoins que Bonaparte dédaigna de prendre en considération. Le Comte Von Bubna avoit préalablement eu le 10 Mars, la conversation suivante avec Bonaparte.

Après l'Audience publique que donna l'Empereur [illegible]

même, mais alors j'aurai acquis le droit d'être sévère envers ceux dont j'aurai défendu les territoires, sans leur assistance. Pour avoir négligé leurs intérêts, les États les plus puissans ont causé le renversement des anciennes Dynasties.

C'est l'intérêt le plus cher de la maison qui a hérité du titre, d'une partie des possessions des Césars, de ne pas permettre aux Russes de commander en Allemagne. Ces peuplades de sauvages doivent être renvoyées dans les déserts d'où elles sont sorties.

Bubna. Mais, Sire, Votre Majesté a tout fait pour détruire l'influence de mon souverain sur le corps politique de la Germanie.

Bonaparte. Oui, cela repondoit à mes vues, qui n'avoient d'autre objet que l'intérêt des Souverains, et la paix des nations. En outre, ne vaut-il pas mieux qu'une grande et généreuse puissance telle que la France, dont le seul but est de répandre également les bienfaits de la civilisation, [illegible]

Rovigo s'approcha immédiatement du Comte Von Bubna pour le désarmer; mais ce dernier recula aussitôt de quelques pas, et mettant l'épée à la main, se prépara à se défendre. Rovigo par un coup d'œil, demanda la volonté de son maître, qui, devenu alors plus calme, lui signifia par un pareil signe, de ne pas aller plus loin.

Bonaparte. M. Bubna ignore-t-il donc que je suis prompt, et que j'ai toute la fierté qui convient au souverain d'une grande et brave nation? J'ai un vif ressentiment des insultes, et il m'a semblé voir quelque chose d'outrageant dans ce que vous venez de dire; néanmoins, quoique vous puissiez vous oublier vous même, je ne veux point oublier ce qui est dû au caractère dont vous a revêtu mon parent et mon allié.

Bubna.—Sire, mon Souverain ne verra dans mon langage que l'expression de ce qui lui est dû.

Bonaparte.—Savez vous bien M. Bubna, que dès demain je puis faire la paix avec la Russie, s'il me plaît de rétablir la Prusse, et même de l'agrandir? Si je place [illegible]

comme je l'avois prévu. Si votre Empereur m'avoit soutenu, il m'auroit épargné bien du sang et bien des larmes. Si votre maître veut sincèrement se joindre à moi, nous pourrons encore rendre le repos au monde, et réaliser le projet d'une paix générale, qui est l'objet de toutes mes méditations et le but de tous mes efforts! On suppose que j'aime la guerre; quelle erreur! Les maux qu'elle entraîne après elle, me font saigner le cœur. Avant de commencer une campagne, j'ai toujours offert la paix, et je l'ai toujours accordée à mes ennemis vaincus. Dans une semaine, j'aurai 300,000 hommes sur pied, et je marcherai sur Magdebourg. Votre Empereur de son côté peut me donner un coup de main à Erfurt; il peut avec deux cens mille hommes, faire un mouvement central, et m'aider à délivrer le Nord de l'Europe, des barbares qui la ravagent. Il doit se joindre à la chaîne de civilisation. S'il me refuse son secours, j'accomplirai sans lui cette grande œuvre: il m'en coûtera sans doute beaucoup plus de temps, j'aurai beaucoup plus d'hommes à sacrifier, [illegible]

1.8 *In February 1813, Thomas published a weekly journal,* Le Miroir Politique, *price 3d (1.25p or £1.50 in today's money).*

1.9 *1833 was a significant year for De La Rue, for in that year the partnership of De La Rue, Cornish and Rock moved from Crown Street to 110 Bunhill Row, Finsbury, which they rented from a Mr James Esdaile for £230 per annum (£27,600 in today's money).*

1.10 Thomas de la Rue's first playing cards. Top row: 1834 – the pack that nearly ruined him; second row: 1840 – the return to convention; bottom row: 1832 – his original pack.

1.11 Augustus Fry, a partner of Thomas de la Rue from 1844 until 1851.

1.12 During the 1840s Warren de la Rue worked on creating an envelope-making machine. Originally envelopes were used flat and unfolded. The customer would have to fold them. Later they were produced folded, this process done by hand. The invention of Warren meant that more envelopes could be folded in an hour than had previously been folded in a day.

1.13 The Great Exhibition of 1851 was important for Britain and it was important for De La Rue as well. It was opened on 1 May 1851 by HRH Prince Albert, husband of Queen Victoria. By this time he had established himself as a popular and, perhaps more importantly, a significant member of British society.

1.14 Warren de la Rue, Thomas's older son (1815–89). Not only did he make a magnificent successor to his father, he also contributed outside the family business, mainly in the field of science. He acted as honorary secretary of the Royal Astronomical Society from 1864 to 1869, and again in 1879–88, and was until his death one of its vice-presidents.

1.15 William Frederick de la Rue, known as 'Colonel Billy' and described as 'an Elizabethan born out of his age, with the charm that overcomes obstacles both human and material – the Cavalier as well as the Colonel'.

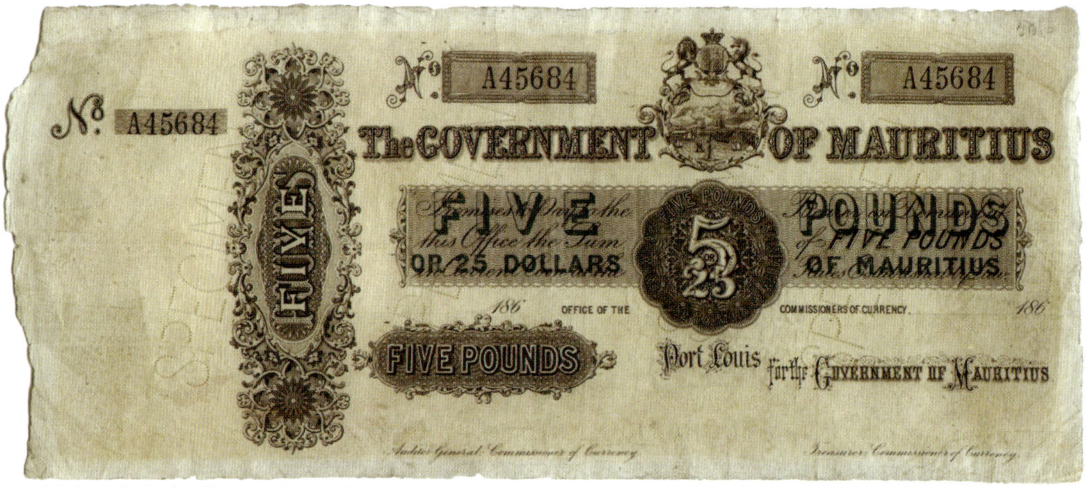

1.16 *In 1859 the Crown Agent General, Penrose Julyan, commissioned De La Rue to print five-pound, one-pound and ten-shilling notes for Mauritius.*

1.17 *During the American Civil War, De La Rue printed stamps for the Confederates. They were designed by the company's brilliant French designer, Joubert de la Ferté, who also engraved for De La Rue, among other things, the Queen Victoria heads used on the early Victorian postage stamps.*

1.18 Warren William, Warren de la Rue's son, worked very hard in the business but was also a keen race-horse owner at Newmarket.

1.19 Sir Thomas Andros de la Rue changed the firm from a partnership into a private company and then, in 1896, into a public company with himself as Chairman.

1.20 In 1905 De La Rue launched the Onoto, a plunger-filling pen that was revolutionary in that it filled on the vacuum principle, the reverse action to a syringe. It was also fitted with a patent shut-off device similar to a needle valve. For more than 50 years, the company made and, at times, heavily promoted the Onoto, but it was never really more than a sideline to the main business.

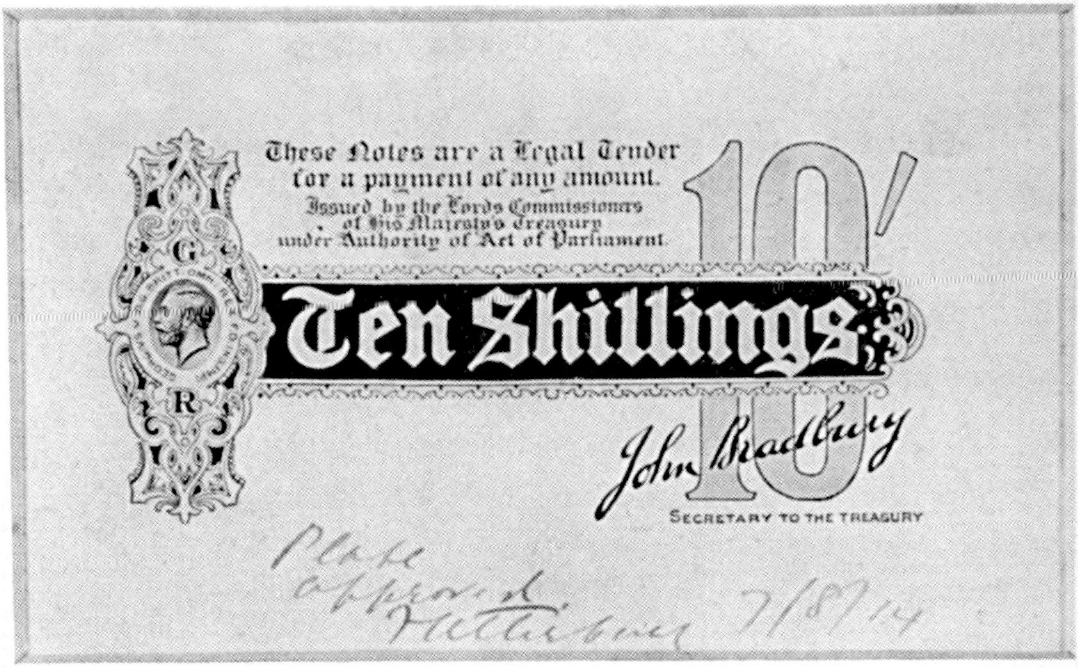

1.21, 1.22 On 5 August 1914, the day after war broke out, the Stationery Office asked De La Rue to 'manufacture 10s Treasury Notes with notepaper supplied by the Inland Revenue'. This was urgent. They would need to work night and day, and indeed every single person worked 24 hours in eight-hour shifts to enable 2.5 million notes to be delivered to Somerset House during the first five weeks of the war. At the same time, De La Rue designed a £1 note that was the same as the 10 shilling note, only slightly larger and in black.

1.23 A photo and cartoon of the two men who rescued De La Rue in the inter-war years, Sidney Lamert (left) and Bernard Westall. They were the first non-family members to be Chairmen of De La Rue.

> postage stamps, the halfpenny and the penny value, supplied to the Post Office; and what is the total number and the cost of the postage stamps supplied to the Post Office last year.'
>
> Mr Hanbury replied: – 'I must decline to disclose particulars of the schedules of prices attached to contracts for the supply of goods for the public service.'

I now beg to give the reason for my action. I served on a Select Committee of the House of Commons in 1888 really to inquire into the contracts of De La Rue and Co., in which I alleged they had charged £500,000 more than the market prices in their stationery contract with the Post Office.

Before that committee had completed its labours it was announced that De La Rue and Co. had agreed to accept a new contract at a reduction of something between £30,000 and £40,000 a year on their previous prices.

On February 24, 1896, I asked the representative of the Postmaster-General in the House of Commons to supply the public with postal orders bearing counterfoils on the plan adopted in certain foreign countries, each counterfoil being marked with the number of the attached order, as well as the amount and office stamp, so as to facilitate detection in case of theft, to relieve the transmitters of small sums from the task of noting these particulars, and to encourage the use of postal orders.

Mr Hanbury replied that larger paper and new and expensive machinery would be required, and the Postmaster-General, would not, therefore, be justified in incurring the expense. An Edinburgh firm of printers thereupon offered to print and supply the postal orders at a reduction of at least 25 per cent on the present prices. On the same day an able Post Office employee submitted to the Postmaster-General a neater postal order, which, with a counterfoil, occupied no more space than the postal order now in use, and would cost less money. The Duke of Norfolk declined both proposals.

I have recently been informed that Messrs De La Rue and Co., were being paid between £16 and £32 per million (including cost of paper) for supplying postage stamps.

The Postmaster-General of the United States of America has just sent me his annual report for 1898–99. He states that he paid last year only £10 per million for the supply of postage stamps; and I challenge comparison between those issued in America and the ones supplied to British public. The former are immensely superior.

It therefore appears that for an inferior ink we are paying De La Rue and Co. three times the price of a superior ink supplied to the American Post Office. Writing without passion and in the position of one who has gained a very large number of postal reforms, I appeal to my right hon friend Mr Hanbury whether there is not here a strong case for inquiry.

When I am told that the Post Office cannot afford the smallest expenditure (such as charging as one word in telegrams the name of each place in the United Kingdom) I have reason to strongly complain of the want of wisdom or honesty on the part of the mandarins at St Martins-le-Grand.

I am your obedient servant.
Roland Hetherington

APPLIED HIS SCIENTIFIC KNOWLEDGE

In 1889 the remarkable Warren de la Rue died. We could write a whole chapter on him, but perhaps *The Times* obituary will suffice:

OBITUARY

MR WARREN DE LA RUE

We regret to announce the death of Mr Warren de la Rue, D.C.L., F.R.S., Ph.D., which occurred on Good Friday. He was the son of the late Mr Thomas de la Rue, and was born in Guernsey in the year 1815. He was educated in Paris, and succeeded his father as head of the firm of Thomas de la Rue and Co., from which he retired in 1880, and which is now carried on by his second son, Mr T. de la Rue. In the course of his conduct of the firm Mr de la Rue applied his scientific knowledge to purposes of practical utility and patented a number of inventions, among them being processes for utilizing earth oils and machinery for simplifying the making of writing materials. The principal scientific work in which he distinguished himself was the application of photography to celestial phenomena. The photographs, when measured by a micrometer which he invented, furnished exact astronomical data. In 1860 he went to Spain with the Himalayan Expedition, and was successful in obtaining a series of photographs of the total eclipse of the sun on July 18. The results formed the subject of the Bakerian lecture, delivered to the Royal Society in April 1862. In conjunction with Professor Balfour Stewart and Mr B. Lowry, he published 'Researches in Solar Physics', founded on observations made at the Kew Observatory under his directions. He also took an active part in making the preparations for the photographic observation of the transit of Venus in 1874. He established a private observatory at Cranford, Middlesex, but it was dismantled in 1873, and the instruments presented to the University of Oxford, where they have been employed most successfully by Professor Pritchard in determining, by means of photography, the distance of 61 Cygni and other fixed stars. In 1874 he fitted up a private physical laboratory, where, employing a battery of 15,000 chloride of silver cells, he has, in conjunction with his friend, Dr Hugo Müller, carried on an elaborate series of researches on the electrical discharge. The results of the researches have been from time to time communicated to the Royal Society and the Académie des Sciences, Paris. 'The Phenomena of the Electric Discharge', was also made the subject of a most interesting lecture, illustrated by a great number of experiments, at the Royal Institution in 1881. Nearly all of the results of Dr de la Rue's scientific work have been embodied in papers and memoirs, which will be found in the 'Transactions' of the Royal Astronomical, Chemical, and other learned societies. He acted as juror and reporter in the Department of Class XXIX, in the Great Exhibition of 1851, was a juror in Class X of the Paris Exhibition of 1855, and presided over Section B, Class XXXVIII, of the Exhibition of 1862. He was a member of the International Electrical Congress, consisting of all the most eminent physicists of all countries assembled in Paris, and of the jury of the Electrical Exhibition held there in 1881. He was also a member of the Consulting Council of the Electrical Exhibition held at the Crystal Palace, Sydenham, in 1882. He has held office in several societies. He acted for some time as honorary secretary of the Royal Astronomical Society from 1864 to 1869, and again in 1879–88, and was till his death one of its vice-presidents. He was for many years president of the London Institution, from which he retired and became secretary of the Royal Institution in 1878, on the retirement of Mr Spottiswoode, who was elected president of the Royal Society, but resigned the post in 1882. He was a corresponding member of the French Académie des Sciences, for the department of astronomy; also of the Imperial Academy of Sciences, St Petersburg, the Philomathic Society of Paris, the Royal Society of Upsala, the Society of Agriculture and Commerce, Caen, the Society of Natural Science, Cherbourg, and the Berlin Chemical Society. Three foreign orders have been conferred upon him: – Commander of the Legion of Honour, Commander of the Order of St Maurice and St Lazare, and Knight of the Order of the Rose, Brazil. Mr de la Rue died, after a short illness, from pneumonia. The funeral will take place tomorrow at Kensal-green at a quarter past 4 o'clock in the afternoon.

Chapter Five

Times Become Harder

1900–1921

Tasteful binding, beautiful printing
Eccentricities
The Onoto pen
The end of the monopoly and crisis
War and serious crisis

TASTEFUL BINDING, BEAUTIFUL PRINTING

What was De La Rue's position in the 1880s and 1890s as the next generation of the family took over the reins?

In 1879 the company had developed the economical, but nevertheless highly accurate, key-plate method of printing postage stamps, and also in that year it produced its first stamp by the intaglio method for the Malayan territory of Labuan.

This system required two plates: the key-plate containing the sovereign's head and frame, which could, if required, be used for several different colonies; and the duty-plate that carried the name of the colony and the value. Various colours were used to distinguish the values in each series. The first of this key-plate series were printed for Antigua and Nevis in 1879.

From 1880 until 1910 De La Rue produced all the stamp requirements of Great Britain, adding the lower denominations to those of higher value that they had supplied since 1855.

There were constant references in *The Times* praising the quality of De La Rue's playing cards, diaries and calendars:

> Some two or three years ago Messrs. De La Rue started some International playing cards which had great success. These cards had all the quaintness of traditional cards, but the honours represented the Sovereigns of the present day, quaintly drawn, and not disturbing to the player.

And, commenting on De La Rue's Christmas cards, *The Times* wrote:

> Messrs De La Rue and Co. issue nearly 100 varieties, many of high class, and none unworthy of attention. Especially attractive, perhaps, are the printings in colour on white satin, some perfumed packets of what may be called the valentine order, and a series representing Oriental girls dancing, angling, beating a tambourine or watching the gambols of goldfish.

Of the diaries and calendars, *The Times* wrote:

> Messrs De La Rue and Co. issue their almanacs, diaries and calendars for the new year with their usual profession. Their annual publications are of all sizes, from about the size of a postage stamp upwards. They furnish calendars suitable for the waistcoat pocket, the desk, the chimneypiece and the wall ... As in former years, Messrs De La Rue show great ingenuity in providing a cover or protection for a diary ... Two of the pocket books issued by this firm are so neat and beautiful that they are almost a work of art.

Three years later, *The Times* wrote:

> Messrs De La Rue and Co.'s diaries are, for the most part, destined more for pleasure or household requirements than for business.

In its review of the almanacs and diaries for 1890, *The Times* wrote:

> All the publications of Messrs De La Rue are characterized by neatness and taste. It is from this firm that we obtain those elegant frames, red or purple, and stamped with gold, which stand on the table and contain the month's calendar.

And for 1896:

> Messrs De La Rue send a parcel, the contents of which are marked by their variety and elegance. The 'Portable Diary' is worthy of special commendation. It is most beautifully bound and contains a purse and receptacles for cards and stamps.

And praise for the quality of De La Rue's diaries continued in *The Times* every year into the new century. In its review of diaries and almanacs for 1906, *The Times* was still recommending the firm's products, writing:

> Tasteful binding, beautiful printing and variety in size, shape and arrangement are now successfully aimed at by most publishers of diaries, but in these and other respects, in their own special department of pocket books, Messrs De La Rue's publications are still far ahead of most of their rivals.

And in the review for 1909:

> Messrs De La Rue's diaries leave nothing to be desired; good paper, beautiful typography, and first-class binding are the rule, not the exception, in their publications, and few firms maintain from year to year such a high standard of excellence.

De La Rue were also printing several journals during this period from 1900 to 1920, including:

Airways & Airports	Monthly	32 pages and cover
Air & Airways	Monthly	56–64 pages and cover
Aircraft Engineering	Monthly	48 pages and cover
The Architect	Weekly	76–96 pages and cover
British Malaya	Monthly	48–64 pages and cover
British Trade Journal	Monthly	96 pages and cover
English Mechanics	Weekly	32 pages and cover
Flying	Weekly	20 pages and cover
Fortnightly Reviews	Fortnightly	132 pages and cover
Hardware Trade Journal	Weekly	80–176 pages and cover
Industria Britannica	Quarterly	48 pages and cover
The Lady	Weekly	48 pages and cover
The Law Journal	Weekly	32 pages and cover
LMS Magazine	Monthly	48–64 pages and cover
Nursery World	Weekly	12 pages and cover
Psychic News	Weekly	12 pages and cover
The Puzzler	Weekly	16 pages and cover
The Tablet	Weekly	32 pages
Theatre World	Monthly	52 pages and cover
Timber Trades Journal	Weekly	108 pages and cover
Time and Tide	Weekly	28–36 pages and cover
The Tourist	Monthly	38 pages and cover
The Transport World	Monthly	88–116 pages and cover
White Star Magazine	Monthly	44 pages and cover

During the 1890s the De La Rue operations in Bunhill Row were visited frequently by royalty. Prince Alfred, the Duke of Edinburgh, Queen Victoria's second son, was shown round the factories, and the Duke of York came for lunch and found it all so interesting he stayed for tea. The Prince and Princess of Wales came at short notice to inspect the stamps that De La Rue were printing for the Prince of Wales Hospital Fund.

The Times reported the visit in May 1897 in great detail under the heading, 'The Princess and the Stamps':

> After performing the ceremony of laying the foundation stone of the new Ophthalmic Hospital, the Prince and Princess of Wales, with Princess Victoria, and Lady Emily Kingscote and Captain Holford, drove to Messrs. De la Rue's Printing Works in Bunhill-row, to witness the process by which the stamp in aid of the Prince's Hospital Fund has been engraved and is being produced. The visit was almost an unexpected one, and certainly the directors of the famous house had had little more than an hour's notice of their Royal guests. Preparation of any sort was, therefore, impossible, in decorations or any other way, but both the Prince and Princess were pleased to say that they waived all ceremony, and wished simply to see how the little triumph of philatelist's art is being turned out. News of the intended visit soon spread, and a large and loyal crowd were assembled outside the works, who gave hearty cheers as the Royal carriages drove up. To receive the Prince and Princess Mr T. Andros de la Rue, the head of the firm, Mr Ernest de la Rue, Mr Shaw, and others of the directors were in waiting, and the Royal party were taken at once in the lift to the Relief Stamping Room, on the fourth storey of the immense factory. Though this was only the passage-way to the object of the visit, the work of stamping crests, monograms, and addresses upon note paper attracted the attention especially of the Princess and Princess Victoria, who examined the plates, the presses, and the method of supplying the coloured paints, with much interest. All this work is done by girls and the Princess asked many questions as to the time taken in acquiring proficiency and deftness, and the amount that a skilled worker could accomplish in the day. [...]
>
> All this Mr de la Rue explained in the most simple lucid manner, and the Prince, as well as the Princess, showed the keenest interest in every detail. Three hand-presses are being employed – two for the blue shilling stamps, one for the red half-crown one – and to these the Royal party next turned their attention. The plates were most carefully and evenly inked, a sheet of creamy-white crisp paper with its special watermark was spread, the screws were turned, and in a few seconds the clearly-engraved sheet appeared. The Prince initialled the first of the sheets he saw printed, and this will be retained as a memento by the firm. Meanwhile, both the Princess and Princess Victoria honoured the workmen with the most gracious notice, asking many questions as to their calling, and a detail which would have escaped most people was observed by the Princess with much concern. It is, of course, necessary that the plate shall be perfectly cleaned between each impression that is taken and fresh ink spread. Almost all is removed with a coarse soft cotton cloth, but the final finish must be put on with the bare hand of the workman, over which a little whiting is sprinkled. The Princess noticed that, and was very glad to learn that from the composition of the ink there was not the slightest danger to health in the practice.
>
> Turning then to the little assemblage, the Prince said: 'Before going I wish to say how very much interested we have been in this process of printing the stamps. I most

earnestly hope that the working classes especially will buy as many of them as possible for doing this will afford them not only an opportunity of paying their shillings to the Fund, but they will also have in them a souvenir of the great occasion of this year.'

Then the visitors' book was brought out – a volume of which the firm was very proud, for it contains many distinguished autographs – and not for the first time did the Prince sign it, as he had paid a visit as a lad, in 1856, to the works. The Princess and Princess Victoria also added their names to it. It is worth quoting, perhaps, a curiously appropriate couplet, which Cardinal Wiseman wrote impromptu above his own signature in it:

> Where else, as here, are perfectly combined,
> Industry, skill, benevolence, and mind?

And how was Britain doing in the late 19th century? Here again is the view of that leading historian of the 19th century, Professor Asa (now Lord) Briggs:

> In the later industrial revolution Britain's lead was cut as other countries, notably Germany and the United States, the latter with far greater natural resources, themselves experienced industrial revolutions, so that by 1913 Germany was producing 13,500,000 tons of steel and the United States 31,000,000 as against Britain's 8,000,000 tons. Textiles, too, faced increasing competition: although there was heavy investment in Lancashire between 1895 and 1914, it was largely in what was by then traditional technology. Coal output rose to a peak of over 270,000,000 tons in the years 1910–14 (as against 66,700,000 tons in the years 1855–60) and coal exports to a peak of 62,700,000 tons. Yet productivity was falling, and in newer industries, like chemicals and electrical engineering, other countries were ahead from the start. [...]
>
> There was ample evidence, too, of both technical and entrepreneurial ability later in the century and in the years before 1914, and one important new invention, Charles Parsons' steam turbine of 1884, which pointed to the future. William Lever's soap enterprise led him to the jungles of West Africa and his successors joined hands with the Dutch in the huge Unilever concern of 1929, the first great European multinational. Ludwig Mond, whose chemical business was eventually to become a key component in the Imperial Chemical Industry, was another tycoon, and William Armstrong, later of Vickers Armstrong, who vied with Krupps in the world's armament business, was a third. It was through enterprise as well as hard work that in 1913 Britain still accounted for a quarter of the world's trade in manufactured goods (as against 37% in the early 1880s). Its share of the world's industrial production had fallen from over 30% to 13%, yet the rate of growth of the national income (2.3%) was not very different from that of the mid-Victorian years.

The last quarter of the 19th century saw a period of unprecedented invention that shaped the modern world: the harnessing of electricity for everyday use by such brilliant men as Michael Faraday, James Clerk Maxwell and Thomas Edison (ranked 28th, 29th and 38th among the most influential people who ever lived by that outstanding

American historian, Michael Hart); the invention of the radio by Guglielmo Marconi (ranked 41st); the invention of the telephone by Alexander Graham Bell (44th); the discovery of penicillin by Alexander Fleming (45th); and the discovery of X-rays by Wilhelm Conrad Röntgen. At the same time Louis Pasteur was making discoveries that would help us to survive nasty diseases and therefore live longer.

ECCENTRICITIES

Amid the accolades that De La Rue was receiving, and the prosperity that the country as a whole was enjoying, the first sign of potential problems ahead appeared when, in 1896, Warren William fell off his horse in Hyde Park. He never fully recovered. Indeed, his eccentricity, never far below the surface, now became marked. Lorna Houseman recounts his way of life:

> He built up an intricate chain supply of umbrellas for himself throughout London, leaving one at White's, one at the Carlton Club, one at Bunhill Row and others at various restaurants. Going to stay with him was a nerve-wracking business. All over his houses notices were displayed (printing by De La Rue). Since he believed in buying the best in contemporary household equipment, numerous instructions were posted as to its use. Apprehensive guests in his town house read that if they got stuck in the lift 'information can be sent by telegraph to the Otis Elevator Company at 4 Queen Victoria Street ... and if at night to the General Hydraulic Power Company at Blackfriars'. On their descent they might find a poster announcing in big black letters: 'IT IS VERY COLD'. Sometimes they supposed their host to have mistaken them for his race-horses; in the hall of his establishment in York Terrace, Regent's Park, were lists advising them of the distances round the Outer Circle, the Inner Circle, and from the Botanical Gardens to the Conservatory Steps (OUTER CIRCLE ... 2 miles, 7 furlongs, 54 yards; 166 yards short of 3 miles; NB 5 times round is 14½ miles 50 yards). He gave similar advice regarding the walk from the hall door to the Piccadilly end of Old Bond Street and the Carlton Club, via Wimpole Street. There was an outcrop of posters concerning his new telephone (the number was Mayfair 5) and his personal telegraphic address (RAINDROPS, LONDON). Among the contingencies covered were alternative arrangements for posting letters when his private post-box was being re-painted. At Newmarket the daily shooting cards read like battle orders, even the coachman's instructions were specially printed.
>
> Visiting valets and maids fared even worse. To avoid disturbing the rest of the house they were told to apply to the de la Rue butler and head housemaid for soft-soled slippers, and be sure to serve morning tea 'in the little pots provided for the purpose'. If visitors did not receive a satisfactory response to their bell-pulling, they were advised to ring three times for Mr de la Rue. Below stairs there was a feast of information ranging from leaflets for making Dr Kussmaul's Fattening Porridge, to hints for working Baker's Patent Decker Oven. The hall boy was given a printed reminder about The Maintenance of the Bicycle, the key of which he was to keep in his pocket, 'and not hide it or leave it around'.

> His neighbours found themselves inundated with printed suggestions. Being the oldest resident of York Terrace he began bombarding the other inmates as to whom to complain to about early milk carts, or why to favour the Akonia Process of Dust Prevention. Not infrequently his requests were benevolent. He urged that generous Christmas Boxes be given to the Garden Night Watchman ('a most reliable man continually controlling the Gardens in all weathers'), as well as donations to the Cabmen's Shelter Fund. Although most of his house regulations were for the comfort of himself and his visitors, he also besought the servants to take precaution against 'the cold coming through the waste-pipe', so that they should not be discomforted whilst bathing in the servants' bathroom.

Eventually his brother, Thomas Andros, persuaded him to retire from his position as Senior Partner, and Warren William went to Tenby in South Wales where he eventually committed suicide. Thomas Andros took full control of De La Rue and immediately changed its structure from a partnership into a private company.

These were the shareholdings by the end of 1898, according to the Register of Members:

	Shares
Thomas Andros de la Rue	21,000
Emily Maria de la Rue (wife of Thomas Andros)	300
Ernest de la Rue	20,500
Florence de la Rue (wife of Ernest)	500
Herbert de la Rue (youngest of the four brothers: Warren William, Thomas Andros, Ernest and Herbert)	5,000
Horace George Bowen and John Gordon Nairne (Bank of England)	5,000
Alexander Dundas Ogilvy Wedderburn and William Palmer Fuller	800
William Palmer Fuller	80
William Auld	50
Francis Country	50
William Teel (Accountant, De La Rue)	50
Thomas Fairhall (General Manager, De la Rue)	50
Thomas Birtles (Warehouse Manager, De La Rue)	50
Alexander Richardson (Manager, Stamps Department, De La Rue)	50
William Wane (Paper Buyer, De La Rue)	50
Albert Hill (Commercial Clerk, De La Rue)	50
Thomas Gunning, (Traveller, De La Rue)	100
Henry Gouns (Stationer in Brighton)	100
Marian Hunt	100
William Shaw (Partner, De La Rue)	120

There were 53,000 shares issued at £10 each, capitalising the company at £530,000 (about £60 million in today's money). The De La Rue family owned 46,000 shares or 87 per cent, the Bank of England 5,000 or 9.4 per cent, and the employees 400 or just under 1 per cent. The De La Rues would have subscribed £460,000 (nearly £50 million in today's money). Interestingly, Dr Müller did not subscribe for any shares.

As we can see, the De La Rue family and their friends retained most of the shares; and Thomas Andros effectively ran it as though it were a private company, with himself as Chief Executive. His position of authority was perhaps strengthened by his being created a baronet, a reward for his work as principal Governor of the Royal Chest Hospital. As Lorna Houseman points out, it would have been more appropriate if his father, Warren, had received such an honour.

Thomas Andros quickly fell out with his younger brother Ernest, who then left the firm and joined the Board of His Master's Voice.

Ernest, later Sir Ernest, de la Rue made a number of contributions both to the company and in the world outside. In De La Rue he foresaw the potential for the firm in the growing popularity of bridge, and, with a few friends, drew up the original laws of the game as it was first played in Britain. Outside the firm he designed and carried out the whole of the decoration of the Royal Albert Hall. In his enthusiasm for horse-racing, he invented the first electric starting-gate. He also produced a system for making papier-mâché splints, which was adopted by most of the hospital supply depots during the First World War.

More significantly for the continued prosperity of De La Rue, Dr Hugo Müller retired, and his technical expertise would be greatly missed. Sir Thomas Andros was punctilious in his attendance at Bunhill Row, arriving every morning at 10.30 exactly and leaving at 4.00pm exactly. However, while there, communication with his staff appears to have been perfunctory. Wearing a high hat, black frock coat and striped trousers, his tours of the works were like a royal procession except that he did not talk to anybody. Furthermore, although his own office was palatial enough, the rest of the plant, badly in need of renovation and modernisation, remained shabby.

A playing card packer, Nellie Cockram, remembered 'very old floorboards and cupboards round the walls, everything seemed very old to me'. The women's lavatories were just holes in the ground that labourers cleared twice a week. And although there was virtually no inflation in the second half of the 19th century, it could not be described as progressive that women on the shop floor were paid the same in the first decade of the 20th century as their counterparts were in 1857. The top rate was twelve shillings a week (60p or £66 in today's money). Frederick Bagley's wages in 1900 were seven shillings a week (35p or just over £30). Sir Thomas Andros *could* be generous on occasion. He once pressed £5 (just over £500) into the hand of David Turner, an engraver who had just completed an excellent piece of work for stamp heads.

Unfortunately, Thomas Andros's high-handed approach eventually led to friction creeping in to De La Rue's dealings with the Crown Agents. Following some problems over supplying stamps to Ceylon, Crown Agent Blake wrote to Thomas Andros when negotiations for supplying stamps to Trinidad began: 'I am most anxious to avoid any recurrence of the kind of correspondence which we had last winter.' And he followed it up with a letter which said, inter alia: 'I return herewith the designs for the Uganda stamp and I am sorry to say that they will not do.'

If Sir Thomas Andros was running De La Rue in an idiosyncratic way, his three sons – Evelyn, Ivor and Stuart – fared little better. They were all bright, and all three went to Cambridge and afterwards joined the family firm. The eldest, Evelyn, enjoyed country life rather than the social life so important to his mother and father, and he married a country girl, May Franklin, whose father was a respected country gentleman with five packs of hounds in Nottinghamshire.

When they were first married, Evelyn and May lived in Westbourne Terrace, Hyde Park, where great-grandfather Thomas had lived. However, Evelyn did not get on well with his brothers, and to escape the constant bickering at Bunhill Row, he and his wife moved out to the Home Counties. Evelyn would then commute to the City – and apparently he once walked, to prove that it could be done. They moved from large house to large house, and though they were rented, they would still spend considerable sums improving them, adding stables, garages, servants' wings and even model farms.

Evelyn became more interested in his hobbies than in the company in Bunhill Row, where he found the in-fighting with his brothers distressing (not that his home life was well-ordered either, as the horse-riding May found domestic life dull and was apparently often late for the meals that she took little interest in preparing). However, Evelyn did interest himself in one product that he became convinced should be developed and marketed by De La Rue.

THE ONOTO PEN

De La Rue had already begun to sell a pen in 1881. It was called the Anti-Stylograph and it looked as weird as its name, with a small piece of hard rubber tube and a barrel-shaped nib. Then in 1884, the company promoted the Swift, the first pen to be fitted with a shut-off valve. It was an immediate success. This is what the *Stationery Trades Journal* wrote about it:

> This pen-holder is one of the greatest successes of the day, and the orders received by the makers show that the public appreciate the advantages of a fountain-pen holder which will fulfil the promises made on its behalf. The mechanism of the pen is very simple, and it is hardly possible for it to get out of order with fair usage. The recommending features of the 'Swift' are that the ink can be regulated in its flow to suit all hands, and that when not in use the ink is effectually shut off at the very point of the pen so that leakage is impossible.

In 1891 De La Rue launched the Pelican, which also boasted a gold nib and had a larger ink capacity. This was also very popular.

Then in 1905 came the Onoto, a plunger-filling pen that was revolutionary in that it filled on the vacuum principle, the reverse action to a syringe. It was also fitted with a patent shut-off device similar to a needle valve. The story of how Evelyn found the Onoto pen was well told by Lorna Houseman:

> Like so many things connected with Evelyn the events which led to the birth of the famous Onoto pen were somewhat bizarre. There was at that time a female impersonator on roller skates by the name of George Sweetser, who also chanced to be an inventor. He too had a fixation about pens. [...]
>
> When he was over eighty and still roller skating vigorously, George Sweetser recalled the interview in a magazine article: 'The stuffing was completely knocked out of me when the gentleman I saw, Sir Evelyn (then Mr) de la Rue pulled out of his pocket an exactly similar pen, his own invention of a month or so prior date to mine ...' After the initial shock the two White Knights recovered themselves. Mr Sweetser did not, he said, think much of Mr de la Rue's invention, not, he hastened to point out, because of sour grapes. 'Oh dear no! but because the filling was a fumble as the piston had to be given four single strokes and the rod twisted twice to engage and disengage the piston'. Mr Sweetser graciously allowed that his visit to Bunhill Row was a blessing in disguise, because if his pen 'had not been anticipated the great Onoto would never have been born'.
>
> To remedy the faults in his model, and challenged by Evelyn's which so closely resembled it, Mr Sweetser purchased an eight-penny 'Houndsditch' pen, converted it and hurried back to Bunhill Row to see the same gentleman. 'When I pushed the plunger down he saw the ink go down in the bottle so knew it must have gone up into the pen.' It was a moving moment. Evelyn uttered the historic words: 'I like that', which as Mr Sweetser pointed out, was not a wise admission. 'If I had been of a certain persuasion the price might have been doubled.' It was obvious that Evelyn wanted the pen badly. He asked the cost, said 'I will have it', and Mr Sweetser came out 'ten minutes after going in, with a big fat cheque'.
>
> This episode may reveal only too clearly that Evelyn's method of negotiating a deal was anything but businesslike. But his inspiration proved to be right. Mr Sweetser's pen was a good investment. Having convinced his father that at last he was on to something worthwhile, Evelyn was allowed to spend the vast sum of £50,000 [it is difficult to believe, but this is about £5.5 million in today's money] on advertising the pen. It was called 'Onoto' for the only reason that its pronunciation was the same in all languages. [Steve Hull, perhaps the leading expert on Onoto pens today, feels it was possible that the pen was named after Ono Tokusaburo, a Japanese watchmaker. He had registered a patent in 1856 for a stylographic pen.] This publicity campaign was the one investment of any note authorised in the reign of Sir Thomas Andros.

Under the onslaught of such intensive advertising the country quickly capitulated, and the Onoto became what it proclaimed to be: *the* pen. Unwilling to be left out, Mr Sweetser made some unusual claims on behalf of his invention. 'It can', he stressed, 'not only be filled in a flash and written with, but could be used to syringe your ears, spray the geraniums with insecticide, and it is ideal for "ink-splashers" as it will carry across the room. Could one ask any more of a pen?'

Steve Hull noted that in the heavy promotion a red pillar box and a young boy – Peter Pen – were used in the advertising. And promotion was not confined to Britain. In France, advertising for Onoto virtually created the market for fountain pens; while in the USA, De La Rue set up the Onoto Pen Company at 262 Broadway, New York.

The pen was advertised as 'Onoto the Pen' at prices up to £10 (£1,000 today), and by the middle of the First World War as the 'All-British-Pen'. The Onoto brand name was spread to inks, diaries and playing cards, and also to fountain pens filled by means of an eyedropper such as the Onoto Landsman and Onoto Valveless.

In the 1920s the Onoto range was expanded, with new models including the 'Streamline' Onoto in 1920, the Onoto ink pencil in 1921, the Onoto safety with retractable nib in 1922, the Onoto Mammoth and lever-filler in 1924, coloured plastic Onotos in 1928, and Onoto desk-sets in 1929.

In 1927, production was transferred to the former Strathendry paper factory mill in Leslie, Fife. In the 1930s, in spite of the Depression, Onoto pens became even more stylish and colourful and several new styles were introduced, including pens with ink visibility in 1935 and the Onoto Magna in 1937.

The Second World War meant restricted production of pens in favour of munitions, and full production was not resumed after the war until 1948, when a reduced Onoto Magna range with a lever-filled version was launched. Other series were introduced, including the K series in 1955, but finally, in 1958, Onoto production at Strathendry was suspended. Production under licence continued in Australia, but even that stopped in 1963.

According to Lorna Houseman, a later Chairman of the company (probably her father, Bernard Westall) reckoned that Thomas Andros allowed the heavy promotional expenditure on the Onoto as a method of spending some of the vast profits being made on the Inland Revenue stamp contracts.

And certainly De La Rue made sure the 'right' people used the Onoto. Field Marshal Earl Haig used one throughout the First World War. Edgar Wallace used one to correct the proofs of his novels. Emmeline Morrison, another novelist, also used one, as did Billy Merson, the music hall comedian. In the Second World War, De La Rue made sure that Winston Churchill used one.

THE END OF THE MONOPOLY AND CRISIS

All good things come to an end, and in 1911 the Inland Revenue decided to split its stamp contracts between De La Rue and another printer, Harrisons. Harrisons had printed for the government but had never printed postage stamps. In spite of this, the Inland Revenue awarded the contract for the higher denominations to De La Rue and the contract for the lower, and more profitable, ones to Harrisons.

Thomas Andros was appalled by this. He is supposed to have told the Secretary of the Post Office that he would see everyone damned before he would share any contract, and that he would only accept all or nothing. The entire contract went to

Harrisons, so the result was that De La Rue got nothing. And, of course, when Harrisons printed the stamps, the quality was not up to De La Rue's standard.

At least Thomas Andros never had to suffer the indignity of posting letters with Harrisons stamps on them. He died within months of the loss of the contract.

However, Thomas Andros's eldest son, Evelyn, did have to suffer the humiliation of being summoned to the Royal Yacht at Cowes by King George V, who, as it happens, was an enthusiastic and knowledgeable philatelist. He showed Evelyn the Harrisons proofs and said angrily: 'Make me look like a stuffed monkey, don't they?' Evelyn agreed that the quality was poor, but had to confess that there was nothing he could do about it.

The Times also commented on the new stamps under the heading, 'A Disappointing Design':

> It is feared that the new postage stamps which made their debut yesterday morning will meet with but small favour among stamp collectors and artists who are anxious to obtain a stamp design that shall be in every way worthy of the nation. Although the difficulties of combining art and utility in the limited area that the postage stamp affords must be recognised, it can scarcely be said that Mr Bertram Mackennal has excelled himself in the new stamps, and it is doubtful whether they are any material improvement upon Herr Füchs's much-criticized portrait of the late King.
>
> In the case of the 1d stamp the design is overcrowded with detail and the general appearance is weak and indistinct. The diminutive portrait of the King is poor and unflattering, and lacks the fine execution which the public has been led to expect. The ½d stamp is slightly more successful, and it would, perhaps, have been better had the same frame design been adopted for both denominations. The engraving of the penny stamp is unsatisfactory, and the printing compares unfavourably with the workmanship of Messrs De La Rue and Co.

Again, there seemed nothing that Evelyn could do.

It was not just loss of face that De La Rue suffered from the Inland Revenue taking away the lucrative stamp contract. They now had to cut back their workforce. The Star Works was closed and half the maintenance men made redundant. How would the three brothers, Evelyn, Stuart and Ivor, cope? Unfortunately, none of them seemed capable of going out in search of new business as their predecessors would have done. Furthermore, in the short term, they (and in particular Evelyn, who was Chairman) had to cope with a misunderstanding over Thomas Andros's will.

Thomas Andros died a wealthy man, leaving not only about £750,000 (about £80 million today) but also some excellent paintings, antiques and jewellery. Each member of the family was allowed to pick one item. Some annuities were left to managers, engravers and foremen at Bunhill Row. When the will was published, just before Christmas 1911, rumours spread through the works that not only would these men benefit, but that *all* De La Rue employees would, according to their years of service.

When we read the notice in *The Times* it is not surprising that the employees at Bunhill Row thought they were going to benefit. Here is the article in full:

SIR ANDROS DE LA RUE'S ESTATE
ANNUITIES FOR EMPLOYÉS

Sir Thomas Andros de la Rue, first baronet, of Cadogan Square, SW, head of the firm of Messrs. Thomas De La Rue and Co. (Limited), manufacturers of postage stamps and playing cards, who died on April 10, aged 62, son of the late Dr Warren de la Rue, the astronomer, left estate of the gross value of £822,041, with net personalty £811,840.

The testator left £1,000 each to Mrs Oswald Chapman of Victoria-street, SW, Miss Fanny Preston of Queensberry-place, SW, Mrs M.A. Worth of Rashleigh, Walmer, Kent and Mr William Palmer Fuller (as executor); the portraits of himself and his wife to his son Sir Evelyn Andros de la Rue, and all his other household and personal effects, horses, carriages, motor-cars, and consumable stores and his residence 52, Cadogan-square, to his trustees upon trust to offer them to his sons in order of seniority for the sum of £40,000, and, failing acceptance by them, a like offer is to be made to his daughter, Mrs Sybil Grantham. He left all his shares, debentures, and money on deposit with Thomas De La Rue and Co. (Limited) to his three sons Evelyn, Ivor and Stuart in equal shares, they bringing into hotchpot any interest in that company given to them by him in his lifetime. He confirmed various family settlements, including the settlement of £40,000 upon his daughter Sybil on her marriage, and he left £40,000 to each of his sons.

He left £1,000 to the Royal Hospital for Diseases of the Chest, City-road, £250 each to St George's Hospital and the London Fever Hospital, and the following annuities to persons now or lately in the employment of Thomas De La Rue and Co. (Limited), to date from their retirement in the case of those still in the employment of the company and to be in lieu of pensions from the company in the case of those already retired: – £500 to W. Wans, formerly paper buyer; £350 to L. Cownley, formerly accountant; £200 to A.J. Hayes, manager of the stamp department; £150 each to F. Watkinson, head engineer, William Godfrey Teed, head of the counting-house, H.L. Birtles, head of the warehouse, and F. Minter, his secretary. He also left £500 to P.W. Potter, secretary of Thomas De La Rue and Co. (Limited); a life annuity of £50 to his late wife's maid, Mrs McDonnell (née Edwards): and a life annuity of £52 to his coachman, Thomas Rawson, if still in his service, in addition to any legacy on account of length of service.

The following legacies are made to servants in his employment or *employés* of companies of which he was a director, if still in his service or in that of such company at the date of his decease: – £500 to each of those of over 20 years' service, £150 to each of those of from 15 to 20 years' service, £80 to each of those of from eight to ten years' service, £60 to each of those of from six to eight years' service, £40 to each of those of from four to six years' service, and £20 to each of those of from two to four years' service.

> The residue of his property he left to all his children in equal shares, the share of his daughter Sybil Grantham being held upon like trusts as declared in her marriage settlement.

Two women sorters were sent to Somerset House to check. Unfortunately, the notices in the newspapers had been misunderstood. It was only Sir Thomas Andros's domestic employees who would benefit, not those at Bunhill Row.

Sir Evelyn now had the unpleasant task of telling everyone the true position, and then had to follow it up with redundancies. For his part, he now had the money to indulge his passion for cars. He teamed up with a Mr Taunton, developed a car called The Taunton, and set up a factory at Liège in Belgium in which to produce it. All was going well, with many cars ordered even before they were completed. Unfortunately, on 4 August 1914, the German army invaded Belgium and the Liège factory was soon appropriated. Evelyn lost £80,000 (£8 million in today's money).

WAR AND SERIOUS CRISIS

Millions of words have been written on why war broke out in August 1914. The *causa sine qua non* was obvious – the assassination of Archduke Ferdinand; the real cause was, and still is, the subject of debate. Some things are certain: the German army invaded Belgium; the British government gave the German government an ultimatum to withdraw; the German army continued to advance. At 11.00am on 4 August 1914 the British government declared war on Germany, and by midnight five European empires were at war: Austria–Hungary against Serbia and Russia; Russia against Austria–Hungary and Germany; Germany against Russia, France, Belgium and Britain; France against Germany; and Britain against Germany. This was not going to be resolved by Christmas as many thought and hoped.

De La Rue had never had to cope with war conditions. The firm was founded just as the Napoleonic wars were about to end, and apart from the Crimean War, the American Civil War and the short Franco-Prussian War and various skirmishes in far-flung parts of the empire, the world had enjoyed 100 years of peace. As we have seen, the company even benefited from the American Civil War. In the end, it would not benefit from the Great War of 1914–18, although in the short term it did receive an order from His Majesty's Stationery Office.

The government anticipated a run on its gold reserves and ordered all gold sovereigns to be handed in. Postal Orders would be used as currency, and on 5 August the Stationery Office asked De La Rue to 'manufacture 10s Treasury Notes with notepaper supplied by the Inland Revenue'. This was urgent. They would need to work night and day, and indeed every single person worked 24 hours in eight-hour shifts to enable 2.5 million notes to be delivered to Somerset House during the first five weeks of the war.

At the same time, De La Rue designed a £1 note that was the same as the 10 shilling note, only slightly larger and in black. In spite of this, the order for printing the £1 note was given to Waterlow Brothers and Leighton. (This was a different company from Waterlow and Sons, although the two Waterlows were cousins.) Stuart de la Rue was upset by this. After all, it was his company that had designed the £1 note, and now Waterlow Brothers and Leighton would be the exclusive printer of these notes, whereas De La Rue would be sharing the 10s notes. The Stationery Office relented and reversed the position in the second contract.

Any joy the company felt would prove to be short-lived. These notes, hastily put together, would be easy to forge, and both De La Rue and Waterlow and Sons (as opposed to Waterlow Brothers and Leighton) realised that something offering greater protection against forgery would be needed. Stuart de la Rue and Edgar Waterlow got together and did a deal. If the government gave the next contract to De La Rue, who would print by letterpress, they would give Waterlow and Sons a shilling for every 1,000 notes. Conversely, if the contract went to Waterlow, who printed using copperplate, they would give De La Rue sixpence per 1,000 (the copperplate process was more expensive).

As it happened, neither won, as Waterlow Brothers and Leighton won with a new and cheaper process called 'photogravure'. This was not the only error of judgement that Stuart would make.

He had been left in sole charge because both Evelyn and Ivor felt it their duty to join the army, and whereas De La Rue began the war with £90,000 (£10 million) in cash at the bank, they ended it with an overdraft of £90,000. Many manufacturing companies thrived during the war. Indeed, there was much comment about profiteers (In the Second World War, profits were capped and any excess taken in tax). De La Rue were given contracts to manufacture shell caps, and they were still printing stamps and stationery for India, but they still managed to lose money.

The main reason was Stuart's acquisition of other companies, prompted by Prime Minister Lloyd George's urging of manufacturing companies to diversify. Unfortunately, none of Stuart's acquisitions enjoyed any synergy, either with each other or indeed with De La Rue. The only thing they seemed to have in common was the parlous state of their finances. One company made the Philip Mead cricket bat (Philip Mead was a famous cricketer who played for Hampshire). Another made the Clyno car. (This is what Lorna Houseman says, but if De La Rue bought the company during the First World War, it made only motorcycles at that point, and indeed supplied many to both the British and Russian armies. It began to make cars in 1922 and became the third-largest car manufacturer after Austin and Morris. However, it went into liquidation in 1929.) Other companies acquired were a boiler business (not Potterton, which was bought much later) and a plastics company (not Formica). None of these acquisitions prospered.

Whereas Stuart carried on the family tradition of helping his fellow man outside the company as a Hertfordshire Justice of the Peace and the Governor of the Royal Chest Hospital in succession to Sir Thomas Andros, he did not carry it on in business acumen. Indeed, at one point he was nearly arrested for forgery when he successfully passed off a copy of a Waterlow Brothers and Leighton note at a bank. By the end of the war, De La Rue was in a poor state; and to compound the problem, Stuart kept his brothers in ignorance of its condition. Both Evelyn and Ivor had survived. Indeed, Evelyn looked back on his army days with nostalgia and even took his wife on a tour of the battlefields. Ivor was not so lucky and suffered a nervous breakdown.

By 1921, the state of the business was so bad that Stuart felt obliged to tell his brothers, and in that year De La Rue finally lost its Indian contracts. The Inchcape Commission had been set up to see what could be done to improve conditions there, and the government asked De La Rue if it would consider setting up a plant in India to meet its printing requirements. Stuart said he would not and the Indian business, so valuable to the company, was lost.

In spite of this difficult position and the loss of the Indian business, Stuart seemed to have pulled off something of a coup, possibly his only one, in recruiting a former Waterlow and Sons managing director, Albert Gronow, as De La Rue's new Managing Director. Gronow lost no time in offering a directorship at De La Rue to the head of Waterlow's printing department, Harold Rapkin, on condition that he brought certain key men with him. They included Waterlow's head designer and engraver and, most significantly, the chief engineer who was just perfecting a rotary printing machine. With them too came a junior clerk, Bernard Westall, who had just married Rapkin's daughter.

The scene was set for Stuart de la Rue's final lapse of business judgement. While Gronow was the boss at Waterlow and Sons, the company had bought Waterlow Brothers and Leighton. Going through the documents at De La Rue, Gronow came across the agreement between Stuart de la Rue and Edgar Waterlow. When he realised the implications of this, now that the two Waterlow companies were as one, Gronow advised Stuart de la Rue that the Waterlow Group should honour the agreement and recompense De La Rue sixpence for every thousand English notes they printed. He sued Waterlow for the money and though it took until April 1923, the court awarded De La Rue £120,000 (about £7 million today) in compensation

Instead of just accepting the award gracefully, Stuart de la Rue said to the Waterlows in open court that he could not understand why they should begrudge paying them when De La Rue had always honoured a similar promise to pay Waterlow for staying out of their stamp monopoly. This was a disastrous announcement, as it became clear that an agreement with De La Rue had gone back more years than had been revealed, and it showed that while Waterlow would have a free run in the export market, the home and colonial markets would be De La Rue's. Indeed, if De La Rue did accept a foreign contract, Thomas Andros compensated Edgar Waterlow by sending his son Stuart from Bunhill Row to Great Winchester Street with the money in a Gladstone bag. Apparently no other Waterlow knew of this arrangement.

This was not the highly regulated business world of the 21st century, but nevertheless everyone was shocked. The Crown Agents, the Foreign Office and the Treasury all demanded an inquiry. Yet again, Stuart de la Rue was lucky to escape with a public ticking off.

The dénouement was nigh. In his desperation, Stuart summoned all the staff to his office one by one and asked them to say what they felt was wrong with the company. Even the junior clerk Bernard Westall was consulted, and his reply was succinct: 'You.' Stuart de la Rue was, of course, outraged and told the Board that either 'that whippersnapper Westall' went or he did. As the only other Board members were two outside investors who had grown increasingly alarmed by Stuart de la Rue's erratic and inept handling of the business, they opted to retain Westall. That, I am afraid, is the last we will read about a member of the de la Rue family. Ivor never really recovered from the war and died at the age of 47 in 1927. Stuart also died in 1927, at the age of 44. Evelyn died in 1950 at the age of 71. He had three sons, Eric, Ian and Victor, and Eric and Ian each had a son, Andrew and Anthony. But the family of de la Rue were not involved further in the management of the company after the early 1920s.

Chapter Six

Hard Pounding

1921–1939

The company is worth nothing
A capital rearrangement
The Bulgarian salesman
100th anniversary (playing cards)
Westall learnt Mah Jong
Beginnings of diversification
The gathering storm
A golden opportunity
Production in China and Burma

THE COMPANY IS WORTH NOTHING

When Stuart de la Rue departed, the company was leaderless. Fortunately, the non-executive directors persuaded Sidney Lamert to take over as Chairman and Managing Director. As Lorna Houseman put it:

> He was the son of an irascible Scottish parson. Like a famous contemporary he went out to South Africa as a war correspondent, but unlike Churchill managed to avoid being taken prisoner by the Boers. On his return he bought with his accumulated savings a substantial interest in an unimportant weekly called the *Investors Chronicle*. It was a lucky buy. The rubber boom arose, stimulating public interest in the Stock Market. The circulation of his paper soared and his fortune was made. Mr Lamert's name began to get mentioned in City circles.

His immediate challenge in De La Rue was to face the debenture holders, who amongst other things had financed the takeover of the Goodall Playing Card Company. Because Stuart de la Rue had allowed a duplication of effort to persist, with the Goodall plant continuing to operate in Camden Town and the De La Rue one in Bunhill Row, this purchase had in no way boosted profits. Mr Lamert found nothing encouraging to report about playing cards, or indeed anything else.

When he launched the debenture issue in 1921, Stuart de la Rue had fixed the interest payable to its investors at the unusually high rate of 8 per cent. There was never the slightest hope of being able to pay it. Mr Lamert told the debenture holders that the Company's assets would not even cover De La Rue's trade debts, and nor were they themselves at the head of the debenture queue. After the loss of the Inland Revenue order in 1911, the de la Rue brothers had issued a first lot of debentures. There would not be a penny left for the second debenture holders.

The latter received the news with profound dissatisfaction. When it was suggested that the one pound shares be reduced in value to sixpence, and that fifty ordinary shares be accepted for every debenture, they remained unmollified. The announcement that there was no hope of a dividend in the foreseeable future scarcely helped, and the meeting erupted into a storm of recrimination against Stuart de la Rue's erstwhile mismanagement. Sidney Lamert stood his ground. He pointed out that the debenture holders had no alternative but to accept his proposals and his resoluteness won the day.

On 26 November 1924, Sidney Lamert gave this sobering news to shareholders:

> While the account of Thomas De La Rue for the 12 months to March 29 show some improvement, a profit of £1,943 being shown in contrast with a loss (after making adjustments) of about £135,000, the position is still unsatisfactory, for the inevitable capital reduction scheme has yet to be carried through. The directors are now considering this matter in conjunction with the committee of 8% Mortgage Debenture stockholders and express the hope that a scheme will be evolved in the course of the current financial year ...

As a result of this financial reorganisation of the manufacturing and sales side of the business, substantial progress had been made, the report states, the output having reached 'record figures'. The company, however, 'will be unfavourably affected by the prospective loss of its contract with the India Government for the supply of postal stores'.

A CAPITAL REARRANGEMENT

Sidney Lamert was forced into a recapitalisation of De La Rue. Holders of 8 per cent debenture stock, which had been oversubscribed when offered on the London Stock Exchange in November 1921, were asked to surrender their stock and to accept only 50 per cent of the face value. In looking at the immediate prospects for the company in March 1925, Lamert told shareholders that they had been losing money at the rate of between £2,000 and £3,000 a week (about £120,000 and £180,000 in today's money) and had been steadily losing at that rate for a considerable time, but that very soon they could stop the loss and be on a profit-earning basis. At the end of the financial year to 20 March 1924, there was small credit balance of about £2,000. As far as the financial year to March 1925 was concerned, he had no figures later than November, but he thought he might fairly say that at the end of that month they were £25,000 better off compared with the same period in the previous year, although they were then already beginning to be affected by the loss of the India contract. Businessmen would understand that the loss of a contract representing, say, £100,000 a year (about £6 million today), even though they were not making a large profit on it, had a serious effect on the question of overhead charges. In his opinion, they would be substantially better off this year than they were last year, and he hoped and believed that next year they would be still better off, working free of the enormous incubus that was over the business now. Pens were doing well, as were playing cards. During several weeks towards the end of last year, they were making and selling 130,000 packs of playing cards a week. Security printing was increasing, and security printing was probably the best hope they had for the future, although it had entailed the provision of a substantial amount of new machinery.

By the end of 1925 prospects were looking better, and Lamert was able to look back on the traumas of the immediate post-war years and the early 1920s with some equanimity. He told shareholders on 8 December 1925:

> Now, turning to the profit and loss account, the balance to credit is £23,666. That compares with the following figures: – In 1921, the first year that this was a public company in the sense that the public was very largely interested, there was a loss of £90,000; in the succeeding year there was a loss of £195,000, but advantage was taken in those accounts to clear up the stock, which had got into a shocking condition during the war. The factories, moreover, were completely disorganized during that period; there was a strike on; production had reached a very low ebb; so I should say that, leaving stock out entirely and simply taking your trading loss in that year, you lost £130,000. The first time I had the pleasure of meeting you (you were then Debenture holders), I told you that I believed the loss would be very quickly eliminated, and that gradually this business could be built up again. In 1923 the loss was converted into a small profit of £2,000. For the next period, in the accounts you have now before you, the profit was £23,000.

Losing the contract in India was very serious. Lamert put it this way:

> I am not one of those people who talk much about luck, but I have a feeling that your luck is largely what you make it, but I do think it rather hard that we should have lost the India contract just at the moment when we were reorganising. I think if India had not taken away that contract, which had been in the house for approximately half a century, the figure we should have been able to put before you as the balance of profit

> in this period would have been at least £20,000 higher. I do not say that we should have made £20,000 out of the India contract. What I do mean is that, taking a very large contract like that out of our business, leaving a very big hole in our turnover, leaving us with disorganised factories and a lot of space that was not earning, meant a difference of £20,000. Income from investments in allied undertakings appears at £12,785. That includes the income we draw from Goodall and Weirs. Goodalls we, of course, run as a subsidiary company, and with regard to Weirs I am glad to say that that unfortunate company has now so far turned the corner, that it is able to pay us interest on the actual cash advances we made to it.

And finally he said:

> You will now want me to say something to you about the general progress of the business. The outstanding feature I have already referred to – that is, the loss of the India contract. It was necessary, immediately we knew that was coming, to take steps to reorganise the factories completely. We had to do so under singular difficulties, because a great deal of the machinery which had been used on that contract was adaptable for that contract and for no other. The India Government are starting a factory of their own. I tried very hard indeed to get them to buy a great deal of the special machinery.
>
> However, they took the view that they would sooner have new machinery, and I am sorry to say they could get it better from Germany. However, the fact remains they did not take our machinery, and a great deal of it was scrapped.

De La Rue's life was made almost unbearable in the early 1920s by no fewer than four legal actions.

First, the firm Warrilows, printers in Birmingham, brought an action against Sir Evelyn de la Rue, Ivor de la Rue and Stuart de la Rue, claiming damages for alleged fraudulent misrepresentation and conspiracy on the sale of 400,000 Ordinary shares in Messrs Thomas De La Rue and Co. Ltd. Actions were also brought by A.G. Gronow, R.H. Ruddock and H.S. Hooper.

Sir Douglas Hogg, in opening the case for Messrs Warrilows Ltd, said that Mr Ruddock, a valuer in the printing trade, acting on behalf of the promoters of a scheme for amalgamating Messrs Warrilows Ltd, Messrs Weir Ltd, papermakers, and Messrs Goodall, obtained an option for one month for the purchase of the whole of the shares in Messrs De La Rue Ltd, which were said to be worth £700,000, and Mr Hooper, Managing Director of Messrs Warrilows, Mr Ruddock, Mr Stuart de la Rue, Mr Underwood and Mr Muir met together to discuss the project. At that meeting Mr Stuart de la Rue told Mr Ruddock and his supporters that, although the stamp contract had been lost, the annual pre-war profits of the company totalled £100,000, of which the profits from the Onoto pen alone amounted to £50,000. The value of the goodwill of the company was put at £427,000, and on the basis of £100,000 a year profit, this figure was not regarded as too large. A further meeting took place on 28 May 1921, the day the option expired, and Mr Stuart de la Rue repeated the figures that he had previously given as to the profits. On that Mr Hooper decided to exercise the option granted to Mr Ruddock on his behalf and to buy the whole of the shares of the company for £550,000. It was further arranged that Messrs De La Rue should buy the share capital in Messrs Goodall and Messrs Weir, and that Messrs Warrilows should buy the whole of the existing capital in Messrs De La Rue, the additional capital to be obtained by public subscription. The sum of £25,000 was paid as deposit. After a later rearrangement, it was agreed that Messrs Warrilows, instead of taking over the whole of the 640,000 shares in Messrs De La Rue, should take 400,000, the remainder to be taken up by Mr Hooper, Mr Ruddock and Mr Gronow, Managing Director of Messrs Waterlow and Sons.

In March 1922, said Sir Douglas Hogg, it appeared that, instead of making £100,000 in 1921, Messrs De la Rue lost £80,000, but as that year was a bad one so far as trade was concerned, it did not occur to Mr Ruddock that he had been deceived. Later, however, matters became serious. In 1923, accountants investigated the position of the company, and their report stated that the profit from Onoto pens was £6,000 and the total profits of the company £35,000 for the year. As a result of the whole unfortunate and disastrous affair, Messrs Warrilows went into voluntary liquidation, Weirs were in very low water, and Messrs De La Rue's shares were practically worthless, the company being carried on in the interests of the debenture-holders.

Messrs Warrilows lost £379,000 and the other plaintiffs also suffered heavy losses. The defence to the action was that any statements made were made in good faith and that in any case they were not relied upon by the plaintiffs, who had every facility for examining the affairs of the company before exercising the option.

Mr Hooper, giving evidence, said that he and his family took over £55,000-worth of shares in Messrs De La Rue. It had been ascertained, he said, that in 1921 that company had lost £80,000 and in 1922 between £200,000 and £300,000. He heard Mr Stuart de la Rue make the statement as to the profits of the company.

Mr Charles, opening for the defence for Sir Evelyn and Mr Ivor de la Rue, said that he was speaking for gentlemen who had lived clean lives, whom no one attacked, whose commercial purity had not been assailed, and who stood before the jury charged with one of the foulest and wickedest things of which a commercial man could be accused. On the most flimsy and uncertain evidence, if the desire of the disappointed plaintiffs were to be realised, these three brothers were to be held up to the whole world as swindling rogues. He asked the jury to say that no such foul stigma rested upon them. The transaction was carried out by Mr Stuart de la Rue because he had been left in charge when his brothers, Sir Evelyn and Mr Ivor de la Rue, were still with the forces during the war. The brothers did not seek to sell the business; they were asked to do so by the optimistic Mr Ruddock, it being suggested that amalgamation would be for the benefit of both parties. The three brothers stood together to face the charge, which they all emphatically denied.

Mr Jowitt, for Mr Stuart de la Rue, said that there was not one scrap of documentary evidence that in any way supported the plaintiffs' case, and it would be a serious thing for any man who sold a business, after the books had been opened for the inspection of the purchaser's accountants, to have the transaction ripped open at the end of two years on the strength of an alleged statement.

Mr Stuart de la Rue, giving evidence, said that he was formerly governing director of Messrs Thomas De La Rue and Co. Ltd. The company had the British stamp contract from 1880 to 1910, and the Indian contract had been with them from 1855 to the present day. The stamp contract was an important part of the business, the profits from this being more than half the total profits. The business was organised for the performance of that contract, and the years following its loss were not normal, because they had to reorganise and turn around. They turned their hands to the trade side and concentrated on pens and playing cards, but the period of abnormality that followed the loss of the stamp contract knocked their profits right down. The position improved later.

Somehow the de la Rues escaped without having to reimburse the litigants, but it was all very time-wasting and, in legal fees, expensive.

Second, Waterlow and Sons brought an action in the Chancery Court to restrain De La Rue from using or selling copperplate printing machinery. This had a serious effect on one of De La Rue's most important activities. The action was finally settled by a payment from De La Rue to Waterlow, with each side bearing its own costs. Lamert told shareholders in June 1927:

> In the annual report the directors had alluded briefly to Waterlow's lawsuit, which, as the shareholders had already been informed, was settled on the advice of counsel. Not only did that lawsuit cost them upwards of £60,000 [£3.6 million in today's money] in cash, but it also had the effect for a period of certainly more than a year of hampering their business of security printing very seriously.

In their turn, De La Rue brought an action against Waddingtons, a printer and playing card manufacturer based in Leeds. This is how Victor Watson recounted it in *The Waddingtons Story*:

> A sales and marketing organisation was brought into existence under the leadership of Clarrie Hirst and playing cards were sold everywhere in this country and shipped in considerable quantities all over the world. The traditional way of selling playing cards through the stationery trade and to advertisers was closely examined and an entirely new concept was devised, centred on selling to the stationery trade playing cards incorporating an advertisement. This became the basis of Waddingtons' 'Beautiful Britain' playing cards which depicted scenes of many seaside and country resorts. It was first subsidised by the Great Western Railway Company and later by the London and North Eastern Railway Company at a time long before the days of British Railways. It enabled beautifully printed cards to be sold through the stationery trade at a very low rate due to this advertising.
>
> From then on playing cards were often in the thoughts of all concerned and it is noted that in October 1922 the Australasian Publication Company were given the sole rights for a three-year period to sell playing cards in Australia and New Zealand. This

coincided with a dispute which arose with Charles Goodall & Co. with regard to the use of the word 'Linen' in connection with playing cards. This dispute seemed to be more concerned with problems in Australia than in this country, but was later amicably settled out of court. It must be agreed that 1921 and 1922 were vital years.

The amazing and rapid success in capturing a large proportion of the playing card market caused some concern to De La Rue. They believed that Waddingtons had copied the designs of their playing card faces and although these designs are traditional there is a question of copyright, particularly when concerned with the ace of spades. They therefore instituted court proceedings in 1924 and sued Waddingtons on the grounds that they were 'passing off'. The case was quite protracted and it seemed that De La Rue would win and that heavy damages would be awarded against Waddingtons. However, when Waddingtons seemed on the point of losing, two exhibits were produced in court which were enlargements of the De La Rue and the Waddingtons ace of spades and this showed the differences to be so great that the Waddingtons ace was not a copy.

De La Rue were not happy about the decision but decided to waive an appeal and the Waddington ace was allowed to stay.

Finally, De La Rue brought an action against Stuart de la Rue in connection with the purchase of the Ordinary share capital of J.A. Weir. This dragged on for a number of years but was finally settled after a payment to the company by Stuart de la Rue, and the company disposed of its interest in Weir in 1927. Lamert told shareholders on 29 June 1927:

> The Weir business, from the company's point of view, had been a most disastrous affair. The former board of directors had paid approximately £400,000 [£24 million today] for it, and, within a few months of its acquisition, it had practically ceased to exist as an asset.

After all this, and with the General Strike in 1926, which Lamert calculated cost the company £10,000 (£600,000 today), he was relieved to be able to say to shareholders at the AGM in June 1927:

> With regard to the position and prospects of the company, he did not wish to harp on the fact of the series of misfortunes, which they had met with. He hoped that those misfortunes were now over. If anyone had told him in 1923 when he first started with the company, what was ahead of them, he thought that he would have said that there was no prospect of getting through. Now, having got through and looking backwards, he wondered how it had been managed. He wanted to express his opinion that the position of the company today, for the first time since he had known it, was sound. They had an essentially good business and he looked with considerable hope to the future. They had got particularly to look forward as their salvation to the copper-plate printing side of the business. The reputation of the great firm of De La Rue was built up as a surface printing-house. For a series of years the house made large profits out

of two letterpress contracts, both of which had now left it. As they could not look to make those profits again out of letterpress printing, they had gone into copper-plate work. Not only had they already established a business, but he thought he could say quite confidently that it was a business with a great future. They could do better and cheaper work than any other house in the trade, and he believed that within the next few years their progress in that department would be rapid.

The shareholders had been informed about the Bank of England contract. It was part of the claim in the Waterlow suit to prevent the company delivering to the Bank of England, and now that the lawsuit was settled they were in a position to deliver machinery, and they were delivering it. They had put in a number of machines and there were more to go in. The work which this contract would bring to the factories for the next few years would be considerable.

With regard to the pens and playing cards, there again the company was making good progress. They had for years been up against fierce competition in the pen business, and that was all part of the price of the Great War. During the war the Americans had the market to themselves, because the company's factories were producing other goods. They were now getting their name and goodwill back, but naturally, the progress was slow. Cards were going ahead very well indeed, and the output was greater than it had ever been. But in the playing card trade prices had been severely cut, owing to competition.

There was one thing that hampered them and was a source of great anxiety to the board, and that was the lack of capital. They had gone through a very drastic reorganisation, but it had not brought them a single penny of additional capital. Altogether, since 1923 they must have spent a sum approximate to £100,000 on the factories. Those who were familiar with the business would know that an expanding concern had more need of capital than one which is stationary. One share-holder had written suggesting that they should cut down the shares to 5s each and make a further issue of shares at 5s. That, of course, was impracticable, for the reason that there would be no justification for writing down the shares to 5s. But while the shares were at their present price, equally they could not make a new issue of capital, and certainly the board would be very slow to suggest putting anything ahead of the Ordinary shareholders because that would not be fair. He wished again to emphasise the fact that for the first time he could say to them that the business was in a sound position.

Furthermore, in spite of all the financial and legal drama of the early 1920s, at least considerable progress was being made on the technical front. A very important development was the introduction and improvement of the De La Rue Recess Printing Press, known as 'the mangle'. This machine solved a problem that had puzzled the printing plate engineers for years, namely, replacing the flat printing plate with a cylinder to hold a pre-curved printing plate, making contact with the impression cylinder that had been developed years earlier. This new machine could be considered something of a breakthrough, and banknote orders began to pour in. By the mid-1920s a new machine was being erected every two weeks, until 44 machines were printing nearly a quarter of a million sheets of print every day.

The Bank of England became interested, and in 1927, after extensive trials, bought machines from De La Rue for printing their banknotes. Eventually the Bank bought no fewer than 28 'mangles' and used them to print thousands of millions of 10 shilling and £1 notes. The machines were still being used in the 1970s. From 1927 De La Rue also supplied the Bank with the ink for them.

The use of dry paper for printing DP (direct plate) was another De La Rue breakthrough at this time. The company's first efforts to print dry were in the late 1920s and early 1930s on pre-gummed stamp paper. Hitherto, DP stamps were printed on damp ungummed paper, dried, and then passed through a gumming machine, dried again and sent forward for perforating. The problems of register were enormous because paper stretches when wet and it never dries to the same size it was before. The introduction of dry printing helped this problem disappear.

Just as De La Rue was performing much better, Stuart de la Rue died after a short illness in Cannes in the south of France. He left property of £111,434 (about £6.5 million in today's money). It was a lot less than the £8 million left by his father in 1911. When his uncle, Sir Ernest, died two years later, he left £261,590.

At De La Rue itself, things continued to improve. Lamert was able to say to shareholders in July 1928 under the heading, 'Value of Liquid Position':

> On the asset side there are one or two items calling for comment. We had added £14,000 worth of plant and machinery, making not far short of £100,000 provided to bring the factories up to date since the capital reorganisation. Work in progress and stock are substantially down owing to the delivery to the Turkish Government of the big note order, which was in progress at the date of the last balance-sheet. Sundry debtors at £84,000 and cash at £8,000 show a considerable improvement on last year. I think I may say, without qualification, that this balance-sheet is the first clean balance-sheet, which has been presented to you, since I joined the company. For the first time, if I may put it so, we find ourselves in the position of the Village Blacksmith, who owed not any man.
>
> I stress this point because, as security printers, we are engaged in a business in which our credit is a matter of vital importance. Contracts with Governments for the supply of bank-notes or other security documents not infrequently run into a term of years, and the customer very rightly is concerned to know that the firm with which he places his orders is certain to be in a financial position to carry them out. When our balance-sheet showed a much less liquid position than it does today, criticism, possibly not uninspired by the representatives of rival firms, was directed to the apparent weakness of our financial position. That, at least, is a thing of the past, and it is an important factor in the situation, because we are confident that on quality and price we can hold our own, and more than hold our own, with any printers of banknotes in the world.
>
> Turning to the report I have very little doubt that there is one sentence which has impressed itself on you more than others. I refer to that sentence in which we say that we confidently anticipate better results in the current year. That sentence was framed advisedly, and we must accept full responsibility for it a year hence. I have had a letter

from a shareholder reminding me that in 1923 I expressed the view that the losses, which the company up to that time had been making would quickly be eliminated, and that in a very few years there would be profits sufficient to justify the reorganisation of capital which your directors then recommended.

At that time no one could foresee the heavy litigation in which we were subsequently to become involved, and which has cost this company in cash alone, and without taking any notice of disorganisation, a sum sufficient to pay a dividend of 5 per cent for some three years on the issued capital. In the course of the present year we have moved the pen factory from Bunhill Row to Scotland, where we anticipate we shall be able to produce much more cheaply.

All our efforts have been directed towards centralisation apart from this move to Scotland of the pen factory, which stands apart. We have closed down the Camden Town factories, and all manufacture will in future be conducted at Bunhill-row. Security printing by intaglio press continues to make sound progress. Not only are we obtaining orders from new territories, notably South America, but it is satisfactory to find out that customers are renewing and extending their contracts. I have already referred in previous addresses to you to the contract, which this company has entered into with the Bank of England in connexion with the printing of the new Bank of England Notes, which, as you know, will presently take the place of the Treasury Notes now in use. This contract is proceeding on lines satisfactory to ourselves, and, I believe I may say, satisfactory to the Bank.

And the good news continued into 1929, so that Lamert was able to say:

Speaking broadly, the position of the company today is that it has ample funds in hand, that it is doing a good and steady and increasing business, and, as we state to you in the report, providing we get no unforeseen setbacks and no general upset in trade which may affect us, we can look forward with considerable confidence to any improvement in the future. (Hear, hear.)

Taking each section of our business separately, our playing cards have done better. Competition is still exceedingly keen, as this is one of the businesses in which prices are cut to ribbons, but our products are holding their own, and I think will continue to hold their own well. The pen business has been a very difficult one this year. I think I explained last year that we could not continue to manufacture at Bunhill-row owing to the heavy cost of operating under trade union conditions in London; so we took the pen factory to Scotland. We took up a certain amount of skilled labour, that is to say, enough key labour to start the factory, but naturally a great deal of labour had to be got locally, and had to be trained, and in the first year we found we were up against substantial difficulties. We have devoted a great deal of time and attention to this matter, and I am glad to be able to report to you today that the pen business is improving. The output is better at the factories, and next year we shall see, I think, better results from that source.

Security Printing Business
Now, I pass to the security printing side of the business. I should like shareholders to understand that, whereas playing cards, stationery and the pen trade may be regarded more or less as steady in that you have a constant output and sales year by year, when you come to a class of work like security printing you are inevitably in a class of work where you get wide fluctuations. That is to say, you cannot be certain that the various countries who are our customers will order large numbers of notes each year regularly and it may be that three or four customers will drop out one year and come in with a rush the next year, so that in that sense we are in a fluctuating business. However, I think we can say this now, that we have all over the world large numbers of satisfied users of our notes, and the tendency is for new countries to come to us for their notes, so we regard the position as highly satisfactory.

President Herbert Hoover was telling the people of the United States of America at about the same time: 'We in America today are nearer to the final triumph over poverty than ever before in the history of any land.' Both Lamert and Hoover, and most other people, were in for a rude shock. Indeed, Lamert began his report to shareholders in July 1930 with these words:

Ladies and gentlemen – A year ago, when we were drafting our report to you, we adopted, after a deal of hesitation and a good deal of consultation among ourselves, a more optimistic tone than we had allowed ourselves in any previous report since the company reorganised. At that time we had just passed through three years in which we had seen expansion of the business in practically all directions; we had seen the profits steadily increasing and we thought that after a long period of waiting we were justified in taking a more optimistic view.

Today we cannot do anything of that sort; the position has become very different and very difficult. I am not going to make excuses or to try to shelter behind the general trade position, because I do not think that is the right thing to do. We have, indeed, a very different story to tell …

I have considered very carefully what I am to say with regard to the current year. Several shareholders have written to me, and I can quite understand their feelings. I am personally the biggest shareholder in this company, and I assure you I do not like dividends being passed. Some of these shareholders asked what is the use of going on with a company which has paid only one small dividend in five years since its reconstruction. I will tell you what, in my view, is the use of going on. If we had stopped at any time during those five years there would have been nothing whatever for the shareholders; by the time we had paid off our debenture-holders and met the necessary expenses I do not believe that the shareholders would have received a shilling.

Moreover, if five years ago the company had had to face such a period as we are now passing through, I tell you frankly that it could not have stood it. In five years what we have done is to build up a business dependent entirely on one or two customers so that it is now a business which has a large number of customers all over the country; it is a solid business and is, I feel confident, capable of standing up to such a

> commercial crisis as this one, which we have got to face. That is the best I can say, but I will add that I do think that when general conditions improve we shall see a substantial improvement in the business.
>
> Although I have to adopt a very different note from the one which I used last year, I am not to be taken as speaking pessimistically; I am speaking in the knowledge that we have got to face the fact that the buying power of our customers is very much smaller than it was. We have got special difficulties in one or two directions. For instance, our biggest customer overseas has always been Australia, and the position today in Australia is either that you cannot do any business at all there, or, if you do any business, you cannot get your money over here without difficulty and loss.
>
> There is another thing. I do not think that we who live in London quite realise the appalling state of the country in the Midlands and North. Recently I went on a tour through Birmingham, Manchester, Bradford, Leeds and Newcastle visiting all our principal customers, and I realised that, having spent most of my time in London, I knew hardly anything of the terrible extent to which they have been affected by the prevailing conditions in these areas.

The bad news for De La Rue continued. The promised large contract for printing stamps for the government of China was postponed, and other security printing orders were also held back.

In September 1931 Lamert was telling the AGM that the drop in turnover in the security printing division could not be made up in the pens and playing cards divisions. In spite of competitive prices, playing cards were holding their own, but pens 'have been unsatisfactory. There are far too many people engaged in this business and ... the market is flooded with American, and to a lesser extent, German products.'

Redundancies were made at De La Rue and the capital of the company reduced from £1,376,000 to £1,012,016 by cancelling capital to the extent of 12s (60p) on each of the issued shares and consolidating the subsequent 8s shares so that every five of such shares should constitute two shares of £1 each.

THE BULGARIAN SALESMAN

At least Lamert could tell shareholders in February 1932 that, following a visit he made to China in May 1931: 'Work on the Chinese postage stamps is now in progress and deliveries are being effected.'

China would become a *very* important customer for De La Rue. Bernard Westall had come to the conclusion as early as the mid-1920s that China, because of the size of its population, should be a prime target, and by good fortune an amazing character called Albert Avramov made a telephone call to De La Rue in 1928.

Avramov was one of De La Rue's most successful, and certainly most colourful, salesmen in the inter-war years.

Born in Sofia, he became involved in the banknote world following a trip on the Orient Express in May 1921. In the dining car he met a Baron Gaston Stalins, a scion of an old Belgian family. The Baron told Avramov that he was a representative of the American Bank Note Company. He was going to make an offer to the Bulgarian National Bank for a new issue of banknotes. Several other banknote firms were also sending agents to Sofia to get the business. In fact, this was his first assignment for the American firm. Avramov offered to introduce him to Marlo Tourlakoff, the Bulgarian Minister of Finance, whom he knew.

The Baron explained that there would be other banknote firms involved. For example, Waterlow & Sons had already supplied the low-denomination leva notes the previous year. That would presumably give them an edge. There would be De La Rue, which was desperate for business. And there would be Bradbury Wilkinson, also of London. To make matters more complicated, Bradbury was a subsidiary of his own firm, American Bank Note. Bradbury had also supplied 1,000-leva notes the year before.

He went on to explain that each of the banknote companies already had an agent in Sofia, an agent on commission only. The agent's job was to find out who was the proper person to persuade, to win over.

In the end Avramov did secure the order. However, he then fell on hard times, and it was almost his last throw of the dice when he phoned De La Rue in 1928 and by good chance spoke to Bernard Westall, by this time Managing Director.

Avramov was a good talker and persuaded Westall to send him some money to get to London. After their meeting, Westall decided to employ him. Westall wanted Avramov to try to break into the secured territory that American Bank Note had in China. He tried him out in Italy first. Mussolini had just come to power and Westall sent him a letter.

In it, Bernard Westall reminded Mussolini that in the 19th century De La Rue had been a key supplier of banknotes and postage stamps for the then unified Italy and had been decorated by King Victor Emmanuel. Now Westall wondered if Mussolini would care to re-equip the state printing works with up-to-date currency presses. Unexpectedly, Mussolini expressed interest and Avramov was sent to Rome. The sale went through.

Lorna Houseman wrote:

> Although the Italian visit was not a real test of his capabilities Mr Westall was impressed by his enthusiasm and resolved to chance sending him to Chungking. He was more than ever convinced that China should be the Company's next target. Through sheer size of population her printing needs were enormous.
>
> Confirming this theory a Chinese enquiry for four thousand million postage stamps came in almost at once. Avramov won it at a good price.

Again, international events helped to advance Avramov's fortunes just in time. A month after the Chinese contract was signed, but before the printing was started in London, the British pound was devalued (21 September 1931) from \$4.86 to \$3.49. In effect De La Rue would be getting 18 per cent more on the order than it had expected. There was a fair amount of to-ing and fro-ing between Albert's and

De La Rue's solicitors in London on whether he was entitled to his percentage of the windfall. They worked out a compromise, but Westall was convinced that he had made a particularly happy choice in sending Avramov to China. He might not have the right appearance, background or accent, but he did have something more important: he was lucky.

With that finger exercise accomplished, Avramov now had to breach the virtually exclusive hold that American Bank Note had on the Chinese note business. It would not be easy. The Americans had been there since 1910 and had become China's largest supplier; indeed, with a few minor exceptions it was that country's sole supplier.

Back in the UK, by July 1932 things were looking a little better. Lamert had been to China again and reported:

> I am glad to say that we have got one more definite order from China. The position in China is difficult, but I do not think it is as bad as the papers make out. From our point of view, the trouble is that owing to contraction of business, the leading banks are cutting down on their issues, and consequently not ordering new notes. However, we have broken into China, and I am very hopeful indeed that ultimately – of course, it is a slow business – we are going to do well in China. From the security point of view our immediate future lies in Europe, and I am glad to say we have recently taken one or two orders, and there are other orders which should come to us. At any rate, there is this to be said, our customers have not ordered from anyone else. Had the business gone by us we should be very much disturbed, but the fact that they have not got orders to give is less worrying. With regard to that, I should like to say that we have to be very careful to see that in all cases we get our money. In some sections of the business I think we could do more work and send out more goods than we do, but we are not going to send out more goods and have bad debts on our hands.

Lamert had some quite good news on journal printing, telling shareholders:

> I should like to call attention to our progress in journal printing. It is about four years since we started this line. We had a few teething troubles like other businesses making a start but our record in journal printing is this: that in four years we have acquired the printing of 22 journals, and have never lost one. It has now become an important section of the business. It is constant and is particularly valuable, because it absorbs overheads steadily.
>
> As to playing cards I am speaking at a time when only three months of the year have gone, but I say definitely that unless something altogether unforeseen happens we are going to have a better year in this section. We have large orders actually in hand on conditions which should leave us with a fair profit.
>
> With regard to our moulding business in Walthamstow, work is plentiful enough, but prices are very low. It is a business very much cut into, but I think we are getting our full share of the orders that are going. Finally there is the pen section. Pens are the Cinderella of this business. We have been criticised for not spending more money on advertising. In the first place we have no pen money to spend at the moment, and

are not going to rob other sections of the business to advertise pens. I think we are all agreed that it would be a wrong policy at the present moment to spend money on advertising pens. Our output and sales have shrunk, but I have a shrewd suspicion that our sales have not shrunk any more – perhaps not as much – as the sales of some of the other companies which were spending very large sums of money on advertising a few years ago. We have the whole position constantly before us, and as soon as the position of the trade justifies it we shall begin to spend more money on advertising.

100TH ANNIVERSARY (PLAYING CARDS)

In these difficult economic conditions De La Rue celebrated its 100th anniversary on 23 February 1932. The firm was honoured with a leading article in *The Times*:

Playing Cards

An article in this issue records that it is one hundred years today since the founder of the firm THOMAS DE LA RUE received the warrant of appointment as maker of playing-cards to the Royal Family, and also was granted a patent for printing playing-cards by typography. The patent began a new era, which succeeded an old era of many centuries' duration, for it seems to be certain that the stencilling of playing-cards filled the long gap between the earliest method, which was painting them by hand, and the typographical process which was patented by THOMAS DE LA RUE and prevails today. One hundred years is a long time in the history of a firm, and the present is certainly an occasion for congratulations and good wishes; but it is a short time in the history of playing-cards. The authorities say that these potent little pieces of paste-board came to Europe, perhaps from Asia, perhaps from the Moors or the Arabs, some time in the fourteenth century. They were being manufactured in England by the middle of the fifteenth century, and were protected not by a duty, as now, but by the flat prohibition of imported cards; and the tax on them (of which MESSRS DE LA RUE are still thoughtful enough to remind a careless world on every ace of spades) came in under KING JAMES I. But nearly a century before that they were already being rescued, as some would think, and ruined, as others might think, by being made use of to improve the mind. Logic, grammar, geography, history – not to mention politics in all countries, and in Soviet Russia irreligion – have been grafted at one time or another on to playing-cards, just as if it was not enough for them to exercise their natural functions of teaching mathematics, of strengthening the memory, and (especially perhaps in poker) imparting control over the facial expression and the tones of the voice.

Three days later, Queen Mary visited the British Industries Fair at Olympia, called on the De La Rue stand, and ordered some packs of cards with pictures of Buckingham Palace.

As we know only too well, one of the actions that made the world Depression of the 1930s deeper and more prolonged than it might otherwise have been was the protectionist approach adopted by many countries, especially the Unites States of

America. The Smoot–Hawley Tariff Act was passed in Washington in 1930 and similar acts were passed in many countries in retaliation. The result was a drastic reduction in international trade.

De La Rue was adversely affected, and on 2 November 1932 *The Times* published this letter from Sidney Lamert:

ON THE CARDS

To the Editor of The Times

Sir – The manufacturer of playing cards starts with paper as his raw material. Two or three sheets are pasted together and the resultant board is enamelled. The enamelled board is then printed, varnished, cut and sorted into packs. At the present stage of our scientific tariff there is a heavy duty of 20 per cent on the raw paper; worked up board gets off with 15 per cent; and the finished packs of cards come in scot free. The effect of all this is that British export in cheap cards, which is dependent on supplies of cheap raw material from abroad, is shrewdly hit below the belt, while imports of American playing cards, paid for in gold, help to knock the pound still lower.

The only effective counter-move would appear to be to move our factories to Germany or Belgium. The house of De La Rue was greatly honoured by being made the subject of a leading article in *The Times* on the recent occasion of its centenary of playing-card manufacture, and we are afraid that if we were in fact to leave this country and set up factories abroad *The Times* would ignore us on the occasion of our bi-centenary. For this and other reasons we propose to carry on as we are. May we write to you, Sir, from time to time, say, every 10 years, until something is done about it.

I am Sir,
SIDNEY LAMERT, Chairman,
Thomas De La Rue and Co. Limited
110 Bunhill Row
London EC1, Nov. 1.

His complaint was reinforced by this letter also published in *The Times* two days later:

On the Cards
The situation described by the Chairman of Thomas De La Rue & Co. Ltd, is an anomaly which will sooner or later have to be adjusted. Attention was given to this matter by prominent members of the Empire Industries Association in the debate upon the Finance Bill. It may be that the Chancellor of the Exchequer cannot see his way for financial reasons to forgo the Excise Duty which is levied on British-made playing cards, but that does not appear to be sufficient reason why foreign playing-

> cards should be allowed to remain in the market on the same basis as British playing cards.

In spite of such difficulties, Lamert was able to report a gradually improving situation in July 1933, telling shareholders:

> Now I should like to say something general about the business. The past has been a very difficult year for all businesses, and especially those operating abroad. As you know, our main difficulty in foreign business is to fix what we are to get in shape of exchange, because it varies so greatly from time to time. We have, I think, so far, been fortunate. We have done well out of exchange fluctuations, but that cannot continue. If anybody in this room can tell me what is going to happen to the dollar or to any exchange, I shall be very grateful. All we can do is to take the balance of probabilities and secure our position as far as is possible.
>
> **Difficulties of Foreign Trade**
> As you, we have big contracts which are settled in United States dollars. That currency is now practically at the old parity, whereas not so long ago it was at 3.40. This makes an enormous difference to the sterling amount we receive. At one time we took a contract with Spain when the peseta was at 28, and we were paid when it stood at 42. We should have made a heavy loss on that contract if we had not been able to sell the peseta forward against payment. I say all of this to warn you that in a business of this sort we have very great difficulties to contend with, and there is always the possibility of a bad upset. I think it would not be unfair to say that at the present moment, with the Economic Conference sitting, the exchange outlook is more uncertain than it has been at any time within living memory.
>
> **Business on a Sounder and Broader Basis**
> As regards business generally, I think I may say that today it is on a sounder and broader basis than it has been at any time since I have been associated with it. Also I think this is the best balance-sheet we have ever been in a position to present to you. Not only is the balance-sheet better, but, what is more important, our business is better. It is on an increase of £100,000 – and certainly it is better equipped to deal with the orders that are coming along. When I arrived at Bunhill Row in 1923 the machinery might almost have been described as 'junk'. That has all been changed. We have modern machinery, and the next thing we have to do is to get it into a modern factory in Walthamstow, and then I think we shall really begin to progress.
>
> Taking the business sectionally, we have done well in the playing-cards. Last year there was rather an unusual boom in cards. There were big orders going, and we got our share of them. We also did well with our moulding. We have within the last few years, had to face a very substantial capital expenditure at Walthamstow in order to provide the necessary presses. The company is now quite in the front rank so far as the plastic moulding business is concerned, and is getting a substantial share of the

> best class of business. All the indications are that we shall continue to remain in the front rank.
>
> Pens have in recent years been a difficult business, and all I can say about them is that we have again definitely begun to progress. We have produced a number of new models, which the trade have taken to very well and our figures are better. Security printing has been referred to in the report and I cannot tell you much more about it. So much depends on exchanges. We must look at the matter broadly. Certainly we have a large number of customers and I think this year is going to be a little better than last year. We had hoped it would be very much better, but all I am going to say is that we think it will be a little better.

Business conditions continued to improve throughout 1933 and into 1934, and Lamert sounded more optimistic at the AGM in July 1934: 'I think I can say to you that the outlook this year is definitely better.'

Playing cards, still the most important part of De La Rue's business after security printing, had been adversely affected by tobacco companies. Lorna Houseman described well the effect of the tobacco companies' marketing tactics:

> Wills, of Imperial Tobacco, tucked two miniature cards into every packet of ten Gold Flake or Capstan, and each complete set of miniatures posted to Wills's Bristol establishment entitled the sender to a pack of normal sized cards. The scheme caught on like a forest fire, and John Waddington of Leeds, the makers of these cards, revelled in it, to the discomfort of De La Rue. The latter did not find their contract with Kensitas to supply five gift coupons for every packet of cigarettes so interesting. The coupons were convertible into tea sets or alarm clocks, not playing cards. John Waddington became swamped with Wills demands, De La Rue helped out by making cards for Waddington, and eventually the tobacco companies came to their senses and abandoned their gift schemes. By this time saturation point had been reached. There was such a glut of playing cards that during the next two years public demand for them was nearly halved. Even so, an amicable arrangement had been made with Waddington, and the firm's playing card profits at last began to pick up.

De La Rue were still finding the pen business hard pounding. Here is Lamert on that:

> The pen business is still difficult, but I am glad to say that we are showing definite better results in our Scotch factory and this year we are going to do more in the way of advertising. It would have been idle to spend money on advertising while the public was not buying, but with a better demand for Onoto products and, we believe, a better buying capacity, we think the policy will justify itself.

The growing banknote business in China received a rude shock in February 1935 when Bernard Westall told the Board that a consignment of 250,000 one-yuan notes, on their way to the Bank of China in Tientsin from Shanghai, had been seized by pirates. De La Rue were not seriously affected by this, though, as a month later Westall was able to report that the Bank of China had placed a new order for 10 million notes 'on terms which were satisfactory'.

By January 1936 the value of orders from China amounted to no less than £400,000 (£24 million). The importance of China to De La Rue can hardly be overestimated. Director Cyril Ashton told the Board that 'money was coming in very satisfactorily from China and the financial position generally was comfortable with £50,000 [£3 million] on deposit'.

Sir Arthur 'Gerry' Norman, who had recently joined De La Rue and who would become Managing Director and Chairman, would say later:

> There were rows of people lined up outside the Star, Crown and George Works. And we were taking them on at a hundred a day really, in order to deal with the workload provided by China. And it's not so long after the Great Depression – there were still people desperately needing work and one of my first jobs was to go down every morning at eight o'clock to the filthy Star Gate, and in a little office behind the smoke-filled cabin of the gatekeeper, one sat down with people who were in tragic circumstances, many of them, demanding, really keen to get work, and refusing people was one of the saddest things one had to do. Fortunately we were able to recruit many of them.
>
> The accent was on taking on people and training them as fast as we could in order to get shipments out. Of course, under that kind of production pressure, it was possible to get incredible loyalties and acts of selflessness. The way people worked – nobody ever thought about going home if there was a case of notes to be got on a ship. Westall had managed to communicate to the whole workforce what China meant, what getting delivered down to the Southampton Docks involved for the Company as a whole, and somehow they rallied to it in a way that would be very hard to envisage today.
>
> The De La Rue spirit, in fact.
>
> It was an incredible spirit, in which the whole army as it were had been motivated to fight the battle. And there wasn't anybody who ever thought of packing up and going home without asking, 'Do you need me any longer?' No nine to five or eight until six – none of that at all. The example provided by getting all these managers to work on until 10 or 11 at night of course had a tremendous effect on people too, because the whole team was seen to be working for the same thing. That was a unique experience.

WESTALL LEARNT MAH JONG

In March 1934 Bernard Westall was appointed sole Managing Director at a salary of £3,000 (about £180,000 today). Sidney Lamert would retire as Joint Managing Director but would continue to serve as Chairman. Westall proved to be a highly successful Managing Director of De La Rue in the generally difficult economic conditions of the 1930s. By early 1936 the Board was recognising his contribution by awarding him a bonus of £500 (£30,000), and in April 1937 £2,000 (£120,000). By 1938 it was £2,500 (£150,000).

Bernard Clement Westall was born in Croydon, Surrey on 29 November 1893. The son of a vicar, he spent much of his childhood in rural Devon, and it was planned that, with his two brothers, he would also enter the church. He was educated at Newbury Grammar School and Queen's College, Cambridge. During the First World War he saw active service in the disastrous Gallipoli campaign and in the trenches in France.

When he was demobilised in 1919, in preference to the church he chose commerce, and joined the printing firm of Waterlow and Sons. After three years there he moved to De La Rue as a progress clerk. As we have seen, the company was struggling and Westall was wondering what to do next. Lorna, his daughter, tells us succinctly in her book:

> At this juncture Bernard Westall requested Mr Lamert's permission to look around for another position. The Chairman agreed, adding sympathetically that he thought Westall was right to do so since he himself saw no future for De La Rue.
>
> But by a strange coincidence a letter arrived the next day from the Government of Siam, announcing its intention to have a new currency issue. It wished to change over from letterpress to copperplate printing and accordingly invited De La Rue to send a representative to Bangkok. Mr Lamert was in a quandary. The Company had been printing the Siamese notes by letterpress for the last twenty years. He was loath to lose one of the few remaining orders De La Rue had. Yet holding no faith in the future of either banknote printing or copperplate, he had not encouraged the development of the rotary copperplate machine. Even the cost of transporting a representative to Bangkok was daunting. Doubtfully he asked Westall if he would care to go. The latter jumped at the chance. Again he had nothing to lose, and the excursion postponed the immediate necessity of finding another post.
>
> Twenty-nine year old Bernard Westall found himself in a four berth cabin aboard a P&O ship sailing to places he had only read about and never expected to see: the Suez Canal, Aden, Bombay, Colombo. Like Lamert he was the son of a parson, a particularly impecunious one, the intensity of the Rev. Arthur St Ledger Westall's beliefs having led him from the Church of England to the Church of Rome and back again. As Father Westall was descended from a long line of clerics with large families and small stipends, he had little money of his own. Scholarships enabled his eldest son Bernard to go from grammar school to Cambridge, where he read Classics like his father, with the similar intention of entering the Church. He took a wartime degree before going out with the Essex Regiment to France, and later Gallipoli. He thought his foreign travels had ended there.
>
> With fifty pounds in his pocket, which was supposed to last for three months, he disembarked at Penang, caught the weekly train from Prai on the mainland, chugged through rubber plantation and jungle, and arrived in Bangkok. There, on the banks of the Menam, the mosquitoes were so powerful that in the evenings visitors were handed a sarong in which to enshroud their legs. Westall got into his first rickshaw

and proceeded unceremoniously to the compound of the Royal Palace, where the Ministry of Finance is situated. He saw the Government's British adviser, who dashed any hopes by stating crisply that he had warned the Siamese against dealing with De La Rue.

When Westall finally obtained an interview with the Controller General, Phya Anaraks Kosa, news of the firm's financial precariousness had preceded him. Why, Phya Anaraks wanted to know, should his Government do business with a company which was liable to go bankrupt at any moment? There was only one answer. Frankly, said Westall, De La Rue needed the order more than any of the other firms and could therefore be relied upon to put in a very low price. He suggested that a clause could be inserted into a contract with De La Rue, stipulating that if the worst happened and the Company went into liquidation, the plates and paper remained the property of the Siam Government and could be handed over to one of the other printers. Still nervous about the Company's future, Phya Anaraks was nevertheless attracted by the notion that if De La Rue were allowed to tender everyone else would have to trim their prices.

The solitary question that remained was the fact that the Siamese required copperplate printing in which De La Rue were known to be inexperienced. That problem, countered Westall, was easily disposed of; would the Government be prepared to have Waterlow, the acknowledged copperplate printers, print the new issue? 'Of course', answered the Controller General. 'Well then', he rejoined, '*a fortiori* you should be satisfied with De La Rue. Perhaps you are unaware that leading personnel in Waterlow have recently transferred to De La Rue?' Agreeably surprised, the Controller General began to soften and granted Westall permission to tender.

Although the first Siamese hurdle was crossed, others lay ahead. When Westall was handed a copy of the specification an immediate difficulty beset him – he had no idea what price he should offer. De La Rue affairs were still so haphazard that Bunhill Row possessed no estimating department. He spent an anxious night in his hot hotel bedroom trying to calculate the potential output of the unfinished rotary copperplate machine, plus overheads, the percentage of wastage and the cost of subsequent operations. That done he borrowed the hotel typewriter, with one finger tapped out his calculation, and he took his offer round to Phya Anaraks Kosa the next morning.

It was a week before anything happened. Idling meanwhile over the pages of the *Bangkok Times*, Westall read that the Siamese Government were experiencing some difficulty with forged customs certificates. He presented himself at the Customs office. The junior official he saw was a contemporary of his at Cambridge, who was called Prince Viwat. In a city of many princes he was destined to become a world figure, not only Minister of Finance and authority at the World Bank, but also the statesman who headed his country's deputation at the Kandy peace treaty conference after World War II.

Prince Viwat was struck by Westall's idea of introducing a security device into customs forms. He persuaded his chief to order some from De La Rue. The little plastics factory in Walthamstow profited too. Insulators were about the only product it was capable of making, and Westall sold a quantity to the Siamese Post Office for telephone poles.

During the enforced wait he was getting acutely short of money. Luckily for him he was an exceptionally good bridge player and was able to supplement his finances. Phya Anaraks eventually lifted his spirits by sending for him again. Only one thing prevented him from giving De La Rue the contract, he confided; how would he know that De La Rue, having quoted a low price, would not be tempted to put it up after completing the first order? 'By multiplying the quantities of notes to be ordered by five, and stipulating delivery over five years', suggested Westall. Phya Anaraks capitulated and gave De La Rue a five year contract.

Westall's nocturnal mental arithmetic proved to be accurate. His estimated figure was within a couple of hundred pounds of the actual cost of the £125,000 order. To Mr Lamert's amazement the Siamese visit had been a resounding success. As a result of it Portals, the papermakers, received a letter from their agents which began: 'De La Rue have a Banknote enquiry for us at last ...' The sentiment was shared to a heartfelt degree by everyone at Bunhill Row.

Ever the thorough salesman, Westall learnt how to play Mah Jong so that he could play – and lose to – the Governor of the Bank of China.

Westall's reputation was made. He was appointed a Director in 1928 and Assistant Managing Director two years later. When Sidney Lamert relinquished his joint managing directorship in 1934, Westall became sole Managing Director and steered De La Rue through the difficult years of the 1930s and the Second World War before becoming Chairman in April 1944.

BEGINNINGS OF DIVERSIFICATION

As we shall see, diversification to add to security printing became an overriding priority for the Board of De La Rue for the next 60 years. It began in the 1930s, or arguably during the First World War.

De La Rue had become involved in the plastic moulding business during the war through a purchase by Stuart de la Rue from the Disposal of Enemy Property Board of a business run by two Germans. It consisted, and still consisted into the 1930s, of two small houses in Walthamstow, east London, with a garden shed that was 'the factory'. Its best customer was a button-making business in Birmingham run by an Allen Clark and his father. The Clarks bought a tiny engineering business in Ilford from a man called Plessey. With this business they made electrical appliances (Plessey would become one of Britain's largest electrical equipment manufacturers after the Second World War), and they bought the plastic parts from the De La Rue shed in Walthamstow. When Westall turned his attention to this business, he bought a 10-acre site in Walthamstow and built a property on it.

Lamert told shareholders of other diversifications:

> There is a great deal of money spent on indoor games and lately we have put on the market several extremely interesting ones. Among them (I daresay some of you shareholders have seen it) is a cricket game known as 'Stumpz'. That is doing very well indeed, and we are hoping for great things from it.

Interestingly, Waddingtons also moved into the games market. Indeed, their great success with one particular game is part of the toy trade folklore. Here is how Waddingtons told it in their book:

> On a certain Friday night towards the end of 1935, Victor Watson handed his son, Norman, a game with the remark: 'Look this over and tell me what you think about it.'
>
> It is recorded that Norman Watson said: 'I played an imaginary game against myself continuing through Friday night, Saturday night and Sunday night. I was enthralled and captivated. I had never found a game so absorbing, and thus Monopoly was first played in England at my home. I was so enthusiastic that on the Monday morning I persuaded my father to make a phone call to Parker Brothers of Salem, Massachusetts, USA, the holder of the rights. Today, transatlantic calls are commonplace but this was the first one ever made by Waddingtons and I was told it was the first one ever received by Parker Brothers from Europe ... A licence arrangement was agreed on the phone and an exchange of letters followed.'

This licence and the next game that followed, Cluedo, made millions of pounds for Waddingtons. Unfortunately, De La Rue's venture into the toy business did not turn out to be so successful, though it did allocate £3,000 (about £180,000 in today's money) to advertising its games in 1934–5 financial year.

By July 1935 Lamert was beginning to sound very confident about the future, telling shareholders.

> Security printing is our sheet anchor, and I can tell you that our security business is going ahead well. There was a time when De La Rue's was what might be called a one-or-two customer business in the matter of security printing, but today we have customers all over the world; their number is increasing and we find that when we have once served a customer he comes back to us. That, I think, is a pretty fair indication that our customers appreciate the quality of our work.

He was pleased with the progress of the moulding business at Walthamstow, but was disappointed by the slow recovery of the playing card business, saying:

> Playing cards are still rather the Cinderella of our business. The backlash – if I may use that expression – of coupon cards is still with us. We tried very hard indeed to get sympathetic treatment from the Government. We pointed out to them that they protected everything except playing cards, but the Chancellor of the Exchequer evidently took the view that it was a very small business and we could get no help from him.

> What we did get – and I very gratefully acknowledge it – was a great deal of sympathy from retailers of this country, who have helped us substantially.

General and commercial printing were progressing satisfactorily, as was the pen division, where advertising had resumed. The games division did not merit a mention.

The following year, 1936, seemed to be all about expenditure on plant and the training of women in the factory to cope with a large order for banknotes from China. Further heavy expenditure was incurred in the plastic moulding division. Lamert told shareholders:

> Next in importance to our banknote printing is our plastic moulding department. When I first joined this company mouldings consisted of small articles, most of them not much bigger than this inkpot beside me, and they were made with small presses. I think presses of about 200 or 300 tons were our largest. As time went on, competition in that class of trade became very great indeed. Every trade in this country where a man can come in with a small amount of capital and buy machinery easily is crowded to excess today. Therefore our policy has been to get into a class entirely by ourselves and to install large and costly machinery. As a result we have at our new factory some of the most powerful machines in the world and we are in a position to supply moulding which no other company in Europe, and, I think I am right in saying, few in America can supply. We have installed absolutely the best and largest moulding machines in the world. That, of course, has been a costly business and it has taken time, but I think the result, the ultimate result, is going to be very much to the advantage of the shareholder of this company.

Pens and playing cards were still difficult, and Lamert put it this way: 'All I can see is that we are holding our own.'

At the 1937 AGM in July of that year, Lamert expressed for the first time concern about the long-term future of security printing:

> As you know, our most profitable source of business is security printing which over a long series of years may become more and more difficult, because the tendency is for countries to make their own paper money. I am going to ask Mr Westall to say something about that because he knows more about it than I do, but looking at it broadly, I think you may reasonably look for a run of a number of years during which security printing will bring you a fair profit, and during that time I think we are going to build up our moulding business, our pen business, and our general printing and stationery business to a point at which we can look forward to the future very comfortably.

Diversification was becoming ever more important to Lamert and his Board.

THE GATHERING STORM

By the time of the 1938 AGM, storm clouds were gathering and they could not pass unmentioned by Lamert, who said to shareholders:

> I have referred to world conditions because so large a part of our business is with foreign countries that it is impossible to ignore the fact that there are at present two first-class wars actually in progress and the state of tension in other countries is such that sometimes it seems that a spark may cause general conflagration, but the manufacturer operating in this country is not less concerned with the enormous burdens which are constantly being piled upon industry, burdens which are almost intolerable at times of prosperity and may become crippling if a general recession in trade should set in.

In view of the dangerous state of the world, Lamert was understandably cautious in announcing in public what contracts had been secured:

> It is, I think, an open secret that we have received large orders for the printing of bank notes for China, but I do not want you to form the impression that China is the only field in which we have made progress. We have secured valuable contracts in a number of other countries, and I do not think it is too much to say that the excellence of our work is now coming to be universally recognised. I am not going to go too closely into all the details of this expansion, because it is not in the interests of the company that everything we are doing should be broadcast, but I may say generally that the whole basis of our security printing business has widened during the year under review, and this encourages us to look forward to the future with growing confidence. Nor does our prosperity rest entirely on the security printing, for our plastic moulding business has shown equally healthy expansion and, as I have told you on more than one occasion, this is a field which opens up very great possibilities.

In 1938 Westall suffered at first hand the threat of Nazi Germany. He went to Sofia, the capital of Bulgaria, and with all the other banknote producers tendered for a new note issue. All reported to the Governor of the Bank, Dr Guneu, and their tenders were read out. In the afternoon, they reassembled and the Governor announced that the order would go to De La Rue. However, the German Minister of Finance, Walter Funk (eventually sentenced at the Nuremberg trials to life imprisonment, he was released from Spandau prison in 1957 and died in 1960), was also in Sofia to discuss the purchase of the entire Bulgarian tobacco crop, and the German Banknote Company persuaded him to intervene via the Bulgarian Prime Minister with the Governor of the Bank.

The next morning Westall received a note from Dr Guneu requesting him to come and see him immediately. The bearer of the message led him via back streets and several locked doors to the Governor's office, where he was told by a tearful Dr Guneu that the Prime Minister insisted he give the banknote order to Germany.

The atmosphere was becoming febrile and Sofia was placed under martial law. Dr Guneu was murdered, and Westall was not allowed to leave his hotel. Eventually he returned to London, dejected by the loss of the order and very concerned about the general political situation. This was at the time of the Munich crisis, and to many war seemed inevitable. He and Lamert realised that De La Rue's offices and factory in Bunhill Row were extremely vulnerable. Should they consider moving, and if so, where?

A GOLDEN OPPORTUNITY

Out of the blue at the end of the 1930s came what appeared to be the answer to their question. They learned that Howard Pillow, the major shareholder in the British-American Bank Note Company in Canada, wanted to sell his holding. To Lamert and Westall this seemed a golden opportunity. Not only would it provide an opening into the Canadian and possibly the US markets, but it would provide an alternative, and much safer, production base.

Pillow, when approached, seemed pleased that his company would remain in British hands, and De La Rue appointed the merchant bank Erlanges to act for them. A director, Mr Kiek, suggested that his son Peter be sent to Montreal to begin negotiations.

Peter Kiek's report was enthusiastic enough for Westall and Lamert to go out to Montreal, where they found Pillow to be extremely hospitable. After drinks at the Ritz Carlton, Pillow took everyone home for dinner with his wife and his daughter, Margaret. The evening went well, and at the end of it Pillow took Westall aside and told him that he would be willing to sell for the price mentioned to Peter Kiek, £250,000 (about £15 million today). A meeting with the company's President, Charles Cowan, was also successful. The lawyers got down to work, and completion was promised for the following Friday.

However, when Friday came, the lawyers asked for one more day. Howard Pillow invited the De La Rue delegation to come to his office on the Saturday morning so that they could toast the signing of the deal with champagne.

Yet again, the lawyers asked for more time and requested that the De La Rue party stay until Monday. This was highly inconvenient, as their bookings to New York and on to London would have to be changed. However, they had little choice, and on the Saturday evening while Lamert and Westall played bridge, Peter Kiek took Margaret Pillow Vaughan to the Governor General's ball (her husband, Murray Vaughan, was away on business). This delay proved to be disastrous. Early on Sunday morning Westall received a call from Howard Pillow, who was apoplectic with rage. Apparently Peter Kiek and his daughter wanted to run away together. Pillow was so angry that he called off the deal with De La Rue and Westall and Lamert returned to London empty-handed. Who was to blame – the lawyers or man's libido?

PRODUCTION IN CHINA AND BURMA

Westall was not a man to sit and mope, though, and he was soon on his way again, this time back to China.

Japan continued to threaten China, and the Chinese Minister of Finance, Dr Kung, was increasingly concerned about the issue of Chinese yuan and the safety of Shanghai. He approached an American company about their setting up a banknote-printing plant in Shanghai. However, the Americans requested guarantees that Dr Kung felt unable to give, and he turned to De La Rue.

Westall set off for China accompanied by Avramov and also by a young new recruit, Arthur, but always known as Gerry, Norman. He had joined De La Rue straight from Blundells, a public school in the West Country, at the recommendation of his housemaster, Rupert Westall, cousin of Bernard. When the three arrived in Hong Kong in March 1939, Norman remained there while Westall and Avramov went to Hanoi to take the one remaining aircraft of the China National Air Company that had not been shot down by the Japanese. But Westall caught malaria, and Avramov had to go to Chungking alone.

Dr Kung insisted that Westall come, and he was able to find an American pilot willing to risk the Japanese fighters to fly him up to Chungking. There was no hotel, but Avramov managed to register them in a clinic run by a German doctor, a strong Nazi supporter. Fortunately, Dr Kung and Westall reached agreement quickly. De La Rue, with no guarantee requested, agreed to build a factory in Shanghai and print China's notes. Westall also agreed to build a second factory in Rangoon in Burma, which would operate if the Japanese took over Shanghai. In return, the Chinese government placed a firm order, according to Lorna Houseman, worth £5 million (£300 million in today's money) for the printing of 2,000,000,000 notes. There was one important proviso in the contract. If it became impossible to print the notes in Shanghai or Rangoon, De La Rue would print them in England.

Westall and Avramov, who had bought the one remaining bottle of French brandy in Chungking for £25 (£1,500 today), took the hazardous journey back to Hong Kong. There they instructed Gerry Norman and left him to organise and supervise the building of the plants in Shanghai, while Frank Richardson did the same in Rangoon.

In spite of the fact that the Japanese had surrounded Shanghai – they were, for the moment, respecting the neutrality of Shanghai's International Settlement – Norman managed to complete the factory in six months. Furthermore, accommodation for all the work-hands was built inside the factory compound so that they could be kept there and news of what they were printing would not leak out. The printing machinery was sent as though it was designed for Goodall's playing cards, as all imports into Shanghai were inspected by the Japanese. The paper to be used was masked by placing 50 sheets of plain paper on top of every ream, the remaining 450 sheets being banknote paper. Finally, the original plates were smuggled in by London staff in their overcoat pockets. Within twelve months the notes were in production, and they were smuggled out at night on dustcarts.

The Chinese orders were now so important to De La Rue that even after war broke out in Europe in September 1939, Dr Kung was able to insist that Westall come out to China again in March 1940 to discuss the situation in Shanghai, which seemed likely to be overrun by the Japanese at any moment. On the way to Chungking, Westall and Avramov visited Frank Richardson in Rangoon, where Richardson had done a similarly brilliant job to Norman in Shanghai in getting the printing plant in full production. From Rangoon, Westall and Avramov flew over the Himalayas via the notorious route known as 'The Hump'. Once in Chungking they could not stay at the Nazi doctor's clinic, which had been wiped out, along with the doctor, by Japanese air-raids. Instead they stayed at the government rest-house.

The Chinese had already arranged with De La Rue that if the Germans overran France, the banknote plant that was in the French concession in Shanghai would be moved to Rangoon. Westall made a further agreement with Dr Kung that turned out to be very important. He secured Dr Kung's approval of De La Rue being able to print the Chinese notes lithographically. This meant that they could be printed anywhere, whereas the more complicated copperplate printing could be carried out only at Bunhill Row.

Westall arrived back in England in April 1940, a month before the German invasion of Belgium, Holland and France. It was clear that the invasion was imminent, and the codeword was sent out to China to close Shanghai and move the machinery to Rangoon. It all got through safely, as did most of the people, despite the submarine menace.

By the time of the 1940 AGM in September of that year, Lamert felt very constrained as to what he could say, restricting himself to:

> A year ago we met you with accounts showing a record profit in the history of the company, and with high hopes that a new era of settled prosperity had dawned for the old house. Within a few months of that meeting everything was shattered by the wanton act of one criminal and we had to face a new series of problems changing almost from day to day. In our report we have told you that drastic alterations have had to be made throughout the factories and we expressed the opinion that, taking everything into consideration, the trading results which we now place before you are not unsatisfactory. It will, I believe, be a satisfaction to many of you to know that this company, in which you have invested money, is certainly 'doing its bit,' in the popular phrase at the present time, both by maintaining a substantial volume of export business, which is so vital to our economic position, and also more directly in producing manufactures which have definite uses in these troublesome times.
>
> **Confidence in the Future**
>
> Finally, I have to say this: it has been my practice in the past to give some forecast at these meetings of the probable results to be looked for in the year that lies ahead. On the present occasion you will recognise that such a thing is not possible. Until the shadow has been lifted we cannot see our way ahead, but on this much we can rely: we have modern factories equipped with the latest machinery, we have a splendid

> body of loyal workers, and we have a managing director who has shown his mettle in the past. I think these things may well encourage us to look forward to the future with confidence.

As he spoke, the final and critical stage of what became known as the Battle of Britain was being acted out in the skies over south-east England.

Chapter Seven

Total War

1939–1945

The truce is over
Portals answers the call
Total destruction
Retreat from Rangoon
The war underground
How did De La Rue cope?

THE TRUCE IS OVER

From 1936 onwards it was clear to many that another war was coming.

The arguments have raged back and forth for more than 60 years over Britain's preparedness, or lack of it, for war in 1939. In hindsight it is easy to see that a further war with Germany was inevitable, and indeed, the leader of the French army in the First World War, Marshal Foch, described the Treaty of Versailles as merely a twenty-year armistice, a remarkably accurate prediction. However, the spirit of the 1920s and early 1930s was one of peace and goodwill. There had to be a better way to settle men's differences than the appalling slaughter that had taken place between 1914 and 1918. It was not only national revulsion at this carnage that led the British governments of the 1920s and 30s to reject the isolated calls for rearmament. There was also a widespread feeling, nurtured by such publications as Maynard Keynes's *The Economic Consequences of the Peace*, that Germany had been treated too harshly. And when Hitler began to rant about the injustice of it all, some were inclined to wonder why the Germans scattered around central and eastern Europe should not live under one government. For example, when the German army marched into the demilitarised Rhineland in 1936, Lord Lothian said: 'Hitler is doing no more than taking over his own back garden.'

Winston Churchill, former Conservative Chancellor of the Exchequer who had put Britain back on the gold standard in the 1920s with such disastrous consequences for Britain's exporters, was by this time in the political wilderness, mainly because of his views on India and other foreign policy issues, but he argued strongly for the expansion of the Royal Air Force. In October 1933 he said to the House of Commons:

> Germany is already well on her way to become, and must become, incomparably the most heavily armed nation in the world and most completely ready for war ... We cannot have any anxieties comparable to the anxiety caused by German rearmament.

Foreign Office Intelligence had changed its mind about Germany's preparedness for war. Original calculations suggested a date some time in 1942, but in 1936 fresh information indicated that the Germans might be ready as early as January 1939. This was one of the reasons for the rapid signing of contracts for Hurricanes and Spitfires before either had been fully tested. The anger of the Air Ministry might well have been better directed at those who had allowed Britain's aircraft manufacturers to be starved of government contracts through the 1920s and early 1930s.

As we now know, Germany did not invade Poland in January 1939 but at the end of August that year, and the anticipated war was declared on 3 September. By that date, 308 of the 310 Spitfires had been built and tested. What we do not know, and never will, is whether Prime Minister Neville Chamberlain was being Machiavellian when he negotiated with Hitler at Munich in September 1938, knowing full well that Britain was not prepared for war. Historians have disagreed ever since about Chamberlain's motives. For example, A J.P. Taylor, Britain's populist historian of the 1960s and 70s, wrote in the Oxford History of England, published in 1965:

> The clearest lesson to be drawn from the crisis over Czechoslovakia was that Great Britain should be more heavily armed, whether for negotiation or for war. Chamberlain, a persistent advocate of rearmament, emphasized this lesson strongly and gave Hitler some excuse for complaining that Chamberlain was as insincere in appeasement as Hitler himself was accused of being.

Chamberlain bought another year for Britain, and for Britain's factories to turn out weapons of war. It is generally accepted that the Battle of Britain came within a whisker of being lost, and that this would have left the way open for a German invasion. Certainly, 'Stuffy' Dowding, commander of RAF Fighter Command, had no doubts about the wisdom of Chamberlain's deal with Hitler, saying: 'It was a very good thing that he did act in that way.'

There was outward euphoria after the signing of the Munich Agreement, when Chamberlain announced 'Peace for our time' (most commentators incorrectly say 'Peace in our time') at Heston airport on 30 September 1938.

PORTALS ANSWERS THE CALL

However, the realists, including Portals and the Bank of England, planned for the outbreak of war in the late 1930s. We saw Portals' progress in the 18th and 19th centuries in chapter two, and the company had continued to make steady progress in the early years of the 20th century.

Then on 4 August 1914, the Foreign Secretary, Earl Grey, uttered the fateful words: 'The lamps are going out all over Europe; we shall not see them lit again in our lifetime.' This was something of an exaggeration – even he lived until 1933 – but the First World War was a cataclysmic event with far-reaching, in many cases disastrous, consequences for millions of people. Tsar Nicholas II of Russia clearly did not realise the implications for both his country and his own family – or if he did, he did not confide them to his diary, where he wrote merely: 'Went hunting today.'

Certainly it was the end of a 'Golden Age' for Britain. (Interestingly, most people in the 1920s wanted a return to this 'Golden Age', including a return to the Gold Standard, whereas after the Second World War, no one wanted a return to the 1930s.) Until 1914, the gold sovereign and half sovereign had circulated as everyday currency for nearly 100 years. After the 1833 Bank Charter Act, Bank of England notes were legal tender in England and Wales only for amounts of £5 and above. On 5 August 1914, with the passing of the Currency and Bank Notes Act, the Treasury was empowered to issue notes of £1 and 10 shillings. Anticipating the possibility of war, the Treasury, assisted by the Inland Revenue, had rushed through an emergency design over the weekend of 1 and 2 August. Notes were printed around the clock by Waterlow Brothers and Leighton, with help on the 10s note from De La Rue, as we have seen. The bank holiday was extended for three days while 4 million £1 notes were printed. These first notes were hurriedly and badly designed. Portals obviously could not produce the paper at a few hours' notice, and the printers were compelled to use paper originally produced for postage stamps. Proof of this haste was provided in 1933 by Lady Atterbury, wife of Sir Frederick Atterbury, Controller of HM Stationery Office, when she wrote to a Sunday newspaper:

> It may be of interest to your readers to know that on the Saturday before the eventful Bank Holiday of August 1914, Sir John Bradbury and a colleague came to my house at Hampstead Heath at night and asked my husband in the Chancellor's name, to get the paper money made ... it was a matter of extreme urgency and the first note was designed in my drawing room in a few minutes by my husband.

For Portals, as for many other employers, one of the greatest difficulties was coping with the loss of large numbers of their workforce who either volunteered or, after the National Registration Act on 15 July 1915, were conscripted into the armed forces.

In August 1914 the first £1 and 10s notes were issued, not by the Bank of England but by the Treasury on plain paper supplied by other manufacturers. In spite of this, the huge demand for security paper kept Portals extremely busy. Indeed, the labour situation allied to the shortage of key raw materials meant that they struggled to cope.

The company responded by buying another mill, Turkey Mill, at Goose Eye, near Keighley in Yorkshire. Renovations and installations were put in hand and the first delivery of Indian rupee paper was made in 1918. Portals was extremely busy during the war. The days of just making banknote paper for the Bank of England were long gone. There was an increased demand for Postal Orders and for millions of forms and certificates used by the armed forces such as Postal Drafts, by which allowances were paid to dependants of serving personnel. These drafts alone were being printed at the rate of 1 million per day by the second half of the war. Furthermore, conditions in India led to an increased demand for small-denomination notes. Then there were repeat issues of National War Bonds and Loans, as well as other security documents.

The Bank of England itself took the opportunity to expand its printing facilities in 1916, when it acquired the premises of the former 'St Luke's Hospital for Lunaticks' in Old Street, exactly one mile door to door from its building in Threadneedle Street. For the next 40 years, Portals delivered its paper direct to 'St Luke's'.

The Great War was finally over in November 1918. Across the world, the news of the armistice was electrifying. Parisians sang and cheered in the boulevards. In New York, 1 million people thronged Broadway. In London, one observer recalled the event: 'I stood at the window of my room looking up Northumberland Avenue towards Trafalgar Square, waiting for Big Ben to tell that the War was over … And then suddenly the first stroke of the chime … From all sides men and women scurrying into the streets. Streams of people poured out of all the buildings The bells of London began to clash All bounds were broken. The tumult grew … Flags appeared as if by magic … Almost before the last stroke of the clock had died away, the strict, war-straitened, regulated streets of London had become a triumphal pandemonium.'

As it became clear to the more far-sighted that another war was inevitable, Portals erected two buildings on the north side of Overton Mill early in 1939 on behalf of the Bank of England. These would accommodate personnel from the Bank if necessary. It did become necessary when Neville Chamberlain broadcast these fateful words on 3 September 1939:

> This morning the British Ambassador in Berlin handed the German Government a final Note stating that, unless we heard from them by eleven o'clock that they were prepared at once to withdraw their troops from Poland, a state of war would exist between us …
>
> … I have to tell you now that no such undertaking has been received and that consequently this country is at war with Germany.

The personnel duly arrived at Portals later in the month.

As far back as 1934, experiments had been made that eventually allowed the introduction into Bank of England notes of a security device of far-reaching importance. This was a narrow thread of special composition, woven uniformly into the paper during manufacture. It became a feature of Bank of England notes and those of most other currencies of the world, and first appeared in 1940 in a new issue of £1 and 10 shilling notes.

Following what became known as the Phoney War during the winter of 1939–40, the situation became much more serious in April 1940 when German forces invaded both Denmark and Norway followed by France in May. France capitulated in June.

Britain now faced the near-certainty of a German invasion. Lord Portal's reaction was to arrange the shipment of two papermaking machines and the Mould Office equipment to Canada, with the plan of installing them at Howard Smith's paper mill in Montreal, where the company could continue to produce banknote paper for India and other foreign countries. When Churchill heard about this, he regarded it as a defeatist gesture and ordered Lord Portal, then a Parliamentary Secretary to the Ministry of Supply, to bring the equipment back. The shipment had already sailed, but when it arrived in Halifax, Nova Scotia, it remained on the ship and returned to Britain. When it arrived back at Overton Mill the workforce reassembled it and had it back in production within fourteen days.

As anticipated, German forces massed in the Pas de Calais in preparation for an invasion of Britain. First, Goering promised Hitler he would clear the skies of the Royal Air Force. During the early part of August 1940 the Luftwaffe began to attack British airfields. Goering, making light of the protests of other Luftwaffe commanders over the difficulties, told them:

> The Führer has ordered me to crush Britain with my Luftwaffe. By means of hard blows I plan to have this enemy, who has already suffered a crushing moral defeat, down on his knees in the nearest future, so that an occupation of the island by our troops can proceed without any risk!

According to James Stokesbury in his book *A Short History of Air Power*:

> The last week of August and the first week of September proved the crucial period for the RAF. In those two weeks the Germans finally got their priorities correct and went after the whole structure of Fighter Command – the radar stations, the airfields, the control mechanisms. They also increased the number of free-fighter sweeps, and, by unremitting pressure, they began to win. Some of the radar went out, a couple of the most forward airfields were untenable and, most important of all, pilot attrition was wearing down the fighter strength. Dowding was scrounging pilots from Coastal Command, the Fleet Air Arm, any place he could get them.
>
> On September 7 Goering threw victory away. Believing the exaggerated claims of his pilots, steadfastly misunderstanding the nature of his enemy, and indeed of air war, he decided the British were already finished. He thought Fighter Command was a broken reed; the battle was won. On September 7 he ordered the coup de grace for

> England. The army and navy were all ready to go; and the tide would be right from September 8 through September 10. The British had put out an invasion warning, and on the afternoon of September 7, more than a thousand aircraft took off from bases across the Channel, formed up in massive units, and droned out towards England.
>
> Park [later Air Chief Marshal Sir Keith Park, he commanded the vital No. 11 Fighter Group during the Battle of Britain] and his 11 Group watched them come with grim determination. They knew it was all over; the thin blue line was fraying out into invisibility. Waiting for their last best shot, they watched for the Germans to break up and head for the airfields and factories; while they did, the huge armada droned stolidly on, disdaining targets in the flat green countryside below. Incredulously, almost too late to do anything to stop it, the British realized the Germans were heading for London itself.
>
> While Park called in every fighter he could find, the Germans bombed the London docks and the East End. Immense fires piled up into the sky, to last all night and be seen a hundred miles away. Hermann Goering, whose pilots sometimes unkindly called him 'Nero' in reference to his pretensions and pomposity [and possibly his addiction to drugs], stood on the cliffs of Calais and warmed himself with the glow of London burning. His cup ran over. He did not know he had just lost the war.

So, the dreaded invasion was at least postponed. However, the bombing raids did not stop, though naturally they were focused on Britain's major cities. During the Second World War, Portals at Overton did not escape completely unscathed. At three o'clock in the afternoon on Wednesday, 26 March 1941, a German bomber came out of low cloud from the north-west over Overton Mill, presumably on its way home from Bristol or South Wales, and dropped a load of high-explosive bombs. The Mill suffered some damage and two employees were injured, but when bombs fell in the Foxdown area adjoining the Mill, a Portals pensioner and the wife of one of the employees were killed. Fortunately, this proved to be the only air-raid of any consequence in the Overton area during the war.

TOTAL DESTRUCTION

On Sunday 29 December 1940 the German Luftwaffe dropped no fewer than 10,000 firebombs on the City of London, and included in the premises destroyed were De La Rue's office and works in Bunhill Row.

The Works Manager of De La Rue's London factories was Clac Prudhoe, a 32-year-old Geordie who had joined the firm as an office boy. He reported to the General Manager, Ernest Gough, and because of the mighty disruption, they and others often spent nights in shelters under the Crown Works in Bunhill Row. Prudhoe and Gough took it in turns to have weekends at home.

Prudhoe spent that last weekend of December 1940 with his wife at their small flat in Harpenden, 25 miles north of London and close to Luton where she worked in a munitions factory. He said later:

> On that Sunday night, we were out walking and, Harpenden being fairly high up above St Albans, we could see that London was really getting a pasting. I said to my wife I must get in early tomorrow.

He arrived at Euston, but there was no further transport and he walked the two and a half miles to Bunhill Row. When he approached Bunhill Row he had to talk his way through the police cordon:

> I was just staggered. Where there had been a four-storey building – the Crown Works, the George Works and the Star Works – all that was left was a tangled heap of machinery and dangling girders. Although most of the fires were out, stocks of paper and other debris were still burning or smouldering. Even as I stood there, another heavy machine crashed down from the top floor, right through the building, to the ground. The whole thing was demolished.

The raid had been timed to coincide with the tidal low-point in the Thames, and water mains were severed in an initial attack using high-explosive parachute mines. Then, with the firefighters impotent on land and the fireboats unable to manoeuvre on the river, came the incendiaries. When, hours later, water was pumped in from more distant mains, the exhaust pipes of fire engines became red-hot through the continued pressure pumping of 20,000 firefighters.

The result was the closest the City of London ever came to the firestorms that later ravaged Dresden and Hamburg. Many of the 1,500 separate fires coalesced into two huge conflagrations, the worst of which covered half a square mile between Moorgate, Aldersgate, Cannon Street and Old Street – the sector with Bunhill Row in its north-east corner. As one observer on the roof of the Bank of England saw it: 'It wasn't just big fires here and there, but a continuous sheet of flame all around us.' The Guildhall was badly damaged, eight Wren churches destroyed and the Port of London reduced to a quarter of its capacity, though other great symbols, like St Paul's and the Bank, remarkably survived. The human toll was 163 dead – terrible indeed, but small on the obscene scale of the wider conflict.

Prudhoe went to find his General Manager, Gough, who had been there when the bombs fell. Gough had the same dismal story of the night before as so many Londoners – no answer to incendiaries because there was no water in the Thames. The company's roof spotters had done what they could with stirrup pumps but eventually they were overwhelmed and just had to let it burn. The company's offices at 110 and 112 Bunhill Row had met the same fate as the factories. Virtually the entire physical body of the 19th-century business had been cremated. However, in one of the night's several miracles, nobody in Bunhill Row had been killed or seriously injured.

While Prudhoe and Gough were assessing the scale of the disaster, local families were being allowed back through the street cordon. Among a gang of children hunting for trophies in the street outside the ruined factories was thirteen-year-old Stan Middleditch, the son of a De La Rue labourer. The Middleditch family had spent part of the night sheltering in the basement of the Crown Works, the father being on duty as one of the company's firefighters. Around midnight, even as some mains water was becoming available, if too late to save the factories, they were ordered to leave the building. They filed down Chequer Street in the light of the flames, with firefighters' hoses playing on them. But by the morning there were some compensations, according to Stan Middleditch:

> I soon became the proud possessor of bundles of Chinese and other banknotes! They were floating or flying about the place and all the local lads helped themselves. There was also the odd bottle of hair cream from other factories in the road.

Bernard Westall was his usual masterly and active self. He decreed that Monday's lunch for foremen and senior managers (a delayed Christmas celebration) at the Great Eastern Hotel should still go ahead. Some of those attending had arrived straight from their homes to receive the appalling news with their first drinks. Over lunch Westall made a short speech, ending with an emotive peroration:

> Today we have seen the burning ruins of our banknote factories. But it is the factories that have been destroyed – we, not they, are De La Rue. New factories will one day be built, far finer than the ones you have been weeping for this morning. Today is the beginning of a new, and let us hope a better, De La Rue.

However, others were to recall somewhat more prosaic passages from their chieftain's address, as did Prudhoe:

> Bernard was very grave, and said, 'Well this is it, nothing we can do about it, we have no factory and are starting from nothing'. He talked to people in a very kindly sort of way but said that for the moment they'd all just have to go home. 'If and when we require you again, we'll let you know. I can't tell you when you're going to be re-employed, because we haven't a place to re-employ you. Arrangements will be made to give you two weeks' wages.' Of course, this was quite generous for those days.

Following the luncheon party there was a meeting between the three executive directors, Westall, Cyril Ashton and Bert Bridge (a fourth, Ian Aird, was in the army), Gough and Prudhoe in a room at the Great Eastern Hotel, when at least one immediate decision was taken. Commercial printing would cease.

During the 1930s, De La Rue had developed a widespread if not very profitable business in printing weekly and monthly journals. Some, like *Country Life*, *Nursery World*, *Time and Tide*, *The Lady*, *Tourist Magazine*, *The Tablet*, *The Fortnightly Review* and *Psychic News*, were generally available at bookstalls; others, such as *Architecture and Building News*, *Timber Trades Journal*, *British Trade Journal* and *English Mechanics*, were aimed at specialist professional groups; and there were several house magazines, including one of the oldest, that of the Port of London Authority.

There was simply no prospect of continuing with any of these publications on De La Rue premises. As Prudhoe said to Westall: 'We have lost all our printing, composing, typesetting and binding machines.' Westall replied: 'Well, it wasn't a very popular activity to begin with. I shall go and see all the publishers and tell them that this business has now come to an end.'

Nor, of course, was there any machinery on which to make the rest of Bunhill Row's products: playing cards, stationery and banknotes. But these would be farmed out in a remarkable process of cooperation with other companies.

The printing of De La Rue playing cards, by now a very small part of the business, was taken in by John Waddington of Leeds. Even before the war there had been an informal arrangement with Waddingtons, and in 1942 the two firms established the Amalgamated Playing Card Company, each owning 50 per cent (initially this was known as the United Playing Card Company, but the name was changed following pressure from American card manufacturers). Thus the De La Rue name, famous on playing cards since 1832, was preserved only by dint of its main competitor's printers.

For the mainstay of the business the answer was more complex. De La Rue relied on two main banknote customers, China and the Crown Agents, the latter placing orders on behalf of British colonies around the world. China was by far the larger, but without either of them the company could not survive.

According to Lorna Houseman's earlier company history:

> Using the Great Eastern Hotel as an office, for now he had no other in London, Mr Westall sent off a telegram. It was addressed to Dr Kung in Chungking (Chinese finance minister and governor of the Central Bank) and it said: 'Factories destroyed by enemy action. Please place additional order for thousand million notes to be printed by lithography' ... Responding heroically, Dr Kung did not hesitate. Back came his telegram: 'Agree'.

The first offer of printing help arrived within a day of the destruction of Bunhill Row, when Victor Watson, chairman of Waddingtons, came down to London to see Westall. The two men, though competitors, had already established a good working relationship through playing cards and related products – for example, De La Rue printed cigarette cards for insertion in packs of Waddington playing cards, and even printed the playing cards themselves when Waddingtons were overwhelmed due to the offer of playing cards from cigarette cards.

This was how Victor Watson wrote about it in his book *The Waddingtons Story*. He made it clear that his father had grown to respect Sidney Lamert thanks to an incident involving De La Rue and Waddingtons during the 1930s. It all stemmed from a new process for producing playing cards that Waddingtons were developing:

> During the development of the new equipment, my grandfather received a communication from Mr Lamert, the chairman of De La Rue, inviting him to call to see something very interesting. My grandfather duly called, whereupon he was shown a letter

which was anonymous and which offered to De La Rue the secrets of the new Waddingtons process. If he wanted to accept the offer, Mr Lamert had to place a notice in a particular newspaper. Instead, the honourable gentleman gave the letter to my grandfather. Back at the factory in Leeds, my father compared the typewriting with the lettering from all the suppliers and found that it matched those from Crabtrees, the electrical engineers in Shipley, near Bradford. My grandfather and father went to see Mr Crabtree who looked at the letter and said, 'It must be Bernard, one of the designers'. Bernard was sent for, confronted with the evidence and admitted that he was the culprit. (Although not essentially part of this account, it is interesting to note that Bernard was known to my grandfather as the son of a professor of Leeds University. Grandfather had reason to be sorry for Bernard, who was so unruly as a boy that he was often chained to a leg of the kitchen table.) He was admonished by Mr Crabtree and taken off the job, but not dismissed. The gentlemanly attitude of Sidney Lamert in regard to this event was probably the beginning of years of fair and friendly rivalry between De La Rue and Waddingtons.

The two men were opposites. Victor Watson left school at the age of twelve; Bernard Westall went to Cambridge University. Victor Watson had been apprenticed to a lithographer; Bernard Westall was the son of a Church of England Bishop and had been born with the proverbial silver spoon in his mouth. Victor Watson had a Yorkshire accent. Bernard Westall had an accent and indeed a way of speaking which made him completely at ease at Henley, Ascot or Lords. He was of military appearance and demeanour; tall, moustached, alert and almost jumpy in manner. He was full of energy, life and laughter. Yes, they were poles apart socially, but they hit it off. They both loved playing bridge, chess, cricket, indeed all the games. They sparked off each other and enjoyed the rivalry and the comradeship which often develop alongside such interactions. After meetings in Leeds and London, they agreed that price fixing would eventually destroy the competitive edge of both businesses and make them vulnerable to attack from others. Instead, they instituted an annual cricket match and other events so that the executives of both businesses would get to know each other, and thus compete fairly and without resorting to anything like unsporting behaviour.

On the night of the bombing of Bunhill Row, Victor Watson happened to be in London, staying, as he always did, at the Waldorf Hotel. When he heard of the destruction of the previous night, he went immediately to Bunhill Row and said to Westall:

> We can't have the Jerries interfering with our rivalry. For as long as war lasts, De La Rue can have half of Waddingtons' playing card production. We can keep the sales forces separate but manufacture jointly.

As a result, not only was the Amalgamated Playing Card Company formed, but Waddingtons undertook much of De La Rue's banknote printing work and rented out part of its Leeds factory.

Victor Watson continued in *The Waddingtons Story*:

> The association of De La Rue and Waddingtons was of great benefit to both companies. It was more than a mere business relationship. It was based on friendship, Bernard Westall was a leader, a man of vision; one who people enjoyed working for because he was imaginative and decisive. He was a man of humanity, capable of great friendship. And he loved life. In the later years when the commercial arrangement between De La Rue and Waddingtons had ended, Bernard Westall continued to be a director of Waddingtons' monthly journal, *Bridge Magazine*. He used to come to Leeds once a year for the annual general meeting with my father, Uncle Horace, Clac Prudhoe (the De La Rue executive who stayed with Waddingtons to run the playing card business) and me as the lad. I wrote the minutes. For example: 'Champagne was served and the directors congratulated each other on the small loss which had been incurred during the year under review'. After the mid-morning meeting we went to Moortown Golf Club for lunch, played golf in the afternoon, then snooker, then dinner and then bridge. When Bernard was about eighty years old, I remember him saying to me, 'I wake up in the morning, say "I've got another day!" and then I pack as much into the day as I can.' I have always remembered that positive attitude, just as I will always remember a remarkable man.

On that fateful day at the end of 1940, Watson proposed that Westall should use part of the Leeds factory for banknote printing. It was a generous, if not entirely altruistic, offer. De La Rue, because of its work for the Crown Agents and also some top-secret assignments for the War Office, operated under the Essential Works Order, which meant it could always obtain the raw materials and retain the labour it needed. Waddingtons' products had no such protection from the exigencies of war, and Watson, astutely looking ahead to supplies drying up, could see a means of keeping at least part of his factory in production.

Gough was sent to reconnoitre the Leeds factory. Waddingtons were expert litho printers but of course had no experience of other key stages in banknote printing, like numbering and finishing. Three Bunhill Row veterans, Alf Caunt, May Suckling and Alice Greygoose, soon arrived to take charge of the new sections in Wakefield Road.

Meanwhile, Prudhoe had set about visiting other printers in London and elsewhere – De La Rue's demand for litho printing was so great that neither Waddingtons nor any other single printer could handle all the work. His brief was to find those who were able and willing to print Chinese banknotes and, when he did, to embark on a process of technical education. In banknote printing, unlike some commercial printing, colour variations from sheet to sheet, let alone damaged type, could not be tolerated. Physical security, too, became a new priority for these firms – installing wire screens and strong rooms and ensuring that waste material could be destroyed under careful control.

Among at least ten companies to take in De La Rue's Chinese laundry were Fosh and Cross, Williams Lea, Waterlow, Sun Engraving, Mardon Son and Hall, Purnell and George Phillips. With Dr Kung's banknotes, or parts of them, being made in

locations spread across England, the inherent problems of quality control and coordination were formidable, as were the logistics of transporting precious parcels around the country under siege. Some notes were printed in one place, numbered in another and finished in a third. Prudhoe's travels, first to find sub-contractors and later to monitor their output, took him from Leeds to London, from Bristol to Dunstable.

De La Rue's work for the Crown Agents took a different route. The actual banknotes may have been destined for Africa, the Far East and the West Indies, but the immediate customer was right on the spot in London, and already very disturbed by security risks possibly lying in the ashes in Bunhill Row. There were printing plates, some intact, some damaged, and many sheets of banknotes, some charred beyond recognition but with clean notes among them. De La Rue had lost its incinerator among all the other machinery, so any sheets containing partly burnt notes were taken to the Bank of England's works in nearby Old Street, where two security officers from the company and the Crown Agents completed the job started by the Luftwaffe.

However, that was not the end of the matter, for many records had also been lost in the blaze. A full audit was impossible. In the end, De La Rue and the Crown Agents had to agree that the starting point for future printing should be from the notes actually delivered to the colonies by the Agents, and all else would be written off – including, quite possibly, some finished notes. 'It may well be true that certain sheets were purloined,' said Prudhoe, 'but there was little looting in those days.'

The Crown Agents were adamant that their business could not be spread around like the Chinese order, and, after much investigation and negotiations by Gough and Prudhoe, they approved the use of one firm only: Wass Pritchard, established in 1901 and with an outstanding reputation for the quality of its litho work. Such was the volume of business for the colonies that Wass Pritchard did little else until De La Rue re-established its own security printing works in Leeds, and it continued to handle other security printing on behalf of the company for many years.

But however resourceful Gough, Prudhoe and their friendly competitors were in stitching together a patchwork quilt of security printers across London and the English countryside, the fact remained that by January 1941 De La Rue's only remaining banknote printing plant was in Rangoon, Burma. It was run by Frank Richardson and a small team of Europeans.

The first news Richardson had of the disaster in London was a cable dated 8 January 1941 that said: 'Star Group Works and office Bunhill Row destroyed. Now relying on your sole production.' Over the next year Rangoon expanded to become the largest security printing plant in Asia, employing over 800 people and producing 12 million notes weekly for the Chinese banks on which, by general consent, the future of De La Rue hung. As Managing Director Westall told the Board in April 1941: 'The future of the company is inextricably bound up by China.'

However, as in Shanghai and Bunhill Row, the global conflagration was soon to engulf Rangoon too.

RETREAT FROM RANGOON

In the autumn of 1941, with the defeat of Soviet Russia by Germany looking inevitable, Japan saw its opportunity to seize the oil and other raw materials of South-east Asia. Its strategy was to advance rapidly through Burma, Malaya, the East Indies and the Philippines and then to establish a defensive perimeter to the south and south-west. The only major threat to this plan was the US Pacific Fleet.

At dawn on 7 December 1941, 366 Japanese carrier-borne bombers and fighters attacked Pearl Harbor, sinking four American battleships, destroying or disabling fifteen other warships and nearly 200 aircraft, and inflicting heavy casualties. Singapore and Hong Kong were bombed the same day, as well as three American Pacific islands. When Hitler heard of Pearl Harbor he said: 'Now it is impossible for us to lose the war; we have an ally who has never been vanquished in 3,000 years.' Within three days of Pearl Harbor, America was at war with Japan, Germany and Italy, while China had joined the Allies.

The Japanese then swept through South-east Asia. By the end of the year they had taken Hong Kong, the Gilbert Islands, Guam and Wake Island and invaded Burma, Malaya and Borneo. In mid-December the British evacuated Victoria Point, the Burmese town nearest to the Thai border. The fall of Rangoon (the name means 'the end of strife'), the Burmese capital that had been under British rule for nearly a century, was only a matter of time.

The city was bombed during Christmas week (as De La Rue managers would have known it). Although the main targets were military installations and aircraft on the ground, there were more than 2,000 civilian casualties and severe damage to morale.

Local manager Frank Richardson later described to his Managing Director how De La Rue's Rangoon factory had suffered a disaster because of the 'paralysing effect of a few bombs' on the working life in the city. On Christmas Eve, the morning after the first raid, only six workers out of 700 reported for duty. A week later there were still only 100 coming in. The air-raid sirens wailed three or four times a day, each incident losing an hour or two's production in the printing factory. Throughout Rangoon the basic services, including transport and food distribution, were completely disrupted.

Westall, knowing none of these details at the time but all too aware of the speed of the Japanese advance, sent Richardson a telegram instructing him to dismantle the plant and take it to China. Within ten minutes of receiving this, on Sunday, 3 January 1942, Richardson started to take the presses apart. No labourers were available, only European staff and a handful of local engineers. Richardson found a building contractor willing to make packing cases for the long road journey ahead, and eventually, through his contacts with the Central Trust of China, he acquired the services of 50 workmen and the loan of a lorry for one week. Subsequently the supply of labourers improved, and enough could be recruited for De La Rue's purpose on a daily basis. Then, on 28 January, came a new order from Westall, who was acting on instructions from Dr Kung: the plant was to be set up in India, not China.

The packing cases had to be strengthened to withstand the rougher handling of sea transport, but loading at Rangoon docks started a week later. It proved very difficult to hire lorries, but Richardson somehow persuaded the military authorities to divert army trucks, as many as ten of them at times, to De La Rue's use, providing a day and night service. In another special concession to the company, Rangoon's port authorities allowed Richardson to have special dockside lighting that enabled loading to continue virtually around the clock, air-raids (of which there were now sometimes eight or nine a day) permitting. However, the Port Commissioners applied one restriction that severely impeded De La Rue's plan to save its most precious equipment: to send to the dock only cases small enough for workmen to handle without cranes. Though Richardson interpreted this as broadly as he could, loading many cases weighing over two tons, he delayed the heavier presses to the last stage, by when, he hoped, heavy lifting tackle might be used.

By Tuesday, 17 February (just two days after the fall of Singapore), Richardson was expecting to finish loading by the end of the week. But the work was cut short on Wednesday, when the docks were cleared for the arrival of an armoured brigade, and no more De La Rue equipment could be shipped out after that. In two weeks about 1,000 tons had been moved from the factory, and this load, accompanied by De La Rue's Arbour, Cater and Smith, sailed for Calcutta on Thursday 19th.

Richardson, in close touch with British army headquarters, reckoned he had at least a week to somehow rescue the remaining equipment. Around noon on Friday 20th, a general order to evacuate Rangoon within 48 hours was published: any cars left in the town after that would be requisitioned or destroyed. Richardson hurried into Rangoon, picked up 30 gallons of petrol and returned to incinerate the remaining 42 cases of security paper. The rest of the day was spent sorting office records and destroying all the non-essentials. By Saturday's dawn, Frank Richardson was on the road to Mandalay.

With him on the 400-mile journey north, in two Morris cars and a Chevrolet, were Downey and Vincent, the Indian members of staff, supplies of food and water, and three packing cases of important records. Richardson was aiming for northern Burma with the intention of descending the passage into India through Assam, a route his military sources had told him was just still passable by car. However, as he explained to Downey and Vincent, he also intended to return to Rangoon if there appeared to be 'a sporting chance of getting the remainder of the machinery out'.

The small De La Rue convoy reached Mandalay, where the intelligence on their proposed route to India was encouraging, and then drove 40 miles north-east to Maymyo to find the army HQ. Military transport was scarce in the region, but Richardson said he could get lorries from Rangoon if the local command could assist with fuel and spare parts. By Thursday, 26 February he was back on the road from Mandalay to Rangoon, complete with letter authorising him to use whatever transport was available and instructing the military authorities en route to supply him with whatever he needed. The ICS (Imperial Civil Service) Commissioner of Mandalay also gave him a letter instructing police and civil officers to render whatever assistance they could.

Downey, Vincent and a local engineer volunteered to accompany Richardson on his return journey. He was at pains to tell them they did so at their own risk. They reached Rangoon at dusk on Friday 27th, to find the town, in Richardson's account:

> Completely abandoned by civilians and very few military in evidence. The aerodrome to the north had been abandoned. Several rows of houses had been burnt down, every house without an armed guard had been looted. Army officers advised me to drive north again immediately.

The next morning, to underline the message, a Royal Engineers colonel advised Richardson to get on the road at once. Instead, he went to see Dennis Phillips, the local secretary of defence who had been of great help to De La Rue in earlier weeks. He confirmed that there was neither labour nor transport available to move cases from the factory.

Still apparently undaunted, Richardson and his three volunteers then drove to the factory. Their route took them along once-crowded roads that were now all but deserted, with everywhere the signs of looting and arson. They called at Richardson's own house, to find that looters had taken everything moveable and destroyed the rest. A dead horse lay in the road outside.

However, they found the factory in the same state as they had left it a week before. There were two letterpress side-frame cases in the road waiting to be loaded, the remainder of the machinery lined up in cases near the entrance.

From the factory they drove back into town to the head office of the Irrawaddy Flotilla Company, only to find the manager standing by with a demolition squad of Europeans waiting for orders to destroy the installation. Richardson's idea was to use a river barge or steamer to float the cases up the Irrawaddy to the head of the new road to India, and then continue overland with lorries when the road was completed. But all that the shipping manager could offer was one cargo ship, which had to leave its moorings that afternoon. The offer, as Richardson saw it, was 'kind, but useless', because of the lack of transport and labour. The shipping manager gave the De La Rue team some food and water and they set off once more for Mandalay, arriving on Sunday night.

On Tuesday he cabled De La Rue in London:

> Regret report journey fruitless for censored reasons. Factory and contents undamaged remaining machinery mainly side frames and cylinders for 8 letter press and 6 copper plate, absolutely essential for factory. Suggest two methods each needing government support. 1. I fly Lashio to Calcutta, obtain 200 coolies or labour for 6 lorries proceed Rangoon. 2. Chinese Government supply 120 lorries plus coolies to bring stuff north for later transport India. 1. preferable. Can India office instruct authorities Calcutta or alternatively will you cable Kung [Chinese Minister for Finance]. Am proceeding Lashio enquire plates and lorry possibilities returning to Mandalay. Richardson.

The next day, Wednesday, 3 March, brought a reply that Richardson may have regarded as being in the highest tradition of head office unhelpfulness to those in trouble in faraway places: 'Consider first proposal impracticable second impossible send stuff via India.' However, De La Rue in London possibly had access to more recent news than did Richardson on the ground. The Japanese were closing in on Rangoon.

On that same Wednesday, Richardson drove another 100 miles from Maymyo to Lashio to seek help from the most senior Chinese army and civil authorities. Extracts from one of the letters submitted on his arrival show him using every argument in the book:

> The company which I have the honour to serve is at present the main source of supply of banknotes issued by the Central Bank of China, the Bank of China, the Farmers Bank of China and the Bank of Communications.
>
> Some weeks ago, on instructions from His Excellency Dr H.H. Kung Finance Minister of the Government of China, we commenced dismantling the machinery in our Rangoon factory for transport by Chinese trucks to the interior of China for re-erection. Before however the first convoy had left Rangoon, His Excellency instructed us to move to India instead and consequently we started to ship the dismantled machinery by sea to Calcutta.
>
> About 1,000 tons had been shipped by the 22nd February, on which date we were ordered to quit Rangoon leaving about 300 tons of essential machinery still in Rangoon. This machinery consists chiefly of the heavy portions, lighter parts having already been shipped. Very few complete machines have actually gone by sea to Calcutta so that without parts now remaining in Rangoon our ability to continue to supply the Government of China with an adequate amount of currency notes will be very seriously impaired. The purpose of this letter therefore is to solicit the kind help of the Chinese Military Authorities in getting this absolutely vital machinery away from Rangoon to the North of Burma with a view to later transport to India when the road now under construction is completed. For the latter purpose I have no doubt the Government of India will in due course supply the road transport.

He continues with a blow-by-blow account of his travels up and down Burma, including a somewhat optimistic assessment of which road should still be open, before making his final appeal:

> I therefore suggest to Your Excellency that it would be very much in the interest of the Government of China to assist us to recover this machinery. It is a special design and of our own manufacture, is irreplaceable at the present time and will aid His Excellency, Dr H.H. Kung, very considerably to solve a tremendous problem that he has to deal with in connection with the issue of paper currency to the whole of China.
>
> Between 100 and 120 trucks with 100 coolies will accomplish this task in little over a week. I will with pleasure accompany such a convoy from any part of Burma

> or China together with such members of my staff as are now in Mandalay in order to ensure that any such machinery as is completely indispensable is loaded.
>
> Your assistance in this matter would be very highly appreciated not only by myself and my Board of Directors in London, but also by His Excellency the Minister of Finance. I await your favourable reply with confidence and have the honour to remain your most obedient servant.
>
> F.A. Richardson, Manager.

Sadly, if inevitably, Frank Richardson's powerful cry for help was to no avail. The Chinese general had to tell him that heavy troop reinforcements were being sent south through Siam and Burma and it was, regrettably, out of the question for lorries or rail transport to be diverted for De La Rue's purposes.

Richardson had one last shot at saving the company's kit. Returning to Mandalay, he managed to hire two lorries and drivers who were willing, at a high price, to drive to Rangoon. Then, back in Maymyo, he obtained British army permission to leave Burma with any military transports that might arrive in Rangoon, as long as this did not delay the departure of the ship. His intention was to pick up coolies in the two lorries somewhere north of Rangoon. He arranged with army headquarters that, when the time seemed appropriate, they would confirm or otherwise 'the advisability of starting our journey'. Unknown to Richardson, even as he made these arrangements on Friday 5th, the Japanese were taking the town of Pegu, which lay across the road to Mandalay just 40 miles north of Rangoon.

Along with the doughty Downey, Vincent and Thompson, who had again volunteered for the trip, Richardson waited for the signal to head south for the last time, cabling London on Tuesday 9th: 'When military advise, am returning to Rangoon with 2 hired lorries. Will telegraph before departure news thereafter will be from Calcutta.'

But it was already too late. The British and Indian troops had ceded Rangoon – and its De La Rue printing machines – to the Japanese on Sunday, 7 March 1942.

There was nothing left in Burma for Richardson and his colleagues so they made their way to India, stopping first in a hotel in Calcutta. There, on 30 March, he received a cable signed by the De La Rue Chairman: 'Very glad to hear safe arrival of all staff.' Two days later came another cable from the Chairman: 'At general meeting tribute was paid to you personally and staff for your very gallant efforts at Rangoon. Further recognition by letter. Congratulations.' Sidney Lamert was not a man to waste words.

They flew across India from Calcutta to Bombay, where they set up one of the world's oddest banknote-printing factories in some buffalo stables in Santa Cruz, not far from the old airport. Despite all their exertions in Burma they had saved only a tiny proportion of their main printing capacity. There were two copperplate machines and one or two letterpress machines, one of them a two-colour press on which tints could be printed.

Improvisation was the order of the day in Bombay, and Charlie Arbour was a remarkable improviser. For example, there was no washing machine for the calico: Arbour acquired a heap of teak, built a barrel and rigged up some side frames, and dug a big hole in the ground for draining the water away. 'Hey, presto!' recalled Richardson, 'In ten days we had an industrial washing machine out of nothing!'

As he later reported, some former office staff followed Richardson from Rangoon to Bombay: 'I didn't pull them out myself but they just turned up from God knows where, the bush telegraph must have told them that De La Rue were now in Bombay, 1,500 miles away from Calcutta where they landed.' They still had to recruit the main workforce locally, though, as the 20–30 people from Rangoon were certainly too few. By Richardson's account:

> [F]or the security finishing department we picked up a number of local girls who were quite nicely dressed but we needed a lot more. On the roads around the factory there were hundreds of Indian girls and women who were labourers and dressed as such. Of course our factory paid a few more rupees so some of these women came to us. The extraordinary thing was that in a matter of three or four weeks, those labourers had completely changed their costumes and were as smart as the rest of them. We were bloody glad to have them.

The main job was to produce banknotes for China. These were delivered in Bombay to representatives of the four Chinese banks and then flown over 'The Hump' to Chungking.

The factory in the old buffalo stables continued to print banknotes throughout the war, then continuing after the war had ended. Richardson and his managers were left largely to their own devices, with no wartime visitors from England and communications entirely by cable. However, Gerry Norman, the former factory manager in Shanghai and now a young bomber pilot in the RAF, did call in.

Frank Richardson returned to England in 1946. After a few weeks he was rung up by General Manager Ernest Gough and told to go to New York. In his words: 'I suppose it was thought that I'd had enough leave.'

THE WAR UNDERGROUND

Corsham, a small market town in Wiltshire, lies nearly 100 miles to the west of London and just ten to the north-east of Bath, the classical showcase for the district's oldest product: stone has been quarried around here since Roman times.

Corsham's commercial heyday was in the mid-19th century when, with the coming of the railways and new techniques in underground mining, it became the main centre for Bath stone. By the 1860s, 100,000 tons of rock a year were being loaded at Corsham station, and by the turn of the century there were fourteen mines close to the town. Most of these were exhausted within the next 50 years, leaving dank, empty caverns below ground, to one of which came a small party of De La Rue managers on a secret mission in 1942.

In that autumn the tides of war were turning. The Russians lifted the siege of Stalingrad, the British 8th Army broke the Afrika Korps at El Alamein, and the Americans invaded North Africa. In London it was a time for exiled governments of Europe to lay plans for the liberation of their countries. Physical reconstruction would take many years, but some actions to restore a measure of normal life could not wait. High on the agenda of the foreign ministers gathered in the British capital was the provision of new currency to be issued immediately their countries were freed.

The main contracts for printing of these notes were awarded to De La Rue by the War Office, following a decision at Cabinet level. It was intimated that the first orders would come through in early 1943 and continue through 1944, and they did. Designers, engineers and printers got to work, and the presses in Leeds (and to no lesser extent Dublin) were soon producing millions of banknotes for Austria, Belgium, Czechoslovakia, France, Greece, Norway, Poland and Yugoslavia. Most were printed litho, a few had one DP side. Though the quantities were vast, the orders were spaced out over nearly two years and only a score or so specially-vetted staff worked on the job at Leeds, under the watchful eye of Clac Prudhoe. Each order was passed to De La Rue by the Bank of England, acting for the War Office, and not by the exiled governments themselves.

Even before the presses rolled, however, there was an obvious problem to be solved: how to ensure the secure and secret storage of vast quantities of notes for an unknown period of time, safe not only from the traditional threats but also from bombs and enemy spies. Many suggestions were canvassed until the search ended in the peaceful Wiltshire countryside, well off the bombers' tracks, in a disused quarry more than 80ft below the ground.

The first impressions of security controller Leslie Norman were far from cheerful:

> The quarry was almost derelict. From the surface a track of rusty rails ran down a slope and then disappeared through the mouth of a tunnel into what had been the quarry workings. Beyond was darkness – and damp. The walls streamed with water and the little light which filtered through gave the cavern an eerie and forbidding appearance. However it was there and then decided that this should be the hiding place.

Within days, relays of technicians and labourers were at work. A shaft was sunk to drain the water that even in the driest weather continued to seep through the walls, and a dehydration plant was assembled below ground to overcome the humidity. Electric generators were installed and the whole cavern was soon festooned with lights. It became, to the De La Rue observers, an Aladdin's Cave awaiting its treasure.

Four galleries were prepared for storing the banknotes, each gallery sealed by a door of solid steel. At the entrance to the tunnel there was a huge twelve-foot drop-door, weighing more than two tons and worked by chains in the style of a medieval portcullis. Outside, on the hilltop, a watchman's tiny hut was the only clue to what was going on below the ground.

All was ready by the spring of 1943 when the notes, packed in tin-lined cases, started to arrive from Leeds. The cases travelled by road in ordinary commercial vans, many of them disguised with advertising posters, and driven by plain-clothes drivers with security escorts provided by the company. A contemporary report describes what then happened in Corsham:

> At the hill-top the vans were carefully unloaded and the cases placed into the trucks, which a few years before had been used to haul the rough quarry-stone. Down the slope to the tunnel entrance, a halt for a security check and then the great portcullis rose on its chains to let the wagons go through. Inside the cave, the treasure-train made its way to one of the four galleries where men stood ready to unload and store the cases to a pre-arranged plan. These cases towered high, tier by tier, tens of thousands of them, almost to the roof.

It is said that there were neither mishaps nor mistakes throughout the operation, over nearly two years – hard to believe, but then there was a war on, and the Official Secrets Act is a powerful weapon. There was some talk that one of the ships carrying notes from Ireland had been torpedoed and the goods lost (yet still invoiced), but no evidence survives. De La Rue's Board minutes at no time refer to Corsham, during the war or later.

There were occasional visits to Corsham by representatives of the exiled governments, accompanied no doubt by anonymous men from Whitehall. When Dr Benes, the once and future president of Czechoslovakia, came to the caves and signed the visitors' book, he marvelled at more than 6,000 cases containing Czech notes. Later, towards the end of the war, these were among the first to leave De La Rue's safekeeping. The cases were driven to a nearby airfield, loaded under Czech supervision into RAF Halifax bombers and flown to a Black Sea port.

Other countries took possession of their liberation currency in different ways. The French notes were handed over to the de Gaulle government in London; the Belgians' money went to the Bank of England; and the Greeks accepted delivery at the quarry. The Polish notes went in five shipments in a Polish vessel, loaded at London docks, and remained in circulation behind the Iron Curtain well into the 1950s.

De La Rue was granted an Essential Works Order on several counts. The contract with the Crown Agents was one, while clandestine activities for the War Office provided further reason for the company's status. In effect the gamekeeper had turned poacher, as the company took to forging documents such as identity papers and ration books for Allied agents to use in German-occupied Europe.

The orders for forgeries were placed by Colonel X and mostly designed by George Meacham of the preliminaries department in the Dufferin Works, the only plant largely undamaged in the Blitz. Meacham and his small team had to sign the Official Secrets Act, as did Ernest Gough and also Lois Lucas (Director Ian Aird's secretary), who acted as courier. She would take completed forgeries to Colonel X and bring back further instructions.

This, however, was small beer compared to the forgeries of the Third Reich, a story that began in 1939, involved a close shave for Giesecke and Devrient, the company's German competitors, and ended with a British lieutenant colonel from De La Rue sifting through the debris of a German bunker.

Shortly after the fall of Poland, Viennese scientist Dr Albert Langer called on Reinhard Heydrich, chief of the Reichssicherheitshauptamt (RSHA), the Reich Security Administration. Langer, a specialist in cryptography and counterfeiting, presented Heydrich with a plan for destroying the British economy by flooding it with counterfeit notes. The scheme was recommended to Heinrich Himmler, head of the police and security forces, who promptly approved the setting up of security printing presses under Langer's supervision. However, the notes produced were of poor quality, certainly not good enough to pass muster with a trusted foreign exchange bank teller in Berlin.

Heydrich and Himmler, still enthusiastic for the main idea, in 1940 sent a senior officer to Giesecke und Devrient in Leipzig, a private company that had been in the banknote business for about as long as De La Rue. Technical Director Franz Helmberger, Germany's leading expert on security printing (and the man who taught the company's long-term chief, Siegfried Otto, his trade), for whatever reason and by unknown means persuaded the authorities in Berlin to rescind the order. In so doing he probably saved the company's life: compliance with the counterfeiting scheme would have led to denazification proceedings after the war, leaving Giesecke und Devrient in no shape to compete with De La Rue and others.

The German firm's own history of its first 125 years (to 1977) is virtually silent on its wartime record, saying only:

> In our view craftsmen and artists in Rome in the later period of antiquity had no need to be ashamed of the fact that they were ruled by Nero. Nor do we feel that we should be ashamed of the honest work we performed under the Third Reich. On those anomalous times, our by no means easy task consisted of continuing the modernisation of our firm, preserving jobs, and above all, carrying on 'business as usual' with foreign countries.

Having been bravely rejected by Helmberger, Himmler eventually turned to Captain Bernhard Kruger, who was in charge of the RSHA section that forged passports and identity cards for Nazi agents. In May 1942, an emissary from Himmler gave Kruger his orders:

> You have been chosen to take charge of a new effort to make British pound notes. The work is to start immediately. Himmler has ordered the following measures: (1) The printing plant, which will have the highest security classification, is to be located in a specially guarded barracks in the Sachsenhausen Concentration Camp [just north of Berlin]. (2) All the men working under you on the project must be Jewish prisoners. In your honour ... the project will be called Operation Bernhard.

There could be little doubt as to why Jewish prisoners were specified: at the end of the work they would be killed. Kruger selected 37 men on the basis of their experience in printing and related trades and took a number of unusual steps to obtain their loyalty – special rations, dental treatment, and even access to a radio on which they would, undoubtedly, tune in to the BBC. He also arranged to withdraw a much-hated Nazi printing supervisor and to trust the prisoners not to sabotage the project. His approach paid off so handsomely that by the spring of 1943 (coincidentally, just when the first new European banknotes from Leeds were arriving in Corsham), counterfeit British notes were passing their first test.

Himmler ordered production of a million notes a month and authorised whatever increases in workers and machines were required by Kruger, who soon had 140 men working in two shifts at Sachsenhausen. The notes were used to pay German agents and to buy small arms parachuted to guerrillas by the Allies, but the original plot, to swamp the British economy with fake notes, was abandoned largely because the Luftwaffe had been driven from the skies over England.

HOW DID DE LA RUE COPE?

This is what the Chairman told shareholders at a postponed AGM in 1941:

> You have already been informed that at end of December 1940, your factories, warehouses and offices in Bunhill Row were totally destroyed by enemy action. The dislocation to business arising from this disaster has only gradually been overcome, and indeed it would not have been possible to overcome it at all had we not received the greatest consideration from other printing houses in this country. To those who came to our assistance, I should like to take this opportunity of tendering our thanks on your behalf.
>
> Shortage of staff has also presented a very serious problem. Some years ago a number of senior officials in the Accounting Department retired and their places were taken by younger men, who have now been called up for service. We have been fortunate in getting back a few of the senior men who retired, but the work thrown on the Accounting side of the business has been tremendous and this is a contributory reason for the delay in presenting the Accounts.

And the destruction continued, so that during 1941 De La Rue lost all its other manufacturing plants – Corfu, Shanghai and Rangoon. As we have seen, the machinery in Bunhill Row was destroyed; in Corfu it fell into Italian hands; and most was moved from Shanghai to Rangoon before that fell into Japanese hands, though some was shipped to India, a factory opening in Bombay in 1942 and deliveries of the vital Chinese contracts resuming in September.

Fortunately, in Britain some machines were transferred in 1940 to a factory owned by Waterlow and Sons, and as the Chairman put it:

> With the aid of good friends in the Printing trade who have come to our assistance, we have been able to carry on the manufacture of Bank Notes on a considerable scale and with a fair margin of profit.

This is what Bernard Westall told shareholders at an Extraordinary General Meeting held on 29 May 1941:

> I think the chairman has so completely covered the ground that there is very little I can usefully add. At the same time now that we are together I would like to take the opportunity of paying tribute to some of our friends and competitors in the Trade. In particular I should like on your behalf to thank Waterlow and Sons for the help that they have given us. They themselves have been blitzed; at the same time they have put at our disposal a considerable part of their country factory. I should also like, on your behalf again, to thank Victor Watson of Waddingtons, Leeds, who has not only been of help to us in the manufacture of playing cards but has been extraordinarily useful to us in the security printing business. His energy and the wonderful way in which he has tackled a very difficult job have been no small factor in the way that we have recovered from the blitz last December. I can only say that it is my earnest hope that those in other trades who have suffered as we have may find their fellow competitors as helpful as we have found ours.

In 1939 there had been 3,000 employees at Bunhill Row producing millions of banknotes, stamps and other security documents. Even though the plant was already fully occupied, the volume of work increased and some of it had to be channelled to the overseas factories. The destruction of Bunhill Row was potentially a disaster but, as we have seen, others stepped into the breach. Because skilled printers were in short supply, litho printing replaced the more complicated Direct Plate printing.

As well as Waddingtons' support after the bombing of Bunhill Row, the Dublin-based firm of Browne and Nolan undertook the lithographic printing of banknotes urgently needed for China. This association with Browne and Nolan lasted for 30 years.

Fortunately for De La Rue, its plastic moulding factory in Walthamstow remained unscathed and worked flat-out during 1940 and 1941. It received a number of government contracts, including one for plastic casings for the 69 grenade. In 1943 it had become so important a division of the company that it was formed into a separate company, De La Rue Plastics Limited, with Herbert Bridge as its Managing Director. Bernard Westall told shareholders at the AGM in July 1943:

> As there is a certain degree of public misconception as to the prospects of the Plastics Industry in the years after the war, it seems to me desirable to make some observations on the possibilities and limitations of your Plastics Company. De La Rue Plastics Limited has a number of advantages which, taken as a whole, entitle us to view the future with a steady eye. First, the company is considerably the largest engaged in plastic moulding. The number of our presses and the complete range of their sizes

> enable us to undertake work of the greatest magnitude. Second, being one of the oldest, if not actually the first engaged in plastic moulding, the Company has a cumulative experience particularly valuable in such a highly technical business. Third, we have a very large Research and Development Department. I think it is safe to say that in the years to come the success of De La Rue Plastics will depend to a very large degree on the success of the Research Department, and shareholders may rest assured that the Directors regard the subject of research and development as the most important of their preoccupations.

Expansion of the plastics business continued into 1944. A Scottish Plastics Limited was formed and a plastic-laminating company, Hammands Industries, was acquired.

During early 1944, negotiation took place to buy Thomas Potterton (Heating Engineers) Ltd. Their principal product was gas-heated hot-water systems for the heating and hot-water supply of private houses, hotels, public buildings, cinemas, theatres, hospitals and factories. The deal for £105,000 (about £3 million today) was signed on D-Day, 6 June. By this time Bernard Westall had succeeded Sidney Lamert as Chairman, and he told shareholders at the AGM in August 1945:

> The efficiency of the system [of Potterton] combined with the extremely low cost of maintenance will, we believe, command a wide sale in the near future. Our connection with the gas industry has given us reason to believe that there is also a wide field for modern economic household gas appliances.

A new company, De La Rue Gas Development Limited, was formed to continue and expand the Potterton range.

CHAPTER EIGHT

A TRULY INTERNATIONAL COMPANY

1945–1960

THE END OF THE WAR
RUNNING ON A SHOESTRING
ALL OVER THE WORLD
CHANGE AT THE TOP AND A NEW STYLE
THE WESTALL CLUB
MORE DIVERSIFICATION
CHARACTERS AT LARGE

THE END OF THE WAR

The Second World War ended, not on one day or at one hour as the First World War had, with its 'eleventh hour on the eleventh day of the eleventh month', but in two distinctly separate months: 8 May 1945 for hostilities in Europe, which became known as V-E (Victory in Europe) Day; and 19 August 1945, which became known as V-J day (Victory in Japan). Both, especially V-E Day, had long been anticipated as British, American and Russian troops closed on Berlin. This again was in stark contrast with 1918, when most people had expected the war to drag on into 1919.

As a result, many businesses supplying war materials had already started to suffer from cancelled orders in early 1945. One such business was De La Rue Plastics, and at the 1945 AGM, Westall told shareholders:

> The past year has been a difficult one for the Plastics Company. As a result of the war situation many Government orders were cancelled at very short notice. Alternative work in this class of industry could not be found at a moment's notice even if the

labour and materials remained available ... I have already indicated that the transition from war to peace would have an adverse effect on our Plastics Company.

Westall also told shareholders:

De La Rue Gas Development

During the past year we have also been able to proceed with our plans for the manufacture of gas appliances. De La Rue Gas Development Limited have acquired the lease of a factory in Gateshead and a smaller one at Elstree. Prototypes of our heaters have been completed, tested and passed forward for trial production. Plant and equipment for quantity production are now being erected. The staff has been enlarged and is engaged on the preparatory phases of production. This result has been brought about by the energy and wise planning of the Managing Director, Mr Leopold Friedman, whose name is already a household word in the Gas Industry. Within a few months from now we hope to see a steady stream of gas appliances flowing from our factories and the name 'De La Rue' on domestic heaters a familiar sight. The Multi-Point water-heater will be the first of our productions to come on the market. In the designing of the De La Rue multi-point heater the utmost care has been taken by Mr Friedman and his staff to ensure that our product will be the most advanced design yet devised. Longer time than was originally anticipated has been spent on the construction of the prototype and on the testing of the apparatus. But the time so spent will be very fully justified by future results. The reports of gas companies on the trials made by them have been extremely encouraging. As for the sales of the 'De La Rue' multi-point, for a long time to come they will be governed by our capacity to produce.

The prototype of the instantaneous boiling water heater is now complete and after completion of tests will also go into production. Apart from the technical aspect, special attention has been given to the aesthetic design. How far we have been successful the public will shortly be able to judge for themselves. The advantages of the instantaneous boiling water heater, both for domestic and other uses, are sufficiently obvious. We are hopeful that there will be a steady demand for this type of heater, which is complementary to the multi-point, for a long time to come.

The third item in our programme is the sink-heater. In addition to the appliances already mentioned, there is a field for a modern efficient sink-heater. This completes the three types of water-heating apparatus demanded by the public. Prototypes are also in hand for a gas grill and a gas copper. One of the features of all our appliances will be the employment of the 'Neat' gas jet. The 'Neat' jet enables the maximum heating value to be extracted from the minimum of gas.

In addition to the appliances outlined above we have also designed and made a prototype of a gas-cooker. The cooker will be made of pressed steel and will contain new features, which will, we believe, make it a distinct advance on any cooker hitherto produced. The manufacture of cookers, however, does not fit in very well, from a technical point of view, with other appliances. We have, however, come to an arrangement with Friedman-Athill, Ltd whereby they will manufacture the cookers and market them through a company in which we each own 50 per cent of the shares.

We hope that this arrangement will prove satisfactory to both parties. During the past year considerable difficulty was experienced by Thomas Potterton (Heating Engineers) Ltd in obtaining iron castings. As a result the Board, primarily with the object of ensuring an adequate supply of castings, purchased the fixed assets, stock and goodwill of the Emscote Foundry Company Limited. It was found convenient to operate the foundry as a branch of De La Rue Gas Developments Ltd. Apart from the manufacture of castings, the foundry is making and selling a gas cooker of a less expensive type than the 'Neat' cooker to which I have referred. New plant has been added to the foundry, which is being modernised. Already production has largely increased both for castings and gas cookers. We are not without hope that in due course the branch will prove remunerative.

General

We cannot expect to finance this considerable programme of expansion for the Insulation [see below] and Gas companies [...] out of our own resources. In due course, therefore, your directors expect to put before you a proposal for raising further capital.

Looking at the picture as a whole, I think our shareholders may be reasonably encouraged to view the future, at any rate for the next few years, with confidence.

During the year three Directors were co-opted. The first, Sir Donald Banks who, as many shareholders will know, was responsible for organisation of those two great wartime expedients, Fido and Pluto [Fido was the Fog Investigation and Dispersal Operation, a system used for dispersing fog from an airfield so that aircraft could land safely, and Pluto stood for Pipe-Lines Under the Ocean, the construction of pipelines under the English Channel between England and France]. We know that Sir Donald's wide experience will be of great value to the Company. The second, Mr J. Eerdmans, the energetic Managing Director of De La Rue Insulation Ltd. The third is Mr E.G. Gough, the General Manager of the Company.

I am glad to say that nearly all the Members of the Forces who have been serving abroad have now returned to the Company and I know it will be your wish to give them all a hearty welcome back. I am sure it will be your wish, too, to pay tribute to the work of the staff which, necessarily depleted, worked so arduously and so well during these long years of war and, most particularly, to Mr E.G. Gough.

During the war, De La Rue's head office had been moved from London to Haywards Heath, and it now returned to 84–86 Regent Street in London's West End. It may be appropriate here to mention Lees House. The lease on this beautiful house in Mayfair had been bought by the company in 1944. Arthur Morrish, the long-serving Company Secretary, recorded his views in the 1980s:

Entertainment in the grand manner has always been a feature of the De La Rue Company. The directors' dining room at 108 Bunhill Row for example was the scene of many a lavish lunch for the Company's security printing customers.

It must be remembered that these customers of a security printing company are highly important people who do not necessarily like to be seen in public being entertained by commercial firms. They are people like finance ministers, governors of central banks, ministers of post and telegraphs. If a finance minister has asked De La Rue to print an issue of notes which makes it obvious that there is going to be a devaluation of that country's currency, he does not like to be seen talking about these things in public. So a very good table was kept at 108 Bunhill Row, until the Blitz.

The chairman of the Company at that time, Sidney Lamert, was a great gourmet and he made sure that there was always a good supply of wine to the directors' dining room. He himself was one of the greatest experts on burgundy in the country and he told me that he lost something like 1,500 bottles of priceless domaine-bottled burgundy when bombs penetrated the cellars beneath the offices at Bunhill Row.

At the outbreak of war the headquarters of the Company and the registered office were moved to Haywards Heath in Sussex. But with a shortage of rail transport and shortage of petrol it was most inconvenient for the directors to keep visiting London to see their customers, and even then the only place to go which would provide the sort of entertainment which the customers and the chair would expect was the Dorchester. So the best was made of what was available.

In 1944 the Board decided to find a house in London suitable for entertaining purposes, presumably at that time, the end of the war had been foreseen. The relevant Board minute in fact describes the house as being suitable for the chairman. The lease of Lees House, 4 Lees Place was bought for £20,000 with some 70 odd years of the lease to run. The Duke of Westminster was the landlord and there were very restrictive covenants on the user and no offices were allowed in the premises whatsoever.

Lees House could well be described as being substantially built in the neo-Georgian style, from the early 1820s, with a large basement and three main storeys, with an attic storey at the top for staff bedrooms. In the basement there was a staff flat and kitchens, cellars, pantry etc.

On the ground floor there was a large entrance hall, an anteroom and a long corridor into a good-sized dining room. On the floor above there was a double room with bathroom and sitting room and further along towards the back of the house a large well-equipped billiards room. On the next floor there are two double rooms, each with their own bathroom, and on the top attic floor were four small single bedrooms and bathroom. This floor in fact had been originally converted into a flat for the chairman, which was the idea mentioned in the Board minutes. The taxman decided that this was not on and the chairman would have to pay a large amount of money if he continued to live there. So the flat was dismantled and converted into bedrooms, which were, although not frequently used, very useful as overflow rooms.

After the top floor flat was converted back into bedrooms, for some reason or another Lees House was not put to the best use. This probably was due to the fact that the staff were rather indifferent and that not sufficient attention had been paid to the equipment necessary for large luncheons, dinner parties, cocktail parties and so on. I think probably also the bedroom equipment, you might say, was insufficient.

So, in 1949 a Committee was set up consisting of two assistant managing directors, Messrs Eerdmans and Gough, assisted by the Secretary, to maximise the use of Lees House to make sure that everything ran smoothly and the necessary service was available in keeping with De La Rue's standards.

So, from 1950 Lees House was put to its proper use and it was the centre of De La Rue entertaining for the next 21 years. As a result of the excellent standards which the Company maintained Lees House became well known, amongst diplomats, politicians and businessmen of all kinds.

The hospitality was lavish, the surroundings impressive and on every occasion efforts were made to gather together interesting and congenial guests. The list of these is impressive. The list includes: King Phumiphon of Thailand, King Hussein of Jordan, President Nixon, President Tubman of Liberia, and five prime ministers – Harold Wilson, James Callaghan, Mr Holyoake of New Zealand and Pibul Songgram and Kukret of Thailand. In addition the Prince of Wales dined at Lees House as a guest of the CBI and not as a guest of De La Rue.

Many trade union leaders were invited to luncheon parties at Lees House, including George Woodcock and Victor Feather during their respective stints as General Secretary of the TUC and of course many leading businessmen of the day, including such people as Sir Isaac Wolfson, Chairman of Great Universal Stores, Arnold Weinstock, Chairman of GEC, Sir Jules Thorn, Chairman of Thorn-EMI and many many others. With such a variety of guests there are inevitably many amusing, and some not so amusing, stories to be told.

Diet was always a problem. Particular attention had to be paid to religious beliefs, so that, for example, the Israeli ambassador was not given pork chops or sausages. On this question of food there is one story which really must be recorded and this concerns the Arab League boycott.

Shortly after the first Arab/Israeli war the Arabs discovered that Thomas De La Rue were printing banknotes both for Israel and for many Arab countries. So they decided to send an emissary from the Arab countries to investigate the set-up at De La Rue and they chose a man who was then First Secretary I believe at the Iraqi Embassy. He asked to come and see the Company and was invited to Bunhill Row where unfortunately none of the directors was available. They were all abroad. He grilled the various senior managers at Bunhill Row as to what the Company did and how it was set up and so on and was then invited to Lees House for lunch, where I, as Secretary of the Company, was one of the hosts.

The moment he was introduced to me he started grilling me as to the Jewish influence in De La Rue. He first of all said, that having seen a list of the directors, most of them were Jews with names like Westall, Houseman, Killearn and so on, which of course was rubbish. When I persuaded him that this was not so he then asked me how many Jewish shareholders there were. I told him that quite a lot of information appeared on a share transfer form, but religion was not one of the items and I could only satisfy him by promising to send him a certificate to the effect that as far as was known, there was no Jewish control of the Company.

After a very sticky start, and a couple of drinks in the anteroom at Lees House, we marched into the dining room where the first course was melon. In order to break the tension, and the ice one might say, Peter Studd (now Sir Peter Studd) said to the butler, 'Where do these very excellent melons come from?' The butler replied quickly, 'Israel'. Well I do really believe that he felt that we had deliberately introduced a Jewish fruit into the lunch to embarrass him and he was extremely annoyed. However, the lunch duly came to an end and the next day or within a couple of days there was a coup in Iraq, King Abdullah I think it was, was assassinated, and he became the Iraqi Ambassador in London and then shortly went back to his own country. No more I may say was heard of this investigation.

There's another story which should be recorded as being of some interest and amusement to an historian, and that concerns a lunch which was given for Harold Wilson when he was Leader of the Opposition. The only other people present were the Chairman, Bernard Westall, the Managing Director, Gerry Norman, and myself.

Being responsible for the running of Lees House I arrived there some time before the others and to my surprise instead of the butler opening the door I was greeted by a small Italian, who from time to time we had used as a waiter. I asked him where the butler was and he said you'd better come and see the butler's wife who was the cook. So down I went to the basement where I found this good lady in floods of tears and when I asked where her husband was she said, ' He went out last night with the dog, came back roaring drunk and he's been drunk ever since and he's incapable of producing a meal, or waiting table, so I'm doing my best with this little Italian.' So I went upstairs and the guests and the rest of the party arrived and after about half an hour of steady drinking, the chairman said to me, 'Are we going to get any lunch?' I said, 'Well, I'm sorry sir, but the butler's got 'flu'. He said, 'Oh, I'm very sorry, do tell him how sorry I am, I do hope he gets well soon.' I said 'so do I', and eventually we sat down to lunch and I don't think anybody quite realised what had happened.

There's another story about Lees House and this time it concerns some Japanese. At the particular time in question Ivan Knops who was technical sales manager was negotiating for the sale of several copperplate printing machines to Japan. The Japanese with whom he was doing business were in London and he asked Gerry Norman whether he might take them to Lees House where they had discovered there was a billiard table. So after a few drinks downstairs they proceeded up to the billiard room on the first floor and I may say that the table, to which I have already referred, was an extremely fine one and was used a considerable amount by the chairman, the various members of the Board and visitors. And to Ivan Knops' horror he discovered after it was too late that none of the Japanese had played billiards before. The result was that when the session was over, the table was a mass of tears, rips and cuts.

The next morning, as I was responsible for the running of the place, Ivan rang me up and asked me how much a new billiard cloth cost. I think I told him it was something like £150, including the fitting, and he said 'Well, I think you're going to have to get a new one', and told me what had happened. 'However,' he said, 'we have now clinched a deal for selling these machines to Japan, our profit on the sale will be enough to cover several hundred billiards cloths.'

Staff at Lees House consisted usually of a married couple, he acting as a butler and valet, and she as housekeeper/cook. There were also several daily housemaids and semi-permanent parlour maids/waitresses. Temporary waiters or waitresses were taken on for big parties.

The original dining room table was rectangular and would seat 24 but in 1953 when Gerry Norman became managing director a round table to seat 14 was purchased in Brussels. It was felt that conversation around this type of table was much more beneficial and easier than that which took place with a long rectangular table.

Lees House was used constantly for entertaining purposes and also as a guest house for visitors from abroad and also for directors spending a night in London. In 1971 however, the rising costs became prohibitive, whilst the increase in London traffic made the journeys from De La Rue House, Regent Street at lunchtime exceedingly time-consuming. So in 1971 the Board took the decision, regrettable to some, to close the establishment, dispose of the contents, and sell the lease.

This eventually took place, the lease with some 30 years to run fetched £105,000 whilst an auction of the bulk of the contents realised about £15,000. One wonders what different figures would have been reached if the 1971 decision had been delayed.

RUNNING ON A SHOESTRING

These were Gerry Norman's memories of the immediate post-war situation at De La Rue:

> I returned to this country in June 1946 and went to see Bernard Westall who was then at 10a Upper Brook Street, alternating between there and the Dorchester.
>
> I had lunch with Cyril Ashton and Bernard Westall and I said to him I didn't really think that I'd be any good for business use after the kind of job I'd been doing and I really needed to think about what I'd like to do. I had the luxury of a tiny ex-gratia award from the service which gave me time to think.
>
> Westall's reaction was, 'By gum there isn't time to think. You don't realise how serious your business is. We have been over-stretching the few good people we've got, and we have an enormous job on our hands at the moment, and I must have everybody that I can get hold of, and I certainly want you.' And, being very young and still wet behind the ears in many ways I caved in. The consideration time was cut down to a very short period.
>
> I was sent to Bunhill Row where I was to work under Ernest Gough, who was then the general manager of the security and banknote side of the business. There I worked alongside people like Ivan Knops, Frank Richardson and Karol Chybinski.
>
> Everything was crisis management, because the piece of string was very short. It was still run by Bernard Westall. It was growing bigger but all the major decisions were taken by him. He used to arrive at the factory most mornings when he was in the country at 9.00am or earlier and he'd be through and out of the factory and back in his office by 10.00. That grew less frequent; he devolved more of the running of the works to Ernest Gough and then the traffic was the other way. When any major

decisions had to be taken, Gough had to go to Brook Street and soon I found myself doing the same thing.

Alan Houseman [a key De La Rue executive in the immediate post-war years] was of course a major figure on the scene at that time and he too was constantly involved on the commercial side. But it was a very difficult thing for Ernest Gough to manage; his production facilities were in Leeds, under contract to Dublin, under contract to Wass Pritchards. We didn't have a factory, except the little bit of Preliminaries and stuff that we were doing in Bunhill Row. And the Anchor Works I think was still going – a small production from that. But it was very dispersed, difficult to manage. Investment had been what was necessary. They'd bought these old hand-fed machines to meet the tiniest demand in the war and all the rest of it. But there had not been any real investment as we would look at it today. In fact, as you know, although a lot of money was put into Leeds, the Gateshead move didn't take place until the 1960s. So there was a whole period of running the thing on a shoestring, but you know, quite successfully.

Ernest Gough made me Assistant Works Manager after a short time, which really meant that I ran errands for him between all the disparate little bits of activity – Stoke Newington, Barratts Grove and all those funny places. We had it all over the place. And demand was fluctuating quite strongly.

The Chairman's statement at the 1946 AGM is most interesting in that it states, at least as far as public consumption was concerned, how De La Rue was emerging from the worst war the world had ever experienced. The meeting was delayed until 18 September 1946, partly because the ever-active Bernard Westall felt the need to visit two very important customers, Brazil and China. This is what he had to say about De La Rue's various businesses:

De La Rue Stationers
Turning to the subsidiary companies, De La Rue Stationers Limited again had a satisfactory year and the profits were substantially greater than for the previous year. We were again handicapped by the restriction on raw materials for the production of playing cards, and the shortage of labour restricted our output of Onoto pens. Although our paper allocation will not allow us to fulfil the demands made upon us for the current year, our output for both playing cards and pens is likely to show a further increase for the year ending next March.

De La Rue Plastics
For De La Rue Plastics Ltd, the past year has been one of reconversion from war-time to peace-time operations. During the war the plant was almost wholly engaged on the production of munitions.

De La Rue Insulation
In the latter half of the past financial year we decided to put into force our plans for the expansion of De La Rue Insulation Limited. A factory is being built at Tynemouth

> which will house not only the existing laminated plant at Walthamstow but the considerable new plant which is now being installed as well as the plant for the manufacture of Traffolyte, which we acquired from Metropolitan-Vickers [see below]. We have also entered into an arrangement with Formica Corporation of America for the manufacture of decorative boards. There is a very considerable demand for this material and when our new plant is in full production, which will not be before the end of the financial year, we may confidently look forward to a very considerable turnover in this new factory. The Managing Director of this Company, Mr J. Eerdmans, has a skilled and enthusiastic staff, and we are hopeful that De La Rue Insulation will in time become a valuable property.

At the end of 1946 and into January 1947, Britain suffered from appalling weather. It was probably the worst winter in the whole of the 20th century. The country was already suffering from fuel and food shortages after the war, and the heavy snow and ice brought many parts of the country to a standstill. Furthermore, the atrocious weather continued throughout February and into March. Industry, including De La Rue, was badly affected.

In the middle of this meteorological disaster Bernard Westall remained as bullish as ever, telling shareholders at an Extraordinary General Meeting in early February 1947:

> During the past 15 years the considerable expansion that has taken place in the De La Rue organisation has been carried out almost wholly out of its own resources. This process is no longer possible, nor, indeed desirable. During the war years, when our Bunhill Row factories were destroyed and our plastics business was engaged almost completely on Government orders, plans were even then prepared for a big expansion, such as has now been brought about. A successful business undertaking cannot remain static. An old-established house can continue for a few years on its own momentum, but without energetic expansion it will then begin to run downhill as did the De La Rue Company in the twenties. In preparing our plans, therefore, we took the view that, whatever difficulties the post-war years might bring, our scheme of expansion should be bold and not tentative, that it should be sweeping and not piecemeal. The first stage was accomplished in the war by transferring to subsidiary companies certain branches of the old company's business. This operation was essential for the proper development of the various activities in which we had decided to engage. The next thing that we had to do was to decide which of our various activities offered the best field for expansion and development.
>
> After a thorough review of the situation we arrived at the conclusion that the laminated section of our plastics business and the manufacture of gas appliances held out the best chances for speedy expansion. The security printing business, of its nature, cannot be developed beyond a certain point. Indeed, I think we may regard the expansion and development of the parent company as having already taken place. Although practically the whole of our plant was destroyed at the end of 1940, all of it has now been replaced and even increased. But any considerable expansion of

> business had to be sought in other directions. Naturally our first thought was of our plastics business. Some time before the war we had developed at Walthamstow a process of manufacture of laminated boards for electrical purposes, and by the end of 1939 we were producing this material on a small scale. Furthermore, our research department had been studying the manufacture of laminated decorative board for constructional purposes. This type of material was being manufactured by the Formica Corporation of Cincinnati, United States, and by Metropolitan Vickers under the trade name of Traffolyte. We decided then that this was a suitable field for our activities.
>
> **De La Rue Insulation Limited**
> A subsidiary was formed, called De La Rue Insulation Limited, and Mr J. Eerdmans was appointed its managing director. To this company was transferred the laminated section, while the moulding business continued to be carried on by De La Rue Plastics Limited. During the war a site was purchased at Tynemouth, and immediately on the termination of hostilities a factory was built there to house various departments of manufacture which had been selected. At the time these decisions were arrived at we felt that the building up of the business of manufacturing decorative boards under our own steam, as it were, would be a slow process, and consequently negotiations were opened up with Metropolitan Vickers on the one hand, and the Formica Corporation on the other. As a result we purchased the Traffolyte undertaking from the former, and from the latter we acquired the manufacturing rights of the Formica products for the British Empire and certain other territories. The plant and machinery required for the making of these materials on the large scale we had envisaged was ordered, and its installation has now been completed; in the course of the next few weeks production at the Tynemouth factory will commence

At the same time as this expansion was planned, De La Rue decided to sell its moulded plastics business, and did so to National Products Limited. Westall reported to the Board on 5 March 1947 that the bank loans stood at £950,000 (nearly £30 million today), but said that the agreement for the sale of the plastics business would be signed the following week, and that the purchase money amounting to over £900,000 should be received shortly afterwards.

Reporting to shareholders at the Dorchester Hotel in August 1947 (needless to say, after the cold winter, the summer of 1947 was one of the hottest on record), Westall said:

> The diminution in the profits of the Parent Company was due in considerable measure to the effect of the power cut on our output last winter – and I may mention in passing that during the stoppage of work our staff and employees were paid in full – and to some extent to the consequent shortage of materials.

In spite of these problems, Westall was able to be optimistic about the current year:

> Since the close of the year [31 March] the output of the factories increased, and at the present time all of them are working to capacity ... Further additions have been made to the plant during the year, and the Rangoon factory is now being re-equipped and production will commence in three or four months' time.

Stationery products and playing cards were proceeding satisfactorily, though the continuous supply of raw materials was a concern. De La Rue Gas Development was an even greater concern. The harsh weather conditions had brought great difficulties for the company, and these were exacerbated by the imposition of a purchase tax at no less than 66.66 per cent on gas water-heating appliances. As Westall said, this was not only 'unexpected but inexplicable. Heating by gas is the most economical method of producing hot water from the point of view of coal utilisation.'

And there, of course, Westall had hit the nail on the head. The Labour government, voted into power (to the surprise of many) in the 1945 general election, had just nationalised the coal industry and did not want to encourage the use of appliances that *reduced* the consumption of coal.

At the 1948 AGM, Westall was almost apoplectic about the imposition of the tax:

> The imposition of the purchase tax in April of last year had a most deleterious effect on the Gas Development Company. We engaged in this enterprise to broaden the basis of the Company's activities, and we did so with the full encouragement and support of the Government. The Minister of Supply, on the occasion of the opening of our Gateshead Factory, used the following words: 'I have already had occasion to congratulate the Company for their enterprise and initiative on the score that the existence and operation of this factory will do the Company good, it will do the workers and the other local inhabitants good, and lastly it will be for the good of the country.' On the same occasion the Minister also said, 'The product which you are immediately producing, the gas heater, is intended not merely for the mansions of the rich but for the homes of even the poorest class of society.'
>
> In view of these statements by a responsible Minister of the Crown, nobody, I think, could have foreseen that the Chancellor of the Exchequer would have selected these gas water heating appliances for the imposition of a purchase tax so crushing as to make it impossible for people of moderate means, to purchase a gas appliance which is the most economic from every point of view for the heating of water. In April last the Chancellor increased this crushing tax to 100%, so that the demand for gas water heaters completely dried up. Now, two and a half months later he has reduced the tax to 66-2/3rds. But taxation at this level puts the heater beyond the range of the lower income group which it was designed to serve. As a consequence, we had drastically to reduce our programme and to discharge a large proportion of the staff who had been trained for this particular work.

In spite of these problems in the Gas Development company, results to March 1948 were very satisfactory, with profits rising from £477,941 to £528,815, the bulk of them coming from the main activity of security printing.

ALL OVER THE WORLD

By 1948 De La Rue were supplying security printing in one form or another – banknotes, stamps or any other documents with a monetary value – to no fewer than 60 countries around the world.

America
- Bermuda
- British Honduras
- West Indies
- British Guiana
- Colombia
- Ecuador
- Brazil
- Paraguay
- Uruguay
- Falkland Islands

Europe
- Scotland
- Iceland
- Holland
- Gibraltar
- Malta
- Greece
- Cyprus

Africa
- Gambia
- Sierra Leone
- Gold Coast
- Nigeria
- Sudan
- East Africa
- Belgian Congo
- Ascension Island
- St Helena
- Angola
- Bechuanaland
- Basutoland
- Swaziland

Africa (continued)
- Nyasaland
- Zanzibar
- Mauritius
- Seychelles Islands
- Somaliland
- Northern Rhodesia
- Uganda

Asia
- Aden
- Transjordan
- Palestine
- Iraq
- Turkey
- Pakistan (including Bahawalpur)
- Jaipur
- Gondal
- Sikkim
- Ceylon
- China
- Burma
- Siam
- Indo-China
- Hong Kong
- Malaya
- Brunei
- Dutch East Indies

Australasia
- Solomon Islands
- Gilbert and Ellice Islands
- Fiji Islands
- New Zealand
- Tonga Islands

Westall spoke at some length at the AGM at the Dorchester Hotel on 30 June about the progress of De La Rue Insulation, saying:

> Last year I informed you that De La Rue Insulation Ltd (your Plastics Company), would be ready for full scale production in September. The principal productions of this Company by the way are di-electric laminated boards for insulation under the trade name 'DELARON' and Formica Boards for decorative purposes. As far as the removal and installation of the plant was concerned, this promise was fulfilled, but the formal opening of our Tynemouth factory coincided with a period of acute shortage of raw materials. This shortage has now, except for certain specialised materials, been overcome. Furthermore, all the labour at Tynemouth had to be trained for the work and this took longer than we had anticipated. Due to these factors we were unable to commence the manufacture of Formica Boards until the end of the year. The various technical difficulties that we encountered have one by one been surmounted and the work now being turned out is of a high standard of quality.
>
> The immediate future of this Company now depends to a very considerable extent on the ability of our foreign customers to obtain import licences for the purchase of our material.

One problem was beginning to surface in 1948, and this entry in the Board minutes of 31 March 1948 may have been a warning:

> The Chairman reported that there was a balance of £4,755 on Current Account and that the Bank Loan now stood at £740,000. Of the £923,855 invoiced to China, £664,758 was now overdue, and it would therefore be necessary to borrow further amounts in order to clear outstanding Bought Ledger Accounts and to meet immediate requirements. The Chairman discussed the position with regard to China and outlined the action he was proposing to take in order to expedite the receipt of future payments.

Mao Zedong had formed his communist Red Army in 1935, but its planned takeover of the government of China was postponed by the Sino-Japanese War of 1937 to 1945. However, in 1949 the People's Liberation Army drove the government out of mainland China into Taiwan and set up the People's Republic of China.

De La Rue lost one of its largest customers, though fortunately new ones were secured. During 1949 a significant contract was signed with the government of the newly formed Pakistan. De La Rue would print all of the country's financial document requirements until the new state printing works (in which De La Rue had taken a 40 per cent stake) came on stream, probably in 1951. Other important orders had been secured elsewhere, including the Philippines.

By the end of 1949 De La Rue's financial position was beginning to give cause for concern, as we can see from the Board minutes of 4 November:

> The Chairman gave a resumé of the Company's financial position and stated that the bank overdraft now stood at £735,000 and that apart from the sum of £300,000 due on the Security Printing side there was not a great amount outstanding in the way of debtors. Of the reserve of £500,000 for Income Tax £300,000 would become payable in January. Mr Eerdmans stated that the Industrial Divisions required a net amount of £100,000 in cash to be able to carry on until the end of the financial year on 1 April 1950. He pointed out that £80,000 was required for the closing down of the Gateshead Factory and £50,000 for the same purpose elsewhere.

However, the storm seemed to pass, and by the middle of 1951 the Directors' Report in the Annual Report stated that:

> Due to the general improvement in the trading results of the Industrial side of your business the need for fresh capital is diminishing, and your Directors have postponed indefinitely consideration of raising fresh capital.

1951 was an important year for De La Rue in the sense that Arthur 'Gerry' Norman, later to be Managing Director and Chairman, became a Director; and Peter Orchard, also destined to become Managing Director and Chairman, joined the company as a graduate trainee.

In 1949 Britain devalued, taking the pound down from $4 to $2.80. As the pound was what was known as a reserve currency in those days, this was a more significant – some would say humiliating – event than later devaluations. Although it did have an inflationary impact because imports, including much of Britain's food, became more expensive, and the Korean War of 1950–53 added to the inflationary impact by causing a rise in the cost of many commodities, the overall impact was beneficial in that it helped increase export sales. The effects on De La Rue balanced each other out, and it scarcely rated a mention in any of the public utterances from the company. In his annual report in September 1950, Westall was his usual confident self, saying:

> During the course of the year new contracts were obtained for the security printing division. It should be borne in mind, however, that the contract for the printing of all documents of monetary value for the Dominion of Pakistan will be transferred gradually to the Pakistan Security Printing Corporation in Karachi, in which the company holds a 40 per cent interest. This will leave a gap, to fill which big efforts are being made with encouraging results.
>
> **Expansion of Industrial Sections**
>
> As long ago as 1943 your directors foresaw the possibility of a contraction in the security printing division, and so, with a view to meeting such a situation, they decided on a policy of expansion of the industrial section of the business. The scale of expansion of the plastic and gas divisions was such that it was inevitable that a considerable passage of time should elapse before these large undertakings could

reach a profit-earning basis. This was increased, in part by the time necessary to train labour required, in part by the quality of the raw materials available and in part – as far as the gas division is concerned – by unexpected heavy taxation. Thus, it is only this year that I am able for the first time to inform the stockholders that a substantial proportion of the profit for the year has derived from the industrial divisions. I am of the opinion that during the current year the major part of the profits will derive from this side of the company's interest.

And he was quite bullish about Formica and Delaron, the laminated plastics products:

In the plastics division sales were double those of the previous year ... we have good reason for confidence in the results of the current financial year.

Finally, at long last, there seemed to be light at the end of the Gas Division tunnel. He told shareholders:

The new gas cookers which we have designed have met with an excellent reception and the output of the factories has been sold for a long time ahead.

CHANGE AT THE TOP AND A NEW STYLE

1952 was a dramatic year in the history of De La Rue. This was how Gerry Norman recalled this period:

1952 was the fateful year we made a loss and the Company was reorganised.

Things were going wrong in 1950/51, none of the Industrial Division (plastics and gas development) and playing cards were earning their corn and the Security business was carrying it all on its back. Great worries were being voiced by people like Alan Houseman, Ernest Gough and myself about the direction in which the Company was going.

I first became director in May 1951 and then I was pushed off the Board at the end of the year.

It was really in a tizzy. There were a lot of politics going on but finally, and as always, Westall grasped the nettle, fired Eerdmans and appointed me as the managing director, with responsibility for the whole ball of wax, reporting to him, which was a pretty subtle thing. From that moment I really moved out of the banknote side and concentrated on trying to find out what one should do with the plastics and gas and all these things, as general manager of the Industrial Division.

So with the departure of Eerdmans and the disintegration of the management of the plastics side, which was now quite big, one of the first things I had to do was to find somebody to run the Plastics Division and that was when Gerard Riddick was appointed general manager at the age of 35 in 1954. He became director of the Company in 1956. He took a firm grip of the business and tried to get it right.

On the Potterton side, we had a headless business. And Ernest Brooks was discovered, by me I think, to be the best guy we could put into that; Poyser was the first man, but he was unsatisfactory and one couldn't rely on what he was telling you.

But despite the problems the Company had got into, having passed its dividend in 1952/3, we were not exactly passive or failing to expand.

The French Formica business, in Quillan, started in 1954. Australia was 1958, Spain was 1956, then Brazil and Colombia (Security), these all came up. Formica in New Zealand was one of the later ones, in the 1960s, but there was a lot in terms of expansion, mainly on the plastics side. And the [Potterton] foundry at Warwick was expanding.

But essential to all of this was the banknote business continuing to provide the funds to enable us to do it; I relied on the tolerance of my colleagues in that business as I tried to get things straight or straighter. There were periods when plastics came in with some good profits; occasionally Potterton did, but not consistently.

Central to this Formica expansion were the negotiations that we had with the Formica Corporation, where we took the view that our lease of the trade mark was an insufficiently strong base on which to proceed with investment in all these countries we've just mentioned. This led to a rather important phase in which eventually we got an agreement under which the trade mark was owned by De La Rue in certain areas of the world, more or less everywhere except North and South America and the Pacific. But the quid pro quo of course was that the Americans took a 40% shareholding in Formica International. [...] Overall it led to a rapid expansion into the Formica business.

Evidently we must have felt sufficiently confident and strong to continue with diversification, because along came De La Rue Bull [see below], and we were building the Gateshead factory which was quite a big investment. We were just about making a deal to take over the Waterlow security business and we were establishing Security Express with Wells Fargo [see below], all around 1959–62. Colombia, Mexico, Brazil were all during this period. Formica Germany too. Then Frigistors and Nigeria 1964 were another very important milestone.

In 1954 the decision was taken to start negotiations with Sidney Flavell to dispose of the Potterton business. Potterton was proving to be a very up and down business and a lot of big companies were moving into gas, which was really the original attraction of Potterton. Margins were being squeezed, the investment load on the Company was going to be a big one and we did have talks with our neighbours Flavell to see whether the two businesses could be put together. I don't think De La Rue at the time ever had any intention of taking over Flavell. It was more trying to spread the risk, even to the point that if we got a reasonable price for Potterton's to get out of it. So there was almost the first de-diversification coming into the business; but it fell away because of Flavell's inability to raise the money.

Pens and Playing Cards

After the Potterton negotiation with Flavell the decision was taken to cease trying to revive the Onoto pen.

We had thought we might get back into the market with this trade mark which had not been supported by advertising all through the growth of the security business. There hadn't been the time or the people to merchandise this properly; we made an effort to introduce new models and revive marketing but it was a failure and we closed the business down in 1957.

By that time we really had very little left of the original stationers business and our play card activity, although we were doing marketing, was on the basis of a joint manufacturing agreement with Waddington in the Amalgamated Playing Card Company. But eventually in 1967 after much heart-searching, because this had been almost the starting point of Thomas De La Rue's success in the 19th century, we decided we would let Waddington buy our playing card interest, on the good reasoning that De La Rue was not in the leisure market whereas Waddington was.

In a sense, it was the behaviour of Dutchman Joe Eerdmans that brought the matter of the top management crisis to a head in 1952. This was how Company Secretary Arthur Morrish explained it:

Eerdmans left Holland just before the Germans invaded and he was in England throughout the rest of the war. As you say, he had his own plastics business at Sutton, Hammans Industries. Very tough, he was ambitious and an immensely strong character. He was a large man too and he bullied. And the big showdown was one of the first crises I had had as Secretary. The Company's Articles have an extremely useful clause which says that a Director may be removed from the Board with the consent of all other members of the Board, it doesn't say in writing.

Joe Eerdmans was a very abrasive, ambitious, tough, large in every way character. He was very anxious to eventually get the Chair, and to start with he wanted to be Managing Director. Some of his methods were a little bit suspect and one I remember in particular concerned Graham Martin Turner who was looking after various factories of the Plastic Division, including the main one at Tynemouth. For some reason or other Bernard Westall was away and so was Joe Eerdmans and some unfortunate, fairly minor, incident happened at the Formica factory. I think it was to do with labour relations, and when Eerdmans came back he was so angry that he gave Martin Turner the sack on the spot.

Now Martin Turner was a protégé of Bernard Westall; he had got him into the Company and all hell was let loose and we had to wait until Westall came back. He was absolutely livid and one morning he sent for me and asked me to bring a copy of Joe Eerdmans' service agreement, and I thought 'Hello, what's up?'. And I went into his office, he looked at it, and he said: 'Right, he gets this, he gets that, okay, call a Board meeting for tomorrow.' So I did and at that meeting, to cut a very long story short, Eerdmans was told that all the members of the Board had agreed that he should be removed from his job and from the Board, in other words as Managing Director of the Plastics Division and from the Board itself. He collapsed at that.

The interesting thing is that we had this article which didn't say that members of the Board had to give their approval in writing. So I was able to get a cable from Lord

> Killearn who was abroad at the time which made up all the members of the Board giving their consent, otherwise we couldn't have done it. It was quite a sensation, and I hadn't been in the Company very long.
>
> The other interesting part of the story happened after Eerdmans left.
>
> The end of the year was September in those days, I think, and the accounts were available sometime after Eerdmans' departure. We made a great loss and passed our dividends which caused an awful lot of comment in the City. One of the comments was: 'It looks as if it could be tied up to Eerdmans' sacking.' And he set out to take us to court. Nobody in the Company ever mentioned that, but it was a sort of logical thought I suppose.
>
> He eventually settled for £18,000 [nearly £500,000 in today's money], but it was a bloody sight less than he asked for. And the man who negotiated this was Eric Davies. In fact that was the absolute minimum; he asked for £50,000, something like that. I had to go and see his accountants, Stoy Hayward, to talk about various bits of his service agreement.

And this was how Morrish went on to describe the eventual result in December 1952:

> Bernard Westall reports that Gerry Norman and Ernest Gough have approached him to resign from the Managing Directorship. After careful consideration, Westall has decided to give way to a younger man at the end of this month. He has held the job for 21 years.
>
> Eric Davies protests strongly at the way Norman and Gough have handled this – grave lack of judgement. Norman explains that it was done in good faith. Westall agrees to remain as Chairman, but Norman has won. Further discussion is deferred to another meeting next week.
>
> At this meeting Westall says the Board has three options: (i) Gough MD, (ii) Gough/Norman Joint MDs, (iii) Norman MD. Killearn and Banks go away to talk; eventually Norman is chosen.
>
> Gough stands down as Assistant MD. In due course he is appointed Managing Director of the Pakistan Security Printing Corporation.

All that left De La Rue with very few executive directors, in fact only two: Norman himself and Alan Houseman, who had been spending most of the previous few years in the Far East. Norman felt obliged to call on the non-executive directors to help. Westall was asked to visit key customers, Sir Donald Banks was asked to take a close interest in recruitment and welfare, and Lord Killearn to increase networking with his overseas and diplomatic contacts. To add to the pressure, the Westminster Bank, apparently disturbed by the company's recent poor results, requested a debenture to secure the company's overdraft and also for a seat on the Board. De La Rue did not accede to either request.

Norman departed from Westall's rather cavalier style and instituted a monthly report to the Board. These reports would prove to be extremely comprehensive, covering all aspects of the company's business and giving Board members, for the first time, a real insight into what was happening.

Furthermore, a Personnel Committee was set up under the chairmanship of Sir Donald Banks. Norman himself and other directors, plus the Company Secretary, were also on this formidable committee whose job it was to implement the Board's decisions on personnel and welfare affairs. It also interviewed candidates for the senior positions in the company.

At the suggestion of Eric Davies, the company solicitor, an outside consultant, Walter Puckey, was asked to investigate the Gas Division. His report was lengthy and highly critical of the management. Following his report, negotiations began to sell the gas company to Sidney Flavell. They proved inconclusive, as we have seen, as Flavell could not raise the necessary funds.

In June 1952 the final dividend was passed and in November the interim was passed.

Gerry Norman had arrived. Things were going to change. Nevertheless, he arranged the setting up of a BUPA scheme (British United Provident Association, a health insurance scheme) for all monthly paid staff members, with subscriptions paid by the company. De La Rue was one of the first companies to have a Group scheme.

What did Bernard Westall, now Chairman, tell his shareholders at the AGM on 29 July 1953 at the rather more modest Winchester House, Old Broad Street?

Profits had collapsed from £649,650 to £161,999 'due entirely to the adverse trading conditions affecting the Industrial side of the business ... On the Security side, business has proceeded in accordance with expectations and a satisfactory profit was recorded, but unfortunately this profit has been largely counterbalanced by losses on the Plastics, Gas Appliance and Stationery businesses.'

While the 'diversification' companies lost money, this was the story on the traditional security printing:

> On the security side of the business our profits were well maintained, and this year, again, there is a satisfactory amount of orders in hand. Since the disappearance of China as a customer, and the decision of Pakistan to make – with our cooperation – their own security documents in Karachi, the effort made to extend our business in other fields has proved very successful. Since the war 19 countries have become customers for bank and currency notes in addition to those who were already purchasing their supplies from the company. This broadening of the basis of the company's security printing business will, I consider, be a reliable source of strength for many years to come.

The most significant event of 1954 was the start of negotiations with a Norwegian gentleman, Holmen, who had invented a counting machine. Agreement was reached for De La Rue to market Holmen's banknote-counting machines, and the company did so for the next 50 years. The first machine was sold in 1957 after test-counting 18 million notes.

At the 1954 AGM, Westall was able to report a much better year. Security printing's profits, though slightly lower, were still satisfactory, and the results from the Plastics Division had improved dramatically. Westall said:

> As stated in the Directors' Report, the Security Printing Division again made a satisfactory though slightly lower profit than that for the preceding year. I do not anticipate that the results of the present year will show any marked change. It is a matter of some satisfaction that the profits of this important section of the Company's interests have been maintained at such a satisfactory level in spite of the loss of so much turnover when China ceased to be a customer.
>
> The main reason for the improvement in the Profit and Loss Account has been the marked increase in the sales of our decorative laminates. These are known by the trade names of 'Formica' and 'Traffolyte'. While export sales had a much better year and, in particular, there was some recovery in our Australasian trade, the main improvement lay in the increase in the Home market. This increased demand has enabled the factory to revert to full-time operation. The use of 'Formica' has expanded very considerably and it is now the recognised material for equipping a modern kitchen. At the same time, it is being increasingly used for canteens, transport services, furniture, shopfittings and for a wide variety of other trades and purposes. The sale of 'Delaron' our industrial and di-electric laminate has steadily improved. While only a quarter of the year has gone by, I think I may hazard the opinion that during this current year a further improvement in the results of the Plastics Division may be expected.

In 1957 De La Rue finally gave up on trying to make a go of the Onoto and other fountain pens. The Strathendry Works in Scotland were closed and the Onoto trademark was sold to an Australian company, Norman Baker and Longhurst. No one could accuse De La Rue of not trying to make a success of this venture, but the truth was that in spite of enormous effort and the expenditure of millions of pounds (in today's money anyway) on advertising, the Pens division had never made a significant contribution to profits. For example, in the 1956 Annual Report, the Chairman had written:

> In the Stationers Division new models of Onoto pens were introduced but the initial cost of publicity, as we anticipated, more than absorbed the gross profits of the additional sales.

1958 brought some significant developments. First, Baring Brothers were appointed the company's registrars and merchant bank. At the same time the parent company's name was changed from Thomas De La Rue and Company to De La Rue Limited. Two subsidiaries – Thomas De La Rue and Company Ltd and Thomas Potterton Ltd – were formed.

Second, in the USA the De La Rue Banknote Company Inc. was registered in conjunction with the Sorg Printing Company Inc. of New York, with De La Rue as the major stockholder. The Sorg Printing Company was a leader in the field of financial, corporate and legal printing in the USA. The new CEO was an American, Perry E. Hudson, currently employed by Sorg. John Shepherd-Barron of De La Rue and J. Sorg Jnr made up the executive committee with Hudson. John Shepherd-Barron had been investigating the market possibilities for De La Rue in North America for a year, and had come to the conclusion that there was a future in the USA for an efficient banknote printer to challenge the existing competition. Because of high labour rates in the USA, most of the production should be carried out in Britain.

Another good reason for basing production in England lay in the difference between the New York Stock Exchange and those of the rest of the world. By a New York Stock Exchange ruling, major corporations listed in New York had to have their securities fully engraved. These securities had an intrinsic value, and the New York Stock Exchange had specified certain high production standards to protect the documents from forgery. This calibre of work was very familiar to De La Rue, who were – apart from currency- and stamp-printing – already printing the World Bank Bonds, the design of which had been officially sanctioned by the New York Stock Exchange in approval of the quality of workmanship.

In addition to definitive stock and bond certificates for listed companies, De La Rue would print inventory stock certificates, as they were called in America. These were a form of bearer certificate issued by companies not listed on the stock exchange and those listed as temporaries. This type of certificate was unknown in Britain. It functioned virtually as a currency note since, if it was lost, it could not be replaced like share certificates in Britain.

Also in 1958, De La Rue signed a five-year contract with the GPO (General Post Office) to print the four UK high-value postage stamps: 2/6, 5 shillings, 10 shillings and £1.

THE WESTALL CLUB

On the personnel front, the Board decided to set up a residential club at Horsted Keynes in Sussex, and made an initial investment of £50,000 (about £1.25 million in today's money).

This club was a converted private house to which were added several bungalettes, the idea being to provide homes for retired work people and members of the staff who were lonely, that is to say, widows or widowers. The Westall Club, as it became known, was run and financed by De La Rue until February 1995, when its assets and management were transferred to the Abbeyfield Trust.

This is what the *De La Rue Journal* said about the new Westall Club:

Good Friends of Horsted Keynes

If you drive out of London, crossing the Thames and heading south through sprawling, anonymous suburbs, taking the Brighton road, you will arrive in Sussex. Turn off the main road and go through Haywards Heath, and then follow the sign post to Horsted Keynes. The narrow lanes will bring you to a village just like hundreds of others in the same county with its church, village green, garages, shops and pubs. If the time is an hour or so before lunch, go into the 'Green Man' and there, if you are from De La Rue, you may find some friends.

Loneliness a stranger

In his speech at the Annual General Meeting in 1958 Mr B.C. Westall said: 'Admirable though it is, the National Health Service does not, and cannot, provide against loneliness.' The Westall Club does. It was formed for people who, having retired from service with the Company and living alone, could spend their retirement in peace and quiet, in the company of old friends, and with the knowledge that they would be well looked after. A Committee was formed to put these ideas into operation.

Mr G.T. Burnett-Brown then conducted a search for premises, and in September 1958 discovered a house, with some 2½ acres of land around it, not far from the Chairman's home. Mr Westall came to view the property the following morning, found it ideal, and gave instructions for it to be purchased at once.

The house, previously a country hotel, is basically nineteenth century, although a part of it dates from 1607. There is an engraved stone to this effect outside the manager's office.

Rooms with character

The first impression you get of the bedrooms is their size. There are nine in all and most of them considerably larger than a good class hotel room. Each is equipped with a modern VANITORY unit. Many of the furnishings were chosen personally by Mrs Westall. In addition to these rooms there is accommodation for guests.

Although all the rooms were originally furnished on similar lines, each is gradually assuming a character of its own, as the occupants move in small personal belongings.

Adjoining the dining room, with its view over part of the Prime Minister's estate, is the sort of kitchen which the modern housewife dreams about. It is large, bright and equipped with every modern amenity. Much of the colour comes from the use of FORMICA plastic for table tops and for cupboard surfaces and doors. Just to keep things in the family, two POTTERTON automatic oil-fired boilers have been installed for heating and the supply of hot water.

Adjoining the main house each 'bungalette' is completely self-contained, with a bed-sitting room, kitchen and a combined bathroom and toilet. The kitchen includes a refrigerator and cooker with FORMICA plastic surfaces to give it a modern touch.

Most of the people at Horsted Keynes, however, spend more time together in common rooms rather than on their own. There are two recreation rooms, a library and a lounge, each equipped with televisions. The lounge has a piano given by Percy Clark, one of the residents.

Help where needed

For most of the residents of the Westall Club, life had an unfamiliar flavour to it at first. By now they have settled down and if you talk with them in the lounge, they will infuse you with their own enthusiasm for the place.

There are few rules. Members can come and go as they please, and even mealtimes can be adapted to requirements if sufficient notice is given.

Conditions of membership are designed to help those most in need. The Westall Club is not a nursing home and each person must be fit and vetted first by the Trustees, Mr Westall, Mr A.G. Norman and Mr Burnett-Brown.

With the coast a little more than half an hour away by bus, nearly everyone has had at least one trip to Brighton or Eastbourne. In addition, Bill O'Keeffe is on hand to take them around the South Downs whenever he has a free moment.

In the village the Women's Institute and the Old People's Institute have opened their doors to Club members. They have all taken advantage of this. Unconsciously each of them is performing a first-class public relations job.

Looking to the future

Talk to any member about life in the Westall Club and he will have a ready word of praise for Bill and Jeanne O'Keeffe. For them as for the others, it was a new departure.

Bill is busy on new projects. A bar equipped with darts and bar billiards has been completed. To create a country club atmosphere, hunting and village green prints are being obtained for the walls.

The good neighbours

The Westall Club is an experiment, possibly the first of its kind in this country. Because its enemy is loneliness, its most striking feature to the outsider is its atmosphere. There is a feeling of warmth here that owes its unique flavour to the fact many of its members have worked together. When we went down to Horsted Keynes virtually everybody wanted to make sure that we emphasised one particular point – that they had the feeling of belonging to a family.

MORE DIVERSIFICATION

In the mainstream business, in 1958 another diversification ball was set rolling when the first talks were held with Compagnie des Machines Bull of Paris, a French company manufacturing and selling computers.

In July of the following year a company was formed, owned 50 per cent by De La Rue and 50 per cent by Machines Bull, to market in the British Commonwealth the full range of Bull automatic data-processing equipment.

Later in 1959 De La Rue diversified further when a new company, Security Express Limited, was set up after John Shepherd-Barron had consulted closely with Wells Fargo in the USA. This is what the *De La Rue Journal* had to say about it:

Security Express

The increase in violent crime in this country has created great alarm, and the police have expressed their concern. Robbery figures for 1959 showed an increase of 20% over those of the previous year. Almost weekly, newspapers have featured many stories of attacks on people carrying money, collecting payrolls or depositing takings.

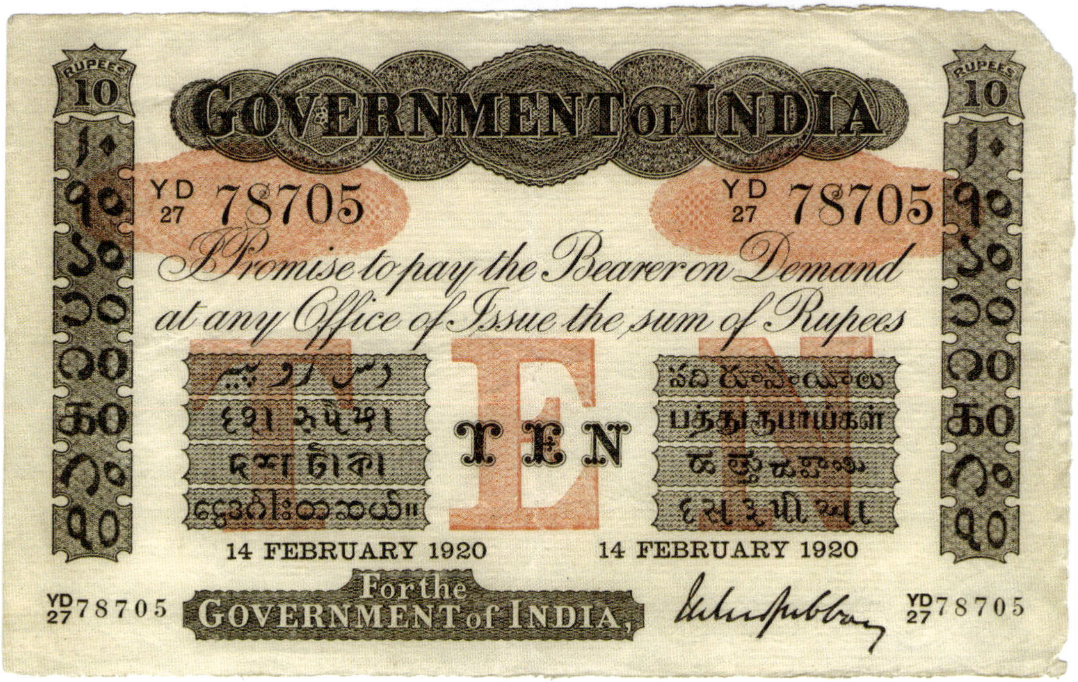

2.1 *A banknote printed by De La Rue for the government of India in 1920.*

2.2 *An engraving for a note to be printed by De La Rue for the Chinese government in the 1930s.*

2.3 Sidney Lamert and Bernard Westall, concerned about the difficult trading conditions of the inter-war years.

2.4 (below) *Bernard Westall explaining De La Rue products to HM King George VI and HM Queen Elizabeth at the British Industries Fair in 1937.*

2.5 The De La Rue works at Bunhill Row in 1938.

2.6 The main entrance at Bunhill Row offices and works in 1938.

2.7 Dufferin Works at Bunhill Row, 1938.

2.8 Sheet examination, Bunhill Row, 1938.

2.9, 2.10 *The Bunhill Row works after the bombing on the night of Sunday 29 December 1940.*

2.11 De La Rue's factory in Rangoon, skilfully brought into full production by Frank Richardson.

2.12 Gerry Norman, Bernard Westall and Sir Donald Banks lead the pirates on a De La Rue company outing on the Thames in the late 1940s.

2.13 Bernard Westall, the man who took De La Rue from the verge of bankruptcy to a formidable international company.

2.14 Lees House, where the De La Rue directors entertained many important overseas clients in the years after the Second World War.

2.15 10a Upper Brook Street in Mayfair, London – De La Rue's prestigious offices in the 1950s.

2.16 Alan Houseman, a key figure in building up De La Rue's business overseas in the years after the Second World War.

2.17 (above) *Den Moore, a key figure in the management of De La Rue from the 1950s to the 1980s. His responsibilities included running Formica for a number of years.*

2.18 (above, right) *David Hosie, another long-serving executive of De La Rue, tragically injured in a car accident in South America.*

2.19 Denis Paravicini, another important sales executive for De La Rue from the 1950s to the 1980s who also managed the company's relations with the Royal Mint.

2.20 Three important De La Rue characters (from left to right): Peter Orchard, CEO and eventually Chairman; Rino Giori, who made a lucrative arrangement with the company to promote together his banknote printing machines; and Ivan Knops, Managing Director of De La Rue Engineering Ltd.

2.21 At the beginning of the 1960s De La Rue set up Thomas De La Rue de Colombia and Gregorio Bautista became General Manager.
Left to right: Gregorio Bautista, Juvenal Villa, President of the Board, and Gerry Norman.

2.22 Bernard Westall with the Prime Minister of Thailand in 1955.

2.23 Bernard Westall with Mumtaz Hassan, the Governor of the State Bank of Pakistan, in 1962.

2.24 The federal government of Nigeria signing a contract with Thomas De La Rue International for the formation of a company to undertake security printing in Nigeria in May 1963.

2.25 Gerry Norman and Bernard Westall with the De La Rue cricket team, an important part of the company's sporting activities over many years.

2.26 On 7 March 1963, Lord Hailsham, Conservative leader in the House of Lords, laid the foundation stone of a new banknote factory for Thomas De La Rue on the Team Valley Trading Estate near Newcastle upon Tyne. With him are Peter Orchard and Gerry Norman.

2.27 The new factory opened in autumn 1964.

2.28 Quality control in the new factory.

2.29 Gerry Norman with Dr Hernando Villa, Colombian Minister of Finance, in March 1961, shortly after De La Rue had formed their company in Colombia with the Bautista family.

2.30 Gerry Norman showing HM Queen Elizabeth some archives when she visited De La Rue's R and D operation in Maidenhead in March 1965.

Thomas De La Rue & Co. Ltd has always had an intense and specialised interest in all forms of security, and it was to see whether we could usefully develop a new security service that Mr J.A. Shepherd-Barron conducted a two month's survey in the United States and the United Kingdom. In the former, since the days of prohibition when gangsterism was rife, Companies anxious to preserve moneys or valuables from theft have had the protection of armoured car delivery services – a welcome safeguard which by its expansion into a very important and flourishing contemporary business has proved its value.

Choosing the team

If such a company capable of offering guaranteed security to anyone concerned when handling money were to be started in this country, what sort of man would one choose as its head? There was, of course, one man pre-eminent in crime prevention and security techniques; a man with fifty years of experience of fighting for law and order, who introduced one of the first forensic laboratories, police boxes and the radio car control system and reached the pinnacle of his career when he became Director General of the MI5. We, therefore, approached Sir Percy Sillitoe, sketched to him the plans we are making and waited for his reactions. He found the idea stimulating and happily consented to become Chairman and Managing Director of a new member of the De La Rue Group.

The new company, Security Express Limited, was incorporated in October 1959 with an authorised capital of £80,000. Its board: Sir Percy Sillitoe, K.B.E., D.I. (Chairman and Managing Director), A.W. Sillitoe (General Manager), J.A. Shepherd-Barron, C. Hans, H.L. Clark, B.C. Wren (alternate) and C.J. Holgate (alternate).

Mr J.M. Bertin was appointed Sales Manager. Led by Superintendent Glyn Jones, the first Operations Controller, who has made a special study of American methods, all the operational members of Security Express Limited are top grade retired police officers.

The service and methods

Security Express Limited will transport, collect or deliver valuables between two locations in complete and absolute safety. The vehicles are specially designed to resist violent attempts at robbery. They will be radio controlled and contain many safety and alarm devices, which for obvious reasons are confidential to the Company and its staff.

In operation it is simple. If you, for instance, use it to carry your payroll by arrangement between you, your Bank and Security Express, the security vehicle will pick up the money from the Bank and deliver it to the cashier at exactly the time required. The service is responsible for the money the moment it takes charge of it, that is both during handling and transit. Apart from the protective measures we have already outlined the money is also fully insured by comprehensive insurance policies. In this way Security Express relieve customer firms of the responsibility of sending staff on what has become a hazardous duty and it will save the cost of employees' time, of transport and of insurance against theft of cash in transit. Moreover the

> deliveries are guaranteed to arrive at the time specified whatever the location and whatever the sum of money or valuable concerned. To begin with there is a payroll delivery service and a daily deposit service which will soon be expanding to cover an envelope filling service and even a complete paymaster service so that not only will the payroll be collected but the envelopes filled and delivered into the hands of the customer companies' staff.
>
> The daily deposit service caters for the needs of businesses such as cafés, restaurants, shops, public houses, who wish to make deposits after normal banking hours. For such customers the money is kept in the strong rooms of Security Express Limited until the banks open next day.

De La Rue set up Security Express Ltd in 1960, taking a 51 per cent interest, while Wells Fargo of the USA took the other 49 per cent. Two or three contracts were quickly secured, and the Chairman told shareholders that 'within two or three years we shall have a network of services linking all the big cities in the UK'.

The beginning of the new decade of the 1960s was a period of worldwide expansion for the Group, as is shown by this memo from Roger Sawtell to Leslie Newman in May 1962.

> **Formica**
>
> 1960 The Formica (NZ) Limited factory at Papakura, near Auckland was opened.
>
> 1962 A Belgian subsidiary of Formica International Limited, Formica Belgium Société Anonyme, was formed in conjunction with S.A. Formica of Paris.
> A Spanish subsidiary of Formica International Limited, Formica Española Sociedad Anónima, was formed in conjunction with their former licensee in Spain.
>
> **Thomas De La Rue International**
>
> 1960 Formation of Thomas De La Rue S.A. de Colombia, followed by the purchase of a factory site in Bogota.
>
> 1960 Formation of Compania Mexicana Impresca de Valores, followed by the modernisation of an existing factory in Mexico City.
>
> 1961 Contract signed with the Bank of Japan for the purchase of 15 De La Rue Automatic Rotary Direct Plate Presses.
>
> 1962 Formation on 1st April of Thomas De La Rue International Limited as part of the re-organisation of the T.D.L.R. Group of Companies.

In the UK, Thomas Potterton Ltd bought the Paragon (Leeds) Sheet Metal Company, manufacturers of warm-air heaters, and De La Rue Instruments was formed as a subsidiary of Thomas De La Rue to run the banknote-counting machines side of the business.

At the same time, as this article from the *Financial Times* showed, De La Rue's basic business of printing banknotes and selling them round the world continued to flourish:

Britain's master money makers

These printers of paper currency for the world are constantly engaged in a battle of wits with counterfeiters and other people who have designs on their product.

On the outskirts of Leeds stands a large brick building that is guarded as tightly as any nuclear installation.

Nobody, no package, gets into or out of the place without careful examination. Security men are everywhere. Periodically, lorries that look like nondescript commercial vehicles roll out through the gates. No armour plating and armed guards are to be seen on the lorries. But each one is rarely out of the sight of the equally inconspicuous police cars patrolling its route.

The lorries are loaded with heavy metal-lined crates whose destination may be Berne, Aqaba, Caracas, Bangkok. In every box is a fortune, often a huge one – perhaps in Swiss francs, Jordanian dinars, Venezuelan bolivars or Thai ticals. All of them have been newly printed by Thomas De La Rue & Co., one of the biggest commercial printers of paper money in the world.

Out of De La Rue's gates every week go approximately 20 million banknotes to governments all over the globe.

Since the company's banknote division designs, engraves and prints the currencies of ninety-two countries, its designing artists must be versatile, able to satisfy the varying tastes of treasuries and national banks. The Swiss, for example, prefer a stark, simple, rather modernistic design for their notes. Iran wants a highly intricate pattern resembling that of a Persian carpet. New Zealand goes in for Maori designs; Cambodia specialises in dancing girls. Many Latin-American countries insist on bills that look as much as possible like US dollars, with presidents' portraits, seals and all.

After the hand-drawn and coloured sketch of a new banknote is submitted to a government and approved, it goes to the engravers. There are only about 100 master engravers in the world who can cut banknote plates of quality. Twenty of them are at De La Rue's. These meticulous artist-craftsmen are similar in character – quiet, pleasant, infinitely patient – dedicated to the job of reproducing a design exactly, in steel. Prima donnas in their way, they cannot be rushed and must not be disturbed. Work benches in the long, pleasantly-decorated engraving room are far apart and one frequently sees an engraver looking out of the window or pacing up and down puffing his pipe – possibly thinking how best to get the effect of a billowing sail or a spectacular mountain.

The intricate designs have more than aesthetic value. They help to baffle the counterfeiter. So does the geometric lathe. This highly complicated cutting machine engraves on a plate the intricate circles, loops and whorls generally used on the border of a note. No human hand can produce even a reasonable facsimile. Nor can one geometric lathe copy the work of another, unless its operator has the formula of the original and can set his maze of cogs and cams accordingly. These lathes cost up to £16,000, are sold only to the most reputable printers and are closely guarded.

There are two other qualities in a well-made banknote that even a forger with the finest of photo-reproduction apparatus cannot approach – the ink and the paper. De La Rue's inimitable inks, mixed according to secret formulae, have been famous for decades. Only a few firms in the world make the peculiarly hard, all-rag paper which has the characteristic crispness and crackle of an authentic banknote. Portals (Laverstoke) Ltd of Whitchurch, Hampshire, furnishes the paper for De La Rue and the Bank of England; Crane supplies the US Treasury; and Office Français des Papiers Surfins et Fiduciaires of Paris supplies the Banque de France. Every sheet manufactured is accounted for, to the last square inch. Most governments have an additional security feature in the paper – the watermark.

No one has yet devised a really satisfactory method of forging a watermark. Nevertheless, the eternal battle between the printers and counterfeiters goes on. 'It's our wits against theirs all the time', said one of the Delarunians, as they call themselves. The firm has used some hard-to-beat gambits. One is the 'security thread', a fine plastic thread inserted into the paper as it is being made. Counterfeiters simulate it by printing a fine line in its place. But the spurious note can be detected simply by running a finger-nail across it.

The increasing precision of photographic copying methods has given the Delarunians many headaches. One of their principal counter measures has been the use of a series of delicate pastel shades which the finest colour cameras cannot reproduce exactly, but which can be distinguished by even an untrained eye.

De La Rue's greatest contribution to banknote printing, however, is its unique presses. At the Bank of England some English currency is printed on De La Rue machines, and two years ago nine of them were installed at the Bureau of Engraving and Printing in Washington.

Until recently it was necessary to wet banknote paper before printing because of its extraordinary hardness. This frequently caused trouble; when the printed paper dried, the lines often became distorted. But the De La Rue presses print with such pressure and accuracy that moistening is no longer necessary, and every sheet comes out absolutely perfect at the rate of 2,500 an hour. This is of particular importance to the United States Treasury, since traditionally it does not use watermarks or tints but depends on the absolute precision and clarity of the printing.

The house of De La Rue was founded in 1813 by an immensely versatile and ingenious printer, Thomas de la Rue, who specialised in fine embossed stationery and playing cards. When postage stamps were introduced in England he turned to them and held the exclusive contract for printing all British stamps for thirty years. Foreign stamp orders from other countries also came pouring in.

At the turn of the century, the tremendous worldwide expansion of industry and commerce brought a sudden demand for paper money in place of the less manageable gold and silver. Some countries tried printing their own, and had disastrous experiences with counterfeiters. There are very few people anywhere with the technical artistry, the mechanical know-how, the complicated and expensive machinery required to make banknotes relatively proof against the forger. When, in 1901, the Government of Siam asked the Bank of England to print its money, the Bank declined but suggested De La Rue, and that is how the huge banknote business started.

Perhaps the severest blow the world of banknote printing ever sustained was the counterfeiting of one government's currency by another government during the

Second World War. The Nazis developed a plan to cripple the British monetary system by smuggling reproductions of the £5 note in to the United Kingdom and scattering them over the world. The counterfeits were good enough to fool experts. Fortunately the war ended before too many of them could be distributed.

It was long thought that the plates for the Nazi 'fiver' had been dumped in Austria by fleeing SS men, and recently counterfeit Bank of England notes were recovered from an Austrian lake and officially burnt. The details of the Nazi plot was a closely guarded secret. But about three years ago the Bank of England began issuing an entirely new kind of £5 note.

'People didn't like the change at first', said an official of the Bank. 'We've had the old, familiar notes for so long. But it had to be.' And that was all he said. The new 'fiver' incorporates every one of the most recent developments in bank security – pastel tints, security threads, raised sections in the paper that can be felt, and other secret features involving inks and paper that do peculiar things electronically. Many of these stem from Delarunians' developments.

'We think', says one Delarunian, 'that we will continue to be able to give counterfeiters – both private and governmental, if need be – a very hard time.'

CHARACTERS AT LARGE

Apart from the directors at the very top of the company, such as Bernard Westall and Gerry Norman, what sort of managers were running and, above all, securing orders for De La Rue?

Peter Orchard, eventually Managing Director and Chairman, joined De La Rue in 1950 as one of the first post-war graduates, and when he spoke to Company Secretary Arthur Morrish in 1985, he was forthright in recounting his entry into De La Rue and early years there:

> It was quite a remarkable performance. We were in our last term at Cambridge, at least John [Shepherd-Barron] and I were, and we were summoned to 10a Upper Brook Street, the thing having been fixed by the Appointments Board. And there we were interviewed by a Committee which consisted of: Bernard Westall, Chairman, Alan Houseman, Sir Donald Banks, Gerry Norman (works manager at Bunhill Row), Arthur Morrish (company secretary and secretary to the Personnel Committee) and Peter Studd (sales manager).
>
> We all marched in and sat down and were asked the usual ludicrous questions: most of the questions directed at me concerned my prowess on the cricket field rather than anything else. And in fact Bernard had a private joke with me which lasted until the day he died – he set out to recruit a fast bowler and look what he got!
>
> After that we were sent out into the park to pass away the time until we were instructed to arrive at the Park Suite of the Dorchester for lunch. It was lunch for twelve, as I recall, and one or two of the people who had been summoned for interview got a bit the worse for wear and were ruled out on those grounds. Out of the six

who presented themselves, three were recruited: John Shepherd-Barron, myself and Ted Pease-Watkin who was Captain of Fives at Cambridge. When we turned up in June of that year, Bill Vowler was added to the congregation; Bill had been working for Shell and had been recruited via Graham Martin Turner. So effectively there were four graduate trainees although Bill wasn't a graduate.

The most horrifying thing about that recruitment exercise was that we were instructed to report, on Saturday June 24th I think it was, to Tower Pier to go aboard the *Royal Daffodil* on what was then the London Outing. Bernard said 'Go, and you'll meet some of the work people'. In fact John Shep and I turned up and everybody ignored us, almost. We didn't know a bloody soul, had a miserable day, terrible induction into the business. John then went away and didn't come back until Wimbledon was over; he got dispensation. In fact I've always said to him I joined the business six weeks ahead of him and have stayed six weeks ahead of him ever since.

De La Rue's graduate recruitment did not continue in that form for very long.

Subsequent batches of graduates were interviewed without this great splendour of the chairman's house and Dorchester lunch and so on. But we've recruited graduates ever since, more or less every year through a period when we cast the net very wide, practically every university in the country was circularised with our recruitment material and it produced very little for enormous expenditure of effort. The entire Personnel department of De La Rue and of the Divisions used to scatter to the four corners of the land in January and February, and very wasteful it was although I'm sure they all enjoyed it very much.

In recent years we have focused on only half a dozen places maximum: Oxford and Cambridge, Newcastle because of local affinities, St Andrews, Bristol and that's about it. If you can't get what you want out of these places then they're unlikely to exist. That was the philosophy.

Nobody thought how we were to be trained. I suspect that on the Monday morning when Ted Pease-Watkin and I arrived together somebody said, 'Oh, God, what are we going to give these chaps, how are we going to train them?' and a programme was hatched up to last something like five months, right up to Christmas.

Now, the training programme, to dignify it with a title it didn't deserve, was to spend according to somebody's judgement (I suspect Gerry Norman's) one week, two weeks, three weeks in various parts of the Security Division. Starting with prelims and working one's way through.

I was lucky because, getting on site first, my training actually followed a logical progress: I started in Prelims and ended up in the production factories, whereas Ted Pease-Watkin and John Shep and Bill Vowler found themselves starting in the Finishing departments, going back to Electrodes, coming to Prelims at the back end and it must have been very confusing for them. Anyway, it was strictly 'Sit by Nellie' type of induction, literally in fact when we got to the Finishing departments. We were just dumped on the managers of these places and they said, 'Here's a graduate, look after him for a week or two, and write a report on him when he's finished'.

Nobody quite knew what to do with us and we wandered about. I got into frightful trouble in the Electrotyping Department for asking Alex Smith how long it took to make a plate. I was taking notes, and he put on his hat (he always put on his hat when he went out of the building) and walked across the road from the Dufferin Works to Bunhill Row to complain to Mr Norman that he was putting spies into his department. He was quite certain this was the thin end of a bloody great wedge which might well include something called work study.

The training programme included a visit to Leeds where we were put in a temperance hotel, I remember. Very wise. I hadn't got an acute drinking problem in those days. A report had to be written and very unfairly, much later in life, I saw my personal file with all the reports that were included in there from various people; I think that Clac's opinion of the four of us was the most amusing and enlightening. He put John Shepherd-Barron first, Ted Pease-Watkin second, Bill Vowler third, and me fourth; in fact he really recommended that I wasn't suitable for industry at all. It's a piece of paper I should never have seen I suppose.

And what about the Chairman, Bernard Westall, who was giving these sober reports to shareholders? This is what Orchard told Morrish:

Bernard was a man of his time.

He was very similar in outlook and attitude to people like Alan Clark of Plessey, Wyndham Portal of Portals, Norman Watson of Waddington; a dictator whose main feeling was that what was good for him was good for the Company. It was an automatic identification.

The Company *was* Bernard and in many ways of course he was a genius, but it wasn't a style that could live for five minutes in today's world. And indeed in most cases it created the problem of succession, because dictators of that kind do not on the whole tolerate people around them who have got opinions of their own or are prepared to say, 'Sorry, you're doing it all wrong'.

Quite recently Gerry Norman made a very true remark when he said, 'In Bernard's heyday you had to be either a slave or a crook to survive'. He didn't appreciate it when I asked him which he was. But this was true, Bernard used slaves to produce and crooks to sell.

The Avramov story has been told elsewhere but in my time we had people like Ken Konstam, Sammy Aftalion, Peter Loopuyt and others, who were all attracted by Bernard, because of their supposed talent for selling. Whereas the general run-of-the-mill Anglo-Saxon was stuck into a works, paid half the amount of salary and told to get on with it and how jolly lucky he was to have a job. This was Bernard's style.

Orchard was also very amusing about the international salesmen employed by Westall:

Some of these chaps made a lot of money, though not many of them hung on to it.

Peter Loopuyt had talked the Company into providing him with a house in Estoril, which is a saga in itself – the Chalet Nini in Estoril. Nini was his wife, she was the prima ballerina of the Danish Ballet and a frightfully good looking woman, very nice too as a matter of fact. Why the hell she was married to old Peter ... one of his favourite tricks was when he introduced his wife: 'My wife Nini, would you like to sleep with her?' Very alarming for a young man anyway; one might find an answer these days but one was rather tongue-tied then.

Kenneth Konstam started as a banknote salesman. He was of course the number two bridge player in the world at the time and he was put on to selling banknotes in the Middle East in Lebanon, which was quite a sensible place for him to start. But then not long afterwards Kenneth graduated to being put in charge of the playing card business, the Stationers Division as it was called, where he was absolutely hopeless. But he was a great charmer, Ken Konstam, he should never have been allowed near business of any kind, let alone ours. Some of the others weren't so charming, but there we are.

What about the others who sold banknotes? They were a later generation in my book. I could write a book about Fitz [see below] and Bob Papworth and Charles Graner.

Charles Graner was an oddity. He was another Bernard invention. He was a Hungarian cavalry officer with a smile like a crocodile. It was a characteristic that he shared with John Innes [see below] as a matter of fact. John always scared me to death when he smiled.

Graner lived in the Bellevue Palace Hotel in Bern, high on the hog for 15 years he must have been, all on the principle that he would secure for De La Rue the Swiss banknote order, which was then printed by Waterlow. We got it in the end, whether he had anything to do with it I don't know, but the entire profit for the first five or ten years must have been sucked up by keeping Charles Graner in the state to which he was accustomed. He spoke French which nobody else could, which was such an advantage.

Bob Papworth was recruited from Reuters in Madrid like his old chum Paul Matthews of Portals, who was almost his exact contemporary. He had this tremendous advantage of being trilingual, with perfect English, French and Spanish, having been educated at the French Lycée in Madrid.

Bob was the most meticulous man you ever came across and one of the nicest. He was impeccable and he used to be given orders because he was so nice, as opposed to John Innes who was given them because he was so nasty. Bob would never push and shove, he wasn't a great salesman in the conventional understanding of the term, but he made it pretty difficult for the customer not to give us the order.

One of the most important De La Rue employees of the post-war period was Alan Houseman, who married Lorna, Bernard Westall's daughter. (It was Lorna who wrote *The House that Thomas Built*.) Lorna had been engaged to Gerard Riddick, a close friend of her brother, Peter Westall, and another important De La Rue employee (see pages 201–4), but she broke it off.

This is what Orchard has to say about Alan Houseman:

He was a man of absolutely astonishing charm, Alan, who knew everybody.

The source of his knowing was in fact his working in the War Cabinet Office for Pug Ismay, he was one of Pug Ismay's boys and he was known in that office as 'Hang Commander Wingover'. But he got to know a lot of people, Jock Colville, and all the civil servants. He was one of the idlest fellows, probably the most lazy man I've ever come across, but men would do things for him because he was such a hell of a good chap; you'd cover up for him, you'd do his work for him and a lot of us did over a long period of time.

There was a famous story which is true. It's to do with Bernard Westall being out in Burma, and the secret marks – we used to put so-called secret marks on banknotes in those days which were deliberate digs in the otherwise regular patterns – which of course the camera picks up as easily as anything else, but this was regarded as tremendously secret.

The set of proofs where the secret marks were was sent not to the general manager of the Central Bank of Burma marked 'personal', but just addressed to the Bank of Burma, and they fell into the hands of some clerk who said, 'What's this?' Now this was the mistake of the Sales Office.

Alan had the misfortune to be sales manager at the time. Cyril Jackson was still a director of the Company, so that makes it some time in the second half of the 1940s. Bernard sent Cyril Jackson a telegram which read 'Sack Houseman, signed Westall'.

Cyril, who was such a nice guy, thought this was a bit steep, and sent for Alan and told him, 'Look, Bernard's told me to fire you', and Alan said to him, 'Well I don't think I'd take that from Bernard if I were you, Cyril. If he wants to fire me let him do it himself, to come back and do it. Why don't we just wait until he gets back. If he fires me then I'll go.'

Cyril said 'Good idea, good idea'. Of course by the time Bernard got back he'd clean forgotten about it. So Alan survived.

Alan's greatest triumphs were really in Indonesia, Thailand and Brazil – a strange mixture. But those were the three countries in which he took a particular and personal interest, and Pakistan in its early days, although the limelight was hogged by Bernard and one or two others. Alan did a lot of the groundwork in his territory and he also found Naja Penty, our outstanding sales manager, which did the Company a lot of good.

Alan couldn't speak any foreign languages whatsoever. He was one of nature's monolinguists. He used to say to defend himself, 'In our business, the selling of banknotes, if you're talking to somebody who doesn't speak English you're talking to the wrong chap'. Which of course, as in everything else he said, had a great deal of truth in it. Because you should have been talking to the Governor of the Central Bank or the Minister of Finance, and it is highly unlikely that people who held these offices in any country would not speak English because they had then, and they have today, to go to Washington to plead for funds at the IMF and the World Bank. So it is very rare to find a Governor or a Finance Minister who doesn't speak English.

Alan Houseman brought off some notable coups. There is one failure which he took very much to heart at the time, his failure to get the Indonesians to agree to a repeat of our Pakistan set-up.

I think Alan's main feat was to get us paid, for the last of the Chinese orders, so we didn't have a bad debt when Chiang Kai-Shek collapsed and upped and offed to Taiwan. We were owed a lot of money and Alan went and got it.

Bernard offered Alan an increase in salary to £5,000 a year or membership of the De La Rue Board.

He chose the De La Rue Board and he joined in 1949. Which turned out to be a very good decision.

Alan was the guy who, apart from teaching me most of the tricks I know in this business, created the style and culture of the Security side, what we nowadays call mainstream De La Rue. He was the compound of a tremendous sense of humour, very sharp brain and great kindness. Alan hated hurting people. In fact he once fired a chap with such finesse that the fellow came out thinking he'd been promoted. A well-known story but absolutely true. And when Cyril Jackson told him what had actually been happening in Alan's office, he broke down and cried.

This was the thing that finally made old Alan crack.

Like so many people with an icy exterior he had in fact tremendous inner tensions and his attempts to save our banknote business in Thailand in 1958/9 led him into a nervous breakdown from which he only recovered for a short while before he died.

The essence of that story was that a fellow called Chote Gunakersen was appointed by General Sarit, who was in charge of Thailand at the time, as Governor of the Bank of Thailand, much to the distress of the permanent officials of the bank.

Sarit then appointed him Minister of Finance as well, with the rather alarming results that his signature appeared twice on Thai banknotes. Chote had spent a lot of time in London in the summer of 1958. When he went back to Thailand in '59 he was contacted by William Hunt who had a poor reputation and was the boss of what was then called Security Colombian Bank Note Company.

William Hunt had crossed swords with De La Rue in many areas at many times and persuaded Chote to buy very large quantities of banknotes from him which he was unable to produce by any respectable method, and the idea was that these should be paid for out of American aid; so the specious argument was advanced that it would cost the Bank of Thailand nothing by comparison to the fantastic prices charged by De La Rue. In fact Bill Hunt charged prices which were very comparable with those charged by De La Rue but, by printing their notes litho, they cost about a quarter of De La Rue's costs. $600,000 was paid by way of an advance to Security Colombian – an unheard of step. De La Rue had never had a contract with the Bank of Thailand, our invoices were met on shipment and that had been going on for 70 years.

Well this is where the plot gets rather confused and memory's not all that hot. But there was an organisation called IBEC, which was a do-gooding aid granting organisation controlled by the Rockefeller family, and it had an office in Bangkok. A girl comes into the story at this point. I can't remember quite who she was, but she had a boyfriend who worked for IBEC and was an idealist and he found out what William Hunt and Chote were up to. And, via his girlfriend, blew the whistle to Alan.

The upshot of it was that the thing became public, there was an allegation that Chote had taken a bribe, that this order was unauthorised. At this point Alan passed the information on to the government. He took advice from old friends like Sung Menerchakal, who had been Governor of the Bank, and he laid before the Department of Justice information which led straight to Chote being put in the cooler. All very embarrassing.

But Alan was put under tremendous strain and I think he was probably threatened at one time, because Hunt certainly and Chote probably were quite unscrupulous people. He had to appear in court. This is where the major strain lay, having to go and give evidence.

There was a very tough cross-examination. His counsel was Kukret's brother; Kukret Promarj, a newspaper publisher by trade, is still going strong and had been Prime Minister of Thailand in the not very distant past, and his brother Senee was a lawyer and Senee Promarj was our Counsel. The net upshot to De La Rue was that the operation was successful but the patient died. Chote was put in the cooler, the contract was cancelled, the Bank of Thailand never got its money back; it wasn't there to be got back, it had been passed around the family.

Then there was the younger generation ...

John Innes was a terrible ethnic mixture; he was a cross between a Scot and a Spaniard which gave him all sorts of characteristics which one doesn't find in the average Briton. He'd been in Consular Service before the war and during the war got promoted into the Diplomatic Service, found himself in Brazil and he was the First Secretary in Rio when Bernard went out there just one day after the war and recruited him into De La Rue. John spoke perfect Spanish and very good Portuguese; it's a feat which is rather difficult in fact, most people speak one or the other and one or the other badly but John spoke both perfectly. He was our man in Latin America for about 20 years, usually living in Rio or Montevideo, again at very great expense, being paid a princely salary.

John had a technique which Alan Houseman always reckoned got him his orders, which was to bore the backside off the customer. Used to sit down in Asuncion or Montevideo or somewhere, week after week, badgering the Bank, ringing them up, going to see them, catching them in restaurants, doing all the things that must have infuriated them until eventually they said, 'For God's sake give this bloke the order and get him out'. There's probably something in that.

Maurice Fitzgerald – 'Fitz' – came next, I think. Fitz was recruited about 1950 and he came from selling tea in South America. His big brother was the boss of Shell in the UK, J.C. Fitzgerald. If you sold tea to coffee-drinking Latin Americans you could sell anything to anybody, that was the idea. Again, his attraction to De La Rue at that time was he spoke Spanish, which so few people did.

So he was given a short run in Latin America and John Innes began to feel his position threatened, so Fitz was switched to the Far East where only English was spoken. And he worked out of Bangkok from the mid 50s onwards, dealing with all those territories which were the most important at that time to De La Rue by far: Thailand, Burma, Indonesia, Philippines and New Zealand. And a very successful salesman he was. He was very very hardworking. Not much imagination, old Fitz, but terribly tenacious and very good at grouting away until he got a result.

> He died quite young, at about 62. He had a heart attack while travelling in Latin America, came back and recovered but then had another heart attack a couple of years later, just after he retired early. I should think that would be about 1968.

Another of De La Rue's salesmen who was a great character was Alexis Napier, or Prince Alexis Melikoff, formerly from Russia, as he was known when he joined the company. He joined in 1948, and this is what he told Arthur Morrish in 1980 of his early days at De La Rue:

> When I joined the company I went into the Production Office where I worked under Eric Barnard who was then a sort of time and motion study man, and added up a whole lot of figures for him about reamages of work going through the factory which was not really interesting but I considered that it is work that you do when one is starting in a company right from the bottom.
>
> After that I worked for John Glennie. All the jobs were on cards on a large board in the Production Office showing reamages of work to be printed and the progression of the work day by day for a whole month. My particular job for John Glennie which in fact was a job which three other people were doing, namely there was Ron Waterlowe, Peter Smith and one other person's name I forget; we were all trainees, was to chase up work in the various parts of the Anchor Works or the Bunhill Row building. And we were dispatched by John Glennie to the various departments. Frequently, we were it seemed all four of us chasing the same job and God help the person who arrived last, which once happened to me in the electro-plating department when I was chasing up a plate, when I was the third person I think to arrive in 20 minutes chasing up this job. And a delightful man called Mr Smith who was the head of the department just spat on me and told me to get out.
>
> Then I worked with Charlie Graner who was the manager responsible for non Crown Agent work, banknotes, stamps and everything for the whole world. And did the clerical work with him. Then I went off to see Bernard Westall to discuss my first trip abroad for the Company at 10a Upper Brook Street. It was very exciting and it was the time when Tito in Yugoslavia was breaking away from Russia and Bernard Westall quite correctly thought that this was an opportunity for a new banknote issue because it seems that the Russians were probably printing the notes for Yugoslavia and they needed another printer. I was very excited about this. To get to Yugoslavia I had to have a visa; I immediately applied for a visa and I waited, I waited and I waited. My name was Prince Alexis Melikoff and it was in that name I applied for a visa, thinking that my title would nullify any Russian Communist phobia that the Yugoslavs might have. Anyway, I was never granted the visa at all and having waited for some time, I think I made the application in September, on Friday 13th January 1950 my first trip for the Company started which was to go to Ethiopia.
>
> The Security Banknote Company were printing the notes for the State Bank of Ethiopia at the time. The Governor of the State Bank was Jack Bennett. I arrived for a stay of I considered a fortnight and one of the first things I did was to go and call

at the Embassy where I saw a very nice person called Leonard Figg who was then Third Secretary.

And I was discussing the banknote business in Ethiopia with Leonard and as an aside complained bitterly about my hotel accommodation at the best hotel which was grim, and Leonard very kindly said, 'Well look, I'm a bachelor, I have a whole house, come and spend a fortnight with me'. I took up this invitation and instead of staying a fortnight I spent seven months. And was then known as the man who came to tea!

I stayed a long time because the Ethiopians were saying that we having submitted our offer, they were saying it would take another two weeks to consider, we shall be ready to place our order in three weeks, and subsequently they asked for tenders from Security Banknote Company and from Bradbury which took time and I asked advice from Bunhill Row as to whether I should come back or stay on, and Ernest Gough said stay on, so I did. And during that time, in fact towards the end of my stay, I had an audience with the Emperor which was fascinating because, well to begin with I had to appear in a tailcoat and striped trousers.

It was quite extraordinary. I borrowed Leonard Figg's tailcoat and striped trousers as he is rather fat or plump, they certainly didn't fit me so I shambled into the audience chamber and one has to bow three times to the Emperor, once in the door, once in the middle of the room and once in front of him and my trousers sort of flopped over every time I bowed.

We talked about the banknote and stamp printing business because he asked me the purpose of my visit and he showed a great deal of interest and in fact gave me an order for a commemorative issue of his father's death which De La Rue printed, I think it was the first stamp we did for Ethiopia.

On this extended trip to Ethiopia, Napier contracted malaria, which developed into jaundice and put him in bed for two months. When he recovered he was sent to Iceland (Napier obviously cannot handle hot climates!). He continued:

After Iceland I then started travelling properly and went to the Sudan which was then getting independence as it was previously the Anglo-Egyptian Sudan under British administration, and being independent of course they did their own banknotes, and I went to see the Financial Secretary who was Louis Chik and started talking to him about producing banknotes. He went absolutely white as a sheet and I wondered what on earth I had said that was not right. It transpired later that half an hour previous to my meeting with him he had a top secret meeting with the Governor to discuss the very subject of a banknote issue and he was initially horrified that someone should raise it from outside so soon thereafter, thinking that there must have been a leak. Tenders were eventually called for this new issue for Sudan. We prepared our designs and Waterlows in fact got the business on price because it was at that time that they had started cutting prices because they needed business badly, which eventually led them to bankruptcy. But the Sudan really was the first time that they started price-cutting.

Napier then moved on to the Middle East, where he again encountered problems with Waterlows' price-cutting. In spite of it he secured a banknote order in Israel:

> I just went to Israel and different prices were submitted with a reasonable contribution. I saw clearly the intention was there to give the order to De La Rue but he wanted a gesture from De La Rue, so on my own initiative I gave him the originals free and he was delighted to confirm the order for us.
>
> Then I was travelling in Jordan and covering Israel at the same time because the order had to be seen through and delivery seen to the Bank etc. and more negotiations subsequently with Israel. I was covering the whole of the Middle East, Syria, Lebanon, Jordan, Iran which was at the time of Mosadec when there were no diplomatic relations between Britain and Iran because of the Anglo-Iranian oil facility crisis.
>
> We were nevertheless managing to print and supply banknotes into Iran and others. Going to the Central Bank no one could speak English so everything had to be done in French and there was a very nice Governor called Mr Nasser with whom we had excellent relations. Then we heard that Saudi Arabia, which was one of the last countries in the Middle East to use coins, were considering having paper currency. So I was sent to Jeddah to check this out and called on the first Governor of the Saudi Arabian Monetary Agency who confirmed to me that this was so, that Saudi Arabia was going to have paper currency, and he explained the way that the Saudi Arabian Monetary Agency were going to set about it, was to issue sort of travellers' cheques called pilgrims' receipts which would be issued to pilgrims in their countries of origin and brought into Saudi Arabia, and would then be exchangeable for gold and silver coins and would then be accepted in circulation.
>
> Initially there was a fair amount of resistance to this new paper currency, but this had been foreseen by the Governor of the Monetary Agency who had asked us to show on the banknote that in the vaults of the Saudi Arabian Monetary Agency there would be equivalent of so many rials in gold, because in the Koran it says wealth should be paid for in work and therefore it's no good getting bits of paper for shoes or anything else, motor cars or whatever you like. And then subsequently these pilgrim receipts were withdrawn and replaced by a proper banknote issue which De La Rue had designed, engraved and printed, in which I was also involved.
>
> About that time Africa was decolonising itself and various people like myself in De La Rue were chasing all the nationals of the countries that were about to get independence, all the key people; mainly the people who were going to be ministers were of course not in the countries concerned, they were either in prison or in exile, or whatever, and they had to be tracked down. I was particularly involved with the French Territories, because I spoke French and the principal person that I was tracking down with Denis Paravicini was the Minister of Finance of Tunisia, or the Minister of Finance Designate of Tunisia, the person who we calculated would be the Minister of Finance of Tunisia because they hadn't got independence yet, called Mr Hedi Nuera. He used to stay in the Hotel Continental in Paris opposite the Formica office. Denis and I used to chase him down the corridors of the hotel because he was never really keen to see us and was rather a secretive man. Nevertheless we eventually tracked him

down and got our talk with him and put over the name of De La Rue we thought successfully enough for him to imprint it on his mind to come to us when his Government was ready to order banknotes.

I then went to Tunisia several times to follow up this conversation with Mr Hedi Nuera and saw various people for by then Tunisia had got its independence, and saw various people in the Government and was always told they weren't quite ready to order our notes. Until word came somehow or other to Bunhill Row that the Tunisians had placed an order with somebody. So I was shot out to Tunis to find out what had happened. And what had happened was that shortly after my last visit to Tunis, in the Government's opinion, the time became right to finally place their banknote order and coincidentally Bradbury's representative arrived calling then. The Tunisians thought there must be only one company in England that printed banknotes, and not two, and promptly gave their order to Bradbury's much to their delight. The name of De La Rue was not as well imprinted on Mr Hedi Nuera's head as we thought. Fortunately I made great friends with the Tunisian Ambassador to England, to Great Britain, Mr Taiev Slin, a very influential person in Tunis because the Slin family were very close to the President. Slin managed to persuade the Government to take half the order away from Bradbury and give it to us. The order was split in half and this was a pure act of friendship on Slin's part, and for several years subsequently the order for banknotes, for Tunisia, has been divided between Bradbury's and ourselves. After that we got the whole business.

Then I did some travelling in the Persian Gulf, Kuwait and Bahrain and was involved in getting the first stamp order for Bahrain, because Bahrain by then had British Post Office stamps overprinted Bahrain; but there was a very nice Englishman called Sir Charles Belgrave who was really the ruler of Bahrain, the Sheikh's right hand, he was called the Adviser, who in fact helped us to get this business. Then West Africa started to decolonise itself and this was an accelerated decolonisation on the British Government's part because they decided to give Ghana independence rather more quickly than even the Ghanaians expected, or even wanted. They were then of course ready to issue, or to order their first banknotes and offers were tendered by ourselves, Waterlows, Bradbury, and lo and behold we got the business, and there was a very ceremonial signing of the contract.

And then I moved on to Nigeria. Ghana having achieved its independence Nigeria wanted to get theirs as quickly, but in fact it was a much more complicated political situation because of all the tribalism, and it took a great deal longer, but the first step as far as banknotes were concerned was for Nigeria to break away from the West African Currency Board which then covered Nigeria, Ghana, Gambia etc. And at about this time it became clear to our management, Bernard Westall, Gerry Norman, and Alan Houseman, that Nigeria would maybe a suitable place to set up a local security printing works because of the population and because of its geographical position. So, parallel with our negotiations to print a new issue of banknotes we offered to set up a local security printing works. This was greeted with absolute horror by the British ex-patriates from the Government downwards because they considered the Nigerians did not have sufficient responsibility to print banknotes in situ themselves.

> Both Gerry Norman and Alan Houseman went out to Lagos, accompanied by myself, to try and convince the British civil servants otherwise; but they wouldn't have it, with the exception of one Englishman, who was a Permanent Secretary with the Ministry of Communications called Mr Will Lewis, who was much more forward-looking than all the others, and with his Minister, whose name I'm afraid I forget, they were the prime movers of the security printing works.

While all these dramas were going on, there were also long periods when nothing much happened. As Napier put it:

> Certainly there were great periods of waiting around with very brief periods of excitement, and the periods were exciting and some were very very exciting indeed.
>
> There was an awful lot of money at stake and really at quite a tender age one was given pretty well, pretty heavy responsibilities to negotiate contracts and prices. Naturally, because of travel and communications, one was away from home for quite a long time and naturally if one was married that wasn't too easy. But, in fact I remember Ernest Gough giving me a slight lecture and advice on what to do in these waiting around periods, and he said, 'On no account sit around doing nothing, either go and watch a football match or go for a walk or do something active, because once you start sitting around doing nothing it's dreadful'. And I always remember that advice. What I used to do is when I wasn't walking, because I used to go around walking quite a lot, was read or paint.
>
> And I took up painting in watercolours and I did some in Jeddah, in Khartoum and elsewhere in Africa and Alan Houseman once got together an exhibition of paintings done by people in Bunhill Row and the judge was quite a well known painter. We exhibited all our paintings and everybody who drew or painted produced their efforts in that old sort of tin shack. And I got first prize.

Everyone has mobiles and Blackberrys these days, so it is difficult to appreciate the difficulties of communicating from Africa 50 years ago. When asked about it, Napier said:

> Well, there were problems of accuracy because telex didn't exist and this is the greatest blessing that's happened to any salesman, the telex, because over great distances you can have a copy of what you send, and a copy of an offer with prices and delivery time etc. So in that way it was uncertain. I used cables, and that took quite a long time.
>
> From Africa it was pretty well impossible. Hardly used the telephone because it was unsafe and one couldn't hear very well. But talking communications, travelling was so different because firstly it took longer, but long distance flights were really much more comfortable than long distance flights now, because there was only one class, and you were looked after and I think it was even better than sort of first class now. But then on the feeder routes, you know the smaller aircraft, things were pretty grotty.

Denis Paravicini, another graduate trainee from Cambridge, joined De La Rue in 1953. After his training (a spell in what was left of the Commercial Print Division and a year at the Leeds security printing factory) he was sent to Europe by Ivan Knops. There he worked for the redoubtable Charles Graner (we have already seen Peter Orchard's view of Graner). Here is what Paravicini said:

> He was a real character. I mean he lived in the Bellevue Palace Hotel in Bern and had done for some years. He was always immaculately dressed in Savile Row suits, he wore a gold rimmed monocle and always walked with a stick, because he had been a great horseman and achieved the record between Vienna and Budapest, and now he was getting a bit arthritic and was having trouble with his leg; but he was a tremendous character. If he walked into a room he immediately attracted everybody's attention by his somewhat fearsome demeanour and the way in which he instructed everybody to do his every bidding. But he did a good job with the colonial banks.

Graner may have enjoyed the luxury and peace of the Bellevue Palace Hotel in Bern in tranquil Switzerland, but Paravicini had to cope with more exciting locations:

> I was told to go to places like Romania, Bulgaria and back up through Hungary, and I even went once on the Orient Express from Belgrade to Sofia. And I had visualised that there would be a nice restaurant on that train but there wasn't, and I had no food for about a ten hour journey, and a German woman with her Bulgarian boyfriend, I think he was, gave me some food, so I was very grateful and I offered to take them out in Bulgaria, to Sofia, for doing this; and anyway, I then got involved in a lot of problems because they wanted me to send money to them subsequently, via Germany, to Sofia. These sort of things happened in Eastern Europe.
>
> But perhaps the most amusing thing is that the chap who I took out was a fairly youngish student, about four years later he was the first Bulgarian to apply for a visa to England; and he sent me the application and I signed it for him and never thought about it again, until one day, working in Bonhill Street in those days, working with Alan Law, I was summoned to Alan Law's office, and Alan Law said to me, 'These two gentlemen here would like a word with you.' So I said, 'Oh yes, where are they from?' He said, 'They're from the Ministry of Defence.' Looking at me, of course, they were MI6 and they said to me, 'Well, why did you, why is the Bulgarian who is the first Bulgarian student who has applied to have studied in England, why should he ask you to support his visa?' So I sat there and said, 'Well, you're not going to believe this.' They said, 'Well, try us.' So I said, 'I actually met him on the Orient Express.' So that was the story, the little things that started my working in those days in Eastern Europe; you never quite knew what was going to happen, because I went to Poland as well and ended up trying to sell Formica bang in the middle of the Poznan riots which was very, very tricky. The bullets were whistling around the town as the workers and the Russian Army fought. Again, we managed to get a contract for putting Formica into an Egyptian railway contract they had, and then of course I ended up in

Hungary absolutely bang in the Hungarian revolution and had actually to flee the country on the last plane out to Prague before the Russians came in.

So it was magnificent, a very interesting time to be in that part of the world, if somewhat hair-raising.

Chapter Nine

Confidence and Trust

1960–1969

I hate freezes
A new factory
Waterlow into the fold
A big anniversary
Export or die
Giori
Minstro or Ministro
Closure of Bunhill Row and the Queen's Award
The Rank bid
'Not in the best interests of shareholders'
'Close personal contact at top level'

I HATE FREEZES

The 1950s had been a decade of growth in the whole of the Western world. Recovery from the Second World War gathered pace as the decade progressed. Ironically, the two defeated countries, West Germany and Japan, grew faster than most. Great Britain grew as well but there were some structural problems, mainly a reliance on what were known as 'smoke-stack' industries such as coal-mining, iron and steel production and ship-building. Furthermore, the UK seemed to suffer more than others from weak management, recalcitrant trade unions and under-investment. This meant that growth was restricted, and the economy also succumbed to inflationary and balance-of-payment pressures, even when growth did exceed a rather modest 2 or 3 per cent per annum.

The Conservative party, led by Harold Macmillan, known popularly as 'Supermac', led the party to election victory in 1959 with the slogan 'You've never had it so good'. However, within two years both the balance of payments and inflation were flashing warning signals and the Chancellor of the Exchequer, Selwyn Lloyd, introduced a mandatory pay pause. This did not amuse De La Rue's Managing Director, Gerry Norman, who said:

> The cure for our economic ills since the last war has been too many 'freezes' on investment, wages, salaries and profits – a completely negative approach. But we can't escape the fact that we are currently in a position of a man who has been living above his means.
>
> This country has rewarded itself above its income and is straining its resources too far. Productivity has not matched the rewards we have been giving ourselves. We have over-balanced – now we must pay for it.
>
> The way to fight off inflation is more goods on the market at lower cost. More goods are needed to meet the needs of everyone who now has increased income to spend. It is important that everyone should understand that the reasons for the Chancellor's pause policy are to make actual increases in wages real in terms of stable prices.

He instituted an economy drive in De La Rue, saying:

> Management must cut their budgets to compensate for these increases and, even more, for the loss of home sales.
>
> We have to maintain the profitability of our company as a measure of its efficiency. If profits fall, dividends go wrong. This makes further raising of money for expansion and prosperity difficult and leads to stagnation and loss of business.

He went on to say that, thanks to its diversification policy, De La Rue was not suffering as much as many other companies, and the fact that much of its business was overseas meant that it was benefiting from continued growth elsewhere in the world.

The Chairman, Bernard Westall, was able to confirm this benefit from De La Rue's overseas business, and he told shareholders in July 1961:

> Of the total capital employed by the Group, 35 per cent is now invested outside the UK. In the last few years nine factories have been established abroad.

On the Thomas De La Rue division, he said:

> The Leeds, Dublin and Gateshead factories are working to capacity and the order book is fuller than last year. A contract has been obtained from the Japanese Government for banknote printing machines. De La Rue Instruments has made

> remarkable strides and increased its trading profits substantially, exporting over 80 per cent of its products.

The diversifications provided mixed results:

> Formica: 'a mixed year';
> Thomas Potterton: 'turnover increased substantially';
> De La Rue Bull: 'progress has been as expected'.

The good performance of Thomas De La Rue continued into 1962 and a new parent company was formed to include all the Group's Security business. It was to be called De La Rue International Limited. The Group Managing Director, Gerry Norman, became Chairman of this new company and Peter Orchard was appointed Managing Director. The mechanical side of the Group now became a new subsidiary, Thomas De La Rue Engineering Limited. Ivan Knops became its Managing Director.

A NEW FACTORY

To confirm its optimism about the future, De La Rue announced in September 1961 that it planned to build what it believed would be the largest banknote factory in the world. It would be built on the Team Valley Trading Estate in Gateshead in the north-east of England and would achieve full production in 1964. The existing security finishing unit at Gateshead would be absorbed into the new factory and a number of personnel plus plant and machinery would be transferred from Leeds. (The Leeds factory had been opened in 1941 in cooperation with John Waddington after the destruction of Bunhill Row.) It was planned that the new factory, covering 250,000 square feet, would employ 1,000 people.

Lord Hailsham, Minister for Science and Technology, laid the foundation stone on 7 March 1963, and said:

> This particular enterprise is noteworthy for many reasons, but also because it has not attracted a pennyworth of Government grant. The whole of the cost comes from private sources.
>
> This is the sort of thing that other people can do. They can get a fine site, full services, an adaptable skilled labour force, good industrial relations, low site values and an admirable countryside.

Continuing its expansion in the early 1960s, De La Rue set up operations in Colombia in South America and Nigeria in West Africa. HRH Prince Philip, the Duke of Edinburgh, visited the new banknote factory in Bogota, Colombia on 14 February 1962 and said in his usual jocular way:

> In the days before the ports of South America were opened to foreign trade, the only way in which Britain could participate was capturing what it could of the fleets which,

> loaded with treasure, sailed towards Spain. I am glad to say that our present trading methods are rather more conventional.

The company in Bogota made a splendid start, prompting this comment from Thomas De La Rue's Managing Director, Peter Orchard, in the 1962 Annual Report:

> As far as our foreign companies are concerned, the Brazilian company made a small profit on trading, which in my view is a splendid achievement ... Slow progress, in a highly entrenched market, has also been made by our New York company. I think that one of the most encouraging and perhaps surprising results of the year has been the success of the company which we have established in Bogota, Colombia, for the printing of security documents.

In Nigeria, the new company would be 55 per cent owned by the Nigerian government, 5 per cent by the Central Bank of Nigeria, and the remaining 40 per cent by Thomas De La Rue International. The new company would build and equip a new factory in which several hundred Nigerians, after training by De La Rue International, would be employed.

WATERLOW INTO THE FOLD

In 1961 De La Rue bought the stamp- and banknote-printing business of Waterlow and Sons. Waterlow was a shadow of its former self and was no longer the fierce rival to De La Rue that it had been in the second half of the 19th century and the early decades of the 20th. In recent years it had become an increasing irritant by quoting aggressively low prices in competitive tenders.

At the end of 1961, Waterlow and Sons Ltd, after struggling with losses for a number of years, was sold to the printer and publisher Purnell and Sons. However, De La Rue bought the plant, machinery and business of printing banknotes, stamps and other security documents.

Waterlow, in its various forms, had been a competitor of De La Rue for about a century. Its founder, James Waterlow, was not dissimilar to Thomas de la Rue, a self-made entrepreneur. He began his career as a legal writer and lived for many years in a small house off City Road in east London, struggling to bring up a large family. His break came when he conceived the idea of employing lithography and printing as a substitute for copying when many copies of a legal document were required. He went into business with his four sons in 1810, just three years before Thomas de la Rue founded his business.

In the 1870s the company divided following disagreements among the brothers, and for many years there were two companies, Waterlow and Sons and Waterlow Brother and Layton. However, the two were reunited in 1920 under the original Waterlow and Sons. As we have already seen, by this time the company was a close competitor of De La Rue and, at the same time, involved with it in various 'trade' agreements; and, of course, De La Rue's great Managing Director and Chairman, Bernard Westall, worked at Waterlow before moving to De La Rue.

Following two outstanding achievements in the First World War – the printing of 4 million £1 notes for the government in five days after the outbreak of war in August 1914, and the production of 78 million ration books and 400 million insurance stamps in nine different values and colours in 1918 – Waterlow thrived in the inter-war years, printing banknotes, stamps, cheques, railway tickets, envelopes, embossed stationery, posters and catalogues, as well as the *Radio Times* and *Listener* for the BBC.

However, the once-proud company had never really recovered from the Portuguese banknote scandal of the 1920s.

The scam was perpetrated by Alves Reis, who forged an order to print $5 million of Portuguese Angolan currency. He then approached the Dutch banknote company, Enschede, which gave him a letter of introduction to Waterlow & Sons. One of Reis's associates went to see Sir William Waterlow, who was keen to replace Bradbury Wilkinson as the supplier of notes to the Bank of Portugal and who therefore received this approach warmly. Inevitably the fraud was discovered and Reis received a long prison sentence.

Waterlow & Sons suffered mightily. Not only did their reputation plummet, but the firm faced long and expensive trials and eventually had to pay the Bank of Portugal $3 million in damages. The scandal led to Sir William stepping down from the family firm and also to Waterlow & Sons abandoning security printing altogether. It was the rest of the company that De La Rue bought in 1961.

For De La Rue the purchase meant three things: some valuable contracts; the elimination of a competitor that had been quoting lower and lower prices; and also the destruction of printing capacity. As the *De La Rue Journal* put it:

> The disposal of plant is already under way. The banknote and stamp printing equipment might well be dangerous if it fell into the wrong hands.

Helping to pay for this purchase was a huge contract worth £2 million (over £30 million today) from Japan for the supply of 21 De La Rue printing presses to print Japanese banknotes.

A BIG ANNIVERSARY

In 1963 De La Rue celebrated its 150th anniversary and was able to report that everything – home sales, overseas companies' sales and profits – was on the upswing. Nevertheless, the company felt that it needed more capital and raised £3 million (about £75 million today) through a placed debenture. Managing Director Gerry Norman explained how the money would be used, when asked if it was for a particular project:

> No, this is general expansion of the business, including major investments like the development of Formica in places like India and Spain, and setting up sales companies throughout Europe where we can. In the case of Pottertons, it's expansion with a capital E; in the case of Thomas De La Rue we have the Gateshead operation which is, of course, a major one, and a large investment going into New York; all these things are taking a considerable amount of financing.

One very sad event of 1963 was the sudden death at the age of 52 of Alan Houseman. He had made an enormous contribution to De La Rue. Gerry Norman said this in a tribute:

> He was a very unusual person, brilliant and imaginative, courageous and unorthodox, selfless and gentle and very mindful of the value and meaning of kindness. These great qualities made it inevitable that he would always be found in the thick of events that mattered, helping, guiding and fashioning the team and the policies which would win greater success in the future. This was how it was right up to his last moments among us.
>
> When Bernard Westall was reshaping the De La Rue business after the long and bitter struggle for survival in the 1920s, he turned his attention to the problem of how to recruit and train young men as potential leaders of the future. Alan Houseman, who was then at Clare College, Cambridge, became the very first of a long line of De La Rue's management trainees.
>
> It was not very long before he was given the chance to manage the printing factory in Corfu, learning the intricacies of security printing the hard way but more importantly, learning how to get on with the nationals of another country. After his return to the UK and a spell in the sales and engraving departments, War brought a new challenge and Alan Houseman, who had already learned to fly at Cambridge, was amongst the very first to rush off and join the RAF.
>
> The award of the Distinguished Flying Cross and the fact of his survival as a fighter pilot in those early days of the War are eloquent tributes to his bravery and skill.
>
> On demobilisation he returned to De La Rue and was soon appointed Sales Manager of the banknote business. It was in the next ten years – hectic and exciting in the extreme – that his genius for selling was really discovered. The word 'genius' implies something indefinable and mysterious, but Alan Houseman's great success seemed to spring from the simple and basic fact that he really liked people, was interested in them and was highly sensitive to the things which made them tick.
>
> He invariably succeeded in making people like him and want to do business with him. The rest, after that, was sheer hard work and loyal determination, seeing things through, disdainful of the niggling detail which never failed to bore him to distraction and regardless of the discomforts and hateful necessity of deserting family and home for months on end. The record shows that, under his inspired sales leadership, the Company's Security printing business grew and prospered wonderfully.
>
> In 1953 his great services were recognised by promotion to the Board of the Parent Company and from that moment he applied himself to the vital task of getting the

whole company to want and to accept the humanist traditions, which he had done so much to implant and nourish at Bunhill Row. This involved struggles – tough ones which again called forth all his great courage – but eventually the day was won and, though he would never have claimed the credit, his influence was responsible for much of what is best in the spirit and outlook which pervades De La Rue today.

No commentary on Alan Houseman and his deeds could ever be complete without a mention of his great capacity for fun. The worst situations inevitably provoked the full brilliance of his wit and humour and there are many who will treasure memories of many a 'bon mot' or shattering comment. His deep sense of fun would cause him to tell many a story against himself and would include his own account of how he was once finally obliged to dismiss one of his bright young colleagues – he so much hated this task and made such a mess of it that when the young man emerged from his boss's office he told everyone he had been promoted.

EXPORT OR DIE

Britain had always had a balance of payments problem. Some thought it was not important but, in the long run, it does matter if Britain wants to be a prosperous country and be able to buy imports from overseas. Foreign currency must be earned. This was understood by the management at De La Rue. Furthermore, if De La Rue were to survive, let alone grow, it had to sell its expertise overseas. This meant sending its salesmen all over the world and selecting salespeople of a high calibre to convince senior politicians and financial officials that they could trust De La Rue to print top-quality postage stamps, banknotes and other financial documents for them. Such salespeople were also going to need resilience and stamina.

One who possessed these qualities was Julian Wethered, who worked for De La Rue all over the world for more than 30 years. A scion of the Wethered brewing family, Julian was educated at Eton and Jesus College, Cambridge where he read History, graduating in 1952. After working for Remington Rand selling dictating machines and being paid £8 a week (about £10,000 a year in today's money), he joined De La Rue at 26 as a graduate trainee on a starting salary of £600 a year (about £15,000 today). After initial training in all parts of the Group – security print, stationery, Potterton and Formica, and spells in the Preliminaries Department and at the Leeds factory – he was sent to Salisbury in Rhodesia (now Zimbabwe) and then East Africa before being asked to take over English-speaking Africa, reporting to Margo Newlands. This is what he said about his experiences in Africa in the 1960s:

> Time to take stock of the African experience, and the changed perspective of relating to De La Rue in London and my family in the Bucks Chilterns. Living in aeroplanes, hotels and out of a suitcase is certainly not for everyone. Being awoken in a Government Rest House in Zambia by a huge Zambian, insisting on polishing the bedroom floor with Mansion House red wax at sunrise, when you've had a late night arrival is disagreeable. Leaving Kinshasa at night, the only European, and refusing to

hand over your spare notes as you go to board a plane can get you into trouble. Especially when a seven foot army Sergeant appears from a side door and bids you in Belgian-French to follow him – suddenly you can't get rid of the useless notes quick enough. Being propositioned in the lift of the Ducor Palace Hotel in Monrovia, Liberia by some mini-skirted ageing bimbo is embarrassing. Asking President Idi Amin to confirm what he has just said could be risky. Waterskiing on Lake Tanganyika, off-shore Bujumbura, Burundi, having been told that crocodiles only stay on the edges of the lake, prompts the thought, 'What if one gets off course?' It encourages you not to prang.

Then there are the oddments, like having lunch with Mark Bostock outside Lusaka in the bush. He drove me out to his house. Hanging on a line were several sun-dried snakes. 'Why those?' I asked. 'I pay the shamba boy a shilling a foot for every snake he kills.' I was impressed and said, 'Why?' The answer came before he could answer, in the form of a four year old boy and a two year old girl. 'They are the reason', he told me. Worth every penny, I thought. Or again when I visited an out of season game park, also in Zambia, and stayed with the English Game Warden. It was a Friday evening, and we left after dark with one of his men, who sat in the back of the Land Rover under a fitted canvas cover. Suddenly in the headlights we surprised a male lion. I still carry the flash of that image as it raised its paw and ripped open the canvas as we passed by. Further down the track we stopped and comforted the distraught ranger who had been sitting on the lion's side of the vehicle. The claws had torn through the material close to his shoulder. So he joined us on the front seat. On arrival at the two rondarvals [African round-houses], we made a circle of the ash from an old fire around where we had supper – this was to deter the snakes who dislike going over ashes. During the night we heard lions, elephant and other weird cries of the bush. Next day my host paid his rangers their wages.

Then there was Africa's west coast. Along with Sierra Leone, the country I visited most was Ghana. Originally known as the Gold Coast and sourcing the slave trade, the old Portuguese castle, in the now capital Accra, has dungeons in which slaves were held before shipment to Brazil. 'The modern state was created by union of two former British territories, British Gold Coast (Crown Colony, 1874) and British Togoland, merging to form Ghana, and declaring independence in 1957. Republic within the Commonwealth, 1960.' (Penguin Encyclopedia, 2004). Kwame Nkrumah was the country's first President. De La Rue were already printing Ghana's banknotes. So my job was to see that they continued to do so, whilst looking for other business meanwhile.

De La Rue's main competitor throughout the world in the 1960s and 1970s was Bradbury Wilkinson, and the De La Rue salespeople would be sure to meet their competitor's representative every time they were trying to secure a new contract or renew an existing one. This was Julian Wethered's memory of his dealings with the Bank of Nepal:

The Bank of Nepal was an old substantial stone-built Indianised style building radiating 19th century dependability and guardianship. Its Governor was a wispy looking man with a poet's soul, and the eyes of a dreamer. It took a while to get on net with him, but I think I partly succeeded. He was graciously courteous and gave me tea whilst he set out the requirement of the Bank to increase their stock of banknotes. He was somehow obsessed with the new portrait of His Majesty King Mahendra, depicting him in his later years, which was to appear on the next series of banknotes. We were in competition, as was almost inevitable in those days, with Bradbury Wilkinson. I had discussed the matter with the Deputy Governor, a man of coarser cloth, whose sole occupation was to drive down the price to rock bottom, and who did not care about the aesthetics and who, I sensed, was inclined towards Bradbury.

My reason for visiting Nepal at this time was to present our sketches for the new order, and also to make contact with a young highly placed courtier, whom I had met in London. In my briefcase I had a cheque made out to The Scouting Association of Nepal, the Chief Scout being His Royal Highness Prince Birenda Bir Birkram Shah Deva, whose wedding was about to take place. All this, of course increased the Wonderland aspect of the whole occasion. I handed the cheque over to the courtier, as a wedding present for the Crown Prince and cherished the hope that I might be invited to the ceremony. But sadly I was not. Thomas Stonor, of Stonor Park near Henley-on-Thames and his wife were; but then he and the Prince had been at school together in England.

It was to be made clear to me that the Governor did not accept the portrait of His Majesty which I had shown him. So I then cabled De La Rue requesting that one of our portrait artists be sent out to work on the portrait. I saw this as the only way we would win the order. Some days later I met Ron Turrell at the airport.

Ron was an intelligent and easy companion, and it was a pleasure to have him around. He was also a skilled and perceptive artist, and it was not long before I was able to present the amended sketch to the Governor. There are certain times when it is necessary to go 'a bit over the top', and this was, as I saw it, one of them. As I have mentioned the Governor was clearly of a visionary turn of mind, who revered the King as something of a demi-god. So, as we scrutinised the royal portrait I said, 'You may notice Governor that Ron has given his Majesty's eyes a quality which brings out his spirituality and wisdom'. I waited fearing he might say 'absolute rubbish'. In fact he said nothing, merely nodded in agreement. A few days later we were given the order for a substantial quantity of notes. Ron stayed on some time in order to tweak a few vignettes and scroll work before returning home.

GIORI

The 1960s was when the long, and sometimes tortuous, relationship between De La Rue and Gualtiero (known to everyone as Rino) Giori came to a head. Much of what is written here stems from an interview with Peter Orchard, the one person who seemed able to cope with Rino Giori.

This is what Rino himself said of his background:

> In 1876 my grandfather, Dino Coen, founded a security printing works in Milan, Italy, called Officine Grafiche Coen. Mostly they did stocks and bonds and bank checks. He had two sons, Augusto and Renato, and one daughter. The two sons succeeded him in running the business.
>
> My family had been in Italy many centuries. Originally, they were Sephardic Jews who were forced to leave Spain in 1492. My father was the first to break the solid, close-knit family tradition by marrying a Catholic. It broke his father's heart. My mother's family had been in textile manufacturing. Her maiden name was Giori.

In 1938 the name of the family firm changed to Calcografia & Carte Valori; the Italian alliance with the Nazis had made the name Coen a liability. In 1939, a Spaniard, Don Luis Augue y Duran, came to Italy, a Franco ally, seeking a firm that could do banknotes for the Franco government that had just beaten the Republican forces in Spain. As manager of the firm's security printing division, Rino Giori was placed in charge of the work. (This was the firm's first banknote order.)

> We were doing about two million notes a day at the peak. All our Spanish notes had Calcografia & Carte Valori in tiny letters at the bottom. Don Luis, a close friend of Franco's, knew of course of the Jewish background of our firm but that didn't matter to him. Assurance of a steady delivery was more important. He never said why he hadn't turned to the German firm, Giesecke & Devrient, but I could only suspect that at the time Spain wanted a semi-independent supplier. We sent the notes to Franco by boat from Genoa. In a sense our notes symbolically represented the first return of the Jews to Spain after more than 400 years. Amusing in a way.

Another reason for the selection of the Milanese firm was that it had two of the most efficient intaglio-printing machines then available. These had been made by a French engineer, Serge Beaune, who had in Giori's words, 'invented the multicolour intaglio'.

Up to then, intaglio printing, which creates a raised surface on paper through considerable pressure, had been largely a one-colour-at-a-time affair. Consequently, it was slow and quite expensive compared to the more readily available offset lithography in which the image comes onto the paper flatly from a rubber roller. The Beaune presses were fairly fast but difficult to operate – encompassing a considerable waste of paper.

> Still, it was a revolutionary process and was faster than any known intaglio presses. In effect, then, our firm, Calcografia, had a headstart on the rest of the world of intaglio printing.
>
> In 1939, my father left for Argentina for racial reasons.

Italy still was far from the murderous anti-Semitic measures of Germany but he thought it wouldn't be long before even Italy succumbed. By 1941, all the rest of Giori's family had fled Italy for Switzerland.

In effect, I was left alone in charge of the large specialized printing plant with 1,100 employees.

I wasn't bothered because I was considered Catholic. And owing to a special decree covering many sons and daughters of similar mixed marriages, I was allowed to take my mother's name, Giori, as my own, instead of the trouble-inviting Coen. The orders for Spain kept on without incident until 1943 when the Germans took over the country just before the Allies landed in Sicily. Now the Nazi racial laws took effect and the fact that I was baptized a Catholic wasn't enough.

Baptism and non-circumcision were not nearly enough for the Nazis. Didn't I have one Jewish parent and two Jewish grandparents? I suddenly became a non-person and since I was in charge of printing the currency of a loyal ally, Franco's Spain, I was also a potential danger. One who had to be deported immediately.

On December 7, 1943 the SS encircled our factory in Milan to deport me ... The officer in charge spoke German only and he was supposed to arrest Mr Rino Coen. In the meantime I had changed my name. I was now called Gualtiero Giori. Gualtiero was my proper first name and Rino was my nickname (Gualtierino).

The German didn't realise the one he was looking for was standing in front of him and he asked where was Signor Rino Coen. I told him Signor Rino Coen was in Switzerland. He said this wasn't possible because they knew he had come to the printing works in a Lancia car around 3.30pm. I insisted, so he asked to place a telephone call and, in German, he took information of the personal data of Signor Rino Coen, which he repeated aloud. Thus, I assisted the description of myself and I gathered I was lost. But God was with me and little by little I started away from him, leaving him on the telephone. I was able to jump from a courtyard to another building which was not encircled by the SS, which enabled me to escape ...

At the end of the war Rino married and moved to Argentina.

In Buenos Aires, Rino looked at the world banknote scene and realised that there were two types of customer. There were the large countries that could either print all their own banknotes or choose to buy at least some of them from the big suppliers: American Bank Note and their British subsidiary, Bradbury Wilkinson, De La Rue or Waterlow. Then there were the smaller countries that could not afford to do their own printing and had to buy from one or all of the banknote suppliers.

Giori calculated that if he could develop the Beaune machine and make it operate efficiently and more economically, he could sell the machines to the smaller countries that could then print their own notes. How was he to put this theory into practice? In 1948 he had the good luck to be introduced to the Argentinean dictator Juan Perón, and he said later:

I studied his political philosophy and it was nonsense. But Perón wanted his country to become a major international power and the way to achieve that was first to develop his nation's 'calling cards' – postage stamps and paper currency.

Rino flattered Perón, who gave him a ten-year contract to develop the intaglio machinery that would turn out a new, impressive issue of postage stamps and currency for Argentina. Under the contract, Rino was able to import all the machinery and the ten technicians he believed he needed.

These technicians made the machinery more accurate and more dependable in being able to lay down five separate colours simultaneously in perfect register on a stamp or banknote.

At De La Rue, Bernard Westall soon realised the potential threat of Giori and his machines, and contacted him. Their early discussions were hindered by a personality conflict between the two. To Giori, De La Rue was still the enemy: he was convinced that they wanted to acquire his machine only to bury it. On 14 April 1950, a letter from Westall to Giori suggests the key point at issue:

> You will, of course, appreciate that the principle of the Serge Beaune is well-known, and, indeed, the original patent has expired, so that the general method of multi-colour printing is now open to anybody. However, if we do not come to terms, and again if we decide to interest ourselves in multi-colour printing, we shall develop it in our own way and with our own processes ... The next point I want to dispose of is the suggestion raised in your letter that we might acquire the rights in your process and machine, but refrain from using it as much as we could. Our only object in endeavouring to come to terms with you is because we believe that there is a big future in printing banknotes on your machine and I also believe that we shall be able to save money and that any royalty payable to you would be more than made up by economics ...

This is what Westall offered:

> Buy one of Giori's machines at cost plus 20 per cent.
> 2.5 per cent of revenue received on all orders printed on the Giori machine.
> 50 per cent of the profits of any such machine sold in the future.
> A $5,000 annual retainer for Giori's 'technical and commercial collaboration'.

Westall invited Giori to London, put him and his wife Maria up at the Savoy Hotel and entertained them lavishly. He even took Maria out to lunch separately to try to convince her to persuade Rino to accept his terms. She would say later:

> Even as he talked I knew nothing would come of this big deal. If Westall believed even for a second that I or any woman could persuade Rino Giori on a business matter ...

She was right. Giori rejected Westall's offer. He had already sold twelve of his machines in Argentina, Brazil, Chile and Colombia, and he reckoned he could afford his own machine-manufacturing plant. Rino Giori's next breakthrough came in 1951 when he met Siegfried Otto, who was trying to rebuild the German banknote-printing company Giesecke und Devrient in Leipzig, which had been bombed out of existence during the Second World War. In spite of the past, when, as we have seen, the Nazis tried to arrest Giori, Otto recalled:

> We hit it off fairly well. I told him his machine had good promise and that my firm would be interested in acquiring a few when it was perfected. I added, perhaps his big mistake was entrusting it to an Italian manufacturer. I felt that as it called for very rigid specifications and had to produce hairline colour registration, he should go to a firm that had lots of experience with fine printing machinery. I suggested the firm of Koenig & Bauer of Würzburg in West Germany and offered to introduce him to Hans Bolza, the head of the firm.

Giori took up his offer and signed a contract with Koenig and Bauer, who have manufactured the machines ever since. He continued to expand his business throughout the 1950s and into the 1960s, and was approached by De La Rue again in the mid-1960s. He said later:

> De La Rue came to me again around 1965. The world market was then divided roughly two-thirds to the Giori machines and one-third to De La Rue which had an intaglio machine but essentially a one-colour device. Ours, of course, was multi-colour, so ours was 40–50% more expensive. Still De La Rue was a very strong company with a lot of push. I was then only 52 but I had to start thinking ahead to the time I wouldn't be around anymore. My son Roberto was then 16, much too early to tell if he would be interested in carrying on the business. Also, when you're a special man you can't transfer your drive and intuition to another. Roberto is now with me in the business and doing very well, but fourteen years ago there just was no way to prophesy. There was another consideration: if we joined forces with De La Rue, between us we would have what amounted to a worldwide monopoly on the multi-colour intaglio machines and other equipment for banknotes and stamps.

This time the two parties reached agreement and formed a 50/50 partnership that was set up in a company, De La Rue Giori SA. Rino Giori was appointed Chief Executive as well as Chairman of the Board of Directors. There were three directors from De La Rue, including Peter Orchard, later to be Chief Executive of De La Rue and ultimately Chairman.

This is what Peter Orchard would say later about De La Rue's association with Giori – and specifically his relationship with Gino:

> I suppose no one would dispute my claim to be the leading Rino-ologist in this company or indeed anywhere else ...
>
> What happened was the big crunch in the period '56–58. The Bureau of Engraving in Washington put out a tender for presses to replace their very antiquated equipment and the two presses available were the De La Rue monochrome press and the Giori polychrome. And it was quite a good bit of buying on the part of the Bureau of Engraving, Henry Holtsclaw was the director at the time. He had the two presses

erected in a room at the Bureau in Washington and a wall erected between them and they were both required to do the same thing simultaneously so that direct comparisons could be made.

Ivan Knops was in charge of the De La Rue effort, he was supposed to be general manager of the Security Division but he was never there because for two years he virtually lived in Washington. Which is how Orchard got his first chance, because I was assistant general manager and I ran the business effectively for a couple of years up to '58. And in the end, amid scenes of great triumph, De La Rue was selected and we sold them eight or ten presses. Giori's press was purchased for the production of stamps but he was sent away with his tail between his legs.

He then came to London to see Gerry Norman, suing for peace, and was told to ... off. 'This is game, set and match, you can forget it,' which in hindsight was a terrible mistake. We could have done a deal with him then on much more favourable terms than was possible later.

In 1961, under pressure from people in the currency business, myself included, who could see the dire threat of uncontrolled Giori, Gerry had another go at negotiating. He failed, and wrote a famous memorandum which says, 'I'm really rather pleased because I don't think this bloke is workable with'. The real problem there, as with Bernard Westall, was that Gerry did not like Rino, still doesn't as a matter of fact. Two more different people you couldn't possibly imagine, and they had no language in common. And you can't negotiate in two languages that don't match with someone you rather dislike or even despise.

They were talking at cross purposes the whole bloody time and Gerry came to me saying, 'This chap changes his mind so often, you can't deal, hopeless, forget it.' So okay, we forgot it. And we forgot it until 1963, March 30th to be precise, one of the dates that stick in one's memory for various reasons. I heard that Rino Giori was in London, went to see him at the Westbury and said, 'Look, I think this fighting between you and De La Rue for the world market for banknote printing is ridiculous and we ought to do a deal'. He said, 'I've heard that before, ha, ha'.

I talked to him in my French which at the time was very poor. I was well stoked up on Portuguese having lived for two years in Brazil; my French was very rusty indeed. But I spoke to him in French and no other language, and still do. Anyway, at the beginning of the negotiation, and because my French was so poor, I had to put up with the frustrations of letting him get in all the smart digs. My vocabulary and my speed of thought in the French language wasn't sufficient to retaliate, which is no longer the case.

Over a period of two years, that took us to 30th March 1965, we had a string of meetings, becoming more serious as he began to trust me and I began to think there was a way through this thicket. I was supported, if that's the right word, at any rate by Ivan Knops. Ivan felt about Rino as Gerry felt about Rino, hated him, and having fought him for two years in Washington and won he didn't relish the idea of any kind of deal. It was rather like Mrs Thatcher and the Falklands – a psychological impossibility to suddenly like someone you've taught everybody else to hate. John Finn, the finance director of Thomas De La Rue International, was a tremendous help. He was a very quiet fellow, greatly underrated by a lot of people, but had an inventive brain.

For two years we met in London, in Lucerne, in Milan, in Montecatini, all over the bloody shop. And eventually hammered out the deal which caused De La Rue Giori to come into existence. The key to it was my willingness, which neither Bernard nor Gerry would ever have conceded, to pay a commission to Giori on the banknote production of Thomas De La Rue.

All the banknotes printed by Thomas De La Rue attracted a commission of 2%, in the end: 2% to De La Rue Giori, which meant 1% for him, 1% for us. The beauty of it was that the 1% for us came through tax-free, so the actual cost was negligible. The insult, if you think in those terms, was colossal. Why would we pay this man money for anything? The answer was, 'It opened the door'. It cost us very little money relatively speaking, but is still resented in the Currency Division, because they never understood how their business was being destroyed by Rino on the rampage running around the world setting up banknote printing plants without a look over his shoulder.

So, Rino signed that deal on 30th March 1965, De La Rue Giori came into being and that created a sole supplier for the supply of banknote printing equipment.

MINSTRO OR MINISTRO

Peter Orchard and De La Rue may have suffered some tough negotiations with Rino Giori, although the joint venture proved to be immensely profitable for both parties for over 30 years, but they were soon embroiled in some more tense negotiations, this time in Brazil.

One day in March 1966 one of the finishing girls in the Gateshead factory told her supervisor that the spelling of a word on the current order for Brazilian currency was different from what it had been previously. As it was a repeat order of a long-standing design for a number of values, the only changes in the content of the notes were in what are called the overprints, in this case the prefixes and the numbers, and the signatures and titles of the Minister of Finance and the Governor of the Central Bank.

Of course, numbers are never repeated, to ensure that there are never two completely identical notes in circulation. On the other hand, in most countries Ministers and Governors change quite often, and Brazil was no exception. On the notes in question, the signature of Sergio Bulhoes appeared on the lower left of the note, as Minister of Finance, and that of Denio Nogueira on the right, as Governor of the Central Bank. To avoid problems of register, the titles were overprinted from the same letterpress blocks as the signatures above them, rather than being engraved and appearing in the main printing.

What the alert girl in the finishing department spotted was that the title beneath the signature of Bulhoes read MINSTRO DA FAZENDA. It should have been MINISTRO DA FAZENDA. No fewer than 110 million notes, a substantial part of the order, had been printed with this error without anyone spotting it. Furthermore, a quick check showed that the error was also on the proofs that had been submitted to, and approved by, the Central Bank.

It could therefore have been claimed, and from a strictly legal point of view no doubt successfully, that Thomas De La Rue was not at fault, since the responsibility for checking and approving proofs, which were as usual submitted before production began, lay with the Bank. While this was technically correct, there was no doubt in the minds of Thomas De La Rue management that the moral responsibility lay with the company, that the goodwill of the customer would be forfeited completely if it refused liability, and that the company would be the laughing stock of the banknote printing world when, rather than if, the mis-spelling was spotted.

It was a particularly awkward time of year for a disaster like this to occur. The company's financial year ended on 31 March, and the cost of reprinting was calculated at more than £300,000 (about £7.5 million today), a very significant sum indeed in proportion to the size and profitability of the De La Rue Group at the time.

At a De La Rue Board meeting held at Maidenhead on 23 March three possible courses were debated. The first was to 'forget' the discovery of the error and hope that it would not be noticed for a long time, if ever. The second was to make some kind of provision in the accounts in the hope that it would not be required, and the third was to throw themselves on the mercy of the customer, suggest various very expensive and unsightly ways in which the error could be corrected on each individual note, and last, if all else failed, be prepared to swallow the cost of the reprint.

Peter Orchard, at the time in charge of the security side of De La Rue's business (Thomas De La Rue International), accompanied by Roy Rochford, the Preliminaries Manager, flew to Rio de Janeiro on 27 March. As it happened, they were both Portuguese speakers, having served together in the Brazilian company five years earlier. They took with them proofs showing what various treatments, such as silvering over or blotting out the offending lettering, would look like.

It was two days after their arrival before they were able to see Denio Nogueira, the Governor of the Central Bank. He, Bulhoes and Roberto Campos made up the three-man 'Equipo Economico' which, under the military rule of Castello Branco, produced what was regarded at the time as something of an economic miracle. In fact, in the end it turned out to be only one of the upturns in the switchback of the economic history of Brazil.

Peter Orchard told the Governor that he had come to see him because there was a potentially serious problem with regard to Thomas De La Rue's current order, and the Governor's decision would be required. He then placed one of the MINSTRO notes on the Governor's desk and asked after careful study whether he could see anything wrong with it. The Governor could not, nor could the three or four henchmen he called into his office.

The MINSTRO error was then pointed out. The Governor said 'Ah', and, after a moment's pause, left the room. He almost certainly phoned Bulhoes for his advice. When he came back ten minutes later he did not ask whether the error could be rectified, having presumably come to the correct conclusion that any rectification

would be unsightly and would cause adverse comment and require explanation. Instead, he asked how soon he could have supplies of the new CR$10,000 notes, which were urgently needed in the inflationary situation of the time. How many did he want? At least 20 million, please.

The TDLR pair went off to send a very urgent and cogent cable (no telephone or even telex in those days) to get a delivery promise out of Naja Penty, the Sales Manager, and Alan Law, the Managing Director of the banknote business. The answer came back within 24 hours. The notes would be ready for shipment in eight weeks, more or less a miracle, and dependent on top priorities everywhere and some luck.

Back to Denio Nogueira. Was that the best that we could do? It was. Would our price for these notes be the same as the previous order? It would. Very well, then, when the error-ridden notes arrived in Brazil, said Denio, they would be sent to the north-east, 'where they can't read anyway'.

Humble thanks, a quick retreat before he changed his mind, an exultant cable and an awful lot of drinking that evening. The notes eventually went into circulation, and it was nearly three years before the error was spotted by a member of the public. Orchard and Rochford returned just too late to vote in the General Election of April 1966.

CLOSURE OF BUNHILL ROW AND THE QUEEN'S AWARD

As De La Rue signed its deal with Organisation Giori, it announced that it was finally leaving Bunhill Row, which had been associated with De La Rue for no less than 132 years. Of course, much of the production had been forced to move elsewhere in 1941. The security printing activities had already moved to St Albans in 1961 and the City Print Division had been closed down in November 1964. Now the remaining De La Rue staff in Bunhill Row would move into new offices in Bonhill Street, and the Thomas De La Rue International personnel in Bunhill Row would move to the Group's offices in Regent Street in the centre of London.

1966 was to prove an interesting year. In the wider economy, a seamen's strike served only to emphasise the UK's vulnerability on the balance-of-payments front, prompting an emergency budget in July (the same month that England finally won the football World Cup). Among other restrictions, a freeze was imposed on all salary and wage levels. For De La Rue the year began well when Thomas De La Rue and Company were awarded a Queen's Award for services to exports. The award was well deserved, as the company had averaged 90 per cent of its turnover in exports for the previous three years.

By the autumn the government measures were beginning to have an effect on the Formica and Potterton companies. In March 1967 Gerry Norman said:

> We shall be reading of poor results from many quarters for some little time to come.
>
> Our reaction in the Group to the complete change of economic climate in the UK which has resulted in short-time working in factories and staff reductions has been to

> accelerate our programme of weeding-out loss-making concerns both at home and overseas, and to make a detailed review of those areas where we can use our resources better and make vital savings.
>
> On the positive side we have been continuing with the launching of new products and maintaining the initiative in the markets in which we operate.

And he added in July, following the annual results that showed a reduction in both sales and profits:

> A tough year – but one in which the decks have been cleared for further expansion – this time accompanied by better profit performance.
>
> The UK economic climate over the past months has hit sales and profits hard. This has coincided with the full after-effects of the policy of weeding out non-profit-earning businesses which I spoke about this time last year.
>
> Now that is behind us. The most vigorous marketing and cost reduction programmes are in action and, given some improvement in the UK economic situation, I think 1967/68 should see a material improvement in profits.

The one company in the Group that had enjoyed a good year in 1966–67 was Thomas De La Rue International, which increased its profits from just over £1 million to £1.34 million (£25 million to £33.5 million in today's money). Norman said this:

> Withdrawal from unprofitable ventures in Mexico and France and USA has left T.D.L.R.I. in a sound state to continue expansion in its own fields and develop new product and services.

Managing Director of Thomas De La Rue, Alan Law, said this of the company's performance and prospects:

> T.D.L.R. largely unaffected by the UK recession, had a very fine year and contributed its highest ever profit to the Group.
>
> Banknote sales made rare inroads into our competitors' share of the market and in particular were on the spot to bring home every contract which resulted from the sudden and violent upheavals in the African continent. The coin section too has made its contribution and we closed down our only loser, Philatelic Services, as it had failed to get off the ground in reasonable time.
>
> I should especially mention the difficulties that the Dublin factory has experienced and overcome and the effort that is now being made to put this operation on a more secure footing.
>
> The Security Print side of the business turned its former hefty loss into a very useful profit and whilst this was undoubtedly helped by the introduction of new processes, it was more especially due to a new, realistic, determined and disciplined approach throughout.

> With the traditional products paying their way, it has been possible to plan and launch a new Automated Printing Unit – the first of its kind in the country – which opens up new markets for new products, using new methods, equipment as well as new people. This 'systems' approach to print undoubtedly offers us great opportunities both this year and in the future.
>
> Nevertheless the banknote side of the business during 1967–68 is still responsible for a very large slice of the cake. It remains as ever vulnerable to the economic disturbances overseas, many of which, contrary to popular opinion, are often outside our control, and it is clear that for these reasons we shall have one hell of a job hitting our target this year.

It was in 1967 that De La Rue came to an agreement with the Royal Mint that they would handle the Mint's sales. The profit contribution was never really significant, but there was the odd coup such as the one described here by Dennis Paravicini:

> But the other one of course which was really a major one was the contract we got for a gold coin for an Arab country, where we put in an offer for 20,000, I think, gold coins, at a very high price indeed for a gold coin of the Sheikh, and the Governor of the Monetary Authority was an Englishman. He took it to the Sheikh who said that he liked this very much, turned to all his sheikhs sitting around him, sitting in a circle as they do in an Arab country, and they all said 'We think it's wonderful too'. And the Governor came back with an instruction to buy a million of these coins and the net result was that we got an order worth £32 million and De La Rue's made at least £800,000 out of it, and the Royal Mint made millions out of this. And of course we knew that they would only ever use 20,000 out of these one million and this is exactly what happened. They went out and they only used 20,000 and there were 980,000 of these things which nobody wanted and so the Governor said, 'We'd better start getting rid of them.' In the meantime the price of gold multiplied; if you remember the time it went from $35 to $400 or something and the Authority made an absolute fortune. It is a perfect example of 'to them that have shall be given', because if it happened to anybody else it would have gone the other way. So we all made an absolute mint out of it. De La Rue made a mint out of it, the Royal Mint made a mint out of it, the customer made a mint out of it and that was a satisfactory story.

THE RANK BID

On 19 November 1968 John Davis, the Chairman and Chief Executive of the Rank Organisation, invited Gerard Riddick, De La Rue's Deputy Chairman and Managing Director, to his office at 56 Hill Street, Mayfair, and told him that Rank were going to make a bid for De La Rue.

He also told Riddick that he hoped the De La Rue Board would recommend acceptance to their shareholders, as he was sure it was in their interest. He said he looked forward to working with the present management and, bidding him good day, requested that he receive a reply by 28 November.

This was a follow-up to a lunch that Gerry Norman and Peter Orchard had been invited to months earlier with Davis and his deputy, Graham Dowson. Apparently it was not clear to Norman and Orchard why they had been invited, as the conversation never focused on anything specific. Orchard said later:

> We had rather assumed that there might be some interest arising from Formica's industrial laminates which were supplied to Rank's television manufacturing division, Bush, but, in the light of later events it is clear that we were being sized up.

Rank's origins were in the film industry, and had been built up by J. Arthur (later Lord) Rank. (Remember the muscle man hitting the gong at the beginning of each film?) When he bought the Odeon and Gaumont British cinema chains in 1947, he created a vertically integrated company that covered films from their conception to production, distribution and showing in cinema chains. In the 1950s, faced with the challenge of television, Rank diversified into other industries, and by the time of the De La Rue bid in 1968, only 18 per cent of its turnover came from cinemas and 5 per cent from film production and distribution. Elsewhere the Group had moved into other parts of the entertainment industry, including bowling alleys, bingo halls and ice-rinks. It also owned hotels and motorway service stations. As it happens, it did have some manufacturing jobs, making cameras, projectors, television and radio sets as well as some electronic and precision instruments. The jewel in the crown, and the main reason for the high valuation of its shares, was Rank Xerox, which it owned jointly with the Xerox Corporation of the USA. In 1968 Rank Xerox represented 48 per cent of Rank's capital base and no less than 79 per cent of the Group's profit before tax.

Riddick made no response to Davis's bid statement but hurried back to De La Rue's head office in Regent Street and summoned the directors who were available – Peter Orchard, Den Moore, who was head of Formica, and Arthur Morrish, the Company Secretary. The Chairman, Gerry Norman, was also President of the CBI (Confederation of British Industry) and was away on CBI business. Freddie King, the Finance Director, was in Rio de Janeiro.

A week later, on 26 November, Norman and Riddick went to meet Davis and Dowson at Rank's head office in South Street, Mayfair. The meeting lasted 45 minutes and Norman reported back to his colleagues: 'At this point of time, Mr Davis is extremely anxious to achieve his ultimate objective with the support of the De La Rue Board.' Apparently, although Norman requested it, no offer price was discussed. Davis said he wanted the two Boards' professional advisers to meet and agree a price on the basis of 'willing buyer, willing seller'.

Davis put forward these arguments for making the bid. Rank, like De La Rue, was something of a conglomerate with a wide difference of performance between its various parts. By far the most profitable part was the Rank Xerox document copiers company, while the rest was 'associated with the leisure and luxury industries which had been severely hit by the Socialist legislation of the present Government'. Davis went on to say that he was within reach of retirement and he wished to secure

Rank's future by acquiring businesses that were less vulnerable to such interference. De La Rue fitted well with his requirements and he saw no difficulties in absorbing and operating it.

In reply, Norman described De La Rue as a 'three-legged dog' and wanted to know how Davis would treat each leg. The answer was that the central-heating business, Potterton, would be sold; Thomas De La Rue, the banknote and security business, would be allowed to continue in what Davis called 'its own specialist way'; and Formica would be merged into Rank's own worldwide interests.

The truth was that it was the diversifications of the 1940s, 1950s and 1960s that had made De La Rue vulnerable to a bid. We saw earlier what Gerry Norman had to say about it, and he concluded:

> Considering that in 1952/53 we hit a low spot and had a total reorganisation, we were soon back on the track of expansion and diversification again. But it was that diversification that led us into trouble which eventually led to the Rank bid in 1969.

When asked about the effects on De La Rue management, Davis said that there were currently seventeen vacancies in senior positions at Rank and that he felt that, providing they were good enough, all De La Rue senior managers would find suitable slots. He anticipated that redundancies were 'likely to arise in some small way' at De La Rue's head office. He offered Norman a seat on the Rank Board and said to Riddick as he and Norman left: 'I'm sure we will make you happy here.'

The next morning, Norman told the full De La Rue Board the details of their discussions and said that Rank was 'strongly placed from a purely financial point of view and that a negative answer to Rank's request for the cooperation of the De La Rue Board in a negotiated take-over would undoubtedly mean, if the bid was persisted with, a long, hard and unpleasant battle'.

'NOT IN THE BEST INTERESTS OF SHAREHOLDERS'

Nevertheless, the De La Rue Board was unanimous and adamant that they did not want to be taken over by Rank under any circumstances. Whatever his own personal views, Norman accepted this view and planned to tell Davis on the Thursday evening. However, on the Wednesday, the London evening newspaper, the *Evening Standard*, carried a story about the possibility of a Rank bid for De La Rue, and Norman immediately rang Davis to request a meeting that evening or first thing on the Thursday.

In the event, he and Riddick met Davis and Dowson at South Street at 8.30am on the Thursday. Norman told Davis of his Board's decision, and when Davis asked for the reasons, Norman refused to give any on the grounds that such disclosure might prejudice any future bid defence. The friendliness of earlier meetings had gone, and Davis said that rejection must be because of the preponderance of full-time employees on the De La Rue Board. Norman rejected this and Davis asked about the shareholders, to which Norman said that without an offer price he could not ask the shareholders.

Norman and Riddick returned to their office, consulted their advisers, and, after a further brief conversation with Davis, issued this statement to the London Stock Exchange at 10.20 a.m.:

> De La Rue announce that the Rank Organisation has made an approach to the De La Rue Board but at the moment no discussions are taking place and no bid has been made.

A week went by, and on Friday 6 December, Rank made a formal offer. It was a mixture of Rank shares and cash valuing De La Rue at 57s 2d (£2.86) against a pre-bid De La Rue share price of 49s 6d (£2.47). (Not much of a premium there!) In the evening, De La Rue issued a formal rejection, saying, inter alia:

> Not in the best interests of shareholders or staff or customers ... unanimous resolve of the Board ... to oppose it.

Peter Orchard, then a Director, later the Chief Executive and finally Chairman until his premature and tragic death in 1996, said later:

> The facts were indeed daunting. Rank had a price/earnings ratio which was nudging 30, while ours was in the low teens. [In other words, the City and major shareholders thought that the growth prospects for Rank were much better than those for De La Rue. It also meant that Rank could easily raise its bid without having to find more cash.]
>
> Thanks to their advertising power (largely from Rank Xerox, then a virtual monopoly in the document copying field), Rank had considerable influence with the press, and John Davis was built up as an industrial manager of great skill and vision. What was puny little De La Rue by comparison?
>
> At the time Rank was 38th in size among British companies measured by capital employed, while De La Rue was 186th.

Rank's sales in the year 1967–68 had been £204.5 million (just over £4 billion in today's money), while De La Rue's had been £42.5 million (£850 million). Rank employed over 50,000 people while De La Rue's payroll was just over 10,000.

The 1960s had been difficult years on the stock market after the excitement of the 1950s. That decade had ended with a boom. Production rose rapidly, and the recovery spread from consumer goods to capital goods. Productivity gained dramatically too, with the increase in employment lagging well behind the rise in production. Exports soared, particularly of cars. These were the days when British sports cars were conquering America, and over 50 per cent of UK car exports in 1959 went to North America, which had taken over from Australia, New Zealand and South Africa as the most important market for British cars. In May 1959, the

British Motor Corporation (BMC) announced that it was planning to step up production in the face of 'overwhelming demand', and after unveiling the new Mini (priced at £497, or about £11,500 in today's money, including purchase tax) in August, it reported that its home market order book stood at three times the level of the year before. British aircraft, too, were very popular with overseas buyers, and the Vickers Viscount became the staple of airlines in many parts of the world.

All this brought an upsurge in company profits. However, the reality of Britain's true position in the world was being masked by this growth in demand. The country was still over-dependent on those smoke-stack industries of the 19th century – coal, iron and steel, ship-building – and was dogged by poor management and low labour productivity.

Anthony Sampson, famous for his book *Anatomy of Britain*, also wrote a book called *Company Man: The Rise and Fall of Corporate Life*, and highlighted some of the reasons for British business weakness relative to its competitors:

> In Europe after the Second World War, British companies appeared to have a long lead over their rivals on the devastated Continent. But the victors' triumph was won at the expense of commercial realism. They remained trapped in their military glory and industrial systems, while the vanquished were compelled to start from scratch, and think again. And the Continental business families re-emerged with their control and motivation revived by the challenge of war, reasserting their continuity and will to survive with more dedication than the British Dynasties.

The pound sterling, in spite of the devaluation of 1949, was still overvalued, a fact that became increasingly apparent as the 1960s wore on. Although Harold Wilson refused to contemplate another devaluation, by 1967 it became inevitable and in November of that year the pound was devalued from \$2.80 to \$2.40.

Initially, especially as devaluation was followed in the spring of 1968 by a tough budget from new Chancellor of the Exchequer Roy Jenkins, the atmosphere in the City was one of gloom. The *Financial Times* 30 Index (there was no FT 100 Index until 1984), which had gone up very little from the 360 it had reached in 1959, started to rise sharply in April 1968 as it was realised that exports and overseas sales, and the constituents of the index that were, on the whole, big international companies, would now be more profitable. The Rank Organisation was a large international company and, through its diversification in the leisure industry, a beneficiary of the increasing prosperity in Britain, where the economy had continued to grow in spite of difficulties with the balance of payments and runs on the pound (governments were obsessed with the balance of payments in those days). This made the City's view of Rank much more rosy than their view of De La Rue. A price/earnings ratio of 30 (i.e., the company was valued at 30 times one year's post-tax earnings) meant that the City viewed Rank as a growth company and that it could easily buy De La Rue, provided the purchase was in their highly rated shares.

John Davis was possibly trying to emulate Jim Slater, the great 'conglomerator' of the late 1960s and early 1970s. A former manager at the large engineering company AEG, Slater had set up Slater Walker Securities in partnership with Peter Walker, a Member of Parliament and later a minister in Edward Heath's 1970–74 administration. (Apparently he realised Walker's worth when Walker sent him a case of a wine Slater had liked – and then followed it up with an invoice!)

Alex Brummer and Roger Cowe described the buccaneering approach of Slater in their biography of James, later Lord, Hanson:

> These deals took place in the fevered atmosphere of the mid-1960s stock market boom. Following a slump in 1966 after Harold Wilson won his second election victory and continued to struggle vainly to resist devaluation, the All-Share index began to rise from a low of 88 points in November 1966 to 180 points by the beginning of 1969, boosted by the eventual devaluation and undeterred by the government's continuing struggle against inflation and the quagmire of industrial relations. These were years in which Jim Slater built his reputation for supposedly infallible investment, which earned him the sobriquet of 'The Master' among his most adoring followers. The Slater years were a time when financial wheeler-dealing was briefly respectable, and when the new breed of 'conglomerateurs' seemed to offer hope to Britain's battered industry.

De La Rue was not highly rated, and indeed its profit record in the 1960s had been patchy. It too had diversified, but whereas Rank could argue, with the exception of Xerox, that its diversification had been effectively still in the entertainment world, there seemed little synergy between banknote and security printing, central heating equipment and industrial laminates. In the 1968 Annual Report, the De La Rue Chairman had said:

> The activities are divided into three main operational groups covering security printing, security transport, security printing machinery, automatic payments systems and their ancillary activities; plastics and chipboard; and heating by gas, oil and electricity. It also has a subsidiary interest in scientific instruments, and in a finance company, in addition to a trade investment in computers.

As for growth, De La Rue could not match Rank. In the five years to March 1968, sales had risen from £30.5 million to £42.5 million (this seems pretty small beer, but multiply by 25 to reach today's values and it looks a bit better). Margins were around a respectable 8.5 per cent, though in the less good years they had fallen to 6.3 per cent.

Furthermore, De La Rue appeared to be unbalanced, with three different 'legs' contributing varying levels of profitability. Thomas De La Rue was doing well, with margins at 14 per cent and annual profits before tax growing at nearly 20 per cent. On the other hand, Potterton's margins were only 3.5 per cent and its profits before tax less than half what they had been five years earlier. Formica's margins were 11.2 per cent but fluctuated sharply year on year. Other diversifications had either been abandoned, for example computers, or were somewhat bizarre, for example pea-sorting machinery.

The implication was: the 'dynamic' John Davis can surely do better than this. Look what he's done at Rank.

The De La Rue Board were likely to face a problem once the shareholders considered the attractions of a bid. None of them had a significant shareholding. The largest stake – only 6,650 shares out of a total of 11.1 million – was that of the Managing Director, Gerard Riddick. Nor did the employees have many either – less than 1 per cent. The company had paid little attention to its shareholders. As Gerry Norman said later:

> All through the Westall period (chairman 1944–63) and for some of the Norman regime (1964–87) it would be true to say that shareholders were given little attention by a management who were bent on conquering the world, outflanking competitors and expanding at all costs (and in all directions!). If the shareholders benefited from time to time it was incidental.

Now, for the first time, the company would have to take its shareholders seriously. Fortunately for them, there were not, as would be the case today, a few financial institutions with large stakes. Ninety-four per cent of the company's shareholders were private individuals who owned 55 per cent of the share capital.

Philip Robinson, the Schroders director looking after De La Rue, was pessimistic, telling the Board they had no chance of fending off Rank and the best that could be hoped for was extracting a higher price.

Others, especially at De La Rue, showed more grit and determination. There was, and still is, a family and team spirit within De La Rue that made the company feel special to the people who worked in it. The general attitude was: 'This is not just any old company, this is De La Rue. I am part of it, I give my all but I appreciate that I am fortunate to be part of this unique company. And I certainly do not want to work for a company that runs bingo halls and motorway service stations.'

One manager said later:

> Because of the personal and paternal nature of De La Rue in those days we were very committed to the Company and the idea of being taken over was pretty horrific.

There was also support from the shop floor. Labour relations, not least in the print industry, were difficult in the 1960s but with this threat of takeover, management and unions came together. Union leaders across the Group wrote to the company, and later to the Monopolies Commission, expressing their opposition. Roger Sawtell made sure that Vic Feather, the Trades Union Congress General Secretary (a powerful position in the 1960s), was 'kept informed of everything, really blow-by-blow'.

One industrial relations manager in Gateshead said:

> The shop floor distrusted management over pay negotiations and that kind of thing, but when it came to the bid there was a great deal of trust, expressed as 'those lads up in the office know what they're doing and we'll just get on with our jobs.'

Furthermore, as Arthur Morrish and Roger Sawtell dug a little deeper into the ethos of Rank, they found out plenty about the way the company was run – virtually a dictatorship. This clearly was not a company for whom any De La Rue executive would want to work. Morrish said that 'Davis, who was used to getting his own way, hired and fired at the drop of a hat with the result that staff turnover in Rank was very high'.

To put their defence in place, the De La Rue Board summoned 40 senior managers to head office in the middle of December 1968. At an evening meeting at the company's splendid neo-Georgian house in Mayfair, Lees House, Finance Director Freddie King, cigarette in one hand, blackboard pointer in the other, and the ever-present large whisky close by, took everyone through a series of charts.

They showed the management and structures within Rank, and that the A and B shares of Rank, and the way the subsidiaries were owned, proved conclusively that the whole operation was indeed run by one man, the unsavoury John Davis. And King did not pull any punches in exposing the private lives – including divorces and alleged sexual aberrations – of various senior executives.

Raymond Hudson, a relatively new De La Rue Board member, recalled later:

> Though it sounds, to put it mildly, rather mean and childish, it was in fact to make a very telling point: 'Is this the sort of management, shareholders, you think can run a business which depends for its livelihood on the right links with heads of state and governors of central banks?' The answer must have been 'No'.

In the end, the company never used this inside knowledge, but it probably worked in terms of inspiring those in De La Rue in their determination to do everything in their power to prevent the takeover. Interestingly, the arts critic Sheridan Morley, writing about J. Arthur Rank nearly 30 years later, said:

> Either he was the man who (backed by a brilliantly astute businessman called John Davis) dragged the post-war British film industry into some kind of shape by throwing £30 million at it, or he was the man who (backed by an extremely unpleasant, wife-beating bully called John Davis) effectively stifled the British film industry and forced its greatest talents ... into often unhappy exile. Either position is just about tenable.

The De La Rue senior managers were instructed to return to their divisions and make sure they performed well. They were also asked to produce detailed sales and profit forecasts for the next two years.

Furthermore, De La Rue did something they had rarely done in the past: they talked to the press, and in April 1969 a very favourable article in the Prufrock columns of the *Sunday Times* appeared under the heading 'The zig-zag path to folding super-lucre'. With photographs of Peter Orchard, David Rowe-Beddoe and Derek Lowther, it said:

> Its designers are to be found in the African bush chatting up chiefs who are experts in local folklore – or even wandering about with their secateurs snipping flower specimens off plants in the Antipodes helping to get the flavour of the country, whether it be florid, quaint or sober, on its banknotes.
>
> That is why Derek Lowther, the company's senior technical manager, found himself on one occasion in an African State checking the symbolic significance of a triangle, a square, a zig-zag, a lizard and a fish, before a thought could be given to incorporating these in designs.
>
> The De La Rue men are dab hands at this sort of detail. Their intelligence network is widespread and is sifting and evaluating political and economic information all the time. Here political in the commercial sense means who are De La Rue's friends in the Republic of Arcadia, and who are its competitor's friends.
>
> Much of this grass roots information comes from its agents on the spot. These are probably ex-Government Ministers or diplomats, men of stature and influence in their own countries.
>
> But overlaying this is the feeling that the company is brimming over with secrecy and a variety of discreet but highly effective security. Its international banknote salesmen – I still find it hard to believe this particular breed of species actually exists – are frequently the repositories of national confidences the like of which would make lesser mortals puke with fright, and which, if broken, could well bring a country's currency under pressure …
>
> You are totally involved in the thinking of important people all over the world. You must have an international outlook and the ability to keep your trap shut. Security is not only built into the product but also management. The company's top security man is a senior professional manager one rung below board level.
>
> David Rowe-Beddoe used to be a banknote salesman in Central America and the Caribbean and is now the boss of six others who cover the world for De La Rue. The first thing to understand about banknote salesmen is that they are emphatically not foot-in-the-door merchants. They do not flick open brown suitcases and say: 'Cop hold of these yins and feel the quality'.
>
> **Selling money**
>
> Selling banknotes is a sophisticated, high level, continuing business. You talk to Finance Ministers and governors of banks.
>
> 'You are selling integrity and quality and the security which is synonymous with them', says David Rowe-Beddoe. The salesman is on the trot seven months of the year and makes continuous visits to his customers, though in some countries less stable than our own there is also a time to keep away. It has not been unknown for questionable gents to approach De La Rue with all sorts of curious currency requests. 'The last thing you do is get involved,' says Rowe-Beddoe.

> How dramatic a contract is – a small country wanting a range of denominations would need 100 million notes and pay about £350,000 for them – depends on the circumstances. With a thing like decimalisation everyone knows in advance. But if a country decides on a new reserve issue the secret is between the salesman and a few others.
>
> Banknotes are sold on quality, security, technical innovation (this is to meet the increasingly sophisticated equipment available to counterfeiters), delivery dates and price. Surprisingly – to me anyway – it is often delivery which clinches a contract.
>
> Central banks sometimes get dangerously near to running out of money, which is something 'neither we nor they can afford to happen,' says Rowe-Beddoe. A memorable issue of one note was put through from design to print in 18 days, which is the sort of service which really gives value for money.
>
> If there is a corps of elite men in the banknote business it is the currency engravers. In De La Rue's London headquarters their status is recognised by individual, soundproofed workrooms, the freedom more or less to keep their own hours and salaries for top engravers which would make middle managers in industry jealous. In the currency engraving hierarchy, a portrait man is No. 1, followed by a vignette engraver – scenes and buildings – with the emblems and letters man in third place.
>
> Derek Lowther says there are 10 top portrait engravers in the world and De La Rue has three of them. They engrave direct on to a steel plate (so did I for a mad few seconds last week and if they ever print my gougings it will be a collector's item) and regard themselves not only as superb craftsmen but also artists. It takes four months to engrave one side of a note and four months to do the other. That's much longer than it takes to spend, isn't it?

The formal bid from Rank on 19 December offered De La Rue shareholders an increase of 55 per cent on their gross income. Norman wrote to his shareholders the next day requesting that they take no action. A detailed rebuttal of the offer followed on 30 December. It showed that De La Rue shareholders would effectively be disenfranchised because they were being offered only Rank 'A' shares, which did not carry voting rights. At the same time it forecast that De La Rue's profits for 1968–69 would be not less than £1.8 million against £1.193 million the year before, an increase of 50 per cent. Norman also warned about Rank Xerox:

> You would be investing in a group which is dependent on Rank Xerox for two thirds of its profit ... the remaining activities have shown no overall profit growth over the last five years.

De La Rue shares rose to 68s, well above Rank's offer. Philip Robinson's prediction seemed to be coming to pass, especially when, on 9 January 1969, Rank increased its offer by over 40 per cent, to 70s 8d. Davis also attacked the De La Rue Board and performance, noting that £100 invested in Rank ten years earlier was now worth £2,800, whereas in De La Rue it would be only £400.

However, Rank's statement not only contained a mistake about De La Rue's profits (which was swiftly and publicly corrected by De La Rue); it also worried the City, in that its forecast of its own profits for 1968–69 was below City expectations. Rank's shares began to fall, as did the whole market as it was realised that all of Britain's problems had not been solved by devaluation. The FT 30 Index slumped from 520 in January to 360 by July.

De La Rue's next move, four days later, was to make a further profits forecast, this time for 1969–70. These, the company said, would be £2.75 million, a further increase of 50 per cent on the forecast for 1968–69 and no less than 127 per cent above those actually achieved in 1967–68. Freddie King had obviously inspired his managers at the Lees House meeting! Every division forecast increased profits, including Thomas De La Rue, which saw significant growth in the sales of banknote machinery through its association with De La Rue Giori and the introduction of two new banking products, security systems, print, and cash-dispensing machines. The Potterton division was also expecting an increase in sales, again helped by new products, and an increased profitability from improved productivity in its factories. Finally, Formica said the same as Potterton – increased sales, new products, greater efficiency.

Whether all this came to pass, we shall see in a future chapter; but for the moment, Gerry Norman told shareholders that all the figures were produced on a basis strictly comparable with the published results of previous years and had been approved by the company's auditors and other advisers. Peter Orchard would say later:

> In those days I do not think the professionals had much idea about how to test assertions by managements and in any case the opprobrium for supporting a missed forecast was not then very great.

Fortunately for De La Rue, the media seemed happy to believe the forecasts. The *Daily Telegraph* wrote: 'De La Rue now looks to have more than a fighting chance of retaining its independence.'

'CLOSE PERSONAL CONTACT AT TOP LEVEL'

For a reason that now seems utterly bizarre, on 18 January 1969, the Board of Trade President, Anthony Crosland, announced that he was referring the proposed takeover to the Monopolies Commission 'for investigation and report under the provisions of the Monopolies and Mergers Act, 1965'.

The public, supposedly, and the Labour government because they thought it would be popular, had become increasingly concerned about 'big' business and its power; and the government was investigating more and more companies that wanted to merge to make themselves more efficient and profitable and therefore, in the government's view, more powerful. Most of the investigations concerned market share and the danger of undue pricing power. Most people could understand the sense of that.

However, the reason given for the Rank/De La Rue investigation had nothing to do with market share – how could it? It was to consider the much wider issue of the public interest, including Britain's balance of payments. (A proposed Unilever/Allied Breweries merger was also referred at the same time. Goodness knows what the reason was – though it was an awful idea – but again, it cannot have been concerns about market share. The Cadbury/Schweppes merger was not referred.)

There must have been more to the Rank/De La Rue referral than met the eye. It turned out that it was due to personalities, or John Davis's personality in particular. Gerry Norman said later:

> Tony Crosland was told by Harold Wilson to pick it up and refer it. I saw Wilson a long time afterwards and he said, 'There's a history between that man and me – he once double-crossed me'. We were very lucky that Davis was in charge of Rank. A bully and unpopular with the government.

It was a victory of sorts, though not, of course, if the Commission ultimately found no reason to block the takeover. Such a decision could be construed as an endorsement of it. Arthur Morrish said:

> After a long, and at times bitter, battle of two and a half months, when morale and company spirit were extremely high, the referral came as an anticlimax. True, it gave the contestants some sort of breathing space but it also involved many of the De La Rue Board and staff in much extra work, often into the small hours, in preparing the evidence which would be required by the Commission.

In its submission to the Monopolies Commission, the De La Rue Board made much of the potential loss of business because of the views of some of its important customers overseas, particularly in Nigeria and Pakistan, who said they would not want to be associated with such a company as Rank. De La Rue's submission concluded:

> To be controlled by a company widely known to be concerned in such activities as ten-pin bowling, dancing and bingo halls, would not assist ... De La Rue's business or its public image.

The commissioners cross-examined the De La Rue directors at great length in both February and March and also paid a visit to De La Rue House in Regent Street to interview executives there. They were suitably refreshed in the De La Rue fashion, and Arthur Morrish would say later: 'By this stage I think they were very much with us.'

Finally, on 2 June 1969, Anthony Crosland accepted the Monopolies Commission's recommendation that Rank's offer for De La Rue should not be allowed to proceed (or strictly speaking, to be renewed, because Rank had withdrawn their offer pending the result of the Commission's investigation). The reason given was: 'because it might be expected to operate against the public interest'.

When the report was published it made interesting reading. Apparently, the Commission had not been concerned about John Davis's almost dictatorial powers:

> While we have taken note of the fact that the constitution of Rank is such that effective control does not and cannot rest with its equity shareholders we have not been influenced in our decision by this fact or by its possible implications.

Nor did it seem concerned by the possible effects on De La Rue's relations with American Cyanamid (see page 236) and Giori, saying that it saw no reasons why these agreements could not be continued or renewed.

However, to the Commission, it was the banknote printing business that was crucial. This is what the key paragraph said:

> De La Rue has expressed to us its fears that this business [banknote printing] would suffer serious damage simply by being taken over by Rank. If this were the only consideration then we would feel that De La Rue's fears were exaggerated and that provided the De La Rue name and management were retained no significant damage would be likely to follow. We accept, however, De La Rue's contention that confidence and trust established over the years by personal contact at top level is all-important to the success of the business and it is on this account ... that we think there is a real risk of loss of business as a result of personnel changes ... several of De La Rue's operations are in fields in which it is the leading company ... so that any loss of efficiency would ... harm the public interest including the balance of payments.

So, De La Rue had escaped and, it would appear, largely thanks to the support it received from its overseas customers for its banknotes. As Barry Isted, long-serving De La Rue employee, ultimately Personnel Director and Company Secretary, said:

> The Company's traditions – and traditional strengths – were deployed to great effect. That virtually all the employees supported the Board, while the managers contemplated mass suicide, is unsurprising, given the ethos (if not the reality) of a family business. That the associated companies weighed in against Rank was also to be expected, given the incongruity of the predator. That so many foreign customers joined their supplier in the trenches is truly remarkable, given the existence of other security printers in the UK and elsewhere.
>
> Undoubtedly the products (especially banknotes) were of the highest quality and the service was second to none, but De La Rue's margin of superiority over its competitors could never be sufficient, on its own, to attract so much loyalty from its customers. That, as the Commission recognised, was down to people and relationships.
>
> In the modern idiom, De La Rue networked to supreme effect among its friends in high places around the world. The network had been developed over many years, through an assiduous attention to personal and national needs and, in equal measure,

great style in entertaining the Company's guests, whether one-to-one or in small groups at Lees House or at the famous diplomatic dinners and other international social events.

For all these assets De La Rue could thank its past. However, many liabilities of history were also exposed by the Rank bid.

The ethos of the family business, paternalism, had led to a measure of complacency. The in-bred Board seemed almost to claim a divine right to rule. The bid was taken as a personal affront. Never again after 1969 would De La Rue believe itself to be invulnerable. Rather, the reverse is true. For, as Chairman Norman remarked many years later: 'It was then a common belief in the City that once a company had been bid for it would be bid for again. It was in play. That certainly concentrated our minds.'

In defending itself against a predator, De La Rue had to step outside its self-contained world and then look inwards as a predator would. What it saw, as opposed to what it said in the public battle, shook the company to its roots.

The battle left many hostages to fortune, not least the unsustainable profits forecast. It threw into new debate a whole raft of former practices, products and philosophies that had been questioned but superficially in the post-war years because they had, by and large, worked well enough to satisfy a quiescent group of shareholders.

How the company reacted we shall see in subsequent chapters.

Chapter Ten

A Tough Decade

1970–1979

Aftermath of the Rank bid
Charging around Indo-China
'Nearly stopped this company'
'We can't get anything done'
'This has to be our bottom price'
Rationalisation
The last post
Crosfield Electronics
Recovery during the 1970s
The twin curse of inflation and recession
Orchard takes over
Into the 1980s

AFTERMATH OF THE RANK BID

De La Rue's divisions had all made forecasts during the battle to ward off the Rank takeover, and some of these turned out to be too optimistic. The historian of De La Rue's merchant adviser, Schroder Wagg, wrote later:

> There was a somewhat embarrassing epilogue nine months later when the De La Rue chairman announced a revised profits forecast for 1969–70 of £1.7 million, the downward revision being explained by an explosion at the firm's chipboard factory and a number of acts of God, Government and omission. Schroder Wagg went to the

> Take-over Panel to explain the discrepancy between the two forecasts and the firms were absolved of deliberate mismanagement.

And Managing Director Peter Orchard said: 'The Rank bid came, the Rank bid went. We bust the forecast we'd given the shareholders by a mile, and obviously things couldn't continue as they were.'

Quite apart from its turnover, profits before tax and margins, De La Rue's performance was to be dogged for many years, and certainly for most of the 1970s, by another figure: '£2.75 million.' This was the forecast made in January 1969, as part of the defence against the Rank bid, for attributable profits in 1969–70. In the event, the figure turned out to be £1.84 million; it was below even this for another two years, and the original target for 1970 was not beaten until 1974 (£3.3 million). In real terms it was not surpassed until 1977.

De La Rue had perhaps become a little complacent, though there was no question that it had worked hard to become, and stay, close to its customers. This was how one long-serving executive of De La Rue recalled the fabulous Diplomatic Dinners, which had been held since 1932:

> Always a proper white tie affair and you had the top people of the diplomatic community as well as the top London bank and business community. Often as not, the Prime Minister and one or two Royals. If you were invited you knew you had arrived solidly in London. The gifts for each guest were truly individual; the kind you expect from a thoughtful Maecenas. One time each guest – and there were a hundred, mind you – found at his plate a box with gold cufflinks – already engraved with his initials. (My friend showed me his pair.) Another time the gift seemed disappointing: an ordinary DLR deck of cards. Perfectly nice, but really – until you looked at the Ace of Spades. On it was your own photo. Can you imagine the detail work necessary to make certain the right picture appeared on the right deck and was given to the right guest on dinner night?

Nevertheless, Chairman Gerry Norman realised that the company would now be under scrutiny and would have to perform well.

And if the results for 1970 were disappointing, those for 1971 were even more so. Whereas profits before tax had grown sharply from £1.94 million in 1967 to £3.25 million in 1969, they declined to £2.56 million in 1970 and £2.145 million in 1971. Chairman Gerry Norman explained:

> The year to 31 March 1971 has been dominated by the struggle to maintain margins in the face of an unprecedented wave of inflation, which has affected every activity in the UK and most of our operation in other countries.

Nor was Norman particularly optimistic about the prospects for 1972 to 1973, saying:

> Shareholders will be well aware of the conditions which have prevailed in the main trading and investment areas of the world in the past year. Rising costs and prices, falling employment, slower growth and monetary uncertainties have all had a depressing influence on business confidence and therefore, on trade and investment levels. In the Board's view, the current year may not show a very great change in this general situation, except that recent government measures in the UK and USA may result in faster growth in the second half of the year. The growth rates throughout the EEC are today lower than in recent years, and inflation will still be proceeding at a damaging rate in most economies in the world if pay and salary increases continue to be seriously out of line with productivity gains. World monetary solutions have still to be found, and the outcome of the battle between trade expansion policies and protectionism is still in the balance.

The first half of the 1970s was a time of great economic turmoil, especially in the UK. The British economy had been struggling throughout the 1960s. The devaluation of sterling in November 1967 had only partially worked because it had not been accompanied by the necessary tough measures. Domestic inflation had quickly eroded the competitive advantage bestowed by the devaluation. In his budget of April 1970, Chancellor of the Exchequer Roy Jenkins had done his best to control soaring public expenditure, but the effect was to produce near-recessionary conditions in 1971. Furthermore, the US economy was at last faltering after almost ten years of uninterrupted growth, and many other of the world's leading economies also suffered a disappointing year. Only Eastern Europe, Australia, South Africa and South America seemed to escape.

Compounding general economic difficulties in the UK, industrial relations sank to a new low. In what proved to be the start of a very difficult decade on the labour relations front, the early months of 1972 saw a rash of damaging strikes. Viewed from the perspective of the early 21st century, Britain was at a very low ebb in the early 1970s. Still clinging to vastly overmanned smoke-stack industries, it had not fully grasped the new technologies. Indeed, the computer was still treated as a novelty by most of industry.

The change of government in 1970, when the Conservative party led by Edward Heath replaced Harold Wilson's Labour party, was supposed to bring an end to the collectivist approach that had been pursued, unsuccessfully in the view of most people, in the second half of the 1960s. Almost as soon as the new government was elected in June 1970, the dockers went on strike and, to the surprise of many, the Minister of Labour, Robert (later Lord) Carr, refused to intervene, leaving the dockers and dock employers to fight it out. The logic was that the interventions during both the Conservative administrations of the 1950s and those of Labour in the 1960s had invariably led to a surrender to trade-union muscle and an inflationary settlement. However, by the middle of 1971 the government's nerve had cracked. The policy of non-intervention in industry was reversed in early 1971 when one of Britain's most prestigious companies, Rolls-Royce, went bankrupt after overstretching itself in trying to complete an order for its innovative new aero engine, the

RB-211. No sooner had the government nationalised Rolls-Royce than it faced another industrial crisis, the collapse of Upper Clyde Shipbuilders. Again, the government swallowed its principles and a grant of £35 million was given to the company.

The most severe defeat experienced by the government came in early 1972 when it caved in to the miners. Furthermore, the flying pickets organised by a new-style miners' leader from Yorkshire, Arthur Scargill, made both the government and the police look clumsy. On 9 January 1972, a national coal strike began, the first since 1926, after the union had rejected the employers' offer of an 8 per cent wage increase. After successful picketing of many key coal depots and power stations, the government appointed a Committee of Inquiry under a high court judge, Lord Wilberforce. Already known for having given the power workers a 20 per cent increase the year before, Wilberforce soon recommended a very large increase for the miners. However, the National Union of Mineworkers (NUM) rejected this offer by 23 votes to two. After further negotiations and concessions, the miners won a total earnings increase of between 17 and 24 per cent and the strike was eventually called off on 21 February. The *Economist*, which had encouraged the Coal Board and government to take a tough line, saying: 'The miners cannot stop the country in its tracks as they once could have done', was seen as too optimistic. The miners seemed to have come pretty close to halting the country.

By the end of 1972 the loosening of credit controls by the Chancellor, Anthony (now Lord) Barber, had created boom conditions in the British economy; and for much of 1973 the problem for manufacturers was not the level of orders but of securing supplies and at the right cost. After the pause in 1971 the world economy was also growing strongly. As we shall see, this burst of growth was to prove very short-lived, but for the moment, the manufacturers' task was to take full advantage.

CHARGING AROUND INDO-CHINA

If general economic conditions in the UK were difficult, what was it like for Thomas De La Rue's salespeople overseas? Certainly, Charles Cardiff was finding it quite exciting in Vietnam, Cambodia and Laos. He said later:

> I spent much time charging around Indo-China. Three of the nicest customers I had and the most interesting that I had there were Vietnam, Cambodia and Laos. As it was Indo-China of course my French came in useful but this was in the dying days of the Vietnam War.
>
> My first exposure to Cambodia was visiting Phnom-Penh and it was just after the American Congress had voted to ban the bombing that the American Air Force were conducting in Cambodia and they were therefore saturation bombing the whole country. It was absolutely terrifying. Although the bombing was taking place some 30–40 miles away from the city, it went on 24 hours a day and because it's all paddy fields and water carries sound, it was as though it was happening across the street. These enormous B52 bombers dropping clusters of three bombs a time and every time they

dropped, the whole air conditioning system clunked and it was quite impossible to sleep at night, and when the bombing wasn't taking place there was small arms fire because the Khmer Rouge were gradually surrounding the city. And I was going there every two or three months in fact.

My last visit was I think two weeks before the Khmer Rouge walked in. I remember taking my then new wife and we checked into a hotel, which was called the Phnom but had been called before the Royale, and it was a three-storey building. We were on the first floor, and I said to her, 'Oh that's good,' and she said, 'Why?' And I said, 'When the rockets come through they're second impact rockets so they don't explode on hitting the roof; they explode on hitting the ground or the floor of the top storey or the ceiling of the second storey, so if you're on the first floor you're alright.' So she slept with all her jewellery on all night long, terrified. And there was a curfew, and there were extraordinary characters that one met: CIA people and other very odd looking people.

But what prospects were there for making any sales in this situation?

Oh, there were marvellous prospects because British aid was limited to a thing called the Foreign Exchange Operation Fund, which was run by a delightful Brit called Edward Fillingham, whom I still keep in touch with; he lives in Portsmouth and became a real good friend of De La Rue's. I met him subsequently all over the place. He was responsible for securing funds from the western companies to support the local currency because there were no funds at all coming into the Cambodian Government, or Khmer Government. He worked very closely with the British Ambassador and I would go and see him and he would say, 'Well, how many banknotes do you think you can sell this year? What's the demand?' And depending on what I told him, that was used as a budgetary limit to report back to the FCO in London and the support for the Cambodians went accordingly, and so we sold quite a lot.

When the Khmer Rouge walked in – and this I subsequently heard from my friend Edward Fillingham, who was flown out by an RAF Hercules to Singapore, and he heard this from his landlord who had managed to escape by walking through the fields to Vietnam, then getting out to Paris – what happened was that the day after the Khmer Rouge walked in, they went to the Bank and told all the people to go out in the street in front of the Bank. They then blew up the Bank and machine-gunned all the employees. They didn't believe in currency. So they blew up the Bank with all the banknotes we had printed and paid for. And I think there were some that weren't even paid for, or they were paid for but never delivered, and all messages and attempts to get messages to them met with no response. They didn't believe in money.

And in Vietnam it was similar because of the war. There were constantly rumours of the banknotes being counterfeited, so as soon as one lot of banknotes were printed another lot were being designed and prepared, so there was a huge consumption of banknotes going on there. In Laos it was rather similar, although I can remember flying with all these extraordinary local airlines they had. Royal Air Lao flew a Boeing 303 and I was sitting on it one day reading the *Far East Economic Review* and the editor's sort of jokey column with stories and anecdotes. He commented that Royal Air Lao were flying this plane which was so old that its proper place was in a museum. As one used to learn, the regular run between Vientiane, which is the capital of Laos, and Saigon touched down at a place called Savanakhet and this was an airport surrounded by hills. As you came down the hills, the Pathetlao, who were Communists were in the hills taking potshots at you. It was all quite exciting in a way. I had no children at the time so it didn't worry me too much.

'NEARLY STOPPED THIS COMPANY'

How did De La Rue cope with all these problems, whether at home or overseas? Realising that changes needed to be made, Deputy Chairman and Managing Director Gerard Riddick brought in a Canadian management consultant, William Allen. Allen had made a name for himself by organising a comprehensive productivity deal at Esso Petroleum's Fawley refinery and by writing a heavily publicised article in the *Sunday Times* under the heading, 'Half-Time Britain'. This said that Britain's problem was that it worked only half the time, with half the effort, for half the pay of its overseas competitors. Many agreed with this summary.

Allen advised plenty of changes at De La Rue, most notably recommending the removal of several key executives and the recruitment of new ones. One of the executives he thought should go was Peter Orchard, then the Managing Director of Thomas De La Rue International. Not surprisingly, Orchard would say later: 'Bill Allen bloody nearly stopped this Company in its tracks with the stupid decisions that he caused Gerard [Riddick] and others to make and the people that he persuaded us to take on.'

Of more than 30 managers that Allen recruited to Thomas De La Rue and Formica, very few survived more than five years. His influence also extended into the Board, as Riddick, without consulting his colleagues, had asked Allen to look into that as well. Again not surprisingly, when Riddick's Board colleagues found out about this, they 'began to get rather angry with Gerard'.

In the event, Allen's services were dispensed with in June 1970, the month his recommendations for Board changes were supposed to have been implemented. Nevertheless, changes were made. In May 1970 the Board agreed that 'The De La Rue Company is a management company' and should take a more hands-on role running the three divisions, Thomas De La Rue International, Formica International and Potterton International. An Executive Committee was set up comprising Riddick, Orchard, Den Moore (MD of Formica) and Freddie King (Finance Director), with John Finn, Company Secretary, as committee secretary. Den Moore remembered that the nickname for this Executive Committee was 'The Colonels' after the group of dictators who took over in Greece. Apparently, to try to make sure their memos (no emails in those days) received instant attention, they sent them on green paper. They were known to the less respectful as 'cow-pats'.

As a result of this reorganisation, Orchard and Moore appointed new operational heads at Thomas De La Rue (Alan Law) and Formica (Keith Bright).

'WE CAN'T GET ANYTHING DONE'

The next big event in the management structure was the removal of Gerard Riddick as Chief Executive. Orchard felt that he never really faced up to the big issues, and the rest of the Executive Committee spent half their time keeping him away from the operational divisions. Many of his suggestions were felt to be the products of convivial late-evening sessions. According to Orchard, the removal of Riddick was hastened by a chance conversation between him and non-executive director Max Stamp in the executive lavatories in December 1971. When Stamp asked Orchard how things were going, Orchard replied: 'Bloody badly, we can't get anything done.' In the end, on Friday, 21 March 1972, Gerry Norman and Stamp dismissed Riddick, and Norman took on the role of Chief Executive to add to his chairmanship.

Norman then acted decisively in reorganising the Group, and by the end of the year he had fourteen people reporting directly to him: the five Group functional heads and nine divisional managing directors. The next most powerful individual within this reorganisation was clearly Peter Orchard, who was appointed Director of Manpower and Communications. He took the opportunity to analyse the business in detail.

Having observed that the Executive Committee had, since its inception, 'spent the greater part of its time on administrative matters ... because of the need to think out its own precise role', Orchard went on:

> However, these factors must no longer remain a reason, or an excuse, for not tackling the main problem. It is no good saying that positive or creative thinking is a waste of time until we are able to place some credence in the forecasts, or until the profit figures lift the share price and enable some masculine action to be taken.

Then, in a remarkably frank diatribe, softened only by the pretence that he was trying to see De La Rue through an outsider's eyes, Orchard assessed the company's problems. In essence, he made ten points:

- The Group did not make industrial sense – it was a rag-bag of different industries with no synergy.
- The individual pieces of De La Rue would be worth more individually than as conglomerated.
- The principle of keeping eggs in widely differing baskets, favoured by many De La Rue managers, was bad for investors.
- De La Rue had little growth because its products were very mature. The very fact that their names were indisputable market leaders indicated that the products themselves were almost certainly over the hill.
- De La Rue's businesses were exceptionally vulnerable to outside factors.
- De La Rue's management was in-bred.
- The business was too dispersed, with too many geographical locations and small units.

- It did not have cash resources or cash-generating capacity to grow at premium rates.
- De La Rue had so seriously deceived its shareholders and the market at the time of the Rank bid that the credibility of the Board, as then constituted, was irreparably damaged.
- De La Rue's inability to fund its borrowings in the short term made it vulnerable to government squeeze and to takeover.

Summarising his conclusions, Orchard wrote:

> If the market and the market-makers continue to believe that these things are true ... the prospects of further growth or indeed for survival are obviously dim ... the share-price will not respond even to improved performance ... if the company is believed to have fundamental weaknesses.

By 1974 things at De La Rue were starting to look a little better, which was more than could be said of the world economy in general, following the oil-price hikes at the end of 1973, and the British economy in particular, with the problems caused by the rise in the price of oil exacerbated by labour unrest and strikes. The *Financial Times* carried out, and published on 5 June 1974, a survey of De La Rue. After noting that it was the largest commercial printer of currency in the world, with customers in 70 countries and a capacity of over 8 million banknotes a day, a staff of 1,800 and a ratio of 96 per cent to 4 per cent export over home sales, it said of Thomas De La Rue:

> David Rowe-Beddoe, 36-year-old Cambridge and Harvard Business School trained Managing Director of De La Rue's Currency Division, often has to travel as much as 200,000 miles a year.
>
> 'The best thing about my job', he says, 'is the people – the entire team with whom I work and the customers we serve throughout the world. I mean that categorically ...
>
> 'Languages are vital on the sales side, and we try to recruit linguists. It's elementary courtesy to try and talk your customer's language ...
>
> 'People tend to think that a craft business like ours by definition must be old fashioned. But our budgeting control procedures, resource planning and performance monitoring is as advanced as can be found in any high technological environment.'
>
> Not many factories can claim to be exciting.

'THIS HAS TO BE OUR BOTTOM PRICE'

One thing that did not change in the 1970s after the failed bid by Rank was the continuing need to capture overseas contracts. We saw how Julian Wethered had enjoyed some exciting adventures in Africa and Nepal while securing contracts. Here he is in the Yemen Arab Republic in the 1970s:

Not long afterwards in the early part of 1970 I was asked to visit the Yemen Arab Republic, YAR (North Yemen). It is situated north of Aden, which at that time was quite a separate independent state (South Yemen). In 1990 North and South combined to become simply The Yemen. To get to Sana, the capital of the YAR, was in itself a journey of interest. I flew to Nairobi and then to Djibouti at the bottom left hand corner of the Red Sea. The aircraft was operated by Aeroflot, the Russian national airline. The First Class section was in the tail, which wagged so much that, feeling sick, I moved into Economy. I was allowed to take my glass of free Vodka with me. The two air hostesses were young, blue eyed, and built like pit ponies. We landed at Al Hudaydah where I was met by our agent and his teenage son, who marvelled at the girth and stature of the two girls as they alighted from the plane. I stayed the night in an hotel there.

In the morning my host, our agent, an agreeable man, came round in his ancient Mercedes and off we went. The journey to Sana, the capital of YAR is about one hundred miles. Half way we started to climb into the mountains, stopping for lunch at a wayside mud domed oven where a seated woman made us fresh unleavened Arab bread. The flattened dough was placed on a broad bladed wooden spatula and flicked up to stick on the roof of the dome over a charcoal below. When baked she deftly recovered it, put it on a plate, filled it with spicy meat and chopped vegetables, rolled it up and handed it to me. It was delicious and sustaining. After lunch we continued into the mountains. Abdul (I forget his real name) explained that I had arrived on the very day that the vicious war against the YAR conducted by Egypt, including the use of mustard gas, had ended after years of struggle. I noticed to my astonishment that there was snow on 3,760m high mountain, and I was told it was unheard of and that some soldiers had been frozen to death there. We entered Sana that afternoon, and I was taken to a large whitewashed mud brick building which was now an hotel occupied by mostly UN personnel. The walls were enormously thick and sunlight filtered through the brightly coloured stained glass windows, projecting their colourful kaleidoscope patterns across the brilliant white walls within, as both a mural and a sundial. The reason for my visit was to discuss the printing of passports with the Minister of Home Affairs. A meeting was due to take place the next day.

What is bizarre for one culture is normality for another. For me the YAR was bizarre. The Minister spoke no English. Our discussions were through an interpreter. During greetings and coffee I brought up a matter which interested me. I had noticed that many men carried AK47 Kalashnikov automatic rifles. All had hooked daggers over their bellies. I decided to wax Biblical and said, 'Minister I have noticed that many people carry weapons. If I, as an unarmed man in your country, were to be killed, what would happen?' The interpreter put the question to His Excellency, who, on realising the import of it looked stern. After a while of contemplation he replied, 'If you were killed we would take ten men from your killer's tribe and shoot them in a public place.' I asked the interpreter to say, 'Thank you sir, I am greatly reassured, and may now walk in your city in the knowledge that I am safe here in Sana'. A huge smile replaced the frowning visage and we both laughed. The ice was broken and after that we got along just fine. 'The Minister he ask me to say about passports.' 'Right,'

I replied. 'During war with Egypt many refugees go live Saudi Arabia. Minister he want to sell each coming back citizen a passport when he return to Yemen. He charge £5 for each, make lot of money, yes?' 'How many refugees are coming home?' 'One million.' 'You want one million passports then?' 'Yes please!' I thought that I had misheard. One million passports would be the largest single order De La Rue had ever had for passports. I promised to get a quotation as soon as possible.

That afternoon I went to the main Post Office. There cross-legged on top of a long high raised counter, chewing the toxic leaf known in that part of Arabia as 'ghaut', sat a man enjoying his afternoon 'trip'. His eyes rolled around a while before obtaining a blurred focus on my face. I handed him the text for the cable to DLR and waited. He somehow managed to hoist in what I wanted him to do and sent off my request for a price and delivery for one million passports. Next day I received a cable asking if I meant one million or only one hundred thousand. I restated 'one million' and sent my reply. The following day I got the price and delivery and the date on which I could expect a sketch for confirmation by the Minister. On returning to DLR sometime later they said that I must have been tipsy and added a nought, or, more kindly, it had got garbled in transmission. But no, it was one million.

Subsequently I returned directly by air to Sana with the full quotation and the sketch for their new passports. On arrival at the airport there I was walking across the tarmac to the terminal building when a tall elegantly dressed man approached me. 'Excuse me for asking but are you British?' 'Yes,' I replied. 'I thought you might be. My name is Carruthers (it wasn't but it will do, on account of memory loss). I am from the British Embassy which we are setting up here. Would you do something for me?' I agreed and he continued: 'You see that plane just landing over there?' 'Yes.' 'Well in a moment our ambassador from Saudi Arabia will alight. You see today the British Government has recognised the new regime in the YAR, the first foreign government to do so since their war with Egypt, and our ambassador is here to present his credentials to the President.' He paused. 'Yes, there he is, I must go and greet him. I say, would you mind staying here a while and I will introduce you to him and those other British people over there. Oh by the way, what brings you to Sana?' I explained and he said, 'That's capital. De La Rue, excellent. Would you mind saying to the Ambassador that you are here and that you might be contemplating putting up an investment in the YAR?' I replied that I would say it was a possibility. It wasn't but never mind. The Ambassador arrived and worked his way down the short line of press-ganged Brits, shaking hands and exuding bonhomie. 'This is Mr Wethered from De La Rue, who is carrying out a reconnaissance with a view to possibly setting up a printing plant here,' said the F.O. equivalent of John the Baptist. 'That's most interesting', the Ambassador beamed down at me. At that point I told him about the passport order for one million pieces to sell to returning refugees to Saudi Arabia. That interested him quite a bit as a nugget well worth a mention in his weekly report to the 'Office' in Whitehall. I had scored points, and we chatted for a while before he took his lanky frame back to the waiting car. I have noticed over the years that being tall assists a diplomatic career path. The upshot was that we got the order to print one million passports. This was in January before I went to Nepal, and it went down well at head office.

In Vietnam, Julian Wethered would need all his reserves of diplomacy and patience, as can be seen here:

The Bank of Vietnam's Governor was a charming civilised man whom over the years I got to know well enough to entertain along with his wife. However, his one-time manager in charge of the day to day running of the banknote issue, a Mr Kye, normally quietly courteous, metamorphosised into an hysterical lunatic when negotiating prices. When I had taken over from Alexis Napier, and we were quoting for a new supply of banknotes, and the haggling over price per thousand (notes are traditionally packed in 'bricks' of one thousand notes) had got down to a unit of US 5 cents up or down, Mr Kye switched into a Mr Hyde mode. He shrieked, 'If you do not come down 5 cents I will give the banknote order to your competitor, how can you cheat the Bank with prices like this. You are robbers.' He advanced towards me. I stood my ground, I could smell his sour breath, we were nose to nose. I replied, 'Mr Kye, I have come down 20 cents already, this has to be our bottom price, the business cannot stand yet another drop of 5 cents. We cannot move.' His face crumpled into a cabbage of hatred and he screamed 'get out'. I thought he might hit me. I thanked him for his time and left.

Quite often as the crunch point looms both seller and buyer become nervous. Adrenaline takes over from reason and self control vanishes. By disengaging there were two options open to me. Either I called Kye tomorrow, when he had cooled off, or I awaited his call. I decided to wait for him to contact me. Grovelling was out, Kye had to think it through, explain it to the Governor, in the hope that the boss would back him, or risk a rebuke for pushing it too far with a trusted supplier, and come back to me and put matters back on track. Diagonally across the open-sided square from the Continental Hotel was the Department of Post's Telex Office. I had got to know the mother-to-be who operated the telex. From time to time I would give her a present of a few Dongs (the national currency) for her layette. This was much appreciated and she tended to prioritise my messages to DLR's new offices in Basingstoke. On this particular day I had returned to my room and typed out my telex giving a brief account of the spat with Kye.

Knowing that we could well manage a drop of 5 cents, I requested, for the sake of good relations with the Bank, and in order to restore 'face' for Kye, we give way as a goodwill gesture. There had been heavy fighting that day and there was a queue of journalists for the telex. The International Press consisted mostly of Americans, *The Washington Post*, *Herald Tribune* and *New York Times* were there, I joined the back of the queue. My little telex lady turned round to beckon the next journalist, spotted me and beckoned for me to come forward, which I did, ignoring mumblings of discontent amongst the others.

Next morning I got the okay to come down a final 5 cents. I returned to my room to await what I hoped would be Kye's call. It came around midday. 'Ah, Mr Wethered, please come to my office at two-thirty, thank you.' I was greeted by a crestfallen Mr Kye who forced a thin smile. 'Please sit down, I have decided to accept the price you gave me.' He waited for my response. I said, 'Mr Kye, De La Rue have asked me to convey to you that, for the sake of our longstanding and highly valued relationship with The Bank of Vietnam, that we have agreed to lower our price by US 5 cents.' Mr Kye's little face lit up into that of a small boy who has been given a new bicycle. 'Oh Mr Wethered, thank you.' Now he could tell the Governor that he had beaten us down to his price. We were friends again and we had gained another denomination off Bradbury Wilkinson. I dined well that night!

RATIONALISATION

In 1970 De La Rue's sales were split 31 per cent Security, 49 per cent plastics, and 20 per cent heating. By the end of the decade this had changed to 76 per cent Security and 24 per cent Crosfield Electronics (see pages 230–2 below). How did this come about?

First, where was the industrial logic in a company that printed banknotes and made heating boilers and plastic furniture? You will remember that Gerry Norman had described the company to John Davis at Rank as a 'three-legged dog'. Apparently, one De La Rue training officer would explain to new recruits that as banknotes and Formica plastic both relied on modern printing techniques and the Potterton and Formica companies both sold products for modern homes, the three divisions had a close affinity. As we have seen above, Peter Orchard for one did not think so.

There had long been the underlying fear in the company that the days of the banknote were numbered, and John Shepherd-Barron had written in 1963:

> In another age, we can see the possibility of doing away with the cumbersome method of buying the goods and services we use today ... The driving force behind the move away from the physical use of currency is the rapidly expanding use of computers in the banking field.

Perhaps the future for De La Rue lay in boilers or plastics and not security printing? If this was ever considered seriously, the events of the early 1970s would have banished such thoughts. By 1973 Potterton had moved from being a low-margin business to a loss-making one (in the previous year losing nearly £1 million, or about £16 million in today's money). In October 1973 the entire Potterton business, excluding its Home Improvements offshoot, was sold to Birmid Qualcast for £5.5 million (about £90 million today). The Home Improvements company was bought by its management.

Chairman Gerry Norman said later:

> The sale of Potterton ... proved very timely. It not only provided the funds for the Crosfield thing but got us out of an industry which wasn't going to see good returns

on investment for a long time in the future ... The financial strength of the business was being sapped by Formica as well as Potterton.

THE LAST POST

If 1973 saw the departure of Potterton, 1974 brought the end of a product with a much longer history in De La Rue. The company withdrew from the printing of postage stamps, which it had been producing since 1855 when Thomas de la Rue had used the typographical skills he had learned with playing cards to start printing postage stamps for the post offices in Great Britain and India. Five years later he secured a stamp order from Mauritius which, fortuitously, wanted paper currency as well, as we have seen. This provided De La Rue with its entry into the banknote market.

The stamp business was heavily dependent on sales via the Crown Agents to the old British colonies – supplying no fewer than 52 of them at the time of Queen Elizabeth II's coronation in 1952 – but it also enjoyed a wide following around the world. It became, however, something of a paradox in the changing shape of De La Rue in the post-war years: a minor product with an almost embarrassingly high profile. Money continued to be spent on attractive philatelic exhibitions but little was invested in new printing methods, and lower-cost competitors ate away at De La Rue's market share. There was a final flurry of activity in the late 1960s with the invention of the Delacryl process, a form of litho printing using a special screen. According to Michael Pugh, who was the product manager for postage stamps in 1968–69:

> We had a five-year product plan at that time which foresaw a £1 million annual turnover, which would have been very significant, but subsequently cheaper litho printers came into the field and we were squeezed out. But we did two commemorative issues for the UK around then.

Despite this decline, the postage stamp remained a unique part of De La Rue's iconography. The place cards at the 1971 Diplomatic Dinner were first-day covers from the new Guernsey issue, 'probably the only stamps in history which have borne the head of a stamp printer alongside the head of a reigning monarch'. When at Basingstoke in the same year, the Lord Lieutenant of Hampshire presented Thomas De La Rue's latest Queen's Award, he in turn was presented with a stamp album of the company's finest products.

Ironically, the eventual decision was taken following a report from, among others at Dunstable, Roy Allen, who was the production manager. He had originally joined De La Rue in 1962 because he was a philatelist and particularly admired the company for its stamp printing. Nonetheless, having now been put in charge of stamp printing, nearly his first step was to say: 'Unless we have major capital investment and do stamps properly we should get out of them.'

The remnants of the stamp printing business (a number of African countries, some from the Far East, fiscal stamps for Turkey, and a sprinkling of commemorative issues elsewhere) were transferred to Colombia with its much lower cost base.

So, what of Formica? It had always seemed a more important and powerful member of the De La Rue family than Potterton. For long periods it achieved more than 50 per cent of the Group's sales. Indeed, in 1975 its sales were 56 per cent of the Group's, and in 1976 it was 52 per cent. But its profits were plummeting. It was a market leader employing 4,000 people, and it produced the highest quality decorative laminates that won numerous awards for imaginative designs. It also made industrial products for high-technology applications and a substantial range of cladding materials for the building and furniture industries. However, as far as De La Rue was concerned, Formica had two drawbacks. First, although De La Rue owned 60 per cent of Formica International Limited and received 60 per cent of the profits, it had to fund 100 per cent of its borrowings. By the 1970s, with the security printing contributing most of the Group's profits (79 per cent in 1976), it was this division that offered a much better investment future. Second, Formica's market position was being threatened by cheaper brands. As with Potterton, a high-quality image was all very well, but most consumers wanted lower prices. Gerry Norman said later:

> The strain was showing very clearly in the Formica arena where a whole host of companies had moved into laminated plastics all over the world. There were hundreds more competitors than in the fifties and sixties; it was an entirely different ball game. That led us to a policy decision to jack up the profitability of the Thomas De La Rue Division ... as hard and as fast as possible in order to put the Company in a strong enough position to be able to divest Formica. Thomas De La Rue's rapid growth in the mid-1970s fulfilled this need and allowed us to resume discussions, which had always been there for resumption, with American Cyanamid.

Negotiations began in 1975 and continued through 1976 until a deal was finally announced on 24 March 1977. The price, which had started at £6 million, was finalised at £9.6 million (just over £100 million in today's money). However, payments were phased over five years, and as we have seen, these were very inflationary years, so the value of the deal to De La Rue diminished sharply. Nevertheless, as Norman said:

> It released us completely from a stranglehold: from that moment the Company got rid of its borrowings and had a strong, positive cash flow.

Indeed, in 1977–78, the first full year after the sale of Formica, profits of the Group rose by 66 per cent and margins improved from 14 to 26 per cent.

In November 1976 the stockbroking firm of Scott, Goff, Hancock and Co. published a long and detailed report on De La Rue. It analysed the company's progress since the late 1960s, and these were its conclusions:

> 1. It has to be recognised that many people in the investment community feel that there is a 'credibility gap' concerning De La Rue. This is largely due to an erratic earnings performance which has tended to obscure the fact that over the past five years certain parts of the business have achieved growth rates well in excess of 30 per cent.
> 2. Substantial changes in the management philosophy occurred in the early seventies which led to sharp improvement in earnings and the disposal of Potterton.
> 3. Both De La Rue, and its associated companies, are very much concerned with the banknote printing industry on a worldwide scale. These activities are discussed in some detail and it will be seen that we expect high growth rates to continue both in the current year and in 1977/78 as contracts taken at increasingly wide margins work their way through. It is quite possible that the underlying trends could ensure further growth in subsequent years but this may depend on the level of the £ and the future of labour relations in the security printing industry. On the other hand, it must be borne in mind that the Thomas De La Rue division is largely recession proof – which could be a very significant plus factor.

Interestingly, the report wondered whether Formica had a long-term future with De La Rue:

> Inevitably, this raises the question of whether Formica International has a long-term future as part of the Group. After all, it is not difficult to argue that De La Rue, without Formica would be worth a great deal more than De La Rue in its present format – on almost any reasonable basis for the sale of Formica. The De La Rue board is committed to a regular review of its operations and it would be very odd if the long-term future of Formica was not examined in great detail from time to time. Are these operations really a source of strength over the longer term? What would be the prospects for De La Rue if the 60 per cent interest in Formica International was sold at an appropriate time? What would be in the best interests of the De La Rue shareholders?
>
> One has only to ask these questions to realise that the case for retaining Formica is not exactly overwhelming. But this does not mean to say that early disposal is likely. Many of the competitors to Formica have been making losses so that, with higher margins possible on new products, there is scope for a marked improvement in profitability. It would be very odd if management did not want to exploit this situation, especially since the very worst time to enter into negotiations is around the bottom of the industrial cycle. Moreover, it has to be recognised that De La Rue would not continue investing large sums of money in this problem area if it was not prepared to take the longer view. We conclude, therefore, that disposal of the interest in Formica International is not something that investors should take into account at this stage.

The stockbroker's conclusion was that De La Rue was a strong BUY.

John White, who joined De La Rue in the same year as the report was published, and who rose to be a main Board director and Group Finance Director, said of De La Rue when he joined:

> I arrived three weeks after David Rowe-Beddoe had gone and Charlie Banks had been appointed. There was an extraordinary climate at the time – here was a business which suddenly had high inflation in the UK and worldwide and banknote volumes going through the roof. Customers had no time to stop and consider restructuring their currencies or anything like that. De La Rue's response to that was already apparent, in the sense that the decision had been taken in 1974 to build the Malta plant, Dublin was being expanded and there was a huge reinvestment programme in hand.

White's observations on the financial controls at De La Rue compared with his previous employer, Glaxo, are very interesting, especially in view of Glaxo's sky-high reputation in the City throughout the 1980s and 1990s:

> They were actually extraordinarily tight by comparison with Glaxo. I'd been working in Glaxo's head office: it was the sort of company that was pouring huge sums of money into research and development, and its whole success was based on getting one, two, three major blockbusters every year or every other year. But the cost controls were not that stringent. In De La Rue there was stringency, and extraordinarily detailed systems had been set up by people like Ted Stonehouse [one of the company's able accountants]. The controls over individuals and individual projects were quite draconian – the analysis of variances and everything coming out of the factories was down to extreme detailed levels. The contrast with Glaxo was very marked.

CROSFIELD ELECTRONICS

While De La Rue was divesting itself of Potterton and Formica, it bought Crosfield Electronics. This was in line with the strategy of being involved in the expanding use of computers in the banking industry. Gerry Norman would say later:

> In De La Rue's planning process, the advent of EFTS, Electronic Funds Transfer System, was very much under the microscope. We were trying to convert our counting machine business – because that was all it was – into a business which could serve the whole banking system and modernise and mechanise banking transactions. We were in paperhandling, in the sense that we had little banknote machines and were beginning to get into cash dispensing, but we had no such thing as a reasonable paper transporter and we had no knowledge of electronics.

John Shepherd-Barron had been watching Crosfield for some time. It was one of the first firms into graphic paper-handling and it enjoyed a high reputation for its technology. Shepherd-Barron introduced John Crosfield to Gerry Norman and a willing buyer/seller situation soon developed. De La Rue wanted Crosfield's technology and Crosfield wanted De La Rue's financial resources. On 24 September 1974 a deal was struck whereby De La Rue bought Crosfield for £5.95 million (£96 million in today's money). At that time Crosfield employed 1,100 people in factories in Holloway in north London, Watford and Peterborough, and in offices in Europe,

Africa and South America. It also had agents in almost every major country. Nearly 90 per cent of its products were exported.

John Crosfield, a former research scientist with ASEA, the Swedish electrical group, had set up the company with a colleague in an attic in 1947. The first two projects were cheque-sorting and printing register controls. By the early 1960s, in response to requests from the five main clearing banks, Crosfield had developed automatic cheque-sorting equipment, and in 1962 he patented a double curvature feeder. This could sort twenty lightweight documents per second. A range of high-speed document-sorting and reading equipment developed from this, and as these machines were selling in a different market from the colour-printing kit, Crosfield Business Machines was formed in 1966.

The Post Office soon became a large customer for Postal Order-sorters, while special machines were developed for lotteries in Germany, France and Spain and for football pools in England. Crosfield equipment meant that 60 people could achieve in a day what 800 people had been doing in a week in the German state lottery. At the same time, Crosfield's business machines were also spreading quickly into banknote-sorting, though not in direct competition with De La Rue Instruments, whose machines were at the smaller end of the range. In this respect their products were complementary. In May 1975, De La Rue Instruments and Crosfield Business Machines were merged under one management as De La Rue Crosfield, a key stage in the evolution of Cash Systems.

John Crosfield's other original project, printing register controls, took off somewhat faster in the late 1940s. He was soon invited by a large rotogravure printer to find ways of removing a production bottleneck in the printing of colour magazines, and he devised a sophisticated yet simple control, the Autotron, which became a bestseller and established Crosfield's worldwide reputation – some 10,000 Autotrons were in use by the time De La Rue bought the business. By the 1960s Crosfield had also developed a range of computerised colour separation and scanning equipment, most famously the Magnascan, for magazine and brochure printers, commonly devised in response to direct requests from major publishing houses like Axel Springer in Germany. In 1970 Crosfield developed the first enlarging scanner, and by 1974 300 Magnascans had been sold around the world.

Corporate finance, however, had always been a problem for John Crosfield, becoming more so with the ever-increasing research and development costs of the advanced technology consumed by the Magnascan family of products. Matters had first come to a head in 1959, when the business was rescued by £24,000 from a Crosfield cousin. Crosfield Electronics' sales continued to grow, with six overseas subsidiaries being established, but there was another cashflow crisis in 1965. This time the saviour was Hambros merchant bank, which bought 26 per cent of the equity and made a substantial loan, placing two of its own directors on the Crosfield Board, one of them as Chairman. At the end of 1971, Hambros put forward a scheme for amalgamation with Muirhead, another electronics firm, but this fell through largely because John Crosfield did not wish to lose control. Keyser Ullman Bank then came into the picture, buying the Hambros shares, but in 1973 there was no further finance available from that source and Crosfield decided to go public. Messel, who were also De La Rue's stockbrokers, prepared a prospectus, but in the spring of 1974 the stock market collapsed and the issue was never made.

By the time Crosfield was talking to Shepherd-Barron and Norman, finance was still a great problem. Barclays Bank had lent up to their limit and the only remaining option was to sell the company to a larger group with financial strength. The American Sun Chemical of New York had made a generous offer, but Crosfield wanted to keep his staff under British management.

RECOVERY DURING THE 1970s

As we have seen, De La Rue was struggling in the early 1970s almost as it had been in the 1950s, and in spite of management changes and the disposal of Potterton in 1974, it was still struggling in 1975. The background economic situation, with rampant inflation and continuing labour unrest, was not helping. In November 1974, Chairman Gerry Norman told employees in the *De La Rue Bulletin*:

> With very few good signs on the horizon, self-help is the only way out of the present difficulties. We cannot look to anybody else.
>
> Price controls operate widely throughout the world, not only at home, and we cannot hope to be unaffected at a time when costs are rising fast.
>
> We must look closely at how we spend our money. Plans for new capital projects will have to be deferred, and some present spending delayed. A cutback in all costs must be made.
>
> De La Rue will be judged by how we stand up to the present economic difficulties and those which are likely to come.
>
> Above all we must have an ability to recover quickly when circumstances allow it. We can start on that now by maintaining quality and service to our customers.
>
> Not all is gloomy. Profits from Crosfield will be included only in the figures for the second half of the year.
>
> Finally I stick to the view which I expressed at the Annual General Meeting that although we cannot escape the effects of cost inflation, high interest rates and the overall decline in both business and investor confidence, we are better placed than most to come good. There will be scars but they will heal.

THE TWIN CURSE OF INFLATION AND RECESSION

The rate of inflation had started to accelerate in the 1960s as successive governments, Conservative and Labour, pursued a policy of maintaining full employment at all costs. This was the avowed, and in many ways worthy, aim of all politicians after the war. No one wanted a return of the high unemployment levels of the 1930s, and each successive government implemented Keynesian policies of keeping demand high using, if necessary, and especially at election times, public money to prime the economic pump. The result, in a Britain with some archaic industrial management and workforce practices, was the creation of greater demand than supply – the classic cause of inflation.

However, this was just a foretaste of what was to come in the 1970s. Anthony Barber, the Chancellor of the Exchequer in Heath's government, pumped money into the economy as never before in 1971 and 1972 following the news that unemployment had broken through the 1 million barrier. (One million unemployed would not be a startling number in 2011 but, after 30 years of full employment, it was considered an appalling number.) Unfortunately, Britain's expansion coincided with a world boom, largely on the back of an inflationary boom in the United States caused by the Johnson and Nixon administrations paying for the increasingly expensive involvement in Vietnam not by raising taxes but by printing money. In 1971 the US turned from being an exporter of oil into a net importer; and in October 1973, when yet another Arab–Israeli conflict, the Yom Kippur War, broke out, the Arab oil producers chose the moment to quadruple the price of oil and to cut back production. The effect on world trade was little short of disastrous. Both industry and consumers had become extremely profligate in their use of oil, which had been getting cheaper and cheaper in real terms over the previous decade. Now it was suddenly expensive and in short supply. In truth it was not in short supply, but some panicked, others speculated and the price rocketed. It was as though the whole world had received a massive increase in its taxes, and the effect was the same. Tens of billions of pounds, dollars, deutschmarks, francs and lire were taken out of the world economy and put in the Arabian desert. Until they could be recycled into the system, the world was going to suffer.

And suffer it did, with Britain, because of its continuing structural weaknesses, suffering more than most. The Barber Boom had not worked. British manufacturers had not invested as much as had been hoped, and the two main results of the expansion in credit had been an explosion in property prices, largely on the back of borrowed money (first from secondary banks and then in their wake from the leading high-street banks), and a rapid increase in inflation. These fuelled resentment from the wage and salary earners, who benefited little from the rising property and stock market prices but felt the impact of rising prices in the shops.

In an attempt to choke inflation, Heath's government tackled the symptoms – rising prices, dividends and earnings – without tackling the cause: too much money. In the autumn of 1973, just before the oil crisis, the government introduced stage one of an incomes policy that would allow index-linked rises if inflation rose above 7 per cent. Because of the oil-price hike, inflation rose quickly above that level, and the automatic pay rises gave a ratchet effect pushing it higher and higher. In the meantime, the National Union of Mineworkers had learned the lesson of craven collapses, when faced with union pressure, by both governments since the war, and especially of the Heath government when faced with their own demands in the early part of 1972.

The NUM submitted a large claim and imposed an overtime ban on 8 November 1973. Heath panicked and declared a state of emergency on 13 November. A month later he declared a three-day week to preserve fuel, and though negotiations with both Arabs and the miners continued, the only results were the continuation of high oil prices and the actuality of a miners' strike rather than just the threat. In the end, and for some people three weeks too late, Heath called an election with the implied platform of: 'Who governs the country, the government or the unions?' The electorate decided it was not sure who should govern the country – the Tories who at long last had shown some signs of standing up to the unions, or the Labour party who might at least get the miners back to work. It gave neither party an overall majority, but gave more seats to Labour. Heath tried to negotiate with the Liberal leader Jeremy Thorpe to form a coalition, but Thorpe would not play and Harold Wilson formed his third administration.

The Labour government gave in to the NUM and when the rest of the unions followed in the headlong rush, inflation soared to 25 per cent (anyone who was paid monthly in arrears was losing out quite sharply). While inflation was soaring and everyone tried to keep pace, financial institutions, and to a lesser extent manufacturing businesses, were suffering severely from the financial squeeze that had finally been imposed in the autumn of 1973. Nearly all the secondary banks went into liquidation or, if it was deemed necessary to maintain confidence, were rescued by the main banks prompted by the Bank of England. Even the National Westminster Bank was forced to make a formal denial that it was in trouble. If the new Chancellor, Denis Healey, had not introduced a corporate tax-saving measure, stock relief, many manufacturing companies would have failed. On the Stock Exchange, prices fell throughout 1974, and the *Financial Times* 30-share index reached 147 in early January 1975 (it had been over 500 as long ago as 1968).

By 1975 inflation was starting to have a serious effect not only on those who had retired and those without the protection of powerful unions, but on British industry generally.

International confidence in the British government, already eroded by the public expenditure explosion and high inflation rates of 1974 and 1975, collapsed completely when the Labour party conference in 1976 adopted by a large majority the nationalisation of the leading high-street banks and the largest insurance companies. In the autumn of 1976 sterling began to fall like a stone.

The Chancellor of the Exchequer, Denis Healey, was forced to make a humiliating return from Heathrow airport on his way to an International Monetary Fund conference in Manila. Instead of going to Manila, Healey went to the Labour party conference in Blackpool, where the new Prime Minister, James Callaghan (Harold Wilson had resigned in the spring of 1976), had already made a blunt speech to the delegates:

> Britain has lived too long on borrowed time, borrowed money, borrowed ideas ... For too long, perhaps ever since the war, we've postponed facing up to fundamental changes in our society and our economy. That is what I mean when I say we have been living on borrowed time. For too long this country, all of us – yes, this conference too – has been ready to settle for borrowing money abroad to maintain our standards of life, instead of grappling with the fundamental problems of British industry.

We used to think that you could spend your way out of a recession and increase employment by cutting taxes and boosting government spending.

ORCHARD TAKES OVER

By 1978, with both Potterton and Formica sold and Crosfield integrated, Gerry Norman was more optimistic, telling employees and shareholders:

> This is the first year in which the Company has traded in its new shape, and the sustained performance of our continuing business confirms our belief that the decision to consolidate our operations and strengthen our finances was a correct one. It is satisfying to be able to report that every single current activity has responded to the challenge by earning good profits, and several have produced greatly improved results.
>
> After the spectacular advance of 1976/77 this was no mean feat, and the Board's confidence that the Company, in its new cohesive shape and with its clear new identity, is fully capable of sustaining and improving upon its present soundly based position is as great as ever. The business is unique in its capability to offer a full range of products and services in its highly specialised fields to international markets.
>
> The central product of the business is the banknote, in which we hold a dominant position in the available world market. It accounts for 40 per cent of our turnover and half our profits. These we regard as reasonable proportions, considering the level of world demand for this important commodity and the opportunities for the supply of related products and services with which our market position and reputation as the world's leading suppliers of currency provide us.
>
> We are in fact making strenuous efforts to project our ability to offer what we call Integrated Money Systems, that is to say the know-how and equipment needed to solve the problems of the production, distribution, protection, verification, accounting, retrieval and destruction of monetary means of exchange. We are also determined to put across the message that De La Rue goods and services possess the characteristics of high performance, high dependability and a high level of after-sales service, because these features are common to everything that De La Rue sells.

As the Formica sale was completed, Peter Orchard succeeded Gerry Norman as Chief Executive of the Group. Orchard had joined the company in 1950 from Magdalene College, Cambridge, where he achieved a First in Classics, and after a spell as a salesman on the security side, he rose rapidly through the ranks until he was appointed Managing Director of De La Rue International in 1962. He was appointed to the main Board the following year, and by the mid-1970s he was effectively in charge of all the Group's activities apart from the Formica companies.

However, though the succession might later seem to have been a foregone conclusion, there had been a number of executives whose stars came briefly into the ascendant, only to wane. Orchard outlived some, out-performed others and outmanoeuvred the rest. Den Moore alone was still there: both he and Orchard said they would be prepared to work for the other one. When the Board voted for Orchard, Moore was as good as his word and remained Orchard's loyal Deputy Chief Executive for the next ten years (taking this appointment in September 1977 after a brief spell assisting with the handover of Formica to American Cyanamid).

An American journalist later described Orchard as:

> [A]bout six feet tall and ... fairly beefy, the ex-athlete – rugby – run to paunch. He's a chain smoker. His florid face is heavily veined and his watery-blue eyes dart at you over half-glasses. The suiting is very dark, even black, so that the heavy gold Rolex and the sizeable gold cufflinks seem more glittering.

The 'Business Diary' in the *Financial Times* wrote under the heading 'Printmanship':

> Peter Orchard emerged yesterday as the successor to Sir Arthur Norman [Norman had been knighted in 1969 following his work as President of the CBI] as chief executive of De La Rue, the world's biggest printers of banknotes. Orchard, Freddie King and Den Moore are the only executive directors the group has.
>
> Although all three are long serving executives of the group, only Orchard has spent his working life in the security and graphics division.
>
> King and Moore came up through what was until three weeks ago the Formica division, the group's only substantial non-security interest. It was then that De La Rue sold off its 60 per stake in Formica to the holder of the remaining 40 per cent, American Cyanamid.
>
> Orchard is a specialist in the Spanish and Portuguese-speaking worlds (De La Rue has operations in Colombia and Brazil) and could tell a tale or two – but won't.
>
> Security printing executives are obliged to be tight-lipped about their work. Sir Arthur, Orchard's predecessor, does however feel free to recall his days as a 'currency smuggler' in Shanghai.
>
> This was in 1938, when as a 21-year-old not long with the firm he slipped through the Japanese lines to set up a banknote factory in the city. The notes, printed from plates smuggled through in mackintosh pockets, were smuggled out for distribution elsewhere in China.
>
> Sir Arthur, a former president of the CBI, is staying on at De La Rue as non-executive chairman. He'll now be free to spend some time in his new job as chairman of the British end of the World Wildlife Fund.

The piece also showed a picture of Orchard with a backdrop of banknotes from all over the world and the caption: 'All other people's, unfortunately.'

INTO THE 1980s

De La Rue finished the 1970s in fine shape. An article by deputy city editor Hugh Sharpe in the *London Evening Standard* in June 1980 summed up the euphoric mood under the heading, 'The laser man at De La Rue':

Peter Orchard, 53, has the expansive air of a man who prints more notes than the Bank of England. As chief executive of De La Rue, he heads an organisation which for 150 years has made money for foreign governments world-wide and which today controls some 70% of the global market for banknotes.

Enthusiastic fans of De La Rue have pushed the shares up to a year's high of 720p, and City rumour has it that a share split is imminent. But Mr Orchard dismisses the idea. 'It's nonsense,' he says.

After 30 years with the company – the past three in the top job – Mr Orchard certainly isn't content with just making money and moving it around. True, note printing and cash security are still the mainspring of the business, but the fastest growth at De La Rue is from electronics. Peter Kraft talked to Mr Orchard about his plans.

In the past, De La Rue's ventures away from its traditional business have not been too happy. It found that Formica, for instance, didn't jell with the rest of the business and shed it.

Getting rid of 'unsuitable' bits and pieces has done much for earnings. Profits – £4,000,000 a decade ago – were £36 million last year, and significantly two-thirds of that growth has come over the past three years while Orchard has been at the helm.

Does his enthusiasm over the growing electronics side of De La Rue mean that the abandoned image of the company as a mini-conglomerate is about to be restored?

'Only in the sense that our interests now cover engineering, transport, electronics and optics', he says. 'But there are threads, common in each, linking them to one main theme – money systems.'

'De La Rue will now venture', he says, 'only into areas where its reputation or expertise will give it an advantage over competition.'

Something which does just that – and which has been the spur behind the 50% rise in the company's share price this year – is Magnascan, a computerised laser engraving device used in colour printing and which has taken a lot of tedious manual effort out of the job.

Going into electronics is all very well, but how will a comparatively small fry in the field stand up to the competition from the Japanese and American giants?

'We're protected because the market for our sort of machine is not big enough for people like Mitsubishi', Mr Orchard says.

'A market of about £100 to £200 million is about our size. We don't want to get into the big time where we would be taking on people like IBM.'

An intriguing runner in the company's stable is De La Rue Systems, which has been losing money for years, but which some in the electronics industry think could become one of De La Rue's biggest money spinners ever.

'Prospects for Systems are good', says Mr Orchard. 'The micro-processor teller takes the labour out of sorting banknotes. It can handle 1,000,000 a day and spot a forgery instantly.'

What plans has Mr Orchard for the company's £32 million cash pile? Nothing immediately it seems. Until he is happy with the smooth running of his electronics bits and pieces, he's going to keep his money safely on deposit.

Then there could be takeovers – 'but only of businesses which support what we are doing, that is, if they centre around money systems and graphics.'

Peter Orchard himself, in his review to De La Rue staff, said:

> On the prospects for the immediate future, anybody who makes a forecast in the economic situation of today, when he does not have to, is asking for trouble. So many things can happen so fast to change the outlook for a Company or individual parts of it. I will therefore confine myself to saying that right now we seem to be pretty well placed to hang on to our share of the markets for our goods and services, even if our margins suffer in some areas, but also that we face the current year with the confidence which comes from having the financial strength to survive trouble, which most UK companies today lack.

There had been another strike at the Gateshead factory that adversely affected the 1980 results, and that prompted Orchard to say in his review:

> **Our most important resource ...**
> During a year in which industrial unrest, rising unemployment and inflation were rarely out of the headlines, De La Rue provided over 400 new jobs in the UK and maintained good industrial relations. Some redundancies, to enable the business to gear its production techniques to the future needs of its markets, were agreed at two plants. Overall, the people of De La Rue worked hard and effectively with only minor stoppages. Support for the national sanctions applied by the engineering unions last summer was short-lived and restricted to one location.
>
> The policies of outside bodies, including governments, employers' associations and trade unions, have some impact but, in the end, they must be of less relevance to the people who work for De La Rue than is the need for the enterprise to remain competitive in world markets and thereby survive at a profitable level.
>
> People remain the most important resource in the business because only they can ensure that we exploit fully all the other resources and opportunities available to us. De La Rue has an excellent record in attracting, retaining, motivating and developing its people. Recognition on their part that the Company's health depends upon its ability to sell its products and services to its customers, and that nobody, at home or abroad, owes the Company a living is the single most important factor in achieving continued growth. Everyone is to be congratulated on his or her contribution to the success of the Company in 1979/80.

The De La Rue Group now consisted of four divisions: Thomas De La Rue, De La Rue Systems, Security Express and Crosfield Electronics.

By far the biggest was Thomas De La Rue, and its Managing Director, Charlie Banks OBE, said:

> Much of the ground lost in the production of banknotes and travellers' cheques through the Gateshead stoppage was recovered. The programme of equipment replacement moved ahead, and the modernisation of the Dublin factory was completed.

The Division felt the effects of political instability in a number of the countries that it serves, causing uncertainty in some of its commercial relationships. TDLR's staff have shown the skills required to overcome these difficulties and maintain the Division's reputation for excellent service. Nevertheless, the risks, inherent in international trading, remain. The order book at the start of the new financial year is, however, in good condition.

Intense pressure on costs and prices and lack of demand for bonds adversely affected the UK Security/Systems Print business. The equivalent operations in Brazil and Colombia did extremely well, the latter greatly supported by its security transport service. De La Rue Smurfit [De La Rue's joint venture with the Irish company, Smurfit] showed a useful advance in profitability.

Jim Salmon, Managing Director of De La Rue Systems, had this to say:

The Division is not yet contributing to Group profits, but the loss sustained was greatly reduced. The performance was significantly better than the budget and there are very real prospects of a positive result in 1980/81. Turnover increased by 38% and the year has started with a substantial order book. Authority was given for a major extension to the Portsmouth factory and the management team was greatly strengthened during the course of the year.

The heavy investment in development has resulted in several new product announcements and introductions. The 3400 Used Note Sorting system was launched and several important orders have already been received. Further progress has been made with the 9100 system, for which major contracts have been obtained and installations completed.

Suppliers of automatic cash dispensing banking systems have shown great interest in the 1300 series. Several major contracts for the supply of components have been signed as well as direct sales contracts for the 1320 Teller Assist version. The new 2100 Banknote Prime Counter and the 124 Spindle Verifier are both selling well. Coin counting and coin wrapping machines have also been launched, thus significantly broadening the product range.

The lottery business shows signs of recovery following the announcement of the 9500 document reading system for which several contracts have already been signed.

Security Express, under Tony Copestick, was enjoying a good run, and he was able to say:

The criminals who attack the cash-carrying companies had a much less successful year and the losses of Security Express from armed robbery were substantially lower than in the previous year. This was due not only to constantly improved security measures taken by the Division but also to excellent work by the Police who made some very important arrests during the year.

Finally, Rowland Dunkley, the Managing Director of Crosfield Electronics, added:

> Turnover increased by 35% and profits showed a modest improvement from £6.1 million to £6.6 million. The profit on sales to a former US distributor were eliminated after that business was bought out by the Division. If these profits had been included the figure would have been £8.6 million.
>
> Magnascan Colour Scanners have again been the spearhead of both sales and profitability and two new models were added to the range. A major extension to the Peterborough factory was authorised to cater for the sustained world demand. The Press Controls business had a successful year but the launch of Lasergravure was delayed. This will now take place in 1980/81.
>
> Two important investments have been made in the US to reinforce the Division's position in the pre-press automation field. A joint venture with LogEctronics has provided a ready-made product and the technology for offset plate-making by laser. The acquisition from Sun Chemical of their Magnascan distribution rights in the US has given the Division access to the US market, the most important in the world, for all its products.

It must have encouraged everyone at Crosfield when Prime Minister Margaret Thatcher mentioned Magnascan in a speech:

> We do have what it takes when it comes to our innate inventive genius. That genius in the nation of Newton, Watt, Arkwright, Davy, Baird, Barnes Wallis, Rutherford and Fleming is alive and well and working all around us.
>
> In aerospace, for example, from jump jets to navigator systems; from swing-wings to angled flight decks for aircraft carriers. What is more, we have Farnborough to prove it. During last week's air-show, Britain's aerospace industry announced orders worth £286 million and these are expected to lead to others to bring the total up to £500 million.
>
> In energy, from pumped storage of electricity to North Sea oil. In machinery, from powered roof supports to the Magnascan electronic scanner.
>
> We are, after all, exporting to the tune of around £1 billion – a thousand million – a week. Just think what could happen when the world economy picks up if we really did put things together.

Of De La Rue at the end of the 1970s, John White would say later:

> It was a most amazing period in which profits just grew and grew, largely through inflation within the colonies.
>
> The Group then was, as to some extent it still is, driven by the banknote side of the business. By the end of that decade, 1979/80, De La Rue's stock market rating was at a huge level. Analyses of the fastest growing companies in the 1970s showed we were very near the top – on top in some charts – in terms of share price which obviously, over a period of time, reflects profitability. So come 1980 we were a Stock Market Darling and very well respected, and a very go-go company.

CHAPTER ELEVEN

LAST CHANCE FOR DIVERSIFICATION

1980–1989

'OUR RESULTS FOR 1981/82 WERE BAD'
TIME TO FEEL PLEASED
AT LAST WE HAVE BRADBURY WILKINSON
'IN MANY WAYS IT HAPPENED QUITE FAST'
AN EXCITING PERIOD
ROBERT MAXWELL ON THE PROWL
SALE OF CROSFIELD
A BID FROM NORTON OPAX

'OUR RESULTS FOR 1981/82 WERE BAD'

The 1970s may have ended on a high note for De La Rue, but tougher times lay ahead. At the AGM in July 1980, Gerry Norman told shareholders:

> The Group has made a slower start to the year than in 1979 and the expected pressures on margins in the UK referred to in our Preliminary Statement are being felt.

And indeed the year 1980 into 1981 did prove to be a difficult one. In the letter sent to all De La Rue employees by Peter Orchard – a practice begun annually in 1980 – he wrote:

> I said twelve months ago that life was going to be tougher in 1980/81, and so it has turned out. Some parts of the Group have been less hard hit than others, but overall our profitability came down with quite a bump. The basic reason for this is that our

> goods and services became more expensive for us to produce and more expensive for our customers to buy. Rising costs in our factories and offices meant that we had to try and raise our prices, and the strong Pound meant that foreign customers had to find more money to buy the same quantity of goods, even if we did no more than maintain our prices.
>
> There are not many signs that things are going to be easier this year either, and that is why it is so important that we do everything we can to hold our costs down. If we can do that, we can hold our prices down, and remaining competitive is what makes all the difference between getting orders and not getting them, and eventually between having a job and not having one.

When asked what the main problems had been, he said:

> We have been operating during a year of world recession on a wide front. This has had the effect of reducing demand and increasing competition. It follows that profitable sales have become hard to achieve, and this has been true in De La Rue Systems and Crosfield Electronics. Other problems, which have contributed to the struggle for orders have been the strength of the Pound, the high cost of production in the UK, fuelled by inflation, and the price of energy. Naturally, as we sell so much of what we make into export markets we have been hit by all these factors. It has been a tough year, but we are facing up to the problems, which have had a devastating effect on so many major UK firms. It is to the credit of everyone in De La Rue that the Group has come through the year, if not unscathed, at least with its head very much above water.

Looking to the immediate prospects for the Group, he said:

> At the start of the financial year order books in general across the Group were in a satisfactory condition, better of course in some places than in others, but it is vital that our rate of selling success shall be stepped up to consolidate this position. Outside factors, particularly the UK inflation rate and the relative value of the Pound, may move in our favour and so make life a bit easier. Equally, the year ahead may see the beginning of the end of the current world recession.

If the year to March 1981 had been disappointing, the following year was decidedly worse and was summed up by Peter Orchard as follows:

> Our results for 1981/82 were bad. Although most Divisions did well in the second half of the year, the Group's overall performance was the worst since 1976.
>
> Although sales increased from £176 million to £203 million compared with last year, trading profit collapsed from £22 million to a little over £13 million.
>
> As one consequence of this unhappy performance, for the second consecutive year there was a net reduction of 209 people in the UK workforce, with substantial redundancies in some Divisions and reductions elsewhere through natural wastage and restricted recruitment.

Political upheavals and economic difficulties in some of our customer countries in recent months have had serious financial effects on the banknote business, costing us something of the order of £9 million profit before tax. This, and the near disastrous showing by the Crosfield Electronics Division in the first half of the year, have been the main factors in the dramatic drop in our profitability in 1981/82.

One of the main problems was the loss of competitiveness of part of the old range of Magnascan colour scanners sold by Crosfield Electronics. Another was the 'political upheavals' referred to above by Orchard. John White remembered the coup in Ghana particularly, saying:

There was one other fairly significant thing that I remember during that period, a rather specific event – the coup in Ghana.

The coup took place on New Year's Eve 1981. It was at a time when we had a huge Ghana order, 900 million, something like that, going through three separate plants. It was the major order in Gateshead, Dublin and Malta, all at the same time. Suddenly we had this coup and a telex came through a couple of days later saying stop all production. You just can't replace the work with something else in such circumstances, so we had three plants virtually at a halt for weeks. The impact on De La Rue's results for the year ending 31st March 1982, combined with the fact that Crosfield had a hiccup at the same time, was significant.

The hiccup may have been quite small compared with what came later, but it was a significant event and lots of people in the City who had been treating De La Rue as a star performer through the late 1970s suddenly said, 'Whoops, what's happened here?' and our credibility took quite a knock.

Ghana knocked all the profitability off the Currency side. We just had this huge gap in production for four to eight weeks, something like that. There were people years later, in the City, who said it was the first thing that really put a question mark in their minds about De La Rue.

When asked whether there were other banknote orders going through the factories at the time, perhaps two or three, White said:

Probably there were many more than that, but in terms of significant orders, it was the most unfortunate timing you could ever get – an exceptionally large order being produced in three plants at the same time, because the pressure for delivery was so big. To get a coup right in the middle of that was just absolutely chronic ... the effect on profits was horrible.

And when asked if Ghana eventually renewed its order, he said:

Yes it did. I think it was Julian Wethered who went out and, over a period of time, rescued the situation, and we got going again. But you never fill a gap in production, it's just lost production. So that was the fundamental reason, aggravated by weak results in Crosfield, that produced the real hiccup for De La Rue as a group in 1982.

Nor was the first half of the year to March 1983 much better. Orchard said in the *De La Rue Bulletin* in the autumn of 1982:

> The first half of 1982/3 has produced results that are nothing to write home about. It is only thanks to a bigger contribution from our associate companies that our overall profit is just ahead of the poor performance of twelve months ago. Our own trading profit is down, and so is the margin (6.6% against 7.6%) on slightly increased sales. The reasons for this lie mostly in two Divisions of the Company, Thomas De La Rue Currency and Crosfield Electronics ... Perhaps the best that can be said about Crosfield is that the loss of nearly £3.9 million for April–September is £1.8 million better than for the corresponding period last year.

Fortunately, the second half of the year was better and Orchard was able to say in the summer of 1983:

> In the end, 1982/3 was a much better year for the Group, with a return of something like the performance levels of the past. But there is still quite a hill to climb, particularly if you think of how much the value of money has declined.
>
> The increase in sales from £203.5 million to £226 million and in trading profit from £15.3 million to £22.7 million looks, and is, a good achievement. However, it falls short of what we did in either 1980 or 1981, and the margin – the percentage difference between what they cost us to produce – also falls far short of what we used to achieve.
>
> On the bright side, most of the Security businesses did well, particularly so in Brazil, Colombia and the Currency Division, although the latter's figures were helped a lot by its ability to reverse provisions made against trading in 1981/82 because of political upheavals and economic difficulties in some of our customer countries.
>
> Less encouragingly, the Group's results were depressed by another poor year from Crosfield Electronics which lost £5.8 million and is recovering more slowly than had been expected. CEL had to launch its new products against tough competition and a background of world recession; sales were up but profit margins remained under pressure. To put this right, the Division's new management have set in train a number of changes and initiatives.

At the same time as these better results were announced, former De La Rue Finance Director (1966–80), Freddie King, also retired from the Board. Chairman Gerry Norman paid him a long tribute in the *De La Rue Bulletin*, and parts of it are worth quoting because not only do they recognise Freddie King's contribution to De La Rue at a critical time, they also give Norman's overview of that period:

> In 1953, on a sales turnover of £5.3 million, De La Rue reported a loss of £131,000 and failed to pay a dividend. This traumatic happening might have been more excusable 30 years later in the midst of worldwide recession, but in 1953 it provided

confirmation that the Company's affairs were in disorder and that a major recovery effort was called for.

The Company's auditors were among those who felt the pressures of the time and they were a small accounting firm, Fuller, Wise, Fisher, which was later swallowed up by Touche Ross in the amalgamation fever which hit the accountancy profession.

Key figure

This was the real beginning of a highly productive relationship between client and auditors that eventually led to the Board's decision in 1959 to invite Freddie King to join the Company as Finance Director of Formica International. To his great credit he eschewed the comparative safety and calm of professional accountancy and plunged headlong into the whirlpool of risk and excitement offered by F.I.L. He soon became a key figure in the rapid expansion of what became the leading company in its field throughout the world outside the USA and South America.

It was no surprise to anyone in 1966, when De La Rue was looking for a Finance Director, that Freddie King was appointed to a task which put him at the centre of a whole series of decisions and events, which have changed the very shape and purpose of De La Rue.

Takeover fight

In the mid-60s, De La Rue was obsessed with the diversification ideas which had been born in the aftermath of the struggle for existence in wartime. The results of the exercise were erratic enough to test the temperament and ability of the toughest of financial bosses and, before he had time to complete the called-for task of reform, the reckoning came in the shape of a take-over bid by the Rank Organisation in 1969. The long and exhausting fight for independence decided by the Monopolies Commission, is almost certainly amongst the clearest and sharpest recollections of a man with an elephantine memory. At the drop of a hat a whole new armoury of skills and know-how was called for and nobody in the Company had been attending business school courses on take-over situations! Once again, Freddie King showed himself ready and able to bear any burden, to deal with any twist to any new problem and, most importantly, to help to move from defence to attack.

New policies

The seventies saw the changes of policy, which led to the acquisition of Crosfield Electronics and the disposal of the Company's interest in Potterton and Formica. In retrospect it can be claimed that this period was perhaps the most significant decade in the whole of the Company's 170 years of operation. Freddie King was not only in the centre of the ring, he was also despatched to all parts of the globe as a negotiator – and there were many who will bear witness to his skills, in that role.

From 1977, the year in which the Formica disposal was finally accomplished, life for the Finance Director must have at least seemed to be calmer with more time being devoted to longer range issues. One of these, dictated by anno domini, was the need to find a competent and hopefully even better successor. In this matter, Freddie King showed a very special flair – he backed the choice of a man who wasn't an accountant. That was no mark of disrespect for the members of his profession, whose role in any business he always rated highly; he believed that financial direction, while requiring a good understanding of finance and accountancy needed good judgement and management skills more than any other qualifications.

A whole man has more to think of than his job, even if high standards of performance mean long hours and endless reading of reports and analyses. The mere mention of Twickenham, Lords or Covent Garden would achieve instant response – indeed, for the unwary such reckless daring could be quite expensive when wagers were offered or placed on the sporting or operatic statistics of a lifetime.

His many friends and admirers will wish Freddie many happy years of good health with a bit more time for the things he has had so few spare hours to enjoy.

TIME TO FEEL PLEASED

By the summer of 1984 life was looking much better, and under the headline, 'Time to Feel Pleased', Orchard was able to tell readers of the *Bulletin*:

> We can all be pleased that the Company has come out of 1983/84 with a good set of figures. Our trading profit went up from £22.6 million to £27.7 million, and when our share of the profits of our related companies is added in, the Group's profit before tax increased from £31.6 million to £37.4 million.
>
> As you might expect, performance has been patchy; not every one of our businesses has done as well as every other. But competition is very tough in all our markets, and there are a lot of companies in a lot of places around the world who are fighting, as we are, to get all the orders they can.
>
> The Crosfield Electronics Division has fulfilled the promise of better things that it was beginning to show halfway through the year, and it has come up with a splendid return to profitability. From a loss of £5.8 million in 1982/83 it has moved to a profit of £5.5 million, a 'swing' of £11.3 million, and what a difference that makes to the health of the Group as a whole!

Perhaps the most disappointing news that Orchard had to tell the shareholders and employees was the closing of the Thomas De La Rue factory in Dublin:

> Nobody can have been happy at the unavoidable need to reduce the capacity of TDLR Currency Division last autumn by stopping production at the Dublin factory. There used to be over 600 people working there, and this was the biggest reduction in manpower in De La Rue for some years. Sad as this was, and expensive too, the Division is undeniably healthier for it, because its costs are now much more in line with the world demand for its products.

In contrast, but as part of the new trend of moving production to lower-cost locations, the same *Bulletin* announced the attainment of full production at De La Rue's Singapore factory, which had been opened earlier in 1984. The *Bulletin* said:

> Thomas De La Rue's new factory in Singapore is now in full production and is proving to have been a sound investment.
>
> It is also proving that Thomas De La Rue's own team that led the design, construction and equipping did a first-rate job, and reflects great credit on people like Nicol McGregor, who was in overall charge, Ronnie Ahrend, who did all the project work, and Keith Elliott, who got the factory into production and is now Factory Manager.

Her Majesty Queen Elizabeth took the opportunity to visit the factory on her tour to Singapore in 1990. It was one of only two factories that she did visit.

The good news continued into 1985, and here are some of the comments of the divisional heads. Brian Malpass of Thomas De La Rue Currency Division said:

> This has been an exceptionally good year for the Currency Division. Certain clients required unusual and unpredictable volumes of banknotes within a short period, and the Division's resources were consequently at times seriously stretched.
>
> However, the Division responded quickly to these demands, and realised the benefits of working at full capacity during the year. Demand for travellers' cheques has picked up recently, and our share of the world market has increased during the year.
>
> The new factories in Singapore and Hong Kong are running smoothly and efficiently and providing good service to the currency issuing authorities in both places. Activity in conjunction with and on behalf of the Royal Mint has been relatively quiet because of low demand for coinage in the world market.
>
> The order position for all products for the current year is good, although margins are under renewed pressure.

Perhaps not wanting to appear complacent or give any hostages to fortune, he finished with:

> This year will be harder as competition intensifies still further. However, our order book is in good shape and provided we keep our costs under control we can continue to take on all comers.

Of the other big division, Jim Salmon, who had received an OBE in the Queen's Honours List in June, said of Crosfield Electronics Division (CEL):

> Crosfield Electronics produced an excellent result, their profit before interest and tax rising from £5.5 million 12 months ago to £9.3 million in 1984/85. The Division also received its seventh Queen's Award, this being the fourth for Technical Innovation.
>
> Although the scale of this improvement was due in large degree to the buoyancy of the US economy, and the US Dollar, since CEL now sells some 40 per cent of its

> production into that market, sales in the Far East have also shown some considerable growth, notably in Japan. The Crosfield Data Systems Inc. business in Springfield, Virginia was closed during the year – however, the Datrax production range is now being produced in Peterborough.
>
> The core products of the business continue to be the Magnascan range of colour scanners and the Studio 800 range of image processing and page composition equipment. These products remain technically superior to those offered by competitors.
>
> The Lasergravure machine and associated technology continues to make good progress in both publications and packaging gravure markets, with some large orders now received from customers in North America where the major market opportunity exists. Press controls products are now performing strongly, thanks to the new products announced earlier this year. A substantial order of Datrax equipment for the *New York Times* represents an important milestone for CEL in the facsimile transmission market.

As with Malpass, Salmon did not want to appear complacent either, and concluded:

> CEL faces the future with confidence. The current order book is in a healthy state, but as far as the next 12 months is concerned, much will depend on the state of the world economy in general and the United States economy in particular.

Peter Underhill said of the De La Rue Systems Division:

> Although this Division's trading result was positive, and represented a substantial improvement over the previous year, it was nonetheless a disappointing performance against both its budget and its potential.

Roger Coombs said that Thomas De La Rue Security Systems Print Division had enjoyed 'a good year'.

> Not only has there been a high demand for passports from overseas customers and for security documents from London financial markets, but the introduction of new methods and equipment into cheque production has given a new lease of life to this sector of the business.

By contrast, Humphrey Miller said that the progress at De La Rue General Services Division, which dealt with identity systems, had been 'disappointing'. He hoped for better things in the future, saying:

> After a very difficult trading year the Division has started to bring new products and services to the market place. The most significant of these is our new association with the Polaroid Corporation of the United States, which should have a major impact on the Division over the next few years.

In South America, Felipe Bautista reported from Thomas De La Rue de Colombia SA:

> This company celebrated its Silver Jubilee during the year – an occasion marked happily by the award of an honorary CBE to its manager over the greater part of its existence, Don Gregorio Bautista.
>
> The business once again made an important contribution to the Group, and during the year took several significant measures to improve further its competitiveness on both the security printing and cash-carrying fronts. In spite of the considerable Peso costs involved, and the remittance of substantial sums to its parent, the company managed to retain comfortable cash balances.

Michael Pugh said of Thomas De La Rue SA (Brazil):

> This company has once again overcome the difficulties of operating in a hyper-inflationary economy and produced a highly creditable result.

The next year, 1986, saw continued improvement, and Peter Orchard gave most of the credit to the Currency Division, Crosfield Electronics and the subsidiaries in Colombia and Brazil. However, the big event of the year was the purchase of De La Rue's long-time competitor, Bradbury Wilkinson.

AT LAST WE HAVE BRADBURY WILKINSON

A fierce competitor of De La Rue throughout the 20th century, Bradbury Wilkinson, a subsidiary of American Bank Note, had become a takeover target by the early 1980s for Peter Orchard, the Chief Executive of De La Rue.

Bradbury Wilkinson was founded at the beginning of the 1860s and there is a record of Jean Ferdinand Joubert, who also worked with De La Rue, issuing an announcement on 12 February 1861 that his patent process for the Acierage of Engraved Plates (Joubert patent) would 'in future be carried on in the establishment of Messrs. Bradbury, Wilkinson and Co., 12 & 13 Fetter Lane, London E.C.'.

The mainstay of the business was the printing of banknotes, but it also built up other lines of security printing such as cheques, share certificates, bills of exchange and bonds. Early banknote customers were in Latin and South America, but by 1865 the company was also supplying banknotes to Australia. In 1871 Bradbury Wilkinson made its first engraving for postage stamps. It did not print the stamps, but the engravings were sent to Hyderabad in India, where they were printed locally. Also in 1871, the company started to work with the Crown Agents. By this time the company was growing too large for its premises in Fetter Lane and moved to Farringdon Road. By this time also, it was printing postage stamps. Records show that in 1876, 90 million España 'postage stamps in nine different colours on watermarked paper perforated, gummed and packed in parcels of 500 sheets' were printed. And shortly after that it received an order from the Crown Agents for printing stamps for the Falkland Islands.

This order was slightly odd, and indeed when they fulfilled it, there were problems. As the Stanley Gibbons catalogue put it, 'the plate used for these stamps did not fit the paper, and therefore the water mark appears in all sorts of positions, a well-centred Crown being scarce'.

The paper was more likely to be suitable for De La Rue machines because it was (and remained for many years) Crown Agents policy to buy the paper themselves and supply it to the printers – and at that time De La Rue had a virtual monopoly of the Crown Agents postage stamp business; in fact they were officially designated stamp printer to the Crown Agents and remained so until about 1915–16. It is not surprising that the policy gave rise to some difficulty when the paper was not ideally suited to the requirements of other security printers. Nevertheless, it was perhaps inevitable, and certainly more economic, that, since the same watermark was required for all Crown Colonies, the Crown Agents should hold stocks of paper available to all printers, particularly for the many short printing runs.

In the 1880s it is probable that Bradbury Wilkinson subcontracted many of its stamp orders, because it was extremely busy with banknote orders from countries all over the world, including Italy, Greece, Switzerland, Bulgaria and Argentina. In 1888 the Argentine government gave them a particularly large order for 11 million banknotes, spread over ten denominations from one dollar to 1,000 dollars. In the 1890s further expansion took place, with orders from Europe and Australia and new customers such as the Imperial Bank of Persia (eleven denominations), El Tesoro de la Isla de Cuba (six denominations), Banco Commercial Chile (four denominations), Natal Bank Limited (four denominations), and Norrbottens Eskilda Bank in Sweden (three denominations), to name but a few.

In spite of this banknote expansion, Bradbury Wilkinson did develop its stamp-printing business. Having produced the first issue of stamps for the Falkland Islands in 1878, in 1890 they printed the first stamps to be issued in Rhodesia. The British South African Company received its charter to administer this territory on 29 October 1889, at which time Cecil Rhodes was General Manager of the company in South Africa. The first issue of postage stamps printed by Bradbury Wilkinson for this territory was released in December 1890 and consisted of eleven denominations from 1d to £10. In the same year, an issue of twelve denominations was released in British East Africa. These were printed by Bradbury Wilkinson but by lithography. Regarding these two issues, John Easton writes in his *British Postage Stamp Design* that:

> Bradbury Wilkinson's lithographed issue of 1890 for British East Africa is a triumph for that process, and a splendid example of the bank-note style of design.

He also wrote that:

> Their design for the Rhodesia issue of 1890 showed that they were equally efficient at designing for the engraved process. The high values show the classic example of a stamp within a stamp, achieved by adding an elaborate frame-work entirely in keeping with the new style.

Between 1891 and 1894, Bradbury Wilkinson printed, by the recess process, a further issue for the British East Africa Company of seven denominations in two colours, while in 1891 and 1895 the first stamps were issued in Nyasaland, then known as British Central Africa.

By 1901 Bradbury Wilkinson's turnover was £104,000 (about £11 million in today's money). It had been as high as £123,660 in 1890 when the Argentine order was still being fulfilled, though it had fallen as low as £25,496 in 1894. Two years later the Chairman, Robert Wilmot Wilkinson, by this time 76 years old, announced that he had entered into a contract to sell the company to the American Bank Note Company. The price agreed was £64,443.11s.4d (about £7 million).

The Americans sent David Woodhull to run the company, while Percy Wilkinson was groomed to take over when Woodhull returned to the USA in 1907. Relations between the British company and its American owner did not always run smoothly. Percy Wilkinson, not well physically, was distressed and disturbed because of an apparent lack of appreciation in New York of the problems that were facing Bradbury Wilkinson and the work they were doing. Woodhull tried to smooth out the situation but received only a characteristically short reply from Warren Green, the Chairman of American Bank Note Company:

> I meant what I said in my letter to Percy – that the profits were satisfactory everything considered. I did not say I am delighted because I was not delighted, I was simply satisfied.

This provided Woodhull with an opportunity of taking up the cudgels on Bradbury Wilkinson's behalf, which he, their Chairman yet also an official of the larger American organisation, could do with far greater effect than anyone else. He had the courage to do so, and again wrote to Warren Green:

> This last year has been one of the hardest England has experienced, business has been simply rotten, the market is quite stagnant and no matter what you tell me to the contrary I know that you personally do not understand the British and Continental business people and their ways of doing business. We have had to buck up against all this last year, also the fact that there was a new American Managing Director at Bradbury Wilkinson and the suspicion that the business of our old customers ... would be handled in a radically different way. You cannot rush the British business man and you can't make him see why he should change for something better even at the same price to something else which just suits him ... Moreover in the Foreign business ... we have been more or less thwarted by the new connection than helped. For a long while we needed the service of a foreign traveller but we held up because you thought

> you might use Dr Reece. We could not use the Baron and were kept back in the selection of the Systems which would be safe for him to exhibit and even after Mr Fritz had perfected his experiments nothing was done as we were waiting to get those of your new tests ... We were not allowed to go to Brazil, where I am sure if we had sent a year ago we could have got an order.

At least De La Rue did not have to cope with a difficult parent. They just had to suffer the eccentricities and, ultimately, the incompetence of the fourth generation of De La Rues running the business.

When the First World War broke out, there was a general belief that 'it will all be over by Christmas'. The bosses in New York seemed to think it should be business as usual, and even suggested it would be a good time for Bradbury Wilkinson to offer their services to the Bank of Belgium. As the Germans were then occupying Belgium, this would have proved a little tricky. The new boss who had taken over from Percy Wilkinson, Leslie Hendriks, could hardly restrain his irritation, and replied: 'As regards to Brussels, either Santini or I would be willing to go but the only way to do so I am afraid, would be to enlist other people and that would leave so very little time for negotiating with the Bank.' He went on to say: 'Under present conditions it is a physical impossibility to get busy in the Balkans as you suggest.'

It is difficult to believe the insouciance of the bosses of American Bank Note, because the American government was certainly aware of the crisis. There were 80,000 Americans on holiday in Europe when war broke out. Rail, ferry and transatlantic services were all severely disrupted as the movement of troops and munitions became the top priority. The international credit exchange system was suspended, so cash transactions became very difficult. An emergency rescue system had to be hurriedly put in place. Meanwhile, President Woodrow Wilson offered his services as a mediator but the belligerents ignored him.

The American parent and British subsidiary continued to bicker over who should try for business in various parts of the world, which led to Percy Wilkinson saying that it seemed 'a great pity that there should be so much friction and almost ill-feeling in reference to who shall or shall not try for particular orders in different parts of the world'.

In view of what we know of De La Rue's negotiations over the printing of banknotes for the Bank of England at the very beginning of the war, the following from a history of Bradbury Wilkinson written in the 1950s is very interesting:

> The first wartime English currency note was issued on the 7th August, only three days after the outbreak of war, and it has been said that no one examining the original 'Bradbury' could doubt that its design and execution were hastily improvised whereas the German note issued on the 12th August was carefully devised before hand. It is not surprising that the use of the word 'Bradbury' as a colloquial name for a British Treasury note should be widely believed to have come from the title of the Bradbury Wilkinson organisation. This was not so; the expression arose from the fact that the

first issue bore the signature of Sir John Bradbury, Permanent Secretary to the UK Treasury at that time.

It was recognised in England that the original £1 note was purely an emergency measure and that it would eventually be withdrawn and replaced by one of a permanent nature. Mr Hendriks and Mr Santini worked hard to secure the order for printing the permanent notes, despite keen competition from Waterlow and De La Rue, but the Bank of England presented a rather severe obstacle. In 1915 Bradbury Wilkinson specimens were given to Somerset House, the officials there being very complimentary and observing that no other firm had shown the enterprise of engraving a note for consideration. This raised hopes at Farringdon Road where immediate consideration was given as to what additional building could be taken over to cope with the work should the Company be successful. It seemed obvious that one of their competitors had informed Somerset House of Bradbury Wilkinson's American relationship and so far as this was concerned, Mr Hendriks told Somerset House quite frankly the true position, pointing out the advantage of such an association, and was assured that, if their note were selected as the best, it was not thought that the fact of being allied to the American Bank Note Co. would be held against Bradbury Wilkinson.

Hendriks felt that, quite apart from the intrinsic value of an order for British notes, the fact of securing it would be very far-reaching. He wrote:

> The India notes would probably follow the lead set by the Home Government; the straits Settlements, who order about five million notes a year through Crown Agents for the Colonies in London and whom Mr Jenkins has been after for nearly two years, are waiting to see the result of our negotiations with the Treasury before ordering surface notes. I got permission from Somerset House to acquaint the Crown Agents for the Colonies with the fact that these negotiations were in progress, and also to show them a note. The Crown Agents have asked us to advise them immediately should the Treasury decide in favour of our note. These two items, and they are very considerable ones, would be I think almost immediately affected in a manner favourable to us if we are fortunate enough to pull through. Beyond that the advertisement would be terrific and it is hard to see just what the effect would be in its beneficial result; but it would certainly bring Bradbury Wilkinson & Co. very much into the limelight and would give us the new plant I have been praying for ever since I have been here.

Waterlows were a long time submitting any specimens to Somerset House, and in September 1915 Hendriks was still hopeful. He reported to New York:

> Things seem to be swinging our way a little, although of course I do not wish to commit myself to any too hopeful statements. I think a change in my style of note is imminent but the official camp seems to be divided between a surface printed note in several colours and our note; the chief attack against our note is on the lines of

> deliveries, which obviously cannot be as speedy as those of a surface printed note, and also price. Through friends who are on the Committee I was called in by the Committee of London Bankers, to advise them with reference to a new note in order that they might make intelligent demand upon the Treasury for a change in the style of note. Of course I made the most of the opportunity, as it was one I had been working for a long time, and I am sure it did our cause no harm. To keep you informed of all the little of almost daily occurrences along what I hope may prove the road to victory would mean writing a book, which even if I had time to do (which I have not) I am sure you would not have time to read. What we both want to know is that we have got the order and I know that your confidence in me is such that you must know that I am not letting any opportunities get past me and as the situation stands today I consider it a wearisome game, but I have strong hopes. It is very difficult to express to you my feelings on the subject for, as you will readily appreciate, I do not want to raise false hopes on your side of the water, so I would like you to view it in the light that we are opposed by a great many Government officials, by the very strong influence of De La Rue & Co. which latter is not to be despised, for, as you know, the de la Rues are rich and influential socially and politically to a greater degree than is possible to a salaried man such as myself. If you look at it in this light, which is a true one, the difficulties to be surmounted are of a serious nature. Being an optimist I think they can be surmounted. Only time can prove whether I am right or wrong. At the same time, the feeling that one is going to succeed is of more help in bringing about a successful outcome than to carry around a feeling that the opposition is too strong to overcome.

Before the end of the month, however, Waterlows submitted their sample; and despite the fact that government officials had told Hendriks that Waterlows had delayed so long that they could be considered out of the running, the specimen was passed on to experts for examination. With characteristic optimism, Hendriks resolved still to leave no stone unturned, though he admitted that one had to 'whistle pretty hard to keep one's spirits up'. In the end the Bradbury Wilkinson engraved note was not accepted.

But although the company did not print the British banknotes, they accumulated as much work as they could possibly cope with at Farringdon Road under war conditions, and sometimes more. Despite these conditions, depleted staff and difficulty in obtaining materials, the security and quality of their products retained its very high standard, and it is rewarding to read in Benjamin White's *Currency of the Great War*, published in 1921 (by Waterlows, their principal competitor for the British notes), the following tribute to one of Bradbury Wilkinson's wartime printings:

> In the course of describing the designs of emergency notes in this and preceding articles, attention has been drawn to the pleasing appearance which some of the specimens present. The crown of success, however, certainly rests on those of Greece, both on account of the beauty of the design and the delicacy of colouring. The engraving is of so elaborate a character that forgery seems to be almost impossible. The glorious

> sculptures of Ancient Greece are reproduced upon these notes in effective fashion. It is a matter for national pride that these exquisite little specimens were manufactured in the United Kingdom.

An employee writing after the war in the *Bradbank Magazine* observed that:

> The war years bringing as they did a tremendous increase in paper currency all over the world made Bradbury Wilkinson & Co., with a shortened staff of men, a veritable hive of industry from early morning until late at night, increasingly late as time went on, and more and more left to join the forces. Time and again it appeared that we should be snowed under with work, and it must be said that it was only the untiring energy and willingness of the whole works that carried us through.

At the beginning of the war there were 80 men in the company's employ, and by June 1915, 45 were absent on military service. Ten had been refused for active service on the grounds of physical fitness and most of the rest were staying in their civilian jobs at the earnest solicitations of the Managing Director. Those who were serving with the forces were receiving half-pay from the company.

After the war (when, as we saw, De La Rue was in dire straits) business boomed for Bradbury Wilkinson in 1920 as banknote orders came in from all over the world. A new factory was built in New Malden, Surrey, and this move proved timely in that turnover in both 1922 and 1923 was over £300,000. (This was far more than the pre-war turnover of less than £100,000. However, wars are always inflationary, and in reality turnover had increased by about 50 per cent rather than trebled.)

Bradbury Wilkinson may have been producing fewer banknotes than De La Rue, but they were still their main competitor, as is clear from this memory of De La Rue executive Charles Cardiff:

> The opposition in those days was all American Bank Note. Bradbury's appeared in the Caribbean, in the English speaking Caribbean, but in the Spanish and French speaking it was the American Bank Note. I certainly had total faith in De La Rue's ability to deliver anything. I knew my product very well, because of the very good training I had, and I was therefore able to speak with some conviction I think.
>
> The first order I got on my own was in a tender in Honduras for the one lempira (named after the river) and it was curious because I think there were two things that helped. One was that our agent had taught the President of the Bank economics at university and when we went in for the offer opening the two old boys sort of nattered away to each other and obviously got on very, very well, the President of the Bank had enormous respect. The other thing, something that has always been important, was understanding the customer, understanding the territory, the culture and so on and translating that into design.
>
> They had given us the design and material, and they wanted the ball court in the Mayan ruins at Copan to be depicted, and they gave us a photograph. I had always been very interested in pre-Colombian culture and the opportunity arose one weekend

to go to these ruins in a small plane with two other chaps where we actually flew between the valleys and never rose above the horizon, and we got to Copan and we were the only people there and had a good wander around. It occurred to me that the angle from which they had taken the photograph for putting on the back of the banknote made it look a very unimpressive thing indeed, whereas if it was photographed from the opposite way with the jungle rising up on the hills in the background it was much better. So, on the Monday when I went back into the Bank I talked to them about this and said, 'You've got it absolutely wrong', and they said, 'Well, let's get some more photographs'. And they got some more photographs and they said, 'You're absolutely right, of course that's the way it should be'. And that's the way it was, and we got the order. Our price I think was $110,000 and the cheapest was US Bank Note who were $75,000, the American Bank Note I think were about $89,000 but we got it all the same.

In those days of course customers were not nearly as critical and as cost conscious as they are these days, and it was therefore possible to get business even at a higher price, and I managed to get the Bermuda contract away from Bradbury Wilkinson at a higher price. I managed to get some of the Haiti business at a higher price from American Bank Note, and I got the first issue of Cayman Islands, which was a small one obviously.

And Bradbury Wilkinson were still very active in the early 1980s. They took the New Zealand market away by building a factory there. In the UK they set up a plant in Saltash in Cornwall to supplement their existing production capacity at New Malden. This is how John White remembered the situation developing in the early 1980s:

There had been a huge growth in banknote volumes during the high inflation of the late 70s. When that slowed down many countries started looking at restructuring their currency – you know, dropping noughts off – which essentially meant a flattening in banknote demand. But at the same time here was Brads putting in new capacity, so inevitably what this produced was the start of a real clash which for several years affected margins. The profitability of the currency business came under competitive pressure, fundamentally from Brads.

And so it was the start of a real battle to try and put them out of business. Through 1983 and 1984, and then into 1985, their results took a real hammering. In fact, it didn't just affect Bradbury Wilkinson, it also affected their parent company International Bank Note (IBN), who started doing everything under the sun – selling off old properties, raiding pension funds – to keep the ship afloat. IBN were getting really desperate.

We started doing huge amounts of analysis on them. We went round their plants where we could, photographed them, and gathered information and literally got ourselves into a position where we knew a huge amount about them in anticipation of taking them over or driving them to the wall. Ed Weitzen who was running

International Bank Note had an amazing ability to survive, we just watched them through these years, 1982–84, as they clutched at straws.

David Hosie, another long-serving executive of De La Rue, said of the takeover:

The Bradbury takeover was probably the highlight of any Thomas man's career because they really were our big competitors. In the late 50s/60s they were about the same size as we were in terms of output. People actually forget that, if we go back to the 1920s, the three big security printers were Waterlows, Brad and De La Rue, and De La Rue was in fact limping out of business until Bernard came in.

Subsequently, of course, Waterlows proved to be the weak link and they never recovered from their fiasco in Portugal and Angola and various other things and so, when we took over the rump of their banknote business, it wasn't actually very big. I think they had about four or five orders when we took over in 1961.

In a sense we were much more aggressive in the marketplace and so as a result, I'd say from 1960 to 1986, Brad lost out in that marketplace compared to us. By '86 we were printing twice as much as they did. Whereas in 1960 I suspect there wasn't much in it.

Brads always claimed a much bigger market than they had, we claimed a slightly bigger market than we had. I think the percentages added together probably came to about 130% so it was difficult to tell.

The real killer to Brads was that, as a result of various disagreements, they made a great error in going down to New Zealand. They had seen us go out to Malta. Interestingly enough, they had terrible union problems towards the end. What people don't realise is that in 1960 Brads were not unionised; they were not a closed shop and yet they went from being virtually free to being far worse – driven by the unions, and of course they didn't have our 1978 showdown with the unions. Also of course we'd moved out of London by going up to Gateshead, and we'd also split Prelims (Design and Origination) from the factory which split the union power to some degree. These were all contributing factors.

When we took them over, Brads had 100 people in Prelims to our 60 and they had full-time shop stewards with offices on the shopfloor. Absolutely staggering. And of course they'd had a series of strikes over the two years before we took them over.

In the marketplace Brads, for various reasons got a bit over-excited and, behind our backs, they did a deal in New Zealand, which was absolutely horrifying. We had printed for New Zealand for 50 years and we couldn't believe it. This was definitely a shock. They actually put a plant up there and that totally contravened any sort of gentleman's agreement. Anyway, the long and short of it was that we opened up in Singapore and Hong Kong in the next few years.

'IN MANY WAYS IT HAPPENED QUITE FAST'

There is no doubt that Peter Orchard had long harboured the ambition of De La Rue acquiring Bradbury Wilkinson. As Barry Isted said: 'Peter had been after Brads since the 60s at least.'

And when, because of the deteriorating financial position of Bradbury Wilkinson's owner, International Banknote Company, a real opportunity arose, Orchard was not going to miss out on it.

However, De La Rue was a public company and John White, recently appointed Finance Director of the Group, was well aware of the necessity of being seen by shareholders to carry out proper due diligence before any purchase was made. When rumours started to circulate that Komori, the large Japanese printing press manufacturer, might be about to bid and Orchard wanted to make a pre-emptive strike, White tried to insist on proceeding with due caution. He said later:

> The fact is he was desperate to do it. I was placed in a very awkward position here because so desperate was he to do it, and to do it blind without any due diligence or whatever that, only six weeks after I'd taken over as Finance Director, I started getting warnings from Schroders and everybody else about director's responsibilities to the shareholders and so on. We went over to New York in the end to negotiate and Ed Weitzen took the classic stance of saying '$56 million – take it or leave it'. And Peter just accepted that because he was so keen to get it. I had a huge run in with him while we were over there, pointing out to him the risks and the thinness of the justification for doing it. It was my first and most serious conflict of interest, between his wish to do it and his belief that commercially it was the right thing against the need for somebody to point out to him that he was taking a massive risk and doing it blind as well.

It all happened so quickly that even the most senior management of Bradbury Wilkinson knew nothing about it. About a week before the deal, Weitzen had sacked the Managing Director, Clive Bradly, and replaced him with John Thorpe. Thorpe, realising the need for better work practices at Saltash, spent much of that week negotiating with the unions. He had just reached what he thought was a life-saving deal with them when De La Rue walked in and told him they had now taken over.

Because it was a secret deal, the four Bradbury Wilkinson locations in England – New Malden, Saltash, Gatwick and Windsor – were raided at dawn like a military manoeuvre by De La Rue personnel who had assembled secretly in hotels nearby the night before. At the Holiday Inn near Saltash, Nicol McGregor, who was in charge of the De La Rue team, marched into the hotel through the revolving doors and straight out again because John Thorpe, the Bradbury Wilkinson Managing Director, was in the lobby. Nevertheless, Thorpe discovered that McGregor was there, because at three o'clock in the morning McGregor received a phone call from him. Thorpe said:

> This is John Thorpe; I'm in the same hotel as you. I've just been told that we're being taken over and that you're down here in order to go into Saltash tomorrow. I'm just phoning to let you know that I'm leaving now. I'm driving up to London and I'll be meeting Brian Malpass tomorrow morning so the field is yours.

When McGregor and his colleagues went to the Saltash factory in the morning they were not sure what to expect. This is how he remembered it:

> The following morning we went to the Saltash factory. I had been instructed to telephone the Factory Manager, a chap called Geoff Martin, just prior to my arrival, so we stopped on the way to Saltash at a telephone box to make this telephone call and I found I didn't have any coins and nor did anybody else, so we couldn't make the telephone call. So we arrived at the factory unannounced. I walked into the reception area, up to the receptionist, gave my name, nothing else, and she asked me to sign the visitors' book. So I looked in the visitors' book and noticed that the guy who had signed in five minutes before me was Chris Harding, the National Officer of the National Graphical Association. And I looked up and across the hall, and on the other side I saw the very same Mr Harding. He looked at me and he obviously thought very carefully and knew immediately what was going on. He looked very grim indeed and I think he left at that point. He knew that De La Rue were taking over Bradbury Wilkinson.
>
> We met Geoff Martin, the Factory Manager. He was okay, he was brisk, he knew what was going to happen.
>
> He'd had a telephone call that morning to say that I would be arriving and would be taking charge of the factory and he was to help us in any way. He was no problem. We got the managers together and told them; they of course were absolutely struck dumb, they were mainly long serving people, as we had in our company at that time. It was a terrible shock to them. One of them was literally struck dumb, he didn't say a word all day, he was absolutely shocked. He looked shocked, he didn't say a word to anybody all day. Poor bloke. So we got the workforce together, gave them the news and told them to get on with their jobs. And I left Ron Dickinson in charge. He had the job of closing the factory down.
>
> It was very grim for them.
>
> John Thorpe's job was to negotiate the closure of Saltash and I sat with him during these negotiations. He did a very good job actually for De La Rue. Very difficult job.

And it was a good buy at the price of $56 million, with $8 million being contributed by Sicpa, the Swiss company that supplied De La Rue with their specialist inks, who wanted to take over Bradbury Wilkinson's ink operation in the UK so that Sicpa could remove the competitive threat, and another $8 million by De La Rue Giori (so effectively half of that came from De La Rue itself). This was John White's view:

> One of the consequences, though, of the Brads thing, and one of the reasons why the financial justification had been so difficult to compile was the fact that there was a

> substantial element of defensive takeover with capacity to be taken out. For example, we had planned to shut the Saltash plant straight away, which incurred extra costs in the short term.
>
> From 1986 through 1989 the additional costs of closing various plants and reorganising everything were undoubtedly a serious drag on De La Rue's profits. In the long run I think taking Brads out and preventing Komori from breaking De La Rue Giori's position, and certainly from the viewpoint of strengthening our position in the banknote marketplace, it was probably beneficial. But for several years it was not, and it will be impossible ever to prove whether or not financially this was a successful acquisition. My instinct is that it probably improved our position in the early 90s, yes, it was probably vindicated.

Others were more positive, some even going as far as saying it was the best purchase De La Rue ever made. White was more reserved:

> No, I wouldn't be quite as ready to say that. When you actually look at the additional costs of closing things and the impact on our results, I would have much greater reservations as to whether it really was. Instinctively, yes, you can say it looks like a great thing to do; financially it was much more marginal.

For his part, Nicol McGregor was happy with the ultimate handling of the banknote side but not with the security print. He said later:

> This was a very interesting period and we were quickly into this under Brian Malpass. We had meeting after meeting, plotting it, planning it and then executing it. It was a very exciting period for the company. I remember Brian asking me just before we did it, 'Are we doing the right thing?' And I said, 'Without any shadow of doubt this has to be the right thing for the business.'
>
> And of course the great thing was that when the takeover took place we had a plan in place, we knew what we were going to do with it, at least on the currency side. That was not true on the security printing side and it was one of the great failures of De La Rue to take a grip on the security print side of the two businesses and put them together. But on the currency side we knew before we went in that we were going to close Saltash, and again Brian said, 'Do you really think this is the right thing to do?' 'Absolutely, no question. We don't need Saltash, we've got these marvellous new factories elsewhere, the last thing we want is another duff plant in the UK.'

AN EXCITING PERIOD

After all the drama of the Bradbury Wilkinson takeover in 1986, the next big event in the life of De La Rue was the 'changing of the guard' in 1987. Gerry Norman, at the age of 70, retired as Chairman and was succeeded by Peter Orchard. This left a difficult decision for the Board in determining who should succeed Orchard as Chief Executive. The choice was between Brian Malpass and the Managing Director of

3.1 Margaret Thatcher, Secretary of State for Education and Science, with Peter Orchard at De La Rue House for the opening of the International Exhibition of Art by mentally handicapped children on 30 November 1970.

3.2 Lord Ashburton, Lord Lieutenant of Hampshire, presents De La Rue Chairman Sir Arthur (Gerry) Norman with the Queen's Award to Industry for De La Rue's export achievement on 20 July 1971.

3.3 (far left) *John Shepherd-Barron (left), with Gerry Norman, was modestly sanguine about claims from others to have invented the modern cash dispenser. 'I've never really thought about being the inventor of the ATM', he remarked, 'but I built the first one, put it in and made it work, so I would say that is invention.'*

3.4 (left) *David (now Lord) Rowe-Beddoe, Managing Director of De La Rue's Currency Division in the 1970s.*

3.5 Bradbury Wilkinson's main printing plant and head office in New Malden, Surrey.

3.6 One of Crosfield's innovative and most successful products in the 1980s was the Magnascan 640 Scanner. The unit on the left is the Input Analyse Scanner unit on which 35mm colour transparencies were mounted on the transparent perspex drum. The control settings were entered through the control panel. The unit on the right is the Output Film Expose unit. A sheet of unexposed transparent film was mounted on this unit. As the transparency was scanned, the information was analysed by the computer housed in the base of the Analyse unit, separated into the four colour channels of information, and sent to the Expose unit. This was used to create and expose the four individual colour-separation films. These films were then used to create the four separate colour printing plates.

3.7 Jim Salmon, the Managing Director of Crosfield, with the Duke of Kent when he visited Crosfield to celebrate its 40th birthday.

H.R.H. THE PRINCESS ROYAL
opened this building
DE LA RUE HOUSE
on 11th December
1990

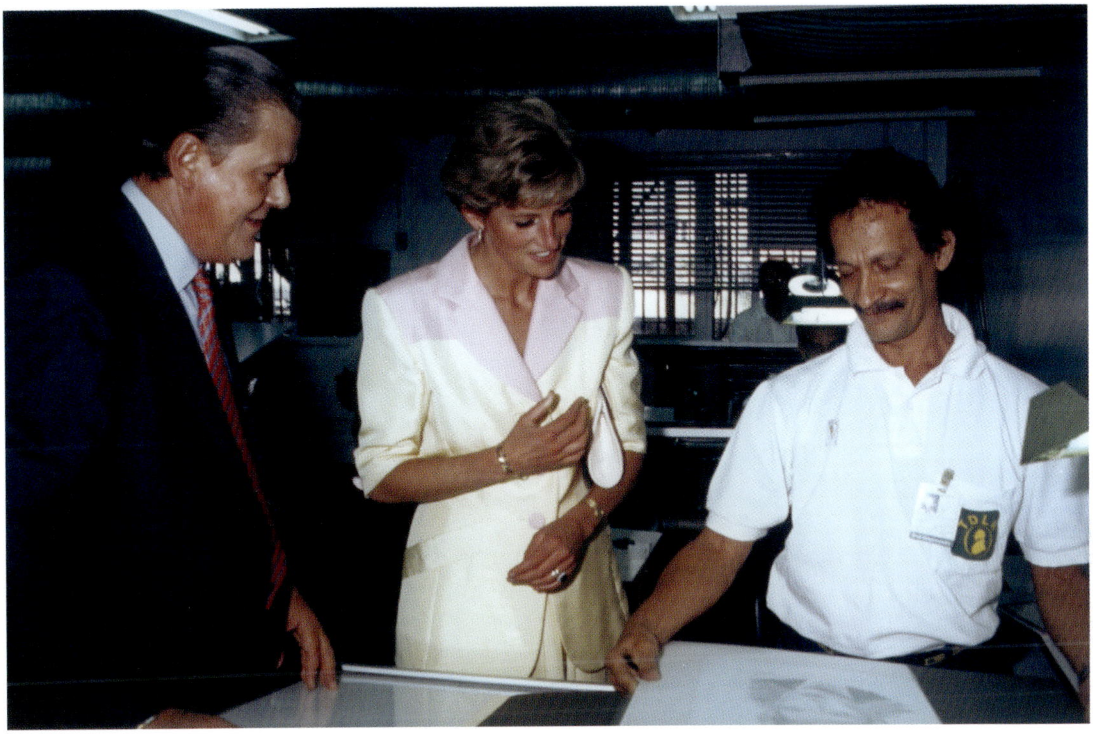

3.10 HRH The Princess of Wales with local Managing Director Alex Hutchinson, while visiting the De La Rue plant in Brazil in 1991.

3.11 De La Rue Sales Director Luke Borwick with the Governor of the Bank of Scotland, Sir Thomas Risk, and Lady Risk at the annual meeting of the IMF.

3.8, 3.9 (opposite) *HRH The Princess Royal opening the new De La Rue head office at Viables, Basingstoke, Hampshire on 11 December 1990.*

3.12 A portrait of HM Queen Elizabeth which was used for portrayal on De La Rue banknotes.

3.13 Chairman of De La Rue, Gerry Norman, with Chairman of Portals, John Sheffield (on his left) and other Portals directors (from left to right): John Lloyd, Julian Sheffield, Charles Cardiff and Philip Conway.

3.14 Chief Executive of De La Rue, Jeremy Marshall (second left), with Chief Executive of Lloyds Bank, Brian (later Sir Brian) Pitman, his wife and Anthony Jackson of Warburgs (left).

3.15 Michael Pugh (right), Director of De La Rue, with the Chairman of the Clydesdale Bank, Sir Eric Yarrow, and Lady Yarrow.

3.16 The 'wet end' of a banknote paper machine at Overton Mill (see Appendix, pages 323–4, for full explanation).

3.17 A banknote papermaking mould cover (see Appendix, page 324).

3.18 An inked intaglio printing plate (see Appendix, page 325).

3.19 Detail of a numbering box used to print sequential serial numbers (see Appendix, page 326).

3.20 Preparing a traditional hand-drawn banknote design (see Appendix, page 327).

3.21 Hand-engraving an intaglio portrait (see Appendix, pages 327–8).

Crosfield, Jim Salmon. The Board was divided and many conversations took place both inside and outside the boardroom. In the event, Brian Malpass was chosen and Jim Salmon confirmed that he was happy to work with him. Salmon became Deputy Chief Executive of the Group.

This is a letter from Gerry Norman, at the time of his retirement as Chairman, to Peter Orchard who was succeeding him, written by hand from 3–5 Burlington Gardens. The letter was written on 22 July 1987, the day of the De La Rue AGM at which Gerry Norman stepped down.

> My dear Peter,
>
> This is the last letter I shall write from 3 Burlington Gardens and I think it right that it should be addressed to you, to whom I and a great many others owe so much for the tremendous job you have done during the last 10 years in particular.
>
> Even before you became Chief Executive you played a central role in re-shaping and re-directing the affairs of the Company and during the last 10 years you have carried through a vitally important programme of change which allows us to claim, without fear of contradiction, that De La Rue is a coherent and well-balanced company which is extremely well placed to make great advances in the years ahead. I do not know of any time in the past when this claim could have been justified and I am sure that most of the credit for this new state of affairs is yours. Your natural modesty will cause you to protest that many others made all this possible and you will emphasise the vital importance of the teamwork which is such a feature of the company's strength, but I know that your own brand of leadership has been mainly responsible for creating such a good team as we now have.
>
> I am not very good at saying these things to you but this letter expresses thoughts I have long wanted to make known to you. I also want to thank you for being such a splendid colleague and good friend over many years. It has been great to work with someone who has been concerned with only one thing in his working life – the best interests of a company which is very dear to us and to all who work in it.
>
> A thousand thanks for many things and all good wishes for another successful and happy decade.
>
> Bless you
> as ever
> Gerry

Gerry Norman's fulsome praise and thanks seemed justified by an article of that year in *Management Today* under the heading, '21 Years of Success and Failure'. First, it summarised the changes that had taken place since 1966:

> The 21st birthday of *Management Today* stands in extreme contrast, in national economic terms, to the situation at its birth in the spring of 1966. Then, high hopes of a sea-change in the nation's economic performance were about to be finally dashed by

> the deepening of yet another balance of payments crisis. After the long cold economic summer of 1966, there was no more talk of the white-hot heat of technological revolution, of managerial renaissance and of national growth nearing 4% annually. It was back to the economic grindstone – for what proved to be most of the years to 1987.
>
> Today, after two decades of disappointments and setbacks that ate far deeper into the economy than the sourest pessimist predicted or feared, optimism has returned. This time, the hopes are not of sea-change to come. Britain's economy is claimed to be well into a revolution that has at last exorcised the demons of the past; overmanning, poor productivity, obstructive unions, uncompetitive costs, excessive bureaucracy, inadequate managements and too many public enterprises with clogged arteries. Led, metaphorically speaking, by the 600 USM millionaires, the new entrepreneurial economy is on the march.
>
> Does the actual experience of Britain's companies back up this hope of positive, lasting and successful change? The hundreds of company profiles that *Management Today* has featured over 21 years contain plenty of examples of failed hopeful strategies and companies.

It then commented on many of the UK's leading companies, and named its Top 10 companies with the best growth in the decade up to 1987:

	% change	
	1976	**1986**
1. BTR	405	3,649
2. Glaxo	271	2,265
3. ASDA-MFI	2,115	1,031
4. Kwik Save	344	988
5. Smith & Nephew	214	1,147
6. Dixons	1,019	2,608
7. Racal	929	807
8. Hanson	1,631	1,895
9. Northern Foods	349	817
10. De La Rue	158	1,151

A decade's growth rating

The article included a photograph of Peter Orchard with the caption: 'Peter Orchard, Chairman of De La Rue: while other industrial holding companies fell from grace, De La Rue made the right strategic decisions.'

In spite of this fulsome praise from *Management Today*, the new team at the top quickly realised that they had inherited plenty of problems. As John White, still Finance Director after these changes, put it:

> With a new chief executive there is always an element of wishing to clear the decks and jettison past baggage – you know, take provisions and say this and that have been

> run appallingly – but there is no doubt that when Brian Malpass and Jim Salmon took over we already had some serious problems around. In spite of the PR success of BW, given the acquisition price, it was a drag on earnings; Printrak by this time, our having decided not to go with IBM in 1985, was beginning to become really quite a serious problem.
>
> Printrak, in fact, that was the first thing to be tackled. Brian sent Jim to Anaheim and he came back saying how serious it was. From memory, it was just shortly afterwards that David Rigg was put in charge and we recruited Bill Deller from outside – Dick Snyder, who had been running it until then, was really taken out of the frame.

Printrak, a fingerprint recognition producer, was one of a number of acquisitions made in the first half of the 1980s, many of them in the USA and prompted by John Shepherd-Barron, who had been sent there by Peter Orchard to look for acquisitions. The others were Faraday, Lethaby, Deltacom and Sygnetron. De La Rue did not pay much for Printrak, buying it from Rockwell for \$1.5 million, and initially it seemed to be an excellent purchase as it was far and away the leader in the market for automated fingerprint ID systems. By 1985 it was attracting the attention of some of the big computer suppliers, who wanted to sell large numbers of computer boxes to police forces throughout the USA. Indeed, IBM approached Printrak and suggested tying their systems to operating on IBM hardware. For some reason, Printrak turned the offer down and soon found themselves in competition with both IBM and NEC. John White concluded:

> The overall gist of all of this was, as may be typical in such circumstances, a considerable degree of hand washing from Peter Orchard and Den Moore: 'Here we are, handing over a great business to you'. Brian and Jim, in my view with considerable justification, were saying, 'No, there are a hell of a lot of problems here'. And that in itself produced a friction from day one in Brian and Jim's relationship with Peter and Den. But the seat of the problem, and stagnation in earnings, were there already.

For the moment, the underlying problems seemed well hidden, and in the autumn of 1987 Malpass was able to report sales up by a quarter and trading profit up by no less than 37 per cent in the six months to September. All the Group's businesses, with the exception of De La Rue Giori ('held back temporarily by some delays in customers' ordering pattern'), were doing well, and the recent acquisitions – Hastech, CSI, Muirhead Data Communications and Bradbury Wilkinson – 'are fully integrated and making important contributions'.

ROBERT MAXWELL ON THE PROWL

The senior management were soon confronted with a serious challenge when it was revealed in October 1987 that Robert Maxwell had picked up 15 per cent of De La Rue's shares.

Maxwell, one of the most mercurial characters in British business from the 1960s to the early 1990s, became a large customer of Crosfield during the 1980s. In early 1987, Scan, published by Crosfield Electronics, proudly announced:

> Robert Maxwell, publisher of Mirror Group Newspapers, has signed a major new contract with Crosfield to install front-end editorial equipment at the *Daily Mirror* offices in London, Manchester and Glasgow. The Crosfield 2400 publishing systems will support a total of 600 terminals, which will make this the largest Crosfield terminal network in support of one newspaper. The *Daily Mirror* is one of the UK's most popular tabloid newspapers with a circulation of 3 million copies.
>
> The order follows the successful launch of the UK's first 24-hour newspaper, the *London Daily News*, which uses a similar Crosfield 2400 publishing system for both editorial and advertising. Robert Maxwell said, 'We have been impressed by the performance of the System 2400 and the support we have received from Crosfield Data Systems. Mirror Group Newspapers is pleased to join BPCC in being Crosfield's partner with this exciting new technology.

For example, on 22 March 1984, one of the largest orders for pre-press equipment had been given to Jim Salmon, then Managing Director of Crosfield Electronics, by Robert Maxwell as Chairman of the British Printing and Communication Corporation (BPCC). Jim Salmon said at the time:

> We have been fortunate to have a strong local partner like BPCC willing to work with us to prove this revolutionary, new gravure technology in a live printing environment. It is a very important milestone for Crosfield.

Much has been written about Maxwell, most notably by the author Tom Bower, who specialises in exposing supposedly successful people whom he considers to be fraudulent. However, there's no doubt that Maxwell fooled a lot of people into thinking he was able, rich and powerful. The preface to Bower's book *Maxwell, The Outsider* sums up well Maxwell's view of himself at the time he bought a significant stake in De La Rue in the late 1980s:

> He stood calmly at the entrance while the packed room fell silent. Over one hundred people had spotted the man who desired immortality but would compromise with glorification. Tall, bronzed and immaculately dressed (bright blue suit, white shirt and dazzling red bow tie). Robert Maxwell, alias 'the publisher', glanced at his watch to judge whether the precise moment had struck for his next public appearance. Behind him stood four uniformed security guards. Hovering in front was his chief of staff, clasping a portable telephone. The publisher places a premium on instant communications. Noticeably erect, on his left, attempting to peer into the room, two secretaries. Their employer prides himself on churning out decisions at a faster rate than most can speak and requires their constant attention to transmit his thoughts instantly. At the rear of the hall waited a photographer. Like recent Presidents of the United States of

> America, the chairman of the British Printing and Communications Corporation wants a visual record of history-in-the-making and the photographer is on permanent call to satisfy his single-minded zeal for self-promotion. Eight floors above hums the nucleus of a growing empire. Even higher, on an adjoining building, is a heliport for the publisher's favoured mode of transport to and from the capital. In the garage below is an immaculate Rolls-Royce. The publisher has always displayed a penchant for the biggest and the most expensive cars. Scattered elsewhere are a mansion, apartments, offices, factories, a luxury yacht and twenty thousand employees.

John White remembered the Maxwell approach well:

> In October 1987 we hit a crucial point – I remember it well, partly because of the great hurricane, when we had a golf match fixed on Friday 16th with Price Waterhouse and Gerry Norman was the only one to get there! On the Monday morning the stock market crashed and within a few days of that, one evening while I was in the office, the phone started ringing furiously with calls from various analysts who said our stock price was going crazy; somebody was buying, what was going on? I remember rushing through to Peter, who had just had his first call with the same questions, and we had a frantic evening. De La Rue stock was virtually the only one to be rising on the London Stock Exchange.
>
> Eventually that evening we reckoned it must be somebody trying to go up to 14.9%, the rules at that time being that you couldn't go any further without making a public statement of your intentions. You could carry on after a short waiting period up to 29.9% if you intended to make a full bid for the company.
>
> Anyway, because we were aware of Maxwell's interest in the company, we took the view that it probably was him and Peter rang him up and said, and I was sitting right beside him, 'Is it you, Bob?', and he said, 'Me what?' And Peter said, 'Buying our shares' – 'Oh, yes'. It was a crazy kind of conversation, sort of a casual and off-hand way.

Maxwell did not make a full bid but lurked in the background, and De La Rue were forced to go on the defensive. For the first time, the company appointed an outside PR company, Valin Pollin, and made a series of presentations to financial institutions. Chief Executive Brian Malpass told De La Rue employees through the *Bulletin*:

> We do not particularly welcome the news that Maxwell Communication Corporation and its associates have seized the opportunity presented by the recent stock market crash to pick up around 15% of our shares. As we have said loud and clear, we have no intention of allowing this large shareholding to influence our conduct of the business in any way.

Unfortunately, life did not become easier during 1988, as Crosfield began to suffer heavily from the need to invest constantly in new products. By the autumn, John

White was making strong warning noises to the Board, and in early 1989 the severe problems at Crosfield were becoming clear to everyone. Competition in digital imaging in the shape of giants such as Kodak, Dupont and Agfa was affecting Crosfield badly. Profits collapsed completely and De La Rue were forced to issue a profits warning. As it happens, they chose 14 February, St Valentine's Day, to issue the warning; and as some other companies including Storehouse and the previous glamour stock, Amstrad, did the same, the City called it the St Valentine's Day Massacre.

Indeed, when the full year results for the twelve months to March 1989 were announced in early June, profits had collapsed from £62.42 million to £26.3 million. At the same time it was announced that Brian Malpass was resigning 'on the grounds of ill health'. In fact Malpass had left the company in March and never returned.

David Rigg, who had joined De La Rue in 1974 and who had come back to head office after spells all over the world in the early 1980s, said of this difficult time for the company:

> You had very powerful personalities like Jim Salmon of Crosfield and somebody of obvious considerable intellectual quality, Brian Malpass, and it was a curious sort of mix, and it seemed to be a group of individuals working as individuals and only coincidentally coming together because somebody had invented a forum for them to come together, rather than a group of people who were seriously working as a team.

Unfortunately, although Peter Orchard had groomed Brian Malpass to follow him as Chief Executive, once that had come to pass and Orchard remained solely as Chairman, Orchard still interfered in the day-to-day management of the company. In the end, Malpass could not cope with this constant interference and resigned.

SALE OF CROSFIELD

Fortunately for De La Rue, a joint venture between the American Dupont and the Japanese Fuji wanted a presence in electronic imaging and approached De La Rue with a view to purchasing Crosfield. Although negotiations were drawn out, eventually in mid-June 1989, De La Rue was able to announce that an outline agreement had been reached for Dupont and Fuji to buy the business for £235 million. Immediately, Maxwell said that he was prepared to pay £250 million. On 15 July, under the heading, 'Maxwell move sparks row at De La Rue', the *Financial Times* wrote:

> Scitex Corporation, a Jerusalem based hi-tech company 27 per cent owned by Mr Robert Maxwell, yesterday went into the London stock market to buy a stake in De La Rue, the troubled bank-note printer and manufacturer of printing equipment in which the ubiquitous British publisher has a 15 per cent stake via the Mirror Group Newspapers.

> As De La Rue's share price surged 50p yesterday to close at 384p, capitalising the company at £541m, a row broke out between the company and Mr Maxwell. Central to this was the fate of Crosfield Electronics, a De La Rue subsidiary. Problems at Crosfield were cited as one of the main reasons for a collapse in De La Rue's profits from £62.42m to £26.3m last year and the business has been up for sale for some months.
>
> It emerged yesterday that Scitex – the shares of which are listed over the counter in New York – had approached De La Rue with a view to buying Crosfield, a direct competitor in the market for electronic equipment used by the newspaper industry. De La Rue denied Scitex the information it was handing out to other bidders on the grounds that it was not prepared to release commercially sensitive information to a competitor.
>
> De La Rue accused Mr Maxwell of betraying confidences in publicising the fact that detailed discussions were taking place over Crosfield. Mr Maxwell denied this, pointing out that De La Rue said it was searching for a strategic link-up for the business when it released its figures earlier this year.

On 23 July, Scitex said it was prepared to pay between £255 million and £265 million for Crosfield, 'subject to contract and receipt of relevant information'. Jim Salmon replied that De La Rue would not consider any Scitex offer unless Scitex could support its claim that there would be no anti-trust problems in the USA or elsewhere if it merged with Crosfield. Between them the two companies held more than 60 per cent of the US and European markets for colour electronic page composition systems for newspapers and magazines. Salmon told the *Financial Times*:

> We need to see a letter from their lawyers saying there are no anti-trust difficulties. Until then we are not prepared to expose sensitive, detailed information to a competitor.

Maxwell continued to oppose the sale of Crosfield, but then suddenly in early August he dropped his attempt to block the sale and a majority of the rest of De La Rue's shareholders voted for the sale to Du Pont and Fuji Photo to go ahead. There was no comment from Maxwell, who was said to be on his private yacht.

A BID FROM NORTON OPAX

No sooner had this happy position regarding the sale of Crosfield been reached than De La Rue received a bid from the printer, Norton Opax, valuing the company at £478 million. Richard Hanwell, the Norton Opax Chief Executive, after an attack on the 'total vacuum of executive leadership at De La Rue', said the enlarged group would have sales of over £700 million and would consist of four main divisions – specialist printing and packaging, currency printing, security printing, and payment systems such as cash dispensers, note counters and currency sorters. Norton Opax assumed that the sale of Crosfield to Dupont and Fuji would proceed, and it would review three other De La Rue businesses – press controls, electronic protection and Printrak fingerprint identification systems – with a view to disposal. It admitted that the acquisition would double Norton Opax's 25 per cent share of the UK market for the supply of plastic credit and bank cards, but felt that competition from overseas would make this position defensible against monopoly objections.

The *Financial Times* speculated that this bid from Norton Opax might be a defensive move against a possible bid from Bowater, who had built up a stake in Norton Opax earlier in the year. Sure enough, such a bid arrived, though this did not prevent Norton Opax from increasing the value of its offer for De La Rue to £679 million in early September. However, on 14 September, under pressure from its major shareholders, Norton Opax abandoned its bid for De La Rue and indicated it would talk to Bowater with a view to accepting their offer.

Chapter Twelve

Rationalisation

1990–1998

'He is very nice and he is very tough'
Challenges galore
On the acquisition trail again
Eastern Europe, a once-in-a-generation opportunity
The end of an era
The National Lottery and Camelot
More closely involved in papermaking
We must diversify
The hangover
Hard times continue
'I feel a spring in my step'

'HE IS VERY NICE AND HE IS VERY TOUGH'

After the excitement of the previous two years, it was announced on 17 November 1989 that Jeremy Marshall would join the De La Rue Board and take up the post of Chief Executive from 21 November. After sixteen years from 1971 to 1987 climbing his way to the top of Hanson Trust, Marshall had been Chief Executive of the recently privatised British Airports Authority until he had left abruptly in August 1989 amid rumours that he could take no more of the interference of the Chairman, Sir Norman Payne. Marshall said of his appointment to De La Rue: 'I started talking to De La Rue among others shortly after that. What I was looking for was an opportunity where I had the space to work efficiently.'

For his part, Chairman Peter Orchard said that he was 'pleased as punch', and of Marshall: 'He is very nice and he is very tough – and that's a good combination.'

After the annual De La Rue Diplomatic Dinner in 1990, Peter Orchard received a letter from Christopher Harding, the Chairman of British Nuclear Fuels. It is worth quoting from, as it praises both De La Rue's hospitality and Jeremy Marshall's abilities. Harding wrote:

> Dear Mr Orchard,
>
> What a very splendid dinner it was last night! I was indeed, absolutely delighted to join you, your colleagues and your other guests for the Annual Dinner that you give in Honour of the Diplomatic Corps.
>
> It was a sparkling occasion with delicious things to eat and drink, excellent speeches and some warm, interesting and stimulating company. I can well imagine and understand why the De La Rue dinner has become such an established and respected feature in the London social calendar!
>
> I greatly appreciated the opportunity of meeting so many friends, both inside and outside the Diplomatic service as well as making a large number of new acquaintances. As a 'new boy' to your Annual Dinner I was enormously impressed by the feeling that it was very similar to a large family party – and I cannot think of a greater compliment to pay you and your team. Throughout the evening there were many very thoughtful arrangements to ensure that we were all made to feel welcome ... not least the fact that we were each personally met by one of your colleagues as soon as we had been received ... a very original and personal touch.
>
> I have known Jeremy Marshall for some 18 years or so and he and Juliette are very good friends. We worked together in Hanson PLC (and I am still involved in that company) and he is someone for whom I have always had the highest regard and greatest respect. I was delighted to hear the reference you made to the contribution he has made in the last seven months since he joined ... but it came as no surprise. He is a thoroughly professional manager with the highest standards, intellectually superb but also combined with an understanding of what is practical and also of the importance of people.

CHALLENGES GALORE

Aside from this goodwill, Marshall faced serious problems at De La Rue. The currency business was satisfactory, but the security print business had been neglected throughout the 1980s and had stagnated. When the results for the six months to 30 September 1989 were announced in December, they showed that the Group's profits had tumbled from £23.4 million to £16.6 million, largely because of a further loss of £7 million by Crosfield (by this time, of course, sold), but also because of losses at Printrak and Remsdaq and Sygnetron (see below) within the security and identity area, also of about £7 million. These losses followed a £14.7 million loss by Printrak in the previous twelve months.

What challenges did Marshall face? There were four strands to the De La Rue Group – currency and security printing, payment systems, other financial products, and associates – and profitability was probably split in the ratio 41 per cent, 26 per cent, 19 per cent and 14 per cent respectively. Geographically, 80 per cent of pre-interest profit was generated overseas. In spite of all the attempts at diversification, the solid earner remained the currency division, where De La Rue's market share, at over 65 per cent, made the company the world's largest independent producer of banknotes. In other security print-based products, De La Rue commanded about 45 per cent of the airline ticket market outside the USA, printing for about 130 airlines, and also enjoyed a dominant position worldwide in passports and travellers' cheques. It also had a strong market position in cheque markets in Brazil, Colombia, Spain and the UK, where it was the second-largest behind Norton Opax. Margins across the security division varied markedly, with the best in the currency division and the worst in airline tickets.

In the payment systems division, the Group was supplying equipment for all aspects of automated banknote processing. In particular it was the world's leading OEM (original equipment manufacturer) supplier to cash dispenser manufacturers. Its mechanisms were installed in 25 per cent of all cash dispensers worldwide. The Group was also a market leader in developing EFTPOS (Electronic Funds Transfer at Point-of-Sale) technology. It was nearly 30 years since De La Rue executive John Shepherd-Barron, then in charge of De La Rue's armoured truck division, which delivered money to the branches of Barclays Bank, had said to himself:

> It is ironic that I am in charge of getting all the money to the branches but there is nowhere I can get money except by going into a bank and I can only do that on Saturday mornings.

Shepherd-Barron then came up with a system whereby cheque-style vouchers carrying a punch-hole code were inserted into a slot and read by a light sensor. Ten £1 notes were then released to the customer. Shepherd-Barron died on 15 May 2010 and this is what the *Daily Telegraph* said in its obituary:

> Shepherd-Barron explained that he came up with the idea of the cash dispensers in 1965 while lying in his bath after finding his bank closed. It was then his habit to withdraw money on a Saturday, but on this particular week-end he had arrived one minute late and found the doors locked against him.
>
> Later that year, he bumped into the chief general manager of Barclays Bank who was about to have lunch. Over a pink gin, Shepherd Barron asked him for 90 seconds to pitch his idea for a cash machine.
>
> 'I told him I had an idea that if you put your standard Barclays cheque through a slot in the side of the bank, it will deliver standard amounts of money around the clock.
>
> 'He said, "Come and see me on Monday morning".'

Barclays commissioned Shepherd-Barron to build six cash dispensers, the first of which was installed at a branch in the north London suburb of Enfield on June 27 1967. The actor Reg Varney, star of the ITV sitcom *On the Buses*, was on hand to be the first to withdraw cash.

As part of his work in developing the self-service ATM, which would dispense banknotes 24 hours a day, seven days a week, Shepherd-Barron also came up with the idea of a four-digit PIN, which subsequently transformed the way people across the world handle financial transactions.

Recalling his Army number, he had originally intended to make personal identification numbers (PINs) six digits long, but reduced the number to four when his wife, Caroline, complained that six was too many. 'Over the kitchen table, she said she could only remember four figures, so because of her, four figures became the world standard,' he recalled.

Shepherd-Barron hit upon the notion of an automated cash machine by thinking of the way chocolate dispensers worked. 'It struck me there must be a way I could get my own money, anywhere in the world or the UK,' he said in a BBC Radio interview in 2007. 'I hit upon the idea of a chocolate bar dispenser, but replacing chocolate with cash.'

With plastic bank cards bearing magnetic strips still to be invented, Shepherd-Barron's early machines used special cheques that were chemically coded by being impregnated with carbon-14, a mildly radioactive substance. Customers placed the cheque in a drawer, the machine detected the material and matched the cheque against a PIN before paying out a maximum of £10 a time. 'But that was regarded then as quite enough for a wild weekend,' he noted.

Asked about health fears, Shepherd-Barron calculated that a user would have to eat 136,000 chemically-treated cheques to suffer any ill-effect.

According to the ATM Industry Association, there are now more than 1.7 million ATMs around the world. In Britain alone a total of £10 billion a month was withdrawn from ATMs last year, with an average of a million transactions per hour.

The development of ATM technology can be traced to prewar New York, where a mechanical device was installed at the City Bank in 1939. But it was dismantled later the same year after customers showed little interest.

Shepherd-Barron was modestly sanguine about claims from others to have invented the modern cash dispenser. 'I've never really thought about being the inventor of the ATM,' he remarked, 'but I built the first one, put it in and made it work, so I would say that is invention.'

And indeed, in its obituary the *Financial Times* wrote:

When Shepherd-Barron was awarded an OBE by the Queen in 2005 for 'services to banking' another Scot, James Goodfellow, stepped forward. He too had played a key role in the development of cash machines and announced that he had a 1966 UK patent.

Mr Goodfellow is certainly credited with taking the ATM to another level by developing the encrypted plastic card and computerised PIN technology that are now used in close to two million ATMs. It is also true that even before the two Scots, others had thought of cash dispensers. American Luther George Simijian patented a hole-in-the-wall device which was tested by Citicorp in 1939 but it attracted lttle demand from customers.

The global ATM Industry Association has no doubts. It credits Shepherd-Barron with the invention of the first functioning cash dispenser and describes him as 'a technological visionary'. It also compared him with Alexander Graham Bell, inventor of the telephone.

Meanwhile, was Marshall equipped to sort out the problems that the De La Rue Group faced?

This was the background of the man on whom so much depended. He was a Cornishman by birth. Not that his parents were Cornish. His father, 'highly educated but retiring and unambitious', retreated to Truro, where he took a humble job on the county council. His mother had a French degree from Oxford and found Cornwall dull, 'but settled to it'. Marshall's upbringing was modest with a strong religious flavour, and he remained a regular churchgoer, saying: 'I don't think I could live without a belief in something beyond the day-to-day.' He was educated at Sherborne prep and senior schools, and as he pointed out: 'My parents went to great sacrifices to send me there but they couldn't have done me a better favour.' He showed an aptitude for figures, and said: 'I have always been rather precise, I suppose.'

At Sherborne he greatly enjoyed the sport, and was still playing tennis and hard games of squash when he joined De La Rue. After Sherborne, he spent most of his National Service in Germany, before going up to Oxford where he read Chemistry while playing lots of tennis, squash and rugby as well as singing in the Bach Passion Choir.

After Oxford he became a management trainee at Wiggins Teape, the paper company. He decided that the British paper industry was in decline (subsequent events proved him correct in this assessment) and moved on to pharmaceuticals, where he became a sales manager at CIBA near Cambridge. He was about to move to Basle in Switzerland when James (later Lord) Hanson tempted him away. Put in charge of integrating two Hanson purchases, Lindustries and Imperial, Marshall earned a reputation as a hatchet man. He disagreed, maintaining that it was a case of releasing the talent: 'Once people were unshackled from the central organisation, they knew what they wanted to do with the business.'

He gave as an example of his more positive actions the turning around of Imperial's sauce division by introducing a second size bottle of HP Sauce and using adverts with the famous boxer, Frank Bruno. At Lindustries he sold the head office for £10 million, thereby releasing a third of the purchase price. Eventually he was lured away from Hanson to become Chief Executive of British Airports Authority (BAA). Here he was not successful, saying: 'You could not have had two more opposite situations than I from Hanson, looking for extreme efficiency, and a public sector company.'

David Rigg soon found out that his sense of humour differed from Marshall's:

> I remember the first day he arrived, he rang me up in my office and said, 'Could you come and see me at twenty-five minutes past three?' I laughed and said, 'Well I can make twenty-four minutes past and twenty-six minutes past but twenty-five minutes past is difficult.' There was a very long silence and he said 'Fine' and put the phone down. I thought, 'That's a good start.'

While Marshall was working on plans to improve the performance of the De La Rue Group, it was announced in early January 1990 that Robert Maxwell had increased his stake to 25 per cent. Marshall said he was relaxed about this, and to the surprise of no one who had studied his career at Hanson, he announced with the results for the twelve months to March 1990 that he had sold the security systems company Remsdaq, along with Crosfield Press Controls. Printrak was also sold to the management for a nominal $100. De La Rue's long-established R&D centre at Maidenhead was being closed, as was the Maryland-based security systems company, Sygnetron.

Henceforward, De La Rue would concentrate on currency printing, security printing and payment systems, though even here there was some cost-cutting as well, with 300 redundancies at the Crawley factory. Finally, the currency factory at Whangarei in New Zealand was closed.

What was the reaction to these sales and cuts? One analyst in the City said: 'Not only is he swinging the axe but it is double-headed and dripping with blood.'

Strong stuff. More measured was the comment in the *Financial Times*:

> Most analysts were upgrading figures for the current year to around the £70 million mark, putting the shares on a nine times rating. De La Rue's record may take some forgiving, but this seems fairly undemanding on fundamentals ... The long-term strategy – how De La Rue counteracts the fact that its core businesses are in mature markets – is still a question mark. But Mr Marshall reckons he has up to two years' grace as the rationalisation benefits work through, and analysts seem to agree.

In the middle of November 1990, when the results for the six months to 30 September were announced, the story was a much happier one. Under the headline, 'Disposals help De La Rue rise 70%', the *Financial Times* wrote:

> [M]uch has been achieved in the last year and there are more improvements to come. Productivity can be tweaked still further and margins should also increase ... Few companies can claim to have survived a cocktail of halved profits, a takeover attempt and Mr Robert Maxwell, and De La Rue shareholders must be grateful for the present calm. In today's economic climate [recession and the imminent Gulf War] the apparent solidity of the group's traditional operations (growth of 4 or 5 per cent in the banknote printing market) is an attraction.

Nevertheless, as the *FT* went on to point out, publicly quoted companies are expected to grow, and it concluded:

> [B]efore long pernickety shareholders are going to ask themselves where the real growth prospects are. The hardest task for the modest Mr Marshall may lie ahead.

For the staff of De La Rue, Marshall had this to say in the winter 1990 *Bulletin*:

> It is with considerable pleasure that we are able to announce half year results which clearly indicate that De La Rue has put the vicissitudes of the last couple of years behind it. The interim profits of £28.3 million are a record which surpasses the previous highest figure of £23.3 million which was attained in 1988/89 in the days when Crosfield was making a significant contribution to the total.
>
> It is particularly satisfying that this result was achieved while so much of British industry is reporting poor figures stemming from difficult trading conditions, but with 85% of our sales generated overseas De La Rue is largely insulated from the UK economy.
>
> This leads me to our major concern for De La Rue factories in the UK, although it applies to all our factories to a greater or lesser extent. If we are to enjoy good pay and conditions then it is absolutely essential that productivity is improved so that our unit costs are competitive. As I am constantly hearing from sales staff, the competition is fierce particularly now that the strength of the pound makes our products more expensive in overseas markets.
>
> During the first half of this financial year there has been considerable activity. New factories have been opened in São Paulo and Tewkesbury and plans for two more in Virginia and Istanbul in Turkey are well in hand. Transfer of work from Gatwick to Gateshead and Dunstable is nearing completion and the newly installed machines at Dunstable are running smoothly. Production at the New Zealand factory has ceased but we have increased our shareholding in ENSEC [a cash-handling and distribution service business] in Brazil and bought out the minority shareholders in the Colombian companies, so increasing our investments there.
>
> The new office and laboratories at Basingstoke have been completed and staff have moved from various older buildings into a superb working environment.

Both Marshall and De La Rue received a welcome New Year present when Roger Cowe wrote this in the *Guardian* on 31 December 1990:

> **Chastened De La Rue now streets ahead**
> Step forward, De La Rue. The printing company was in terrible trouble at the start of the year. It had been saved from takeover only by the bidder itself having been devoured. But it was still labouring under the threat of a 20 per cent shareholding with Robert Maxwell.
>
> During 1990, however, that threatening stake has been spread around the City, and more importantly for these purposes, the company has reported profits virtually doubled from the previous year's disastrous low. The resulting growth in earnings of over nine times has rocketed De La Rue to the top of the Outlook table, which is based on a composite of earnings growth, cash flow and dividend cover.

> De La Rue has done well in 1990, but its performance is exaggerated by the depth of the fall in 1989. And its recovery has sadly been based on selling much of its future.
>
> The company best known for printing bank notes had come a cropper (like so many others) when it tried to develop vaguely related businesses with an electronic angle, such as security systems. Now it has retreated to printing and the manufacture of cash machines. Fine for De La Rue, bad for the rest of us as the next century's work goes abroad.
>
> Nevertheless, congratulations to the company for its dramatic recovery.

The good news continued to flow in the first half of 1991. In the currency division, competition from state printing works (known as SPWs) had not worsened, though the SPWs nibbled away at prices and therefore margins. The one area where they could not compete with De La Rue was quality. The company employed fifteen of the 50 to 60 capable engravers in the world. These craftsmen, who served a four-year apprenticeship, tended to remain with De La Rue for life, and brought a skill and artistry to banknote design that no SPW could match. Market growth in this division remained good, reflecting inflation, world population growth and increasing urbanisation, and De La Rue still had about 65 to 70 per cent of the available banknote-printing market. In the short term, De La Rue was getting excited about the potential in Eastern Europe following the break-up of the Soviet Union. At this point, the company felt that the main beneficiary of this development would be De La Rue Giori selling its banknote-printing equipment. Following the closure of the Whangarei plant, the loading at other plants had improved and Sri Lanka and Colombia were performing especially well.

The much-trumpeted threat from Lonrho's Harrison & Sons subsidiary was dismissed by De La Rue. It had failed to make progress even in Africa, where the influence of Lonrho's Chief Executive, 'Tiny' Rowland, was supposed to be especially strong.

In the security print division, City-related business had been poor as markets coped with the recession; and competition in the UK cheque market was intense, with banks applying heavy pressure on prices. Brazil and Colombia were making reasonable profit contributions and Faraday, printing plastic cards, was performing well, helped by new business from AT&T.

Payment systems, which now consisted of De La Rue Systems, Garny and Fortronic, was doing well. De La Rue Systems was performing steadily, with good sales of banknote-counters and sorters, achieving sales of £60 million a year. The German company Garny, which made and installed banking automation equipment and physical security systems such as safes, vaults and alarm systems, had recovered from the disruption in German banking circles caused by German unification, and was performing well. De La Rue increased its stake from just over 50 to 60 per cent. Finally, Fortronic, the smallest of the three operations in this division with sales of about £10 million, was nevertheless growing fast, reflecting demand for its terminals for the electronic transfer of funds at the point of sale. It was joint market leader in the UK, Germany, Norway and Spain.

By this time, Marshall was saying that his strategy for De La Rue fell into four categories. The first was the exit from high technology, and this had been accomplished during 1990. The second was the improvement of core businesses and the reduction in central costs, and much of this had also been achieved. The third was the growth of selected existing businesses, and a start had been made on this. The fourth was the selection of areas for strategic expansion. Not much had been achieved here, but research on it had begun. It was felt that any acquisition would need to be quite substantial, so that it really was a strategic move rather than just an 'add-on'.

In early June 1991, when the results for the twelve months to 31 March 1991 were announced, comment was highly favourable. For example, the *Financial Times* said:

> The City expected De La Rue to report another big increase in profits but few predicted an increase of much more than 40 per cent, let alone the actual rise of 53 per cent ... Marshall has done an excellent job in focussing the group on its core businesses. The profit increase was partly due to the high proportion of sales (86 per cent) abroad and the disposal of loss-making operations in the UK and the improving profitability of its current British businesses.

As always, the *FT* sounded a warning note:

> Profits are expected to continue to grow, but not at the same rate ... The time is approaching when Mr Marshall, like Lord Hanson, his former boss, needs a deal to maintain the group's momentum.

Marshall himself was not getting carried away, and in the *Summer Bulletin* he said, under the heading, 'Tough Going Ahead':

> Compared with those of many other companies, the annual results which we have just announced shine out like a beacon. After all, in times of recession in many parts of the world, not many companies are reporting a doubling of profits after tax, but last year De La Rue's profits before tax went up from £38.5 million to £58.9 million, and after tax they increased from £21.5 million to £40.5 million.
>
> Unfortunately, under closer inspection the underlying situation is not so impressive. First, the results reflect a recovery from some very poor figures during the previous two years, and we are not yet back to the profit levels achieved as far back as 1988, even before allowing for the effects of inflation. Second, we need to concentrate on improving the performance of the continuing operations.
>
> We can survive, and thrive, in these mature markets only if we are ultra-efficient and more skilled than our competitors, and this is what we are now working to achieve.

> Inevitably, there have been some difficult and painful decisions to make in protecting our business, such as the recent redundancies at Gateshead, but if action had been delayed any further, we would only have been putting the rest of the business at risk.
>
> The obvious major cost-saving measures have been set in train, but the task is never complete and there is still ample room for improvements, particularly in our working practices in some of our manufacturing plants. We all need to work together towards better productivity and the highest quality to keep De La Rue's name as the foremost in our selected fields.

He went on to say that the De La Rue balance sheet was now strong, and that finance was available for investment if it could be shown to be justified. As examples he cited the recent opening of new factories for De La Rue Card Technology in Tewkesbury, for Faraday National near Washington, DC, and for the Brazilian company's cheque-printing business in São Paulo, as well as the new £16 million operations centre in Basingstoke.

ON THE ACQUISITION TRAIL AGAIN

In October 1991 Marshall made his first major acquisition when De La Rue bought the Swedish money machine-maker, Inter Innovation, for £94.7 million. To finance this acquisition he announced a Rights Issue of £160 million. The issue was at 350p, a 21 per cent discount to the 448p that the shares had reached before the announcement. Most comment was favourable, and Lex in the *Financial Times* gave its approval, saying:

> A £100m rights issue might seem a touch unnecessary for a debt-free company wanting to make an agreed £95m acquisition. But the cash call is a measure of how things have changed at De La Rue. Two years ago it was labelled a prime takeover candidate, with a string of loss-making subsidiaries testifying to a decade of misdirection. Now management has slimmed the group down to two businesses covering security printing and payment systems. It wants the extra money to pursue other quarry once it has finished digesting the Swedish manufacturer of cash-handling machines, Inter Innovation.
>
> While the printing of bank notes is a relatively mature business, providing banks with machines which do away with the physical handling of cash by hordes of back-office staff is in its infancy. By acquiring a market leader on an exit multiple of just 14, De La Rue is making a sensible bet. If shareholders need further inducement to take up their rights, a promise that the acquisition will immediately enhance earnings and a pledge to increase the final dividend on the enlarged share capital by at least 9 per cent should do the trick.
>
> Yesterday's six-month results suggest De La Rue's main businesses are performing well enough to justify its strategy – a 15 per cent increase in earnings and an 8 per cent rise in the interim dividend. Judging by the mild reaction of the share price, this is one rights issue which will not be left with the underwriters.

And the *Investors Chronicle* also approved, commenting:

> The deal makes De La Rue's payment systems division the largest in the group. In true Hanson style, immediate benefits will flow from closing Inter Innovation's head office in Stockholm and merging sales, service and research teams. De La Rue also gains access to new counting and sorting markets – Inter Innovation's safe and vault manufacturing subsidiary is the third largest in the US – and improves its distribution network.
>
> But the pay-back period on Inter may be protracted. Marshall predicts a banking revolution in which automated telling systems – cash dispensers in secure safes – will replace human sorters and counters. In the process, banking halls will become more open-plan as bars and grilles come down. Marshall believes a lot of fat can be taken out: '1.6 million people are employed in US retail banking. The scope for rationalisation is enormous.' But with American banks folding and merging at unprecedented rates, it might be more than just people who get the chop. Investors can only take Marshall's vision on trust. At least he's earned it.

This acquisition of Inter Innovation would take the sales of the payment systems division past the sales of the security printing operation, i.e. the currency division and the security print division. As Jeremy Marshall said in the summer edition of the *Bulletin* in 1992:

> The need for automation of money handling operations has become very apparent, particularly in the labour intensive retail banking sector. Prospects for increased sales of our banknote counters, sorters and teller cash dispensers are most promising providing we can continue to offer well designed, up-to-date, reliable and cost effective equipment.

EASTERN EUROPE, A ONCE-IN-A-GENERATION OPPORTUNITY

The results to 31 March 1992 reflected the benefits of cost-cutting and increased productivity, with profits up 29 per cent from £58.9 million to £76.2 million. Furthermore, after strong cashflow from most of the Group's operations, net cash rose to £112 million, earning interest of £3.9 million. This compared with an interest charge of £2.1 million in the previous year. On the whole, Lex in the *FT* was complimentary:

> De La Rue shares have outpaced the market by 140 per cent over the past two years, a performance which owes more to growing faith in the management than to any fundamental shift in the outlook for its business.
>
> Eastern Europe offers one of those once-in-a-generation opportunities to boost the bank note order book; but it remains a relatively unexciting if cash generative activity with average volume growth of 4 per cent a year.

Jeremy Marshall had said:

> Thus we had moved from the Baltic Republics through Ukraine to build up a CIS [Commonwealth of Independent States, made up of countries formerly in the Soviet Union] Eastern Europe team which covered the Central Asian Republics, and that led us into the printing of the Polish banknote issue, which took us back to the 1920s when we used to print for Poland, which we won in competition against the state printing works. We still print some of the Polish currency.

Lex continued:

> Complementing that steady annuity income, though, is the more interesting payment systems side recently strengthened by the Swedish acquisition, Inter Innovation. The process of integration means that Inter's first year contribution will not be visible, so investors will have to take the company's word that the rights issue promise to avoid earnings dilution stills holds good.
>
> Price pressure from Japanese companies at De La Rue Giori and tough trading conditions in Nigeria may cause some current year forecasts to be shaved. But while there were inevitably a few profit takers yesterday, the shares look worth supporting in the long run on a forwards multiple of 17.

And the good news continued, with half-year profits to 30 September 1992 up 48 per cent to £46 million. Marshall was able to say:

> I am delighted with the continuing progress De La Rue is making, which is reflected in these results. Security printing has continued to grow strongly, while the addition of Inter Innovations to payment systems has proved to be a valuable acquisition. In spite of depressed economic circumstances, prospects for De La Rue remain good.

Nevertheless, picking up business in the countries that had formed the former Soviet Union was not straightforward. John Burbidge-King, Director of Sales of the security paper and print division from 1989 until 1996, made that very clear:

> There were very few hotels and the telephones didn't work. It turned the clock back some 50 years in terms of selling. The sales people even had to take in their own food initially, it was that bad ... Very few people spoke English ... I think the one thing that struck us as a big surprise was that then people were a lot happier, they enjoyed partying. We drank gallons of vodka, my liver's probably riddled because you can't sign a deal without drinking and once you've opened a bottle of vodka you finish it.

In the autumn/winter edition of the *Bulletin*, Burbidge-King spoke of the potential of the new markets in the old Soviet Union:

The new markets following the break-up of the old Communist bloc have indeed provided a tremendous opportunity for both Currency Division and Security Print Division but, let there be no illusions, everyone under the sun has also identified it.

We have set up special teams including linguists fluent in Russian, Polish, Ukrainian, Czech, Slovak, Hungarian and Serbo-Croat to take on the competition and I have no doubt that in many cases logic will prevail as customers recognise that De La Rue is the most skilled and reliable source to which they should turn.

He had anticipated the break-up of the Soviet Union for some time:

Towards the end of the 1980s we all, certainly in Thomas [De La Rue], had a sensation, talking to people, that there was going to be a change in the Soviet Union.

Michael Pugh and I sat in the office one morning just before the coup, and said, 'It's going to go wild, what resources do we have?' Well then sure enough within days Gorbachev got ousted and we all saw it happening. We talked to the Foreign Office again and they were so amazed that it had happened they didn't believe that it couldn't go back again. But we could see because, you must remember, currency is a sovereign product: it had gone too far to deciding they were going to get the basics of a currency, a passport, an airline and a national anthem, and we knew all about these plans ...

Estonia and the other Baltics moved first but then one began to see it elsewhere, the whole Union was going to break up. Then Gorbachev was ousted and Yeltsin was elected President in democratic elections in the fall of that year. Two months later I went on a momentous trip, in my view, with Giorgio Coen of Giori, to Kiev, which was the first proper Soviet Union state that I ever visited. We went to discuss a banknote printing plant ...

Many of them wanted autonomy straight away and they knew of Giori through Goznak in Moscow, the State printer for the former Soviet Union which bought Giori equipment.

So we went to Ukraine to set up a state printing works.

That was the most fascinating project. When I asked if Thomas could therefore print something in the meantime the answer was no because they wanted to set up a printing works. However by the following spring, virtually within a couple of months of going there, we were printing Ukrainian coupons, sharing with a French printer. The coupon – *karbovanet* – was an interim currency which is still currency even today [1996]. We started printing the coupons and ended up printing all the coupons for the Ukraine.

The next step was that Giori were unable, through all the well-tried sources, to finance the plant, and De La Rue took a very brave decision which was also a very correct decision, to finance wholly the printing plant for Ukraine over a period of some two years.

One of my colleagues, Trevor Jones, and I were flying back from Tbilisi when we ran out of fuel. We were in a Tupolev 144, I think, and about half an hour after take off they told us we would not have sufficient fuel to get to Moscow, where we were going to connect back to London on a British Airways flight, but we were landing in Sochi, which is in Russia. Really what they were doing was they deliberately took on only half the fuel on the basis that the Russians would move aircraft on and give them some fuel, because they couldn't afford to buy it.

So we landed in Sochi and Trevor and I were getting itchy about our connection in Moscow, it was winter and cold. We had learnt by that stage to take our own stuff – there was no food on the aircraft except chocolate, whatever we could scrounge or whatever we had brought out with us. I went out to relieve myself at the front, the Tupolev's quite an old aeroplane, very packed, very close. Couldn't see a tanker anywhere, and a Soviet tanker is a very clear, big yellow thing with Aeroflot on it, and standing sort of at the doorway at the front of the aircraft there was obviously the captain and crew and a guy in overalls with big rubber gloves who probably was the tanker driver.

There was a litre of vodka, salami, tomatoes and these guys were partying.

I came out and they said, 'You American?', and I said 'No.' They said, 'You look American, have a drink'. And they handed me a glass, it was a tumbler, like a tooth mug, of vodka, and I knew at this stage you drank with these guys and they were clearly getting drunk so I said, 'Well this might be an academic question' (the captain spoke English), 'when are we going to Moscow?' And he said, 'You British, you're so humorous' and he picked up the bottle and pointed to what was left of the quart. 'We leave for Moscow this time', pointing to the bottle.

They filled up, the tanker driver was happy, he was drunk as well, filled up with fuel, three quarters of an hour flight to Moscow. That's the way it was.

Burbidge-King gave credit to Russian and Russian-speaking colleagues for all the help they gave:

We brought two nationals into the Company: Dr Svat Buchlovski, who was then heading up the Warsaw Pact Dissolution Committee and Anna Shevchenko, from the Ukraine, who later interpreted for John Major, Her Majesty the Queen, and for most of the Ukrainian Presidents that have come to the United Kingdom.

Thomas has always had a Latin American, an African, a Far Eastern culture, even a techno-culture from the Islamic countries, and we now had to import another new culture to make the whole system work.

We had to learn that very quickly, so we had to have everything printed in Russian, hence Svat Buchlovski and Anna Shevchenko were very helpful in the early days of helping us to style the way we operated. Russians don't say please and thank you, they are very direct people, so we had to change the whole way we operated.

The problem we had initially, driven by Jeremy Marshall quite rightly, was what resource we had. Finding that resource was exhaustive. Where do you find it? The person who came up trumps right in the beginning was Alexis Napier of course, a White Russian. Alexis helped us enormously through the whole thing but was close to retirement and wasn't there to help with the rest of the drive, but he was a tremendous asset at the beginning.

THE END OF AN ERA

January 1993 brought the shocking news that De La Rue's Chairman, Peter Orchard, had collapsed and died at Bishop's Stortford railway station. There were many eulogies to him, but perhaps we should quote most extensively from the obituary in the *Independent* written by the former Personnel Director and Company Secretary, Barry Isted, who had worked closely with him and knew him well:

> Peter Orchard could well have been a career diplomat, soldier or classical scholar. He had the talents and tastes for all three professions, but chose instead to work as an international businessman.
>
> Orchard and De La Rue, the world's largest currency and security printing company, were made for each other. Outgoing and gregarious, yet subtle, blessed with the gift of language (in all senses), and a pragmatist with vision, he was at ease in a competitive and political marketplace. He also had a keen sense of company tradition and sought to maintain its standards whenever he thought them threatened by passing fashions.
>
> By 1950, when Orchard joined De La Rue, the business had entered its conglomerate phase which was to last, in various forms, until 1977 when he became chief executive.
>
> De La Rue for long periods had difficulty in defining its own identity. Though its core business was, and is, the undisputed world leader, there was always the fear of over-reliance on the banknote as a product. If, on occasions, Orchard led De La Rue towards technologies for which had no special feeling, he never lost sight of the fact that the company's standing in one field was its most priceless asset. He lived to see, as chairman, De La Rue regain a clear identity, as a balanced and innovative group of currency, security print and payment systems businesses. It was a fitting culmination to his career.
>
> After school at Downside, in Somerset, then four years in the army as a captain in the 60th Rifles and an instructor at the School of Infantry, Orchard went to Magdalene College, Cambridge, where he took a first in the Classical Tripos. Typically, however, he always believed he was offered a graduate traineeship by De La Rue because the company cricket XI lacked bowling talent.
>
> As a natural linguist, ambassador and negotiator, he rose quickly through the security side of the company. In 1959, at the age of 32, he was managing director in Brazil, a country for which he retained a lasting affection. By 1962, he was managing director of Thomas De La Rue International, joining the De La Rue main board in 1963. Other appointments followed – he was an imaginative and influential personnel director for three years – until he succeeded Sir Arthur (Gerry) Norman as chief executive in 1977. In this role, he ran De La Rue for the next decade in partnership with his close friend and deputy Den Moore.
>
> When Gerry Norman retired in 1987, Orchard succeeded him as only the fourth chairman in De La Rue's history as a public company. Though non-executive, he continued to devote his energies to the company and to travel widely on its behalf. He

never lost touch. Indeed, for six months in 1989, he was required to act as chief executive, until Jeremy Marshall's appointment.

Here is Orchard talking about his limericks, for which he was famous:

> I love them. They have three attractive qualities. They're Anglo-Saxon, they're masculine and they're upper-class. The French and Germans don't bother with them and the women don't like them. I suppose it's a slightly intellectual disease. When I was younger I used to try them first on my wife and the typical reaction would be: 'That's not funny', or, more likely, 'That's disgusting'. Well, I no longer try them on her, not since the last time we were in Lipari Island on vacation and I tried one out, 'There was a young man of Lipari …' It had a certain elegance but it was fascinatingly filthy, I must say.

This is what Orchard had to say about his competitor, Otto Siegfried:

> Otto, that SS Panzer colonel … keep in mind that the Germans are great in planning, in meticulous execution … they just bowl you over and start making you fearful until the very end when you find out that they've neglected the small key item.

And on his competitors:

> 'A word about our competitors: we treat each other with respect, justifiably … but,' broad smile, 'we've also driven them off the face of the bloody earth in the banknote race.'
>
> Cash, banknotes, had its enemies out there, Orchard admitted, but 'you will not succeed in knocking out the private citizen's desire to control his own cash. Money is great: it's also unrecorded. The banknote is still the most efficient means of transaction invented. It will be around a long time you can be sure.'

Losing a man of Peter Orchard's ability, experience and close connections was a shock and a blow to the company; but in the short term, at least, the good news on the profits front continued to flow. When the Group's results for the twelve months to March 1993 were announced in June, Lex in the *Financial Times* waxed lyrical about the company's new balanced portfolio:

> British consumers wrote 3 per cent fewer cheques in 1992 than the year before as they made greater use of debit cards. This trend could have proved an embarrassment for the printer De La Rue, but it remained unperturbed; the company also specialises in payment systems. This breadth of activity enabled De La Rue to record a 34 per cent increase in profits last year. Its banknote business – given a fresh burst of life by former communist countries issuing new currencies – provides a steady income stream. Its presence in payment technology, strengthened by the acquisition of Inter Innovation, gives good growth prospects.

De La Rue's attractions are clear enough and it deservedly stands at a 15 per cent premium in the market.

Furthermore, De La Rue's success was being noticed internationally. In the USA, the *Wall Street Journal* wrote a long article on 26 April 1993 which said, among other things:

How can a cautious stock-picker get a piece of the action in Eastern Europe?

By buying shares in De La Rue PLC – especially now, many analysts say.

Here's a British company that has struck gold in the Wild East by helping new democracies automate their banks and print their own currencies and passports. Despite the region's reputed riskiness, the century-old banknote printer is racking up steady gains in profit and dishing out dividends as reliably as a utility.

The company's prospects in the east are making many analysts set aside past qualms about the stock's high price. Shares in De La Rue settled at 702 pence ($10.92) on Friday after a day of heavy trading on London's Stock Exchange, leaving the price/earnings ratio at a steep 21.5. But analysts suggest that buyers who balk at the price may be shortsighted.

S.G. Warburg Securities analyst Mike Murphy has long rated the stock a buy, but as recently as November suggested that it was somewhat overvalued. Now, he's more enthusiastic.

'It's looking more interesting and offering more value,' he says. De La Rue not only offers good management and good fundamentals, he adds, but is also getting a big boost from the development of Eastern banknotes and an increased use by banks of machines that count and sort the notes.

Mr Murphy expects the stock to perform well in the short term as well as in the next three to five years. 'It's due for a good run' between now and the release of the preliminary results in June, he says. In fact, the stock has picked up steam; it has risen more than 6% since January 1, while the *Financial Times*-Stock Exchange 100 Share Index has been treading water.

Charles Pick, an analyst at Nomura Research Institute Europe, is also upbeat about De La Rue. He and his colleagues at Nomura boosted their recommendation on the stock to 'buy' from 'hold' after they visited the company about a month ago.

'The basic message we detected was that the year ended pretty strongly,' Mr Pick says.

A Focus on Swiss Associate

Like Mr Murphy, Mr Pick sees improvement in both of the company's key activities – banknote printing and payment systems. But he is particularly enthusiastic about the performance of one of the company's associates, 50%-owned De La Rue Giori SA of Switzerland, which makes most of the world's banknote printing presses. This is a volatile business, because its sales volume is low and gyrates wildly from year to year.

'It sounds as though they've had some very good orders and shipments in the second half of last year, particularly in March,' Mr Pick says.

The Giori factor has prompted Nomura and others to increase their profit forecasts for the company.

The stock isn't risk-free, of course. Analysts voice concern about the company's exposure in Germany, where an economic slowdown could begin to pinch Garny in the next three to six months. Another concern is that De La Rue could lag behind cyclical stocks if the British recovery becomes strong. That's because De La Rue earns the bulk of its profits outside Britain, and is largely insulated from the ups – as well as the downs – of Britain's economy.

Such concerns make James Capel more cautious than other firms that watch De La Rue. David Parsons, one of two people at James Capel who track the company, says they are counselling investors to hold the stock. For Mr Parsons, it's largely a question of price and timing.

'De La Rue has been a very good performer throughout a recovery situation, from when new management came in in the late 1980s,' he says. Now, he adds, investors in the British market are looking for stocks of companies expected to gain from the UK recovery.

Even so, Mr Parsons agrees that De La Rue is a solid growth stock for investors who like to sleep soundly at night. He just feels it would be more attractive if it were about 10% cheaper.

James Capel is also concerned about De La Rue's net cash holdings. 'They have a cash pile of £125 million, possibly more,' Mr Parson says. 'Obviously, the interest received on that will be less in the 1993–94 year than it was in 1992–93, with interest rates having fallen so much in the UK.'

But the cash is a source of suspense as well as concern.

'The big question,' Mr Pick of Nomura says, 'is when they do the next big deal.' After all, he notes, De La Rue hasn't made a really big acquisition since it shelled out £94.7 million for Inter Innovation in 1991.

'It remains a good story,' he says with relish.

THE NATIONAL LOTTERY AND CAMELOT

In July 1990, David Rigg, then working in the Thomas De La Rue division of the De La Rue Group, met Ian Jones, a South African who had worked for De La Rue for many years, in La Tartine, a wine bar at the bottom of Floral Street in Covent Garden opposite the Garrick Club. Jones said to Rigg: 'Do you know that there are only two countries in Europe that don't have a lottery? Albania and the UK.' Of course, De La Rue printed the tickets for many of those other countries, and Rigg thought: 'What a good idea for the UK to have one.'

With Margaret Thatcher running the country there was no chance of the Conservative government allowing a national gambling scheme. However, in December 1990 the Conservative party replaced Margaret Thatcher with the more flexible John Major, and Rigg set about persuading the government that it would be a good idea. Not only would a vast majority of voters like the idea, worthy schemes and buildings could be financed without calling on taxpayers' money. Furthermore,

HM Customs and Revenue were beginning to worry about the loss of revenue from spending on other countries' lotteries.

It would require a consortium to provide the investment and the skills, and Rigg was instrumental in putting together a group with those skills. The five original shareholders of the Camelot Group were: Cadbury Schweppes plc, De La Rue plc, GTECH UK Limited, Racal Electronics plc, all with 22.5 per cent of the company each, and ICL plc with 10 per cent.

Cadbury Schweppes was a large international company in confectionery and soft drinks, with brands famous in over 170 countries. Its annual sales were £3 billion and it employed 36,000 people worldwide.

Cadbury Schweppes' contribution would be to find the best retail outlets, recruit them, handle the negotiations, provide the sales force and understand the British consumer. GTECH UK was a leading supplier to government lotteries, designing, installing, maintaining and operating lottery systems for more than 60 state, provincial or federal governments throughout the world. Its customers included the national lotteries of Spain, Ireland and Belgium, and it also ran 26 lotteries in the USA. Racal Electronics was a world-leading electronic communications company with 12,000 employees throughout the world. ICL provided information technology services, computing hardware and applications software globally. And finally, De La Rue, as we know, was a world-renowned security printer and had been involved in the lottery industry worldwide for twenty years.

The Chairman would be Sir Ron Dearing, former Chairman of the Post Office and director of British Coal, Prudential and Whitbread. Chief Executive would be Tim Holley, a director of Racal, and other directors would be Norman Hawkins of Cadbury Schweppes and Alex Burstin of GTECH. Financial Director would be Peter Murphy, formerly of accountants Price Waterhouse and most recently Director of Finance at De La Rue's largest division. Finally, Director of Communications would be David Rigg, Director of Commercial Development at De La Rue.

Dan Atkinson summed up neatly what was in store in the *Guardian* on 2 October 1994:

> When the day arrived in May 1994, for the director-general of the Office of the National Lottery, Peter Davis, to tell Peter Brooke, heritage secretary in the Conservative government of John Major, which consortium he had chosen, Brooke raised no objection. Nor did Major when Brooke rang him to tell him of Davis's choice. For some days these were the only three who knew, but there was plenty of speculation and many thought Richard Branson would win as he had cunningly promised to donate all his profits to charity. Altogether, there were 20 large companies involved in the eight consortia who had bid.

On the day itself, Wednesday, 25 May at 9.50am, officials at the Office of the National Lottery began positioning eight faxes on separate machines. As the faxes went out, there were seven disappointed recipients and one triumphant one. According to Matthew Lynn in the *Sunday Times*, Branson was joined by Lord

Young, the chairman of his consortium, and 45 of the team who had helped put their bid together:

> As the fax came through there was a stunned silence of incredulity and sorrow. Young attempted to mollify his younger partner in the venture but to little avail. While those around him opened the bottles of champagne laid on for the celebrations in a brave attempt to drink away their disappointment, Branson lost the good humour for which he is celebrated. Tearing up the fax he abruptly disappeared from the house, walking alone through the streets of Holland Park to the offices of his old friend Simon Draper, the man with whom he had built up Virgin Records ... For him, it was a moment when only his oldest friend could console him.

What was the atmosphere like in the offices of Camelot at Covent Garden? Camelot had based itself there, and it was agreed that Dearing and Holley would stand guard over the fax machine. They had worked out a deal already: if they won, Holley would make the announcement; but if they lost, Dearing would break the sad news.

A fax came through at the promised time, 10.00am, but it was a long diatribe from an eager lawyer in Hong Kong. A frantic phone call told him to desist. As the crucial fax finally came through, Holley picked it up, read it, and handed it to Dearing, saying: 'I think you'd better read this.'

Needless to say, when Dearing read it, he was slightly bewildered by Holley having handed it to him. Everyone looked on in silence and then, as it became clear that they had won, the cheering broke out. Apparently, it was so loud that they heard it in the police station over the road. Sir Ernest Harrison, Chairman of Racal, asked David Rigg where the party was, to which Rigg replied: 'I was too superstitious to organise one. But I'm sure there is a bar somewhere that will sell us a drink.'

They settled on the Dorchester Hotel. They could afford to celebrate. As Lynn concluded:

> For the five companies involved in Camelot, taking the lottery is a vindication of almost three years' hard work. For each, it will be a profitable contract. The profit margins will be slim but even with a margin of 1%, Camelot will make profits of well over £50 million once it is up and running.

Furthermore, the members of the consortium were also suppliers. Racal established the interconnecting communications links and supplied modems and other technical equipment. Cadbury Schweppes built on its links with 10,000 small outlets that were set to grow to 40,000, while De La Rue printed the numbered slips and till rolls.

The National Lottery was a huge success that inevitably brought criticism once it was realised how much money was being made by members of Camelot, and also the size of bonuses being paid to the directors. When the Labour party won the general election in May 1997 and assumed power, the new Secretary of State for the National Lottery, Chris Smith, made three suggestions to the new Camelot Chairman

Sir George Russell. He asked Camelot to repay £7 million of interest from unclaimed prizes to the good causes fund; he suggested that directors pay some or all of their present and future bonuses to charity; and he gave Camelot six weeks to come forward with plans for operating as a non-profit organisation.

The directors and the companies within the consortium were not impressed, and there was talk of mass resignations and withdrawal. Smith's case was not helped by Raymond Snoddy showing in a detailed article in the *Financial Times* that the National Lottery was the most efficient lottery in the world for the second time, contributing more to good causes while paying more in tax than any other lottery. It contributed 43.67 per cent of its income, while the French national lottery contributed barely half at 24.9 per cent.

MORE CLOSELY INVOLVED IN PAPERMAKING

Success for De La Rue carried on into the first six months of the year to March 1994, and by the autumn of 1993, the group's cash pile of £200 million was becoming something of an embarrassment in view of the rights issue raising £160 million two years earlier. Only £94 million of it had been spent on the acquisition of Inter Innovation. Where was the next big, effectively promised, acquisition? De La Rue seemed to be disposing of companies rather than buying them. In 1992 it had sold its Colombian company and in June 1993 it announced that it had sold its Brazilian company for £30 million to the United States Banknote Corporation. De La Rue said that the Brazilian company did not form an integral part of its global security business and was not involved in the production of currency. It intended to continue to supply currency, passports and other high-security documents to South and Central America, but these would be produced elsewhere and paid for in hard currency. (Brazil had long been suffering from near-hyperinflation.)

Of the 33 years that De La Rue had been involved with the Bautista family in Colombia, the *Bulletin* said this:

> When we decided to go into Colombia in the late fifties, we had the good fortune to recruit Gregorio [Bautista], who was then director of the Imprenta Nacional (the Stationery Office of Colombia) and had before that been in the banknote printing works of the Banco de la Republica. Under his brilliant management, the security printing activity was profitable from the very first day, as was the security transport operation when it came into being a few years later.
>
> Thomas De La Rue de Colombia soon came to be recognised as the flagship of British investment in Colombia, as a succession of British Ambassadors can testify. [...] For his efforts in support of practically every British activity in his country, Gregorio was appointed an honorary OBE in 1972 and promoted to CBE in 1984, a very rare honour.
>
> In recent years, intensified competition in the security transport field, and the spread of terrorism in the country, reduced both the profitability of the business and its attractiveness as a foreign-owned enterprise. We came to the conclusion last year

> that although our Colombian investment had, over the greater part of its 33-year history, been a valuable source of both profits and cash to De La Rue, its future would best be served if it passed into new ownership.

However, Marshall said he was not going to be rushed into making an acquisition for the sake of it. He told the *Evening Standard*: 'While we do have targets in sight I'm not going to be rushed into paying too much. I'd rather play a waiting game.'

In early 1994, talks to achieve the long-awaited significant acquisition began when De La Rue opened discussions with the papermaker, Portals. The two sides failed to reach agreement on price. Inevitably, perhaps, news of the talks leaked out, and in May the Portals share price soared, prompting De La Rue to say, yes, the two companies were in discussions about a merger.

Marshall was irritated by the leak. Up to that point, talks had been proceeding at a leisurely pace. They had begun over a friendly lunch at the Savoy the previous autumn, when Marshall met his opposite number at Portals, John Lloyd, to discuss how the two groups could work more closely. De La Rue was already buying a quarter of its paper from Portals, and the latter, with a new machine about to come on stream, was keen to increase the tonnage. For its part, De La Rue was attracted by Portals' sophisticated anti-counterfeiting devices integrated in its paper. All kinds of joint schemes were discussed, but eventually Marshall felt that a full merger was the best way forward. Relations then became strained when, on 24 May, the *Daily Mail* wrote under the heading, '"To the manor born" row sours De La Rue's bid':

> Relations between paper maker Portals and its supposedly friendly bidder, De La Rue, have turned frosty following an embarrassing revelation about perks for the Portals chairman.
>
> De La Rue, chaired by Jeremy Marshall, has upset Portals after suggestions that it was the source of reports that Portals chairman Julian Sheffield had been living for 14 years in a £3m-plus Hampshire mansion owned by the company.
>
> Laverstoke House, sitting within a 4,000 acre estate on the River Test, has been owned by Portals, and before that its founding family, for more than a century. At least some of its furnishings are believed to be owned by the company.
>
> The fact that the £124,244-a-year chairman lives there, paying a rent which the company refuses to disclose, is not revealed in the annual report. The only mention was in a circular for an extraordinary meeting four years ago.
>
> Under company law, all non-cash benefits to a director have to be revealed – unless the board decides they are not material to the accounts.
>
> Portals finance director Lars McBride insists: 'We're a very big company and this is a small asset.' He says the fact that it is no small asset to Sheffield is irrelevant. Estate agents say the mansion, which is near some of the best salmon and trout fishing in the world, could be rented for upwards of £100,000 a year. De La Rue made its friendly bid approach to Portals, the maker of half of the world's banknote paper, two weeks ago.

> 'This is a surprising action from somebody who purports to be acting on a friendly basis,' a spokesman huffed. 'It suggests to me they may feel they want to go hostile. But Portals wants to remain independent and they will have to pay a great deal of money.'
>
> Observers feel De La Rue may have been trying to dampen the Portals share price, which has soared from 630p to 795p (up 32p yesterday) in recent weeks. Analysts say De La Rue could have to offer up to £10 a share to get Portals' board approval, valuing the group at almost £650m.

On 27 May the two companies published the following statement: 'The boards of Portals and De La Rue announced that they have been unable to reach agreement on the terms of an offer. These talks have therefore been terminated.'

However, Marshall and his colleagues were convinced that Portals was a sound, strategic buy, and they returned with a higher offer in autumn 1994. Finally, on 20 December it was announced that Portals had accepted De La Rue's offer of £10.50 a share, valuing Portals at no less than £682 million. The next day, the *Financial Times* wrote under the headline, 'Increased offer turns on leaks':

> It was perhaps appropriate that the final stages of negotiations between De La Rue and Portals should be disrupted by a burst water pipe.
>
> The eight month courtship, involving two separate approaches, has sprung so many leaks that it has prompted at least one Stock Exchange inquiry, emergency statements to calm nervous investors and enormous volatility in the Portals share price.
>
> Aside from its leaking pipe, last weekend's meeting at Schroders, De La Rue's advisers, marked the final attempt by the fiercely independent Portals to dissuade De La Rue from making a formal offer for the specialist paper making group.
>
> Mr John Lloyd, Portals managing director, said the board had eventually been swayed by the amount of money on offer. 'We believed we had a great future as an independent company, but at the end of the day, we must look after the interests of our shareholders.'
>
> One adviser to Portals said that he was rejecting the De La Rue offer of £10.50 a share in favour of prompting a hostile bid from the banknote printing group. 'I felt we would be looking at closer to £12 a share in a contested takeover.'
>
> Mr Lloyd said, 'the board, our banks and advisers all said the De La Rue offer was a good one. It's as simple as that.'
>
> He added that the company's renowned low corporate profile, reflecting the corresponding high profile of its international central bank customers, was a factor in not wishing to get involved in a protracted takeover battle.
>
> De La Rue has also emphasised the need to maintain its conservative and measured reputation in the security-conscious banknote industry. In both its approaches the group stated that it would not make a hostile bid, stressing it was seeking the agreement of the Portals board.
>
> However, from the beginning the discussions were plagued by leaks, to both the stock market and the press. After the first approach in May, the two companies were

forced into confirming the talks after the Portals share price jumped 20 per cent in four days. The Stock Exchange subsequently launched an inquiry.

The shares tumbled a week later after talks were terminated. Sources close to the negotiations said De La Rue offered about 900p a share which was rejected.

'We remain determined to convince them of the logic of the deal and we analysed the situation further over the summer and came back with an even stronger case second time around,' said Mr Marshall.

Early this month there was a re-run of the spring. Portals shares shot forward, followed by emergency statements and talk of a Stock Exchange inquiry. However, De La Rue came back with a higher offer. And finally, an acceptable offer.

'It's a very full price they are paying, but in the longer-term it should be a good deal,' said Mr Alastair Irvine at Smith New Court.

He added that without any obvious costs being taken out by the merger, short-term benefits were few. 'Strategically De La Rue has done the deal to increase the durability of its banknote business. They believe security is more in the paper side than in the printing.'

Mr Marshall said that the group would review Portals' core businesses, including tea bag production and the protection and control division. He said it was likely they would be sold if the sales were not earnings enhancing.

One part of the business definitely being retained is Portals' mansion in Hampshire, home to Mr Julian Sheffield, the group's chairman. He is to join the De La Rue board and Mr Marshall said his agreement to stay in the house until August 1996 would be honoured.

These were the reasons for the acquisition that De La Rue gave to both its own shareholders and those of Portals (a number of financial institutions had shares in both companies):

Reasons for the Offers

Technological change is accelerating in the markets served by De La Rue and Portals Limited (the supply of banknotes and other security printing, cash-handling systems and transactions systems to commercial banks and state entities worldwide). In terms of the provision of banknotes, the increasing availability to counterfeiters of inexpensive sophisticated colour copying machinery has created demand for notes featuring a combination of security features, and this demand will grow in the future. Some of these features are found in the paper on which the notes are printed and some in the printing process itself.

Existing features in paper manufactured by Portals include:

- watermarks
- a range of speciality threads, including
  - windowing
  - clear text

- machine detectability
- colour shift

Existing features added by De La Rue at the printing stage include:

- specialist inks
- intaglio printing
- printing and numbering devices
- application of holograms and foils
- application of machine-readable features

De La Rue and Portals believe that the next generation of banknote security features will include combined paper and print characteristics. With representation in paper manufacturing as well as printing, the Enlarged Group will have both the technological expertise and the strong customer relationships to enable it not only to combine these existing features, but also to identify and exploit new developments in both print and paper technology, shaping the market demand for high technology banknotes.

However, the technological links go beyond the printing of banknotes. For example, De La Rue continues to develop actively the incorporation of holograms into the design of banknotes and other documents. De La Rue believes that there is also considerable demand for the development of security features in banknote paper which can be detected by proprietary sorting equipment designed and supplied by De La Rue's Payments Systems Division.

Through the ability to develop new products which include print, paper and other security features, De La Rue and Portals will reinforce their positions in the provision of banknotes, initiating and leading technological change and exploiting the opportunities which will emerge. They will deliver a fully-integrated banknote manufacturing service. In due course, customers will be offered notes that are more secure, more durable, more easily readable by sorting machinery and more acceptable in a wider range of dispensing machinery. Furthermore, the Enlarged Group will be able to provide these banknote manufacturing services alongside the complementary functions such as design of cash handling equipment.

The acquisition of Portals represents a further logical step in a series of strategic moves by De La Rue in order to build a group providing services in all areas of currency production and handling. Building upon the establishment in 1965 of De La Rue Giori, the leading supplier of banknote printing equipment (in which De La Rue holds a 50 per cent interest), De La Rue has in particular acquired:

- in 1986, Bradbury Wilkinson, a leading security printer which manufactured banknotes and other security printed documents
- in 1989, control of Garny, strengthening De La Rue's position in the German market for cash-handling systems and security equipment, as well as the provision of bank design and furnishing services

- in 1991, Inter Innovation, whose main activities comprised the manufacture and supply of automated currency handling systems, the manufacture and supply of physical security products and the service and maintenance of such machinery
- in 1993, Case ICC, a leading UK manufacturer of equipment for sorting and counting coins
- in 1993, the remaining shares in De La Rue Holographics, a manufacturer of holograms.

De La Rue will continue to seek appropriate acquisition opportunities.

The acquisition by De La Rue of Portals will bring together the leading commercial banknote printer and the leading banknote paper producer worldwide. The Enlarged Group will be a leading provider of printing and paper manufacturing services both to the commercial sector and to State-owned print works ('SPWs'), offering a full range of services comprising:

- manufacture and supply of paper
- design and origination services
- printing of banknotes
- licensing and sale of anti-counterfeiting features
- technical advisory services

Although De La Rue will continue to buy paper from other manufacturers, it will be in a position to optimise the use of Portals' capacity over the long term.

Portals is a supplier to a significant number of SPWs, which account for 88 per cent of the world banknote printing market. De La Rue believes that this access, combined with De La Rue's relationships with SPWs and with the Enlarged Group's range of technological features, will allow the incremental sale of high-denomination, high-security banknotes which will offer the optimum security features in both print and paper manufacture, leading to increased sales of higher quality banknote paper and banknote manufacturing services.

De La Rue expects that the acquisition will result in a moderate enhancement to the earnings per share De La Rue would otherwise report in respect of the year ending March 1997, the second full year following the acquisition. The extent and timing of earnings enhancement will depend primarily on the strength of worldwide demand for banknotes and on the ability of the Enlarged Group to increase volumes through its marketing and development activities.

WE MUST DIVERSIFY

What attracted De La Rue to Portals? Just as De La Rue felt the need to diversify, so did Portals.

By the early 1960s, Portals' long life – nearly 250 years – as the supplier of banknote paper to the free world, outside the large papermaking countries such as the USA and Canada, was coming under threat. For example, in 1962 the Indian government decided to build its own security paper mill and provide its own banknote paper requirements. Although this had long been expected by Portals, nevertheless it meant the loss of a large customer.

This was Portals' position:

> Fundamentally it had only one product – mould-made security paper in the one form of watermarked banknote paper. It sold to 119 issuing authorities, was the largest manufacturer of banknote paper in the world devoted entirely to the manufacture of security paper, a point greatly in its favour with its customers. For two hundred years and more it had been required to make more paper each year. It could increase prices with costs, and achieve a gentle progression of profits.
>
> In the mid-1950s, however, a French company, Arjormari, came into the act, and in the mid-1960s a mill was set up in Germany by Giesecke & Devrient, who again nibbled away at the market. And when Portals set up a mill for the Indians, its production at its papermaking plant at Overton Mill dropped by 20 per cent. An adequate return on investment could no longer be taken for granted. Portals did not regard a marketing orientation as a great cure-all in this situation. Marketing in this context was a matter of optimisation of profits from a fairly fixed market. It was hard, for instance, to sell to more countries, but there were ways of making existing markets more profitable, and the aggression comes in maintaining market share.
>
> The market itself did not operate in a very conventional fashion. There were three sources of contracts, and three only. First, orders could come from currency printers, De La Rue or Bradbury Wilkinson. Secondly, an issuing authority would order paper and print separately; or thirdly an issuing authority could order paper to be delivered directly to its own printing works. In all these, what was being sold was security, and only secondarily paper. The market was not primarily price-sensitive. It demanded a high minimum standard of quality as licence to do business and only then did a price factor enter in. Portals therefore did not launch new products, like a detergent company, on an unsuspecting market but had to decide which aspects of its one product could be improved to increase the confidence limits of its customers. It had also to provide a broad range of devices like security threads, sensitising materials and watermarks.
>
> The key, then, to the market was technical excellence, particularly in the research and development side. It is for this reason that Portals Ltd had involved itself in very detailed study of the forecast requirements for banknote paper for the following ten years.

The company needed to look for new pastures, and Chairman John Sheffield decided to buy his way into water-treatment. There was industrial logic, not just his recognition of the potential of the water-treatment industry. The first acquisition was the water-treatment business built up by Sir William Paterson, and this was followed by Candy International, Houseman and Thompson, British Berkefeld Filters, Bell Brothers and Permutit. By the end of the 1960s, Portals had bought its way to a dominant position in the UK water-treatment market.

The difference with this new side of Portals' business was that with water-treatment it was in a number of industries rather than just one – for example, swimming pool filtration units, chlorine dispensers, chemical cleaning and under-pressure tapping machines.

One person who knew both De La Rue and Portals very well was Charles Cardiff. He worked for De La Rue in the 1960s and 70s but felt at one point that his progress in the company had stalled, and at the end of the 1970s he left to join Portals. He set out his views of Portals:

> It was a bit like De La Rue in those days, very clubby ...
>
> I don't think the culture was as different between the two companies as it was by the time of the acquisition. Portals was immensely feudal, it really was. The Board sat there, pontificated, gave out orders and everybody jumped to attention and carried them out without question. And the Board met every two weeks and effectively ran the business. That's the Portals Limited Board. It was quite a small business and it was very much into the banknote side of things and it was similar in that there was another side, in the same way that De La Rue had systems or whatever it was called in those days ...
>
> In Portals there hadn't been that many people brought in. The ones that came in like John Mahler and Bill Wood had stayed and had a very strong impact on the business, and I think Bill Wood for all his faults did an awful lot to modernise the business. Then they had someone like John Lloyd who was homegrown, who again had a modernising effect on the business. In the, what, 25/26 years I was with them it was interesting to see the transition in a business which hadn't invested very much for a long time, and the decision to invest and make very heavy investment to modernise. In De La Rue, Portals was seen as a sleepy sort of business. I can remember in the two years that I was responsible for Sales, part of my responsibility was for buying banknote paper and the director of Portals who was responsible, the only contact other than the telephone in those two years I had with him was that he took me to lunch once. So they were used to a market where basically they sat back and waited. They were order takers and very much a production-led business.

In 1985 Brian Malpass did a deal with Philip Conway, who had just completed his first year as Managing Director of Portals, whereby Portals conceded a 5 per cent per annum reduction of the paper price for three years. Cardiff felt that this would be an appropriate moment to try to consolidate relations between the two companies. However, it was not to be, and Cardiff blamed De La Rue, saying:

> De La Rue did not wish to have with Portals the sort of close commercial relationship that we would have liked. That a strategic alliance of some kind should be formed was always dismissed virtually out of hand, by De La Rue.
>
> And we tried all sorts of ways, we tried through salesmen talking to salesmen rather than necessarily doing it at a higher level and were told to call off my salesmen, they were to stop interfering in De La Rue's business and so on. So relationships were

not good. I realised that one couldn't go back to the halcyon days of cricket matches and so on, although one did get the cricket going again in an effort to try and improve relationships. Even old friends in De La Rue clearly had been told 'Keep them at a distance.'

The most surprising thing about the bid, for me, is that it took so long coming, and I can remember talking to David Rigg and I said to him, 'Why don't De La Rue bid for Portals? It's such a logical thing to do.' And my understanding is that Peter [Orchard] was totally opposed to it. He felt it was wrong, it would be disloyal to all his old contacts at Portals, and so on. I don't know, there was a personal thing there. He really didn't feel it was the right thing to do, that was my understanding.

Gradually, as the 1990s progressed, Portals made significant progress in building anti-counterfeit measures into its paper. This had become even more important as colour photocopiers became ever more sophisticated. Philip Conway would say later:

Finally, a few words on security thread manufacture. As I said, the technological advance which thrust Portals ahead of its competitors [to whom it granted licences that earned royalties approaching £0.5m at one stage] was windowing of security thread, for which we shared the Queen's Award for Technological Advancement with the Bank of England (who conceived the idea). This is also the security feature which, in my opinion, tilted the balance in Portals', i.e. the paper's, favour versus the features added by the security printer. Ultimately and perversely it probably contributed to Portals being acquired by DLR.

With this feature in our armoury, we took the view that we had to control in-house manufacture of security thread which until 1993 we had purchased from a firm in Horwich, Lancs called Nathaniel Lloyd. In that year I concluded negotiations to buy the company for £1.8m, which we then renamed Portals Packaging Tapes. (It did make tear tapes for cigarette packets, food items and for parcels etc. and we did not want to draw attention to its main activity, hence the innocuous name.)

Lex in the *FT* gave its guarded approval of De La Rue's acquisition of Portals:

Portals' shareholders may be disappointed its board failed to fight: a contested takeover would probably have raised the final price paid by De La Rue. But in an industry where customers are governments and discretion is a byword, the damage wreaked on both businesses during a hostile bid could have been significant. Shareholders are being offered a fair price for a fair business.

The rationale for combining De La Rue's printing expertise and Portals' paper technology is impeccable. Governments are increasingly concerned about counterfeit banknotes. De La Rue will be able to marry the two groups' anti-fraud technologies, offering worried customers a comprehensive service. Portals' paper distribution network will also help De La Rue market its high-denomination, high-margin banknotes to governments which are unwilling to invest in expensive technology for low-volume print runs. Finally, De La Rue will be able to market verifying machines based on paper technology to clearers and central banks.

Fears that De La Rue is deepening its exposure to paper money when a cashless society is on the horizon are groundless. Use of cash is set to expand rapidly in the developing world, while a cashless first world will remain a pipe-dream in the foreseeable future. Nevertheless, concerns remain. De La Rue needs to allay fears that competing banknote manufacturers will be unwilling to buy paper from its new subsidiary. Given few opportunities for cost cutting, the group will also have to demonstrate the synergies of putting the companies together are real. The acquisition is sensible if not sensational.

There was some criticism of the price paid, which valued Portals at over 30 times current earnings. Jeremy Marshall had always maintained that he would not overpay for acquisitions. He defended his offer by saying that the rising profits forecast by analysts for Portals, and the recently announced £100 million order from India, had meant that a higher offer was necessary.

Questor in the *Daily Telegraph* made a point that would become only too relevant in the years to come:

'Gearing will be over 100 per cent'

Most analysts judged the acquisition price to be expensive, but thought the deal would ultimately prove profitable for De La Rue. 'They are getting a cracking good business for the money,' said Alistair Irvine, an analyst at stockbrokers Smith New Court PLC. 'Portals' customers in the state-owned area should open up a lot of business for De La Rue. It's a good-value deal.'

Christine Munro, an analyst at Hoare Govett Investment Research Ltd., added that a company 'doesn't get good strategic moves like this cheaply.' Ms Munro said the combined group would provide 'a full range of expertise in producing bank notes from start to finish. That is likely to give them access to a new customer base.'

If we return to Charles Cardiff, the *De La Rue Bulletin* saw him as the ideal man to comment on the takeover and the problems as well as the opportunities that would lie ahead. In the spring 1995 issue it led with an interview with Cardiff:

Q. How is morale at Portals after the acquisition?

Understandably, there has been some unease which only the passage of time will fully cure. But any concern is misplaced as it is obvious that De La Rue acquired the business because it was perceived to be well run and because the combination of the two companies could only make them both stronger.

After all, it's all about perceptions – I know that some people think that Portals was all men in tweeds, shooting and fishing. But the truth is that we have been a well-run company producing a high quality product. We have won the Queen's Award for Technological Achievement, two National Training Awards in three years and there is ISO 9001 accreditation at Overton, Bathford and Portals Packaging and Tapes.

Q. And how have Portals' customers reacted?
The first thing I did was to write to our customers to reassure them of both the continuity and the separation of the business. The acknowledgements and replies I've received have been most encouraging and we will be making visits to provide further reassurance. I know they are carrying out the same exercise at Bathford, where they make security paper for high security documents.

Q. For those of us not directly involved in that side of the business, what is the difference between the banknote paper produced at Overton and the security paper produced by Bathford?
Banknote paper is made from cotton waste because it has to be strong enough to be used over and over again. Cheques are a one transaction item so they are made from wood pulp.

Q. What do you perceive to be the advantages of the merger of De La Rue and Portals?
There are several. Now Thomas De La Rue salesmen can sell a balanced portfolio of paper and print integrated features. The fact that these two kinds of features are not competing with each other is better for the customer, so it's better for us.

The Overton and Bathford sales forces can also alert Thomas De La Rue to any overspill opportunities from SPWs [state printing works].

I am particularly excited by the opportunities in the area of Research and Development. It must be possible to develop features that are mutually dependent in both paper and print. The R&D teams will join forces at Basingstoke under Ken Wade, who was Technical Director at Overton, and is now Divisional R&D Manager.

There are also advantages to be gained from treating the two businesses as two departments of the same organisation to bring costs down.

Q. Any final thoughts?
Yes. It seems to me that the banknote industry and those who serve it depend on two things and two things only – quality and security – and whatever we do we must ensure that these are the twin pillars on which we continue to build the business. Any strategies that deviate from that can only bring trouble. Historically, both De La Rue and Portals have always stuck to this rule and I know that is how we will succeed in the future.

THE HANGOVER

No sooner had the ink dried on the purchase documents (and everyone could feel pleased with a job well done and a strategic objective achieved) than De La Rue was forced to give a profits warning on 7 March 1995. Somewhat unfortunately, the *Financial Times* had published an article entitled 'Picking a stock with potential' only three days earlier, and had included eulogies about De La Rue:

> For Sally Walden, who manages the UK Growth unit trust for Fidelity Investments, De La Rue is one of her favourite growth stocks. The company has a licence to print money, being responsible for printing the banknotes of many countries round the world, and expanded recently by acquiring Portals, one of its main paper suppliers.
>
> Walden says De La Rue dominates its market and has both healthy margins and the ability to generate cash. There are also good growth prospects in developing nations (such as the nations which emerged from the break-up of the Soviet Union), as well as markets where central banks have traditionally printed notes. 'Those banks that do so don't have the expertise in fighting counterfeits that De La Rue has,' she says. Portals add to the group's anti-counterfeiting expertise.
>
> According to REFS [Really Essential Financial Statistics], De La Rue has achieved compound growth in earnings per share of 40.6 per cent a year over the past five years. Shares in the company have risen 267 per cent since the start of 1990, far outstripping the FT-A All-Share index.
>
> Analysts are forecasting earnings per share of 57.5p in the present year, a 21.8 per cent increase on last year's 47.5p. For the year to March 1996, the consensus forecast is 61.2p, a growth rate of just 8 per cent. The main reason is the effect of the acquisition of Portals, for which De La Rue paid nearly 31 times historic earnings.

Possibly as a result of this piece, two days later De La Rue said: 'The board currently considers it likely that there will only be modest growth in headline earnings per share in the first full year following acquisition.'

When your company has come to be considered a 'growth' stock, a word like 'modest' will send the shares crashing, and sure enough it did. They fell 143p. Jeremy Marshall was forced to say: 'Nothing has changed on the Portals front in the short time since we bought it. We're perfectly happy with what we have found now we're inside.'

Lex in the *FT* was critical of the way in which De La Rue had made its announcement:

> De La Rue's statement to the market yesterday was not supposed to be a profits warning, but was so clumsily formulated that the effect was far worse ... However the specific issues which formed the meat of yesterday's statement were not addressed. Some investors doubt management's claims that these negative elements have emerged only recently.

This prompted Marshall to write to the *FT* editor, and his letter was published in full two days later. Marshall, particularly incensed by Lex's inference that De La Rue were withholding relevant information, wrote:

> One can never predict accurately how markets will react to information and, in these nervous days, overreaction should not obscure the responsibility that directors of public companies have to ensure all market participants receive information equally ... companies acting in a responsible manner should not, in our view, be treated

> cynically as Lex implies in at least part of its March 8 column, nor be accused of withholding material information during a sensitive period.

When the results for the twelve months to 31 March 1995 were announced in June, profits showed a healthy rise of 13 per cent to £146.6 million. When questioned, Marshall said that current orders in the banknote business were good, though not at the record levels of recent years. The performance of the payments systems division would depend on whether Garny recovered (its profits had halved to £5 million). On the whole, the press and the market reacted reasonably favourably.

In his message to De La Rue employees in the summer issue of the *Bulletin*, Marshall said he was delighted with the purchase of Portals:

> The benefits of combining the Portals security papermaking businesses with our security printing operations are proving to be even more promising than first thought. There are further developments for new anti-counterfeiting devices in the pipeline and the sales organisations are already benefitting from a unified approach.

He said that, 'by the year 2000, De La Rue will be the undisputed leader and recognised expert for "money products" throughout the world'. But the Group could not afford to be diverted by 'unrelated activities', and other companies in the Portals Group would be sold. He continued with an appeal to everyone to redouble their efforts to show 'inspired initiative and drive', saying:

> We need to find new applications such as those which have added extra value in the past. Recent examples are the major orders for state-owned banknote printing plants in the Ukraine and Kazakhstan, the establishment of our own plant in Kenya, the purchase of the M.B. Clarke cheque printing plant and the Shell contract for smart cards.

The disappointing news of the spring and early summer continued in the autumn, when De La Rue announced its half-year results to September and issued another profits warning. The shares reacted badly, falling 20 per cent, and analysts cut their full-year profit forecasts. Marshall said: 'We are still strong performers. The group strategy will not change because we have no real weak points.' When asked what he thought of the share price plunge of 166p to 734p, he said: 'We had a very high premium rating but no one walks on water.'

He pointed out that the world market for banknotes had been growing at 4 per cent, while De La Rue's business had been growing recently at 20 per cent, and added: 'It was obvious that this could not continue and we have tried hard to dampen analysts' expectations about the future.' He went on to say that investments being made in all areas of the business would bring some recovery in 1996, but warned: 'There will be some improvements, although I do not want to hype up the prospects for growth. This business is far more volatile than it is given credit for.'

At the beginning of 1996 the Managing Director of the payment systems division, Robert Gardner, was replaced by Haydn Abbott. Marshall said he was particularly keen to benefit from Abbott's marketing experience. Almost at the same time, the company announced it was selling its Hong Kong banknote manufacturing plant to the Hong Kong government for £21.9 million. De La Rue intended to retain export work, which accounted for 45 per cent of plant volume, and would transfer the production to its Singapore plant.

There was no relief from the gloom of 1995 when results for the year ending 31 March 1996 were announced in early June. Profits were only marginally down at £147.9 million. They would have been considerably worse but for a windfall of £17.4 million from National Lottery operation Camelot, which was up £15 million on the previous year. In the two main divisions, banknotes had been hit by increased demands for expensive security measures, following a wave of counterfeiting. Furthermore, excess capacity in the industry had led to price-cutting. Cash Systems fared even worse, with profits halving to £20 million after an £18 million exceptional charge to cover restructuring costs. Marshall said the business had been hit by reduced demand for cash-handling equipment, particularly in the USA after the recent wave of bank mergers.

The market did not like the results and marked the shares down again. Questor in the *Daily Telegraph* was fairly savage. In an article under the heading, 'De La Rue looks devaluation prone', he wrote:

> It is only 18 months since Jeremy Marshall, De La Rue's chief executive, waved a £50 note in the air to demonstrate the clever security designs in modern banknotes. That was when De La Rue, with its shares at 954p, agreed its £682 million bid for Portals, one of the major makers of the specialist paper beloved by Mr Marshall.
>
> The notes themselves might perform well, but De La Rue's own paper – the equity – has proved horribly prone to devaluation. After three profits warnings and a drop of almost a third in the share price, Mr Marshall's halo has disappeared and De La Rue looks a mundane, if cash-generative, business operating in a mature market.
>
> If there is a consolation for shareholders it is that the shares would be out of sight without the Portals acquisition. Thankfully, Camelot has also come along and now contributes almost all the profits from associates.
>
> The Portals purchase now looks like a defensive move to avoid the pain that was about to arrive in the banknote market. With its advanced technology, Portals has done its best but it has not been enough to save the group.
>
> To be fair, Mr Marshall has never pretended life would be rosy. He used the term 'bonanza' to describe the unrepeatable profits from the break-up of the Soviet Union when every newly-independent state wanted a set of new banknotes.
>
> Eventually, capacity will come out of the market and it is a fair bet De La Rue will still be standing at the head of the pack in a market growing at 4pc a year. It has a near-monopoly in some parts of the world and can afford to take the game into new technological areas.

> But it will not happen quickly. It is even conceivable Mr Marshall will still be complaining in six months' time.

Even before the next results were announced in November, there were signs of the pressure that Jeremy Marshall was coming under. On 20 October 1996, Kirstie Hamilton wrote in the *Sunday Express*:

> Anyone needing lessons in how to get rid of shareholders' money should visit Jeremy Marshall, chief executive of De La Rue. Until recently Marshall was known as one of Britain's brightest managers, and De La Rue had the advantage of a luscious-sounding business: it literally prints money.
>
> But like everyone, Marshall makes mistakes, and his was a big one. De La Rue paid the fanciest of prices, £682 million, for Portals, the specialist paper maker, in December 1994. Even those on the receiving end of the bid couldn't believe their luck, but De La Rue was adamant it was doing the right thing.
>
> Since then three profits warnings have followed in quick succession, and the shares have crashed from a high of 900p last year to 585p on Friday. The market keeps expecting good news, but it hasn't happened yet. Marshall blames 'events conspiring against us'.
>
> The Marshall fan club is now dwindling. Other chief executives who have begun to think they can walk on water should watch and take note. Unless Marshall can do something to revive De La Rue's fortunes soon, he may find events conspiring against his role in the company.

In the event, although De La Rue announced profits for the half-year to 30 September down 13 per cent, comments about stabilisation of prices in the banknote business and management changes and restructuring in the Cash Systems division, and also promises of better times ahead, helped the company's shares to rise a little – the first time that had happened for two years.

At least in early 1997 there was some very positive news to announce when De La Rue bought the Lonrho security printing subsidiary, Harrison & Sons. Harrisons was the leading supplier of stamps to the Post Office and also printed banknotes, travellers' cheques, passports and other security documents for governments around the world.

Harrison & Sons was a very old company. *The House of Harrison*, published in 1914, claimed that their forebears were 'not unknown in the annals of printing' in the middle of the 16th century! Certainly in the 19th century they could list customers such as the Admiralty, the Chancellor of the Exchequer, the India Board, the Home Office, the Board of Trade, the Council Office, the Colonial Office, the Foreign Office, the Irish Office and the Tax Office.

The company had moved to High Wycombe from Reading in 1933 after winning the contract to print British postage stamps. It had printed all the special issue royal stamps since 1934, and thanks to this it had enjoyed three royal visits, beginning with Queen Elizabeth in 1952 to see the first stamps of her reign. This was followed in 1972 when Prince Philip and Princes Andrew and Edward came to see the stamps for the Queen and Prince Philip's silver wedding, and finally Prince Andrew and Sarah Ferguson came in 1986 to see the stamps for their wedding.

Harrisons was bought by the conglomerate Lonrho in 1979 and considerable rationalisation took place, entailing a reduction in the workforce from 1,000 to 500.

Harrisons' sales in the year to 30 September 1996 were £27 million, and it made a loss, after reorganisation costs, of £4.6 million. De La Rue were paying a nominal sum and taking on Harrisons' net debt of £14.4 million. The turnover of £27 million would add a mere 10 per cent to De La Rue's existing turnover in its security printing division. However, as *Print Week* pointed out: 'De La Rue has eliminated a "major annoyance" from the security printing market.' For example, De La Rue had recently lost the contract to produce Singapore's two lower-value, and therefore higher-volume, notes when Harrisons quoted a lower price, despite De La Rue having a plant in Singapore.

Furthermore, in acquiring Harrisons' postage stamp business, De La Rue not only re-entered a market it had abandoned generations ago, it added a possibly new and more profitable diversification from banknotes. Meanwhile, the Group's other recent acquisitions, three cash-handling businesses – Brandt in the USA, Associated Cash Handling in South Africa and the Brazilian cash-handling and distribution service business Ensec – as well as McCorquodale Security Cards and Applied Systems Institute in the USA, which it had bought in 1995, were all attempts to build up the hopefully more profitable Cash Systems division. It was also in the process of buying Philips Smart Cards.

HARD TIMES CONTINUE

The purchase of Harrisons was something of a side-show in the continuing fierce market conditions that De La Rue was facing. When the results for the year to 31 March 1997 were announced in early June, the market reacted badly and De La Rue's shares fell 13 per cent. The company blamed the market conditions especially in the banknote division, where over-capacity was hitting volumes and margins (at least the company had just taken one competitor out of the market!). Furthermore, Jeremy Marshall was forced to admit that: 'We do not expect any significant advances in sales volumes in the immediate future.'

And in cash-handling, the supposed growth area, operating profits fell no less than 42 per cent to £22.1 million because of investment in new products and lower sales of high-margin products. At least here Marshall talked of profits moving ahead in the current financial year. Even Camelot's contribution was slightly down at £15.9 million against £17.4 million.

To Jeremy Marshall the glowing headlines and fulsome praise of just two years earlier must have seemed a lifetime away. He would not have enjoyed reading the City Comment in the *Daily Telegraph*:

Marshall plan that could be one to rue

Printing money is not the same as making it, but the management at De La Rue seem rather slow to grasp this point. Banknote printing is getting more competitive, while there is a disappointingly slow market for those old fashioned coups which saw a new despot's head on the local currency. Worst of all, the world is not inflating like it used to, so paper money does not become worthless before the note has worn out. None of this is exactly new, but the result is another fall in profits, and a share price at its lowest for six years. The board's strategy seems to consist of wait and see, and to hope that the competitors tire of such poor returns and switch to something else.

This looks forlorn, rather like Jeremy Marshall's cheerful whistling about the lottery and the value of De La Rue's stake in Camelot. Common sense, he says, will surely prevail, and the operator will keep its licence. He may be right, but do not put your banknotes on it. Never mind, there's always the single currency to look forward to, along with the smart card which De La Rue expects to produce rich returns, someday. None of this sounds very convincing, and shareholders who have watched the shares fall 60pc in two years might wonder whether this Marshall plan is going to work.

Chris Porter of *Printweek* studied the company closely and his assessment of De La Rue's prospects was more balanced and optimistic:

Despite the dominant scepticism toward De La Rue, it is still a fundamentally good company. And, say analysts, it is worth more than its current market value – which fell £140m following the announcement of the profits fall. Here's why …

Firstly, following the acquisition of Harrisons, De La Rue has a new market to develop – stamps – and it starts as the market leader in the UK. Secondly, De La Rue Holographics doubled its profits this year and Portals and De La Rue Giori also did well, both having won significant contracts in India.

Then there are banknotes. Although De La Rue has seen a huge 10% fall in banknote profit margins, the company is weathering the overcapacity storm better than its competitors. Finch [analyst at Credit Lyonnais] points out that its current 15% banknote margin is impressive when compared to its European competitor, Giesecke & Devrient, which reported 4% margins this year. And having taken out one of its most aggressive competitors, this success looks set to continue. The restructuring of its UK print operations will cost the company £14.8m but will begin to show benefits of £7m a year from next year, Marshall promises.

Smart moves

The profits from security print are the bedrock of the group's investment in other areas.

So far, smartcards have been something of a drain on profits. But the £56m acquisition of Philips Smartcards has given De La Rue a place alongside market leaders such as Gemplus, Schlumberger and Bull in a growing market, positioning the company well for the future.

Jeremy Marshall told *Printweek* he expects to see the market for smartcards 'quadruple within the next few years' – an explosion that will more than justify the expense.

De La Rue's long-term strategy is to invest in these 'exciting new technologies' in the drive towards becoming a 'cash to cards group'. And the importance of technology to the group has been underlined by the recent replacement of the directors of the Cash and Transactions Systems division with more technically-minded successors.

'It's all about tapping into new technology in the banking sector of De La Rue', says Finch. 'The company has to re-brand itself so it is not seen as a "mere printer". It needs to be seen as a service provider to the worldwide banking sector.' Finch believes that De La Rue had adopted a sensible, evolutionary approach and will not be tempted to bet on a sole, potentially explosive market, as it did with Crosfield Electronics in 1990.

These projects are seen as a necessary step for long term survival and prosperity, says Finch: 'De La Rue is a well run, profitable company but it is in a transition stage.' This is an industry-wide problem as commercial currency printers are affected by a general lack of inflation and relative political stability, which has affected the demand for new banknotes. De La Rue's core earnings are not living up to expectations in terms of profits and its new businesses still have large development costs. But it's surely not as bleak as it's painted.

'I FEEL A SPRING IN MY STEP'

Results for the six months to September 1997 were reasonably well received and there was hope that the corner had been turned. Unfortunately it was a false dawn, and on 19 February 1998 De La Rue was forced to issue yet another profits warning and say that it expected to halve its dividend for the current year. Furthermore, it announced that Jeremy Marshall, Chief Executive since 1989, would retire in April, two years earlier than planned. De La Rue's shares fell no less than 25 per cent to £2.70, down from £10.39 three years earlier.

Now comment in the press and from analysts was pretty savage. Even the new De La Rue Chairman, Brandon Gough, former senior partner at accountants Coopers and Lybrand, who had succeeded the Earl of Limerick, was forced to admit: 'We can be fairly accused of having taken our eye off the ball.'

One analyst was somewhat more brutal:

> Someone needs to pick this company upside down, beat it with a big stick and see what falls out. Every business needs to be re-examined and made to justify its existence. The remedies being suggested are completely limp-wristed.

Jeremy Marshall himself, no doubt partly relieved at the lifting of the unrelenting pressure, sent an upbeat message to his colleagues at De La Rue:

Although my much publicised retirement falls on April 18th, my 60th birthday, I can joyfully tell you that my life of relentless-lifelong-more-than-fulltime-but-nevertheless-fulfilling employment ends next Friday March 27th.

I feel a spring in my step, a weight from my shoulders, even light headed but, be assured, continuing confidence that I can from a more leisurely location watch De La Rue again basking in the success which it deserves.

Chapter Thirteen

Recovery and Back to Basics

1999–2003

'Completely unacceptable'
The euro
Printing for the Bank of England
Banknotes for Iraq

'COMPLETELY UNACCEPTABLE'

Ian Much, aged 53, was appointed to become De La Rue's new Chief Executive on 1 September 1998. His most recent position was Chief Executive of T&N plc (the former Turner and Newall), where he had spent ten years. He had joined T&N first as Managing Director of the industrial and engineering division and subsequently the bearings and industrial division. During his career, Much had worked for a number of international companies in both the UK and the USA. His two-year period as Chief Executive of T&N was marked by a significant improvement in the company's financial performance through modernisation and a more market-orientated approach.

Chairman Brandon Gough said of the appointment:

> Ian's excellent operational track record and his experience in changing corporate culture to one that is marketing and customer-focused will stand him in good stead as he faces similar challenges at De La Rue, a company whose products and services are second to none but whose priority is to improve its financial performance. Ian will be building on the firm actions we have taken over the last six months to ensure that we meet this objective.

The first results Ian Much announced, the six months to 30 September 1998, did not make good reading. Trading difficulties caused by financial problems in Asia, and a loss in Cash Systems, meant that the Group's pre-tax profits crashed no less than 80 per cent to just £7.8 million. Much described them as 'horrible' and 'completely unacceptable'. De La Rue's shares plunged further to 133p. By March 1999 the company was cutting jobs. Five hundred redundancies, or one sixth of its workforce, were announced at Cash Systems, and seventeen of the division's 22 sales offices around the world were to be closed. Much also replaced the matrix organisational structure with three business streams, each with a managing director, saying that the previous system had been confusing and the distribution system inefficient, with central overheads too high. He added: 'There was a lack of responsibility for profits and a lack of clear reporting.'

In August 1999 it was announced that De La Rue was in discussions to sell its smart card division to the French company Oberthur. The company's view was that, although the division promised rapid growth, it was currently too small and would require too much investment. Its market share was about 8 per cent. Oberthur, also a banknote, security document and lottery ticket printer, had built up an 11 per cent share of the global card market following its acquisition of Kirk Plastic of the USA and the card division of Syseca, a Thomson CSF subsidiary. The City was generally impressed by the sale and the price achieved, and De La Rue's shares rose 7.5p to 375p. This was a long way below the £10-plus achieved in the mid-1990s but it was also a long way above the 133p of twelve months earlier. And in November, the Group pleased shareholders further by announcing better than expected half-year profits – an 80 per cent rise – and by saying it would return £104 million to shareholders by way of a scrip and cash issue. Ian Much was able to say that the Group was considering acquisitions again and that the restructuring of the banknote division, so that it could concentrate on higher-margin business, was now complete. Tempus in *The Times* was able to say that De La Rue was 'finally winning back some friends in the City'.

The good news continued into 2000, and in May the company announced that pre-tax profits for the twelve months to 31 March were up 31 per cent. Much was able to say:

> This brings us to the end of chapter one. The second chapter will be about sustainable sales growth and that bit is a lot more fun.

He was becoming excited by the prospects for the Global Services division, which provided a wide range of security services such as passports and passport control systems, brand protection and supply chain security services, as well as internet security systems. The division had also developed an electronic system for pre-paid mobile phones that avoided the use of vouchers. By November, when the next interim results were announced, Francesca Raleigh of West L.B. Panmure was able to say:

> There was a very robust performance from continuing businesses. The recovery at the end of the cash systems division suggests that they are on track to hit a 10 per cent margin by the end of the year. The strategy of improving the mix at the security paper and printing division has also improved margins.

THE EURO

The next big event for De La Rue was the introduction of the euro in January 2002.

The path to the European single currency was a long one, beginning with conceptual studies in the 1960s and 70s, but it finally began to gain real momentum with the Delors Report in 1988. Plans for a single currency by the year 2000 were enshrined in the 1991 Maastricht Treaty, and the European Monetary Institute (EMI) – the forerunner of the European Central Bank (ECB) – began planning for the single currency. The denominational structure of seven notes was agreed at the end of 1994 and the Madrid Summit in December 1995 settled on the name 'euro'.

The EMI had identified two potential design concepts for the euro during 1995. One was entitled 'Ages and Styles of Europe' and the other was for an abstract design. Both concepts were intended to lead a pan-European design style with no identification of any individual countries. By February 1996 design briefs were ready and the EMI launched a Europe-wide competition to find the design of the euro.

On receipt of its invitation to the design competition, De La Rue arranged an internal contest among its design team to produce potential entries for the competition, which was due to close in September 1996. Rivalry was fierce, with most members of the design team submitting an entry, but the De La Rue jury eventually selected entries from Stuart Rost and John Stevenson. There were three other UK entries for the design competition, two from Harrison & Sons – Colin Braun and Terry Thorn – and one from Andrew Ward at the Bank of England.

The designs were duly submitted and the ECB jury met in September to draw up a shortlist of five designs from each theme, which were further assessed before the winning design – by Austrian designer Robert Kalina, based on the Ages and Styles theme – was selected in December 1996. Further development of the aesthetic design, together with the selection of the anti-counterfeiting security features, led to the approval of the final designs by the Council of the EMI in February 1998.

Following design approval, the development process then moved on to origination – the creation of the detailed line artwork and engravings and their assembly into the final printing plates. This process was carried out by a number of banknote origination facilities across Europe, and De La Rue was asked to work on the origination for one denomination alongside the Spanish national print works. The simplest way to undertake the work was for one organisation to do one side of the note while the other prepared the reverse, and this was what happened, but it nevertheless required careful co-ordination between the teams in Basingstoke and Madrid to ensure the two sides subsequently fitted together.

By September 1998 all the origination was complete and the process moved into a pilot production stage. De La Rue's Gateshead factory ran pilot production on two denominations of the new currency and the process was used to collect extensive data on production tolerances and parameters, to identify any production problems with the new designs, and to help develop the quality management methodology that would be used in subsequent production. By the middle of 1999 the pilot stage was complete and production of the new currency began.

Historically, De La Rue's market position in the printing of European banknotes had not been particularly strong, being confined to Luxembourg and the provision of part-printed sheets to Portugal, which were then finished locally. The other countries all had local sources of production, which in most cases were state-owned, and this meant that the printing opportunities for the company were limited.

The Banco de Portugal operated a plant near Lisbon, which took sheets printed to the intaglio stage from commercial banknote printers and then numbered, applied the signatures and cut them into finished notes. This arrangement was essentially a consequence of the infamous Waterlow incident in the 1920s (see chapter nine), but as part of the move to the euro, the Banco de Portugal became interested in enhancing the capability of its plant to fully print euros from white paper. Following extensive discussions it was agreed to establish a joint venture company (Valora) in Portugal, 75 per cent owned by the Banco de Portugal and 25 per cent by De La Rue. De La Rue provided the technical support for the development of Valora's printing capabilities and the joint venture was highly successful in printing Portugal's euro requirements. The company eventually sold its share in Valora to the Banco de Portugal in 2008.

The ECB, which was formed from the EMI in 1998, estimated that the volume of euro notes required for the launch and initial logistical stock was 13 billion banknotes, and the production of this requirement was allocated by the ECB to the individual eurozone national central banks. The central banks then typically allotted their share to their local print works. Following the decision that Greece would join the euro area, the estimated volume was increased to 14.25 billion and by 2001 the figure had risen to 15 billion pieces.

The launch date for the new currency was set for 1 January 2002 and EU legislation allowed for a maximum period of six months for the process of redeeming the legacy currencies, but many countries opted to impose shorter periods. With a large volume requirement and a fixed deadline, the pressure was on the printing works to achieve the required volumes. Inevitably, and despite the extensive pilot programme, there were some difficulties in production.

De La Rue had detected that all was not well with the euro production schedule. The Gateshead plant had the printing capability and available capacity, but did not possess the specialised automated inspection equipment that had by then become the norm for euro production. Time was of the essence, and the De La Rue management team faced the dilemma of whether to purchase the requisite equipment ahead of any possible euro orders, as to wait, given the lead-times from the manufacturers, would mean missing the boat. The decision was taken and over £4 million was committed.

By early 2001, after a further series of technical issues, the ECB had become sufficiently concerned that there could be a shortfall against the volume requirement that it decided to establish its own Central Reserve Stock (CRS), representing about 10 per cent of the original volume, to act as a contingency against production shortfalls or unexpectedly high demand. Events then began to move quickly and a consortium of four private-sector European printers, including De La Rue, plus the Austrian state print works, was formed to provide the capacity required to produce the CRS. Almost in parallel, two national central banks also approached De La Rue for support in meeting their requirements.

Thus, by the spring of 2001, the company had three separate euro orders to process, together with the small matter of commissioning new automated inspection equipment and establishing the ECB's particular quality management system in Gateshead. This was a classic De La Rue challenge, and the organisation successfully met it in characteristic fashion.

ONE, which was what the in-house magazine was now called, said in March 2002:

Customer Service takes the strain

Normally, the launch of just one new note in a single country would be a big operation, says Ian Richie, Cash Systems director of customer service, as he outlines the challenges of the euro launch. 'But we were talking about a whole new currency across 12 countries – it was a momentous event for the European service teams.'

The statistics speak for themselves. More than 20,000 machines upgraded and more than 130,000 replacement cassettes shipped to customers in the run-up to euro launch day on 1 January. In the month that followed, more than 30,000 customer queries were received from customers and 20,000 service visits made.

There was a huge peak of activity in late December as many of our customers, especially banks, needed to have their machines upgraded in the short window between Christmas and New Year's Eve, explains Ian. 'Speed was absolutely crucial – it was a bit like a Formula 1 pit-stop.'

All in all, the changeover has been a big success. 'For many of our customers, the euro launch could have been one big headache,' he continues. 'Our speed, reliability and quality helped them through a tricky period, and our long-standing reputation for providing outstanding service has been enhanced.'

'The achievement is due to the dedication of the service and support teams across Europe. Many people worked right through Christmas and New Year, and everyone showed great commitment to the cause.'

The service and support team in Germany were among those working flat-out to ensure a smooth euro transition. The company's squad of 150 full-time field service engineers was bolstered by up to 130 sub-contractors as the team coped with the peak in demand for upgrades and visits. A specialist call centre was set up and, at one stage, was dealing with 1,400 customer calls a day.

'It was a major management and logistical challenge,' recalls Markus Koch, customer service director in Germany. 'As well as co-ordinating the efforts of our own teams, we had to select and manage a range of third-party providers.

'Our people worked long and hard right through weekends and public holidays, and we made sure everyone was recognised for their efforts. Motivation was high and there was a great team spirit.'

And De La Rue's printing plant at Gateshead was the only site outside the eurozone given a contract to print the new currency. The company invested £4 million in the plant in order to win the contract. New finishing machines were imported from Germany, and electricians from the Gateshead factory spent a month in Munich being trained on the new equipment.

The contract for printing significantly boosted De La Rue's income for the year to 31 March 2002, way above what Ian Much had been predicting a year earlier. In the event, the boost to sales in that year was £60 million or 9 per cent of the company's revenue. It also helped to boost earnings by 15.7 per cent.

Meanwhile, on 11 September 2001, which became known as 9/11 (the telephone number used for emergencies in the USA, a coincidence appreciated by the perpetrators of the attack), the world was stunned when at 9.00am Eastern Standard Time a passenger airline was flown into one of the Twin Towers in downtown Manhattan, New York. A few may have thought it was an accident, but when, 40 minutes later, another airliner was flown into the second tower, no one was under the illusion that these were anything but deliberate attacks. The realisation was reinforced when another aircraft was flown into the Pentagon in Washington, and finally when a fourth aircraft crashed in Pennsylvania, killing all those on board.

The mighty USA was under attack on its home soil, the first time since the Japanese attack on Pearl Harbor in December 1941. The President, George W. Bush, was visiting a school in Florida and was quickly bundled into the presidential aircraft and flown around while it could be ascertained how serious the situation was and whether any more attacks were likely. Needless to say, all other aircraft throughout the USA were grounded.

Many businesses throughout the world were adversely affected by the events of 11 September 2001, if only by the uncertainty created.

However, for De La Rue there was some potential upside. The terrorist attack focused attention on identity documents as a growing market for the company. Ian Much made the point that De La Rue was placed to benefit: 'September 11 has brought into sharper focus what we were already seeing.'

However, after the excitement of the launch of the euro in early 2002, things started to go wrong again later in the year. Orders for cash-handling machines declined, and there were delays in receiving banknote printing orders and some restructuring of the division producing travellers' cheques and security threads. All combined to produce a loss in the six months to September 2002. The company issued a profits warning in July and, in the nervous stock market atmosphere following 9/11, De La Rue's share price fell sharply. In September the company announced that it was closing the High Wycombe factory it had acquired when it bought Harrisons.

PRINTING FOR THE BANK OF ENGLAND

One bright note amid the gloom was struck in December 2002 when De La Rue announced that it had reached an agreement with the Bank of England for the company to print British banknotes.

The Bank of England has been issuing banknotes since its foundation in 1694. The first notes were hand-written on Bank of England paper, but from 1725 part-printed notes – now on Portals-produced paper – were sourced from commercial suppliers. In 1791 the Bank took banknote production in-house and began printing in the basement of its main offices in Threadneedle Street, London. During 1916 the Bank acquired the site of the former St Luke's Hospital and banknote production was transferred there in 1920, although during the Second World War some equipment and staff transferred to the Portals site in Overton, Hampshire as a contingency against the threat of enemy action.

After the Second World War, the search began for a new location to construct a purpose-built banknote-printing facility, and a site in Debden on the outskirts of north-east London was selected. The new printing works, which opened in October 1956, featured a large, open print hall able to contain all the printing presses in a single space.

During the 1950s the Debden printing works was producing the equivalent of 2 billion banknotes per year, but over time the volume declined. This was due to a number of factors including the replacement of lower-denomination notes – the 10 shilling and £1 – by coins, major changes to improve the efficiency of the circulating cash cycle, and the gradual development of alternative payment means, such as cheques and plastic cards. Although requirements were periodically boosted by the introduction of new and more secure designs – such as the 'E' series in the 1990s – by the early 2000s it was forecast that the Bank of England's note requirements would not fill the available capacity at the plant. The possibility of using the spare capacity for export work for other central banks was briefly explored, but this inevitably brought it into conflict with the commercial banknote printers, and the Bank was never entirely comfortable with a department of a public-sector central bank engaging in commercial operations.

Consequently, in February 2002, the Bank began a strategic review of the printing works and considered three options, which were: to downsize the plant and focus on producing Bank of England notes with very limited other work; to sell to a commercial organisation; or to retain ownership and try to fill the excess capacity with export work. The latter option was rejected relatively quickly and the review focused on the first two options.

The downsizing option was soon labelled as 'managed decline' as the implications of more closely matching the printing works' capacity to the anticipated level of Bank of England demand were assessed. In parallel, the Bank held exploratory discussions with a number of commercial organisations, including De La Rue, to consider how the option of selling the printing works could be realised. Although the Bank had identified three core requirements – security and quality of note supply, the interests of the staff at Debden, and reduction in costs – there were a number of models that could have been used for the sale process.

In early July 2002 the Bank issued a tender for the sale of its printing operations, so that it could fully assess the second option. The model it had chosen was to sell the production assets (the printing presses and such like), transfer the production staff to the selected bidder, lease the production space at Debden (the site was used for other Bank activities including one of its cash centres), and offer a supply contract for its notes for a minimum period of seven years.

The response was required by the middle of August and the Bank's request generated a huge amount of activity within De La Rue, presenting, as it did, the possibility of a significant expansion of the size of the company's currency business. The work involved in responding to the tender was extensive, requiring inputs from a wide range of departments including finance, legal, manufacturing, human resources and technical specialists. The large state-printed banknote market had always been attractive but very elusive, and the tender presented the opportunity to demonstrate how the state printing of banknotes could be successfully transferred to the private sector. It was hoped that a successful outsourcing by the Bank of England of its note production could act as an example that might, over time, encourage other central banks with their own printing works to follow suit.

Four organisations responded to the tender, and the evaluation process involved, among other things, a visit by a Bank of England team to Gateshead. De La Rue successfully made it on to the shortlist and was then engaged in discussions to clarify various further details. In December 2002, the Bank assessed the outcome of the strategic review and decided to pursue the outsourcing option with De La Rue as its partner.

In many ways the Bank's decision was merely the beginning of the main part of the work, as a frantic three months then ensued to finalise the legal agreements and fill in the massive detail that was required in key areas such as the quality system. The legal documentation was an interlocking web of agreements on the sale and purchase of the assets, the lease of the space at Debden, the transfer of staff (including the complex area of pensions), and the supply contract. As part of its proposal, De La Rue had undertaken to implement a new quality management system in Debden, based broadly on the statistical sampling type approach used in Gateshead for euro printing. Although the Debden printing works had already started some work along these lines, the implementation of the whole system in three months was a major achievement.

The various agreements were finally signed in London on the evening of Friday 28 March 2003 and, on the morning of 1 April, a small De La Rue transition team arrived in Debden and started work. It proved to be the beginning of a highly successful relationship.

Meanwhile, early 2003 brought no relief, and in February De La Rue was forced to issue another profits warning, the third in eight months. By this time the build-up to an invasion of Iraq was gathering pace, and the company said that general political and economic uncertainty was partly to blame for the decline and delay in orders and therefore lower profits. The rest of 2003 proved better. As *ONE* wrote in the December 2003 issue:

> De La Rue has made an encouraging start to the year with improved interim results ... Currency was the star of the show after turning in excellent first-half results. The papermaking business saw a big jump in work and the first deliveries of the major order of banknotes for Iraq also played a part ... In Cash Systems, revenues were down as tough trading conditions continued ... In February the business announced 300 redundancies to reduce costs in the face of a downturn in Europe ... After a recent strategic review Global Services will cease to exist as a separate division.

BANKNOTES FOR IRAQ

On 7 July 2003, three months after the fall of the Saddam regime in Iraq, the Administrator of Iraq, the US diplomat Paul ('Gerry') Bremer, announced the introduction of a new currency. This decision was taken for five reasons. First, it was deemed politically and economically sensible to have a single currency for a single country. Second, it made sense to have a secure currency that could not be counterfeited. Third, a break with the inflationary past was needed. Fourth, a convenient range of denominations was also needed. And finally, it was deemed politically sound to have a neutral currency without a portrait of the dictator, Saddam Hussein.

How did De La Rue become involved? Simon Gray and Jacob Nell, two British currency advisors working in Downing Street and the Bank of England, who were chosen to supervise the introduction of the new currency, wrote this in their book *A New Currency for Iraq*:

> *The new notes.* The new notes were printed in the denominations 50, 250, 1,000, 5,000, 10,000, 25,000 dinars, using modified versions of the existing plates for pre-1990 ('Swiss') dinar. The main banknote printers, De La Rue, were chosen on the basis of their experience, the speed with which they could fulfill the order and the competitive price quoted. They formed a consortium with three other banknote printers, including the Spanish FNMT [Fabrica Nacional de Moneda y Timbre] whose contribution was generously financed by the Spanish government, to print the notes simultaneously in seven different countries. The initial order was for two billion notes worth six trillion dinars, planned to cover the existing note issue and provide a 30% buffer stock. However, the initial order was supplemented by three supplementary orders, firstly to provide more low denomination notes, and then to ensure an adequate supply and buffer stock, when demand for the new dinars turned out to be much higher than demand for old dinars. In total 2.25 billion notes worth 6.4 trillion dinars were printed and delivered by the end of the currency exchange in mid-January

2004, and a reserve of a further 1 billion notes worth a further 6 trillion dinars were printed and delivered by June 2004.

One early decision was to print the banknotes in paper, not in polymer. Polymer would last longer but would be more expensive, and in view of the general political and economic uncertainty, the cost of printing and reprinting was considered important. It was decided that the banknotes should include these features: 100 per cent cotton paper, a registered cylinder mould-made watermark, security threads, lithographic printing, front and back intaglio printing, letterpress numbering, a machine-readable authentication and Optically Variable Ink, printed in intaglio in the highest two denominations.

It was soon apparent that De La Rue were the most obvious choice as the lead printer. Not only were De La Rue the most experienced of those competing for the contract, especially in the Middle East, they were the only firm that could meet the 15 October deadline. Once serious negotiations began, De La Rue offered what was deemed to be a competitive price, and also agreed to bring all the banknotes produced at its plants around the world to its UK storage facility. In the event, De La Rue used its plants in Sri Lanka, Malta, Kenya and the UK. An initial slight complication was the offer by the Spanish government to pay for its government-owned printing works to print some of the notes free of charge as part of its contribution to the coalition effort for the reconstruction of Iraq. This contribution was co-ordinated with DLR, and the Spanish printed 250 million of the 2,000 million 250-dinar notes while De La Rue printed the other 1,750 million.

Gray and Nell may have made it sound as though De La Rue were the obvious choice, but the business could have gone elsewhere without the contacts and hard work of the company's John Black. Formerly of Bradbury Wilkinson, Black moved to the Gulf States to replace John Burbidge-King, who had been appointed Sales Director of Printrak at the end of the 1980s, and he lived in Bahrain from 1988 to 1998. He was instrumental in securing new banknote contracts for De La Rue in Iraq after the first Gulf War. A key person was the Director of Vaults and Issues at the Bank of Iraq, and Black got to know him well when he was sent to the UK to witness the destruction of obsolete Saddam Hussein notes. This contact was to prove critical in De La Rue's negotiations to print the new Iraqi notes as by this time he was Deputy Governor of the Central Bank of Iraq.

Once printed, the banknotes were packed into cases containing 50,000 notes and moved to the global distribution hub, a secure warehouse at Manston freight airport in Kent, where they were built into pallets for loading on an aircraft. The aircraft, which were Boeing 747s, each carried about 90 tonnes (or 22 to 25 pallets) either directly to Baghdad International Airport or into a transit hub in the United Arab Emirates (UAE), where they would be stored pending trans-shipment on a small 707 aircraft to Baghdad. Because of the threat of missile attack, the landings in Baghdad were scheduled for just after the breaking of dawn. This meant late evening take-offs from Manston. It beggars belief, but the local council in Kent imposed a fine of

£52,000 on the currency flights because only humanitarian flights were allowed to take off after 23:00 hours.

This fine was the least of their problems. As Gray and Nell put it:

> Arrival in Baghdad was very dramatic, with the enormous B747 planes corkscrewing down in the secure airspace above the base in the early dawn to minimise any low-altitude presence that could be reached by a ground to air missile fired from outside the base ... A major complication arose when a DHL aircraft was hit by an anti-aircraft missile over Baghdad airport on 22 November. Nineteen of the 27 flights had successfully landed in Baghdad at the point this incident occurred. The understandable initial reaction from the operator was to put further flights on hold pending the outcome of an investigation ... After some days it became clear that, although the airfreight contractors were willing to continue flights, the insurers had serious concerns ... They were quoting $200,000 per flight, some ten times higher than before the DHL hit ... The situation was difficult, since additional currency, particularly of low denomination notes, was urgently needed ... After some intensive discussions, and a reconnaissance trip to an airport in the UAE, Hannover Aviation put together a creative solution. This involved the B747s flying into the UAE and storing the currency in a secure warehouse ... A separate, African-based airfreight contractor who was prepared to take the risk of delivery into Baghdad on his own account was then hired to fly the currency in smaller aircraft (707s) from the UAE into Baghdad.

The Iraqi population needed to be told of the change to the new currency, and here again De La Rue were involved in two ways. First, the old notes in circulation would need to be collected, counted and destroyed. This was how Gray and Nell described part of that operation:

> The most substantial piece of equipment supplied to the banks by the ICE [International Currency Exchange] operation was 1,200 note counting machines, an average of five per exchange location. A number of these machines, plus a small number of larger counting machines, were retained by the CBI [Central Bank of Iraq] to support its own exchange and verification operation. The tender asked for offer of electric counting machines for use in large volume transactions (75–100,000 notes per hour), capable of counting aged and worn banknotes of varying sizes, reliable and easy to operate with little or no maintenance required, for delivery to Baghdad. After sifting over a hundred offers, the tender committee chose the models proposed by De La Rue, at a total cost of about $900,000, as meeting the specification and offering the lowest price, and they were delivered with the currency shipments. Initially the bank engineers reported that the counting machines did not function well with the Iraqi dinars, and kept jamming or miscounting the notes. The Saddam dinars were quite a challenge since they had been printed on poor quality paper: many were very dirty, taped together and with corners missing. With time pressing, De La Rue sent an experienced engineer to tackle the problem. Distributed machines were recalled and he

managed, working with the engineers of the CBI, Rasheed and Rafidian banks, to finish manual recalibration of all the counting machines before the exchange started.

Second, publicity was needed. The new notes were unveiled in early October 2003. This was done by the Deputy Governor of the Central Bank on special presentation boards to representatives of 25 news organisations. This was supported by the distribution of 120,000 posters and 550,000 handbills displaying the new currency. There were also quarter-page advertisements with pictures of the new currency in the leading Baghdad newspapers. This presented a security risk, and in order to protect the integrity of the images provided by De La Rue for this public information campaign, the images were released to the printing company only in the presence of an armed security escort, who was responsible for seeing that no additional copies of the banknote were made. Furthermore, the banknote images had 'sample' written across them and were printed in slightly different colours from the actual banknotes.

ONE explained what a marvellous job De La Rue did to supply 1.75 billion banknotes to Iraq:

> Iraq has a new set of banknotes thanks in large part to the record-breaking achievements of hundreds of De La Rue people.
>
> The order was placed with De La Rue on 17 July 2003. Six weeks later, the first 300 million notes were ready and were shipped to Baghdad in mid-September. Further consignments followed at regular intervals.
>
> To complete such a large order in just four months required an extraordinary effort from teams across Currency and Tapes & Holographics.
>
> The print factories in Malta, Sri Lanka, Kenya and the UK all switched from five-day to seven-day working weeks. In addition, employees in Malta and at the Portals papermaking facility in Overton signed up to working during the site's summer closures.
>
> To create the origination materials, the Portals studio and Prelims team created paper, print designs and origination materials in record time.
>
> Meanwhile, Tapes & Holographics employees faced the challenge of producing millions of metres of security thread in five weeks. The first supplies of security threads were needed for papermaking within days of the order being confirmed, with follow-on supplies to ensure Portals could achieve its delivery programme. Production staff worked 12-hour days, seven days a week to ensure deadlines could be met.
>
> **Consortium leaders**
>
> One of the biggest challenges facing De La Rue was to lead a global consortium including other paper manufacturers and print companies.
>
> The project team had to oversee operations at the various production sites and ensure high quality and security standards, throughout. Solutions had to be found to a range of technical issues, including the different equipment used by the partner companies.

All in all, it is an outstanding feat, according to Currency division director of manufacturing Mark Jeffrey. He says: 'Iraq's Coalition Provisional Authority made a very public commitment to having new notes in circulation by 15 October. The world was watching and the pressure was on us to deliver.

'No other organisation could have delivered an order of such scale and complexity in such a tight timeframe. At times, it was a rollercoaster ride, but teams at all sites involved responded superbly to the challenge.

'As well as making a significant contribution to our revenue, the achievement reinforces our position as the world's leading producer of banknotes.

'My thanks and congratulations go to everyone who contributed.'

Pulling out the stops

To deliver the Iraq order, De La Rue had to:

- Create factory materials in record time
- Manufacture Iraq banknote paper within 10 days of the order
- Print the final banknotes within six weeks of receiving the order
- Manage a major sub-contracting operation

These De La Rue manufacturing sites played vital roles in delivering the order:

- Currency
  - Malta
  - Sri Lanka
  - Kenya
  - Gateshead, UK
  - Debden, UK
- De La Rue Tapes & Holographics

And the efficiency with which the company dealt with the Iraq order meant that it was able to tell the market that its first-half profits for 2003–04 would be better than expected. *The Times* reported on 27 May 2004:

> De La Rue, the money printers and cash machine maker, yesterday unveiled a 21 per cent jump in full-year profits as it reaped the benefits of a huge contract to provide two billion new banknotes to Iraq. [...] The company had to charter 27 Boeing 747s to deliver the currency.

Afterword

It is always difficult to decide what date to pick for ending a company history. If the company is still operating it is creating new history every day.

We have chosen 2003, following the successful deal with the Bank of England and the winning of the contract to supply banknotes to Iraq, as an appropriate moment to end the story for the moment. It showed De La Rue and Portals at their best after nearly 200 years, or nearly 300 years in the case of Portals, of ups and downs, triumphs and disappointments.

Both companies began as family businesses and remained as such for over 100 years in the case of De La Rue and for nearly 250 years in the case of Portals. By 2003, merged together, they were, and still are, the largest commercial currency printer and papermaker in the world. They have constantly been at the centre of national and international events.

I think it is a great story and I hope you have enjoyed reading it. The Appendix that follows will explain both how a banknote is designed and printed and how suitable paper is prepared for it.

BANKNOTE PRODUCTION

HOW TO MAKE A BANKNOTE

De La Rue is now the largest commercial producer of banknotes in the world, and it is useful for a reader of this book to have a basic knowledge of how a banknote is produced and the contributions that De La Rue and Portals have made to that process over the last 300 years.

Paper

Paper is produced by draining a very dilute suspension (0.3 per cent) of a fibre in water (combined with some other chemicals) through a fine metal gauze, which collects the fibres on its surface as the liquid drains through. As the layer of fibres builds up, the very wet embryonic paper is taken off the gauze and goes through a series of drying processes to remove the residual water and produce the dry paper.

Banknote paper is specially made by what is known as the cylinder mould-made process, whereas most of the everyday paper we handle uses a different manufacturing method (called Fourdrinier). Furthermore, banknote paper is made from cotton fibres (mainly in the form of by-products from textile manufacture). In contrast, everyday paper uses processed wood-pulp for fibre. Cotton produces a more durable paper and, particularly when combined with the subsequent intaglio printing process, also contributes to the distinctive feel of money. This unique feel is an important part of the security of the final note.

In the cylinder mould-made process the fibrous suspension (known as 'stock') is pumped into an open tank, which contains a rotating cylinder. The surface of the cylinder is covered with several layers of phosphor bronze gauze and the stock drains through the gauze layers, leaving the fibres on the surface. The residual water in the centre of the cylinder is pumped away. The cylinder is rotating during this process and, as it rotates, the fibre collects on its submerged surface, becoming ever thicker. The very wet paper (around 75 per cent water by weight) is then drawn off the cylinder surface onto a belt ('couching') and the process of drying then begins (see figure 3.16). This consists of a series of stages including vacuum sucking, pressing (similar to an old-fashioned mangle), and heated cylinders. Subsequently, materials are coated on the surface and the paper is finally dried using hot air in a non-contact process. The final stage is smoothing the surface ('calendering') using pressure applied by metal rollers so that it is fit for printing.

The key security aspect of the mould-made paper process is that the surface of the cylinder (the 'mould cover') includes an embossed three-dimensional image of the watermark (see figure 3.17). As the stock drains through the cover, the resulting paper is thinner where there are ridges in the embossing and thicker where there are depressions relative to the nominal surface. When the resulting paper is held up to the light, the thinner areas appear lighter and the thicker areas appear darker compared to the surrounding paper. This enables the distinctive watermark image to be easily visible to the public. The three-dimensional master embossing is created by highly skilled designers from two-dimensional reference images. It is possible to produce a form of watermark by the Fourdrinier process, but this is stamped into the very wet paper after it has been formed on the couche, rather than created at the time the paper itself is being formed, as in the mould-made process. As a consequence, Fourdrinier watermarks are unable to achieve the same degree of tonal range as is possible with the mould-made process.

Watermarks are first thought to have been used in Italy in the 1200s, and were employed in banknotes issued by the Stockholms Banco in Sweden in the 1660s. They have been used in Bank of England notes since 1697 and have become a de facto security feature in banknotes.

The next key development in enhancing the security of banknote paper was the security thread, which is the narrow metallic strip seen by holding the note to the light. The idea was developed by the Bank of England in the 1930s and was translated into production by Portals, initially being used on the £1 note in 1940. With the introduction of colour copier technology in the 1980s, the 'windowed' thread was developed by the Bank of England and Portals, and was used on the £20 note from 1984. In this development, the thread periodically surfaces on one side of the note so that the reflective metallised coating on the thread is visible. The visible part of the thread has a metallic appearance and is intended to reflect the light from the scanning device, producing a dark, non-metallic appearance on the reproduction.

The windowed thread was so successful that the idea was further developed in subsequent years by the addition of wider threads incorporating sophisticated holographic or colour-shifting materials to enhance the visible impact of the exposed area of the thread.

Printing

Banknotes use three main printing processes:

1. Offset printing – which is used to print the highly coloured background 'tints' that cover the majority of the note's surface.

2. Intaglio printing – which is typically used for the main text and key motifs on the note (such as the portrait) and gives the note its distinctive 'feel'.
3. Letterpress – which is used to apply the unique serial numbering to each note.

In addition, many notes now incorporate additional processes, most notably:

1. Screen printing – which is used to apply special colour-changing inks.
2. Foil blocking – which is used to apply holographic foil-type features.

Offset printing

In offset printing an image is transferred from an inked plate onto an intermediate 'blanket' cylinder before being applied to the sheet of paper. The process was originally developed in the late 19th century and used 'lithographic' plates, which rely on the incompatibility of oil and water to produce an image from an essentially flat plate with separate oil- (which attracts ink) and water- (which doesn't) receptive areas.

Litho was first used on banknotes in the 1920s as a means of increasing the colour range used on notes in response to the growing threat of counterfeits produced by photographic origination. In the latter, the counterfeit was created by photographing the note to produce the printing plate, and the introduction of more colour was a means of making this process more difficult. The counterfeiters responded by using a series of coloured filters to separate the different colours on the note into individual plates, so a series of features were developed to intermingle or subtly vary the colour across the note to increase the difficulty of colour separation.

In the 1950s, De La Rue began to use a different type of offset plate. This had raised areas for the image (similar to letterpress) and the process involved inking the top of the raised areas before the image was then transferred to the blanket. This did not require the use of water and strictly speaking is 'dry offset', but is often referred to as 'litho' or 'dry litho'

Intaglio

Intaglio, also known as copperplate or in De La Rue jargon, 'DP' (short for 'direct plate'), is an ancient printing process that dates back to the earliest periods of printing. It is based on the use of an engraved plate, where the image is carried as a recess in the plate. The plate is inked, forcing some of the ink into the recessed areas, then wiped to remove ink remaining on the surface of the plate (but not in the engraved recesses; see figure 3.18); then the plate is applied to the paper under high pressure and raised temperature. This releases some of the ink out of the engraving and onto the paper to produce the printed image. This image consists of a relatively thick film of ink, which, together with an even higher embossing effect created in the paper by the pressure of the process, gives the note its distinctive 'raised' feel. Another factor contributing to the feel of the note is the calendering effect of the hot plate under pressure on the paper in non-image areas.

Intaglio was used on the earliest modern banknotes (Stockholms Banco in 1661 and the first Bank of England notes in 1694) and enables very fine images to be printed in strong colours, as well as giving the note its unique feel. The process, which is complex and relatively inefficient compared to more modern non-security printing processes, is now used almost exclusively for high-security printing.

Letterpress

This is essentially the printing process originally developed by Gutenberg in the 15th century. It involves the use of a plate with a raised image, which is inked and then applied directly to the paper (i.e. without the use of a transferring blanket cylinder). It is used to apply the unique serial numbers on the notes, plus in some cases other elements that may vary between different print runs of a particular design, such as the date or the signatures.

The serial number process involves the use of a 'numbering box', which is a frame that carries wheels bearing raised images of numerals (see figure 3.19). The raised numeral is inked and printed and, as the press rotates, a cam mechanism turns the wheels in the box to the next number in the sequence.

Screen printing

This process has been used in non-security printing for over 200 years, but its use in banknote production is relatively recent. The process involves squeezing ink through a fine mesh, which is open in the image areas but blocked off in the non-image areas. From the security printing perspective, the key attribute of the process is its ability to print inks containing relatively coarse particles. The screen printing process can take place either onto white paper at the paper mill or in the banknote printing works.

This became relevant in the 1980s when the development of colour photocopiers and electronic scanners changed the nature of the counterfeiting threat. These devices were capable of separating colour much more rapidly than using cameras and filters, and also enabled non-skilled users to create passable counterfeits. One potential solution to this threat was the use of iridescent or colour-shifting materials, but, by their nature, the particle size of these materials was too large for them to be used in the offset, intaglio and letterpress processes. The first note to use an iridescent screen ink was a Dutch 100-guilder in 1992, but it has now become a relatively common process in banknote production.

Foil blocking

The introduction of the foil blocking process into banknote production was also a response to the development of colour copiers and electronic scanners. This was driven by a desire to apply so-called 'optically variable devices', such as holograms, to banknotes to produce a feature whose visual properties could not be emulated by printing from a scanned image.

There are a variety of ways of applying such devices, but most are produced using hot foil blocking, where the hologram mounted on a carrier film is applied to the paper using heat and pressure. This activates the adhesive on the hologram, sticking it to the paper, and the carrier film is then lifted away. As with screen printing, the foil blocking process can be carried out either onto white paper at the paper mill or in the banknote printing works.

Two main variants on the feature have developed: either a discrete registered 'patch' or a continuous foil 'stripe' running the full height of the note. The first use of a holographic-type device on a banknote was the Austrian 1,000-schilling in 1989 and De La Rue's first use of a hologram was on a Kuwait series in 1992.

Design and origination

A precursor to all the production process is the design and origination of the banknote. This involves creating the aesthetic concept of the note and, following approval of the design by the customer, then originating the detailed artwork, engravings and films that will be used to produce the production dies and plates. In De La Rue, the design and origination processes are conducted in the Preliminaries department (usually referred to as 'Prelims'), which consists of a team of highly skilled specialists.

In papermaking, the traditional approach was to begin with a sketch or photograph of the watermark subject, which was then engraved into a block of wax. The differing thicknesses of wax simulated the differing paper thicknesses in the finished paper. Following approval, the wax was then used in a mould-making process to create a pair of metal dies for stamping the watermark image into the gauze mould cover.

From the 1980s onwards, digital techniques were developed whereby the subject was created as a greyscale drawing on a computer that was converted by software into a virtual three-dimensional image. This image was used to drive a computer-controlled milling machine to produce the stamping dies.

For print, the aesthetic image was traditionally created by the designer as a montage of elements, typically including some printed sections, such as geometric border patterns, together with hand-drawn or watercolour pieces, such as the portrait (see figure 3.20). Following approval of the design, the detailed work would then begin to originate the various components required for the final production materials.

Offset printing required the production of a photographic film for each plate. Early offset-printed notes typically used up to two plates on each side, with modern notes now using up to four on each side. In traditional photo assembly, each film for plate manufacture was made up from a large number of individual pieces of film. These individual pieces would consist of images of hand-drawn artwork for motifs, special line patterns etc., and would be assembled manually in a complex series of photographic and masking processes, rather like assembling a jigsaw.

Intaglio engraving traditionally consisted of the individual skills of portrait engraving, vignette engraving, geometric pattern work and lettering. The portrait engravers were considered as the leading craftsmen and would convert the aesthetic image from the designer into an image consisting of fine lines and dots by engraving into a piece of steel (see figure 3.21). Geometric pattern work was created on specially built De La Rue mechanical lathes that used cogs and wheels to create the unique patterns.

Finally, all the elements were brought together to produce a proof for customer approval, which was essentially a hand-printed banknote including all the elements in the final production note.

Digital technology started to have an impact in print origination in the 1970s. The original application was to replace the geometric lathes with a computer-based pattern generation system called 'HRD' after the large, laser-based High Resolution Displays used by the operators. The design process was then converted to a digital system, with colour prints from computers replacing the hand-made montages. Finally, the use of high-resolution image setters (originally developed for the semiconductor industry) enabled the process of film assembly to be moved onto computer, with the resultant films being output on the image setter. Digital technology is now also applied to intaglio origination. This still allows the unique security nature of the intaglio image to be retained, but allows more efficient control over the depths of the engraving.

Bibliography

Bender, Klaus W., *Moneymakers* (Wiley-VCH, 2006)
Blakey, George, *The Post-War History of the London Stock Market* (Mercury, 1993)
Bloom, Murray Teigh, *The Man Who Stole Portugal* (Carroll and Graf, 1922)
Bloom, Murray Teigh, *The Brotherhood of Money* (BNR Press, Ohio, 1983)
Brummer, Alex and Cowe, Roger, *Hanson* (Fourth Estate, 1994)
Bunt, John P., *The De La Rue Definitives of the Falkland Islands, 1901–1929* (John P. Bunt, 1986)

Cooley, John K., *Currency Wars* (Constable & Robinson, 2008)
Crosfield, John F., *Recollections of Crosfield Electronics, 1947 to 1975* (Crosfield, 1991)

Dodds, John, *The Age of Paradox: England 1841–51* (Victor Gallancz, 1953)
Duggleby, Vincent, *English Paper Money* (Spink, 1994)

Easton, John, *The De La Rue History of British and Foreign Postage Stamps, 1855–1901* (Faber & Faber, 1958)
Evans, Eric, *The Forging of the Modern State* (Longman, 1983)

Gilbert, Martin, *A History of the Twentieth Century* (HarperCollins, 1999)
Gray, Simon and Nell, Jacob, *A New Currency in Iraq* (Central Banking Publications, 2005)

Harrison, C.R. and H.G., *The House of Harrison* (Harrison & Sons, 1914)
Houseman, Lorna, *The House That Thomas Built* (Chatto & Windus, 1968)

Kynaston, David, *The City of London: A World of its Own, 1815–90* (Chatto & Windus, 1994)
Kynaston, David, *The City of London: Golden Years, 1890–1914* (Chatto & Windus, 1995)
Kynaston, David, *The City of London: Illusions of Gold, 1914–45* (Chatto & Windus, 1999)
Kynaston, David, *The City of London: A Club No More, 1945–2000* (Chatto & Windus, 2001)

Mackenzie, John, *The Victorian Vision* (V&A Publications, 2001)

Newman, Oksama and Foster, Allan, *The Value of a Pound* (Manchester Business School, 1995)

Portal, Sir Francis, *Portals: The Church, the State, and the People* (Oxford University Press, 1962)

Roberto, Richard and Kynaston, David, *The Bank of England* (Clarendon Press, 1995)

Sampson, Anthony, *Company Man* (HarperCollins, 1995)
Sandbrook, Dominic, White Heat (Little, Brown, 2006)
Sandbrook, Dominic, *Never Had it So Good* (Little, Brown, 2005)
Sked, Alan and Cook, Chris, *Post-War Britain* (Penguin, 1984)

Tiratsoo, Nick, *From Blitz to Blair* (Weidenfeld & Nicolson, 1997)

Vander Weyer, Martin, *Closing Balances* (Aurum, 2006)

Watson, Victor, *The Waddingtons Story* (Northern Heritage Publications, 2008)
Wiseman, W.A., *Great Britain: The De La Rue Years, 1878–1910*, Vol. 1 (Bridger & Kay, 1984)
Wiseman, W.A., *Great Britain: The De La Rue Years, 1878–1910*, Vol. 2 (Bridger & Kay, 1990)

Index